ORGANIZATION THEORY AND THE MULTINATIONAL CORPORATION

Organization Theory and the Multinational Corporation

Second edition

Edited by
Sumantra Ghoshal
and
D. Eleanor Westney

Second edition published 2005 by
PALGRAVE MACMILLAN
Houndmills, Basingstoke, Hampshire RG21 6XS and
175 Fifth Avenue, New York, N.Y. 10010
Companies and representatives throughout the world

PALGRAVE MACMILLAN is the global academic imprint of the Palgrave Macmillan division of St. Martin's Press, LLC and of Palgrave Macmillan Ltd. Macmillan® is a registered trademark in the United States, United Kingdom and other countries. Palgrave is a registered trademark in the European Union and other countries.

ISBN 10: 0–333–54622–9 hardcover
ISBN 13: 978–0–333–54622–2 hardcover
ISBN 13: 978–1–4039–0670–0 paperback
ISBN 10: 1–4039–0670–X paperback

This book is printed on paper suitable for recycling and made from fully managed and sustained forest sources.

A catalogue record for this book is available from the British Library.

A catalog record for this book is available from the Library of Congress.

10 9 8 7 6 5 4 3 2 1
14 13 12 11 10 09 08 07 06 05

Printed and bound in China

This volume is dedicated to the memory of two highly valued colleagues, whom we lost too soon

Sumantra Ghoshal (1948–2004)
Gunnar Hedlund (1949–1997)

Contents

Contents

Tables and figures

Acknowledgments

This volume had its origins in a panel for the annual meeting of the Academy of International Business in San Diego in October 1988. The Program Chair, Donald Lessard, had chosen as the meeting's theme the challenge of building a stronger discipline-grounded theory base for future research in international business. At his urging, the two editors of this volume joined forces with Bill Egelhoff to organize a panel on "Organization Theory and the Multinational Enterprise." We followed this up with a workshop on the topic at INSEAD in September 1989, to which we were fortunate enough to attract a number of leading contributors to both fields. As editors, we owe our greatest debt of gratitude to the participants in this workshop: Howard Aldrich, Christopher Bartlett, John Daniels, Jacques Delacroix, Yves Doz, William Egelhoff, Cathy Enz, Michael Gerlach, Gunnar Hedlund, Jean Francois Hennart, Carlos Jarillo, Martin Kilduff, W. Chan Kim, John Kimberly, Bruce Kogut, Mitch Koza, Andre Laurent, W. Richard Scott, Andrew Van de Ven, David Whetten, and Sidney Winter. Many other hands also lightened our task. Four of INSEAD's doctoral students acted as rapporteurs, providing the authors with detailed notes of the discussions: Carlos Cordon, Dana Hyde, Harry Korine, and Gabriel Szulanski. INSEAD provided both administrative and financial support for the workshop, for which we continue to be extremely grateful.

Ruth Lewis of INSEAD managed the complex logistics of the workshop, and Loretta Caira and Vaira Harik at MIT provided invaluable help in preparing the manuscript. Loretta Caira was also of crucial importance in the preparation of this second edition.

Finally, this second edition owes an immense debt to the encouragement and gentle persistence of Stephen Rutt, the Publishing Director for Economics, Business, and Management of Palgrave Macmillan, without whom it could never have been completed.

Notes on Contributors

Christopher A. Bartlett is the Thomas D. Casserly, Jr. Professor of Business Administration Emeritus at Harvard Graduate School of Business Administration. He received an economics degree from the University of Queensland, Australia, and both Master's and doctorate degrees in business administration from Harvard University. Prior to joining the faculty of Harvard Business School, he was a marketing manager with Alcoa in Australia, a management consultant in McKinsey and Company's London office, and general manager at Baxter Laboratories' subsidiary company in France. His academic interests have focused on the strategic and organizational challenges confronting managers in multinational corporations and on the impact of transformational change. He has published eight books, including (co-authored with Sumantra Ghoshal) *Managing Across Borders: The Transnational Solution*, and *The Individualized Corporation*. He has authored or co-authored over 50 articles which have appeared in journals such as *Harvard Business Review, Sloan Management Review, Strategic Management Journal, Academy of Management Review*, and *Journal of International Business Studies*. He has also researched and written over 100 case studies and teaching notes.

Jacques Delacroix is a Professor of Management in the Leavey School of Business at Santa Clara University and a former Director of its International Business Program. A native of France, Delacroix emigrated to the USA in 1963 and obtained his PhD in Sociology from Stanford in 1974. From 1974 to 1978 he taught at Indiana University; from 1978 to 1983 he founded and managed an international business consulting company in San Francisco. His most recent publication, in the *Independent Review*, examines critically the case for the cultural exception to free trade, with reference to motion pictures and television programs. His current interests center on the interrelation between the globalization of the entertainment industries, on the one hand, and the emergence of new collective identities, on the other. He lives in Santa Cruz, California with his artist wife, Krishna.

Yves L. Doz is the Timken Chaired Professor of Global Technology and Innovation at INSEAD, where he was Dean of Executive Education (1998–2002) and Associate Dean for Research and Development (1990–5).

He is a graduate of the Ecole des Hautes Etudes Commerciales (Jouy-en-Josas, France) and received his doctoral degree from the Harvard Business School, where he was an assistant professor from 1976 to 1979. His research on the strategy of MNCs, focusing particularly on high-technology industries, led to numerous publications, including four books, in particular *The Multinational Mission: Balancing Local Demands and Global Vision*, co-authored with C. K. Prahalad (1987), *Alliance Advantage* (1998), and *From Global to Metanational: How Companies Win in the Knowledge Economy* (Harvard Business School Press, 2001), co-authored with José Santos and Peter Williamson, two INSEAD colleagues. Professor Doz currently carries out research on strategic partnerships and technological cooperation between companies, on global competition in the knowledge economy, and on the competitive revitalization of international companies.

William G. Egelhoff is Professor of Management Systems at the Graduate School of Business, Fordham University. Previously he was on the faculty at New York University. He received his PhD and MBA degrees from Columbia University. Prior to returning for his PhD, he worked in various planning positions with Esso and National Distillers and Chemicals Corporation. His research deals with strategy and organization design in MNCs. He has written a number of articles and book chapters in this area, and also a book entitled *Organizing the Multinational Corporation: An Information-Processing Perspective*. Recently he edited a book entitled *Transforming International Operations*.

Sumantra Ghoshal held the Chair of Strategic Leadership at the London Business School until his sudden death in 2004. He received doctoral degrees in international management from the MIT Sloan School of Management and in business policy at Harvard Business School. His research interests ranged widely. He was a recognized leader in the study of strategic and organizational challenges facing large, complex organizations, and in recent years he wrote extensively on the impact of organizations on society and of management theories on managers. He was the author of 12 books, including (in addition to those co-authored with Chris Bartlett) *Strategic Control* (co-authored with Peter Lorange and Michael Scott Morton) and *The Differentiated Network: Organizing Multinational Corporations for Value Creation* (co-authored with Nitin Nohria). His many articles appeared in a wide range of scholarly journals, and one of his last articles (co-authored with Linda Gratton, "Integrating the intrapreneurial enterprise") won the Beckhard Prize as the best article of 2002–3 from the *Sloan Management Review*.

Mauro F. Guillén is the Dr. Felix Zandman Endowed Professor of International Management at the Wharton School and Professor of Sociology in the Department of Sociology at the University of Pennsylvania.

He previously taught at the MIT Sloan School of Management. He received a PhD in sociology from Yale University and a doctorate in political economy from the University of Oviedo in his native Spain. His current research deals with the diffusion of practices and innovations in the global economy. His book *The Rise of the Spanish Multinational Firm* will be published by Cambridge University Press in 2005. He is the author of *The Limits of Convergence: Globalization and Organizational Change in Argentina, South Korea, and Spain* (Princeton University Press, 2001), *Models of Management* (University of Chicago Press, 1994), and, with Charles Perrow, *The AIDS Disaster* (Yale University Press, 1990). His research has appeared in a variety of academic journals, and he serves on the editorial boards of the *American Sociological Review, Administrative Science Quarterly, Academy of Management Journal, Academy of Management Review,* and *Journal of International Business Studies.* He is a former Guggenheim Fellow and Member in the Institute for Advanced Study in Princeton.

Gunnar Hedlund was a Professor of Business Administration at the Stockholm School of Economics, from which he had received his doctorate in 1976, until his death in 1997. For ten years (from 1980–90) he was Director of the Institute of International Business at the SSE, an institution with which he was associated from its inception in 1976 until his untimely death in 1997. He was a visiting scholar at the Wharton School, the European Institute for Advanced Studies in Management in Brussels, and Stanford University. His publications appeared in a range of journals, including *Strategic Management Journal* and *Human Resource Management,* and, with Christopher Bartlett and Yves Doz, he edited *Managing the Global Firm* (1988).

Jean-François Hennart is Professor of International Management at Tilburg University. He received his PhD degree in economics from the University of Maryland. He is the author of *A Theory of Multinational Enterprise,* which pioneered the transaction cost explanation of the multinational enterprise, and has published extensively on transaction cost approaches to the multinational firm, joint ventures, and modes of foreign entry, in such journals as *Management Science, Journal of International Business Studies, Business History, Organization Science,* and *Strategic Management Journal.* His current research continues to focus on the relative efficiency of prices and hierarchy in organizing international interdependencies.

Martin Kilduff is Professor of Management at Penn State, and currently serves as Associate Editor of *Academy of Management Review* and *Administrative Science Quarterly.* Professor Kilduff received his doctorate from Cornell University, and spent two years at INSEAD in France prior to joining Penn State in 1990. Much of his work focuses on social networks, including the book (co-authored with Wenpin Tsai) *Social Networks and Organizations* (Sage, 2003), the article "The social networks of high and low self monitors: implications for workplace performance" (*ASQ*, 2001), and the forthcoming article (co-authored with Herminia Ibarra and Wenpin Tsai) "Zooming in and out: connecting individuals and collectivities at the frontiers of organizational network research" (*Organization Science*).

W. Chan Kim is the Boston Consulting Group Bruce D. Henderson Chair Professor of Strategy and International Management at INSEAD Business School, France. Prior to joining INSEAD, he was a professor at the University of Michigan Business School, USA. He has served as a board member as well as an advisor for a number of multinational corporations in Europe, the USA, and Pacific Asia. He has published numerous articles on strategy and managing the multinational which can be found in *Academy of Management Journal, Management Science, Organization Science, Strategic Management Journal, Journal of International Business Studies, Harvard Business Review, Sloan Management Review*, and others. Professor Kim's current research focuses on strategy and management in the knowledge economy. He is a Fellow of the World Economic Forum at Davos and the winner of the Eldridge Haynes Prize, awarded by the Academy of International Business and the Eldridge Haynes Memorial Trust of Business International, for the best original paper in the field of international business.

Bruce Kogut is Professor of Strategy at INSEAD. Until December 2002, he was the Dr. Felix Zandman Professor at the Wharton School, University of Pennsylvania, where he headed the Reginald H. Jones Center. He received his PhD in International Management in 1983 from the MIT Sloan School of Management. He has been a visiting scholar at the Ecole Polytechnique, Stockholm School of Economics, Wissenschaftszentrum, and Santa Fe Institute. He works in the area of international direct investment, the theory of the MNC, country competitiveness, development economics, technology policy, and privatization. He has published over 40 articles in leading scholarly journals, including the *American Sociological Review, Review of Economics and Statistics, Management Science, Organization Science*, and *Journal of International Business Studies*. In 2003, Peter Cornelius (now Senior Economist, Shell Corporation) and Bruce Kogut published an edited book on *Corporate Governance and International Capital Flows* (Oxford University Press). In the same year his edited volume, *The Global Internet Economy*, was published by MIT Press.

Renée A. Mauborgne is the INSEAD Distinguished Fellow and Affiliate Professor of Strategy and Management at INSEAD in Fontainebleau, France, and Fellow of the World Economic Forum in Davos. Professor Mauborgne has published numerous articles on strategy and managing the multinational, which can be found in *Academy of Management Journal, Management Science, Organization Science, Strategic Management Journal, Journal of International Business Studies, Harvard Business Review, Sloan Management Review*, and others. Her research has also been featured in the *Economist, The Times* of London, *Wirtschaftswoche, Global Finance, The Conference Board, L'Expansion, Børsen, and Svenska Dagbladet*, among others. Professor Mauborgne is the winner of the Eldridge Haynes Prize, awarded by the Academy of International Business and the Eldridge Haynes Memorial Trust of Business International, for the best original paper in the field of international business.

C. K. Prahalad is the Harvey C. Fruehauf Professor of Corporate Strategy and International Business at the Ross School of Business at the University of Michigan, Ann Arbor. He received his BSc in physics from the University of Madras, his MBA from the Indian Institute of Management, and his DBA from the Harvard Business School. He was Visiting Research Fellow at Harvard, Professor at the Indian Institute of Management, Ahmedabad, India, and Visiting Professor at INSEAD, France. His research and consulting interests center on the role of top management in large, diversified MNCs. He has published widely on the subject in professional journals and has co-authored *The Multinational Mission* with Yves Doz (INSEAD, France), *Competing for the Future* with Gary Hamel (LBS, UK) and *The Future of Competition* with Venkat Ramaswamy (UMBS, USA). His latest book is *The Fortune at the Bottom of the Pyramid: Eradicating Poverty Through Profits*. He is a three-time winner of the McKinsey Prize from the *Harvard Business Review* and has won the best article awards from the *Strategic Management Journal* and *Research and Technology Management*.

Sandra L. Suárez is an Associate Professor of Political Science at Temple University. Her current research deals with the democratic impact of new information technologies. She has published articles on the politics of language, labor control policies, and Internet diffusion in comparative perspective. She is the author of *Does Business Learn? Tax Breaks, Uncertainty and Political Experience* (University of Michigan Press, 2000), and several articles in *Polity, Studies in International Comparative Development, Telecommunications Policy*, and *Comparative Politics*. She has been a fellow of the Center of Intenationional Studies at the Woodrow Wilson School at Princeton University, the Ford Foundation, and MIT's Poltical Science Department.

John Van Maanen is the Erwin Schell Professor of Organization Studies in the MIT Sloan School of Management. He has also taught at the University of Surrey, Yale University, and INSEAD. He has published a number of books and articles in the general area of occupational sociology, including

Tales of the Field (1988) and *Qualitative Studies of Organizations* (1998). Cultural descriptions figure prominently in his studies of the work worlds of urban patrol officers in the USA, police detectives in London, fishermen in the North Atlantic, and happiness providers at Disneyland. He is also one of the authors of *Managing for the Future*, a text on organization processes written with Sloan School colleagues.

D. Eleanor Westney is the Society of Sloan Fellows Professor in the Strategy and International Management group at the MIT Sloan School of Management. She received a BA and MA in sociology from the University of Toronto and a PhD in sociology from Princeton University. She has worked extensively on Japanese organizations, and is the author of *Imitation and Innovation: The Transfer of Western Organizational Forms to Meiji Japan*. Her research has focused on the cross-societal transfer and adaptation of organizational patterns, organizations and social change in Japan, and the organization of multinational corporations. In addition to numerous articles on these subjects, she is one of the co-authors of *Managing for the Future* and co-editor with Anil Gupta of the volume *Smart Globalization: Designing Global Strategies, Creating Global Networks* (2003).

Remembering Sumantra Ghoshal

Sumantra came relatively late to academic life, and yet in a career of just over two decades, he accomplished much more than most of us do in twice the time. He arrived at MIT in 1982 in his early thirties as a high-flying mid-career manager in the Indian Oil Company dispatched to a 12-month Masters program at the Sloan School of Management. By the spring semester he had succumbed to the call of the academic world and was already taking some PhD-level courses; in the fall of 1983 he entered the PhD program in International Management at Sloan. That same autumn he took a doctoral course at the Harvard Business School taught by Chris Bartlett, who was just beginning the fieldwork for his research on the transnational model of the MNC. Excited by Chris's research, Sumantra decided to add a second doctoral program to his already full schedule, and in the fall of 1984 he embarked on a DBA in Strategy at HBS. He quickly became not a research assistant but a research partner in Chris's research, beginning a collaboration and a deep friendship that lasted for the rest of Sumantra's life.

Finishing two doctoral degrees in a three-year period, in two different fields with two completely different dissertations (the MIT dissertation in IM focused on international environmental scanning in Korean firms, the HBS dissertation on transnational networks) was not enough to keep Sumantra fully occupied. He also signed on as a research assistant for a book on strategy being written by Michael Scott Morton and Peter Lorange, and he became so important a contributor that he was made third author on the book (Lorange, Scott Morton, and Ghoshal 1986).

The capabilities that Sumantra demonstrated during his brief but action-filled graduate student years continued to distinguish him throughout his career. The most obvious was the phenomenal energy that enabled him to achieve so much in such a short time (and that gave rise to the rumor at Sloan that he was really triplets). More significantly, just as Sumantra was able to succeed simultaneously in two different graduate programs in two institutions with significantly different cultures and expectations (differences that were more marked in the 1980s than they are today), so he was able throughout his life to combine active engagement as a consultant and advisor to some of the world's most powerful and complex firms with a steady stream of publications in the leading academic journals. Sumantra believed strongly that management research that did not have an impact on managerial practice was not worth doing. He also passionately wanted to leave a lasting imprint on the academic world of theory—to be cited by generations of graduate students long after he was gone. Life for Sumantra was never "either/or"; he wanted "both/and."

His work with Chris Bartlett on the transnational model of the MNC achieved this dual ambition to a considerable degree. Few research-based publications in international business have reached such a wide managerial audience and had such a strong impact as their 1989 book *Managing Across Borders* (and its 1998 revised edition); no body of work in IB has been so widely cited by social scientists. The careful design of the research (one US, one European, and one Japanese MNC in each of three industries), the focus on cross-border innovation processes, and the parallels with the domestically focused work in organization studies on new organizational forms all contributed to the academic impact of the book—an impact enhanced by the many journal articles that Sumantra and Chris wrote based on the research. The transnational project continued to provide data for significant subsequent work, most notably the book Sumantra wrote with his long-time friend and colleague Nitin Nohria, which was based in part on Sumantra's HBS dissertation research and which won the 1998 Academy of Management Terry Award for the best management book of the year (Nohria and Ghoshal 1997).

Increasingly, Sumantra was drawn to the challenges of taking effective managerial action in the enormously complex, multi-business MNCs of the late twentieth century. This was the theme of his 1997 book with Chris Bartlett (*The Individualized Corporation*) and of his passionate critiques of the transactions cost paradigm that dominated so much management research, which he believed grossly over-simplified and distorted the motivations that drove individual and collective achievement. Not satisfied with critiques, however, Sumantra wanted to build a new theory. He had begun reading deeply in social psychology and in both western and Indian philosophy to find insights on which to build a new and better theory of effective action. He died before this work really developed.

Sumantra used to say that he transformed his life every decade. He spent just over a decade as a manager; he taught at INSEAD (which he enjoyed enormously) from 1985 to 1994, and he had spent a decade at his new academic home, London Business School. All of us were watching with great interest to see what Sumantra would focus on next. None of us thought that the next transformation would be that we would lose him.

Sumantra was enormously pleased when Macmillan proposed a second edition of this volume, and even more pleased that the chapters in this book stood the test of time remarkably well, and he hoped that a new generation of doctoral students and scholars would find it useful. We little thought, when the two of us decided that we would dedicate the new edition to

Gunnar Hedlund, a brilliant and creative colleague whose untimely death we both mourned, that by the time the final stages of the new edition were in process Sumantra himself would be gone. This edition is therefore dedicated to Gunnar, as we had both decided, and to Sumantra, who should have been here to rejoice in its completion.

D. Eleanor Westney
January 2005

1 Introduction and Overview of the Second Edition

Sumantra Ghoshal and D. Eleanor Westney

The goal of the first edition of this volume in 1993 was to build a bridge between two fields that had not developed a particularly close relationship: organization theory and international management. The 1980s had seen the rise to dominance of important new paradigms in both fields. In organizational sociology, theory building had increasingly focused on the interactions between organizations and their environments. On the other hand, the international business (IB) field had witnessed the emergence of new models of the multinational corporation (MNC), premised on changes in business environments that demanded increasing interactions across MNC subunits operating in different national environments. The potential for creative interaction between the two fields seemed obvious. As an organization operating simultaneously in many diverse environments, the MNC (the primary focus of the field of international management) would seem to present a promising arena for developing and testing organization theories about the relationships between organizations and their environments. Yet organization theorists had rarely addressed the opportunities or the challenges offered by its study. On the other hand, within international business, studies of the MNC tended to draw eclectically rather than systematically on organization theory, and to favor older paradigms such as contingency theory over the newer approaches. The 1993 edition of this volume aimed to broaden the span of interaction between organization theory (OT) and the study of the MNC by spotlighting the most promising theoretical perspectives provided by OT and articulating their relevance to the analysis of MNCs, and by presenting some theory-oriented discussions of some of the key issues in the study of the MNC.

Over a decade has passed since the publication of the first edition of this volume. We can report that the bridge has been built and is beginning to bear more traffic, although not so much as we might wish and not as bi-directional as we had hoped. In the introduction to the first edition, we stated that "With the possible exception of contingency theory, no paradigm from the major theories about organizations and environments has had a major impact on the study of multinational enterprise, and no research on MNCs has drawn significant attention from organization theorists" (p. 1). This is no longer true. The paradigms represented in this volume have provided the foundation for a growing body of research on

MNC organization within the IB field, and the explosion of interest in the complex cross-border phenomena covered by the umbrella term "globalization" has led a growing number of social scientists in many fields, including OT, to scan the IB literature on MNCs.

In contrast to the 1980s, the decade of the 1990s was, in both fields, a time of extending and building on existing theoretical paradigms rather than of generating new ones. The paradigms represented in the 1993 volume have shaped much of the organizational analysis of the MNC in the last few years. When the two editors sat down together to discuss a second edition (at the prompting both of the publishers and of colleagues whose students were finding it difficult to get their hands on a copy), we quickly came to two decisions. The first was that the individual chapters were remarkably robust, and could stand largely as they were. Second, we could not identify any new paradigm in organization theory that should be represented in the second edition. Whereas the 1970s and 1980s had witnessed the rise and elaboration of several influential new OT paradigms (including resource dependency, population ecology, and institutional theory), the 1990s had been a time of building on these paradigms rather than the development of new ones. We did believe, however, that the area of comparative cross-national analysis of business environments and organization had expanded enormously in the last decade, with significant consequences for one of the key issues in the study of MNCs: country effects on MNC organization. This work built on established theoretical paradigms, rather than generating new ones, but we believed that the second edition would benefit from a chapter that reviewed this literature and spelled out its implications for the study of MNCs. Therefore we asked Mauro Guillén to take on this task, and the chapter by Guillén and Suárez is the result.

In this introductory overview, we survey briefly the evolving relationship between the study of MNCs and organization theory, and then provide a brief overview of each chapter.

THE ORGANIZATIONAL ANALYSIS OF THE MULTINATIONAL CORPORATION

From the earliest days of the emergence of IB as a field of research, the theory of the MNC was dominated by economics. For economics, the MNC was a critical anomaly (which it has *not* been for organizational theory): in a world of efficient markets, a firm would produce in its home country and either sell abroad through exports or contract out its proprietary know-how to firms in other countries, for an appropriate fee. Explaining why MNCs existed was a fundamental theoretical challenge for economists, and therefore, understandably, an economics-based paradigm drove the earliest and the most voluminous stream of theoretical work on the MNC. (For overviews of this literature, see Dunning 1974; Calvet 1981; Casson 1987.) In this paradigm, firms extend their organizational boundaries across national borders in order to exploit firm-specific advantages for which there are imperfect markets (Buckley and Casson 1976; Dunning 1977, 1993; Rugman 1981; Caves 1982). The work of the 1970s saw the parent organization as the generator of those advantages, which were exploited through overseas subsidiaries. Subsequent work suggested, however, that the firm-specific advantages of the parent that gave rise to the initial expansion across borders may well erode over time and be replaced by emergent advantages derived from the multinational network itself (Kogut 1983; Dunning 1993).

The more organizationally oriented research on the MNC that emerged in the late 1960s and early 1970s drew primarily on contingency theory, which was then the dominant OT paradigm in business schools. Early work (e.g. Stopford and Wells 1972) focused primarily on developing a typology of MNC structures and entry modes, and on the problems of maintaining headquarters control over national subsidiaries (e.g. Doz and Prahalad 1981). By the mid-1980s, the focus had shifted to the changing strategy and organization of MNCs in the face of increasingly global competition—that is, of growing interaction and interdependence across markets. Not surprisingly, contingency theory remained a conceptual anchor of the development of these models: as Christopher Bartlett (1986) noted, the conceptual framework for this approach, developed at the Harvard Business School, was strongly influenced by the concepts of differentiation and integration of Lawrence and Lorsch.

The strategy and structure of MNCs were portrayed as a response to two major environmental factors. The first included a number of the "forces for global integration," including growing homogenization of markets and market segments across societies; the geographic dispersion of lead users; and the growing parity in technology among countries. The second category, "forces for national differentiation," included state intervention to maintain a local presence in certain industries, distinctive tastes and preferences, and distinctive marketing and distribution systems.[1] The two forces were seen as orthogonal: in a growing number of industries, firms were seen as subject to simultaneously increasing environmental pressures for global integration and responsiveness to local conditions.

In keeping with the strategy–structure tradition, the scholars working in this area quickly moved to identify the organizational structures associated with these strategies. By the mid-1980s, an increasingly widely used typology distinguished two kinds of MNCs. First were multi-domestic MNCs, whose organization had developed in environments with strong forces for local responsiveness, in which national subsidiaries focused on their local markets, carried out production and marketing activities locally, and had a significant measure of autonomy from headquarters. This model contrasted with "global" MNCs, which developed in industries where forces for local responsiveness

3

were weak and forces for global integration strong, and which concentrated their production and administrative activities in one location (usually the home country) in order to reap the cost and control advantages of economies of scale (Bartlett 1981, 1986). In the early 1980s, leading figures in the strategy field portrayed firms with a "global" strategy in this sense as the exemplars of the successful international firms of the future (e.g. Hout, Porter, and Rudden 1982).

Increasingly, however, interest centered on those firms that faced simultaneous pressures for high levels of global integration and of local responsiveness. The vulnerabilities of the global organizational structure had been revealed by the volatile exchange rates of the 1980s, which exposed a firm whose production was concentrated in one country (especially the Japanese firms that had been the exemplars of a global strategy) to unpredictable variation in costs relative to revenues. Simultaneously, global firms were facing the challenges of dispersing manufacturing activities in order to reduce their political risk and exchange rate exposures, and multi-domestic firms were seeking a division of labor among their subsidiaries that would enable them to capture greater scale economies within their multinational network. In other words, a growing number of multinationals seemed to be trying to move toward a model that combined elements of the strategies and organizations of both the global and the multidomestic. Academic work in this paradigm began to concentrate on the organization of this "transnational" (Bartlett 1986; Bartlett and Ghoshal 1989), the "multifocus" firm (Prahalad and Doz 1987), or the "heterarchical organization" (Hedlund 1986), as it has been variously dubbed.

The new MNC was, for these scholars, an organization that differed substantially from earlier models and that was considerably more difficult to manage. The most significant departure from the older models was the growing interaction across subunits, as value chains became increasingly distributed across locations, and as subunits increasingly specialized in a set of activities that they performed to regional or global instead of national scale. Both the capacity to innovate and the capacity to exploit innovations became increasingly dispersed across locations, and technological and organizational innovation was no longer the prerogative of the center. The closer interactions and linkages among subunits were often accompanied by a much looser array of joint ventures and strategic alliances with external partners, at both the individual subunit and the corporate levels.

The relationship between the changing model of the MNC and changing environments for international business raised the possibility that macro-organizational theory could contribute to understanding more clearly the emergence and form of the new MNC. The workshop at INSEAD in 1989 that provided the impetus for this volume brought together a group of leading organization theorists (including Howard Aldrich, Jacques Delacroix, John Kimberly, Richard Scott, Andrew Van de Ven, and David

Whetten) and many of the leading researchers on MNCs (including, in addition to those represented in this volume, John Daniels, Carlos Jarillo, and Andre Laurent). We found, however, that building a bridge between these two fields was not as simple a task as it seemed. The two groups were divided by a mutual skepticism about the value of interaction and exchange. For the organization theorist, the skepticism has focused on the distinctiveness of the MNC as an organization: What is it about the MNC that makes it theoretically interesting? For the more phenomenologically oriented MNC scholars, OT has, at times, appeared to be focusing rigorously on the uninteresting, developing little by way of concepts and tools that can illuminate the complexity of large multinational organizations.

The uniqueness of MNCs: The debate over degree versus kind

Organization theorists, along with scholars from other disciplines, have derived some of their skepticism from the failure of international management scholars to articulate clearly what distinguishes MNCs as a class of organizations and what theoretical import such features have. Most researchers who focused on the MNC in the 1980s had focused on what differentiated the new model of the MNC from older forms, but had not articulated clearly what differentiated MNCs from domestic companies. One feature of the MNC is clearly distinctive and defines the category: its activities span national boundaries—but what is the theoretical import of this distinction in terms of organization theory? Economists and political scientists in the field of international business point out the many implications of transacting intraorganizational exchange across the boundaries of sovereignty: the multiple denominations of a firm's value given that its cash flows are in multiple currencies; the multiple denominations of external and internal authority; the multiple market structures represented in the variety of customers, competitors, suppliers, and institutional contexts in different countries; and the differences in location-specific factor endowments in those countries (Sundaram and Black 1992; Kostova and Zaheer 1999). Other international management scholars highlight differences in social organizations, cultural norms, and individual orientations across countries as additional sources of plurality inherent in multi-country operations (see the articles by Westney, Kilduff, and Van Maanen in this volume).

Are these differences a matter of degree, or a matter of kind? To the organization theorist, acutely aware of intra-country differences (particularly in a country as large and as diverse as the USA), the distinction of differences between Boston and Dallas, on the one hand, and between the USA and Canada (or even Germany) on the other, appears blurred.

Further, even admitting the additional environmental and organizational complexity entailed in multi-country operations, it is not clear that this complexity contributes in any way to the task of building and refining theory. The objective of theory is to simplify by focusing on the essential. To the extent that a simpler empirical setting can allow for testing and enhancing theory, choosing a more complex setting is merely bad research design. Therefore, the question of degree versus kind matters. If it is merely a difference in degree, the only rationale for the theorist's interest in the MNC is to delineate the range of variation within which a theory is robust. The MNC will be of particular interest only to the extent that the theory in question is focused on any of the specific variables or outcomes that are likely to be influenced by that variation. If, on the other hand, the MNC is indeed a distinct kind of organization, with characteristics that make existing theoretical models and paradigms inappropriate or inapplicable, then it would clearly provide the opportunity both for extending and enriching current theories and for building new ones. To many organization theorists, it appears that those in international management who study the MNC have so far failed to make this case.

Managing complexity: The debate on rigor versus relevance

Many of those who study MNCs, on the other hand, have been equally skeptical of the contributions that organization theory can make to their quest to develop a deeper understanding of the environmental, strategic, and organizational challenges of multinational management. Given their phenomenological and often normative orientation, as well as their association with and affinity for senior management personnel in the largest and most visible MNCs, they have been uncomfortable with the assumptions, motivations, and methodologies of the dominant streams in modern OT.

Their argument focuses on the issue of complexity. The integrated MNC is a particularly complex organization, the different parts of which are dispersed in very different contexts that are nevertheless increasingly interconnected. Such MNCs are internally differentiated in complex ways, yet integrated to respond to the interdependencies across the different organizational subunits. The complexity caused by such differentiation and interdependence has been at the heart of the efforts in the international management field to understand how MNCs function.

Faced with what they see as a need to analyze and understand the internal working of such complex organizations, international management scholars despair at what they see as a trend in organizational theory to move increasingly further away from the messiness of organizations, either by redefining the theoretical quest or by simplified assumptions about individual and organizational behavior. Organization theory increasingly became more a theory of environments than of organizations, they claim. Their case studies of significant change in specific and non-randomly selected MNCs contradict the premise of strong inertia in many of the dominant approaches to organizational analysis, and their rich contextual observations of internal management processes and individual behavior in companies—many of them non-American—make them deeply suspicious of theories premised on the pervasive opportunism of the rational actor in transactions cost theories.

The article by Yves Doz and C. K. Prahalad that leads off this volume presents a clear version of the critique, as the authors lay out and justify their 20-year efforts to develop a new and different paradigm to guide research on MNCs. Building on their extensive field research and consulting experience in a wide variety of US, European, and Japanese MNCs, these two pioneers in the international management field first identify a set of requirements for a paradigm that can be helpful for analyzing these complex organizations. They then review seven major strands of OT to suggest that whereas most of the theories can be useful for some specific and relatively narrow set of questions, none is robust enough to serve as a broad conceptual map to guide MNC-related research. The authors then lay out the paradigm they themselves have evolved—the "global integration/local responsiveness framework"—and suggest how this approach can meet many of the paradigmatic requirements they have identified.

Organization theorists can and undoubtedly will take issue with this review. The search for grand theory is not very popular at present, and for good reasons. Doz and Prahalad's review of the seven theoretical strands can also be blamed for being too broad-brushed and selective. Finally, the contingency flavor of their integration/responsiveness framework can invite all the criticisms of contingency theory that have been made over the years. But the review does present in sharp relief the motivations and demands of those who study the MNC, and thus puts forward a wish-list for the future theory-building effort that this book aspires to trigger. It also fosters a degree of humility and modesty in the bridge-building task, suggesting how much clearly remains to be done.

If Doz and Prahalad set up the challenges, the other chapters in this volume suggest ways in which these challenges can be approached. Each chapter attempts to develop a theoretical approach to the study of some specific aspects of MNC-related phenomena. Although the emphasis on theory and phenomenon varies among the authors, each attempts to explicate both the theory and the MNC context to which it is being applied. Most of the contributions deal with broad, overlapping issues, and they span levels of analysis. The first five chapters draw on a range of macro-organizational theories to describe and analyze the environment and organization–environment interactions in the context of MNCs. The next six chapters focus more on the organization of MNCs: their structure, governance, and culture and norms.

ENVIRONMENT AND ORGANIZATION–ENVIRONMENT INTERACTIONS

The emergence and rise to dominance of open-system models have made organization–environment interactions central to most strands of OT.

Effective exchanges across the organization–environment boundary are key to an organization's survival, and the fit between its internal structures and processes and the characteristics of its environment influences the effectiveness of such exchange. Although they may use different language systems, different criteria for survival and effectiveness, and different assumptions regarding flexibility, inertia, and choice in adaptation to environmental changes, almost all branches of OT—including contingency theory, resource dependency, population ecology, and institutionalization theory—appear to accept these fundamental propositions regarding organization–environment interdependencies (Thompson 1967; Lawrence and Lorsch 1967; Pfeffer and Salancik 1978; Scott 1987a; Hannan and Freeman 1989).

Virtually without exception, however, organization theorists have ignored or underemphasized the case of diversified organizations whose various constituent units are located in different business or geographic contexts. Each organization, in most paradigms, confronts a particular kind of environment, shared by other organizations. Most empirical work has focused on single-activity organizations operating in only one geographic area. Population ecologists studied newspapers in Argentina and Ireland (Carroll and Delacroix 1982; Delacroix and Carroll 1983) and social service organizations in Toronto (Singh, House, and Tucker 1986); institutional theorists researched educational organizations (Meyer and Scott 1983; Tolbert 1985) and hospitals (Scott 1983) in specific parts of the USA; and proponents of resource dependency analyzed organizational structures and processes in selected American universities (Pfeffer and Salancik 1978).

In contrast, the MNC consists of a number of national subsidiaries, each of which is located in a particular national environment. Each of these environments might share some characteristics with other national environments because of interdependencies and cross-linkages; it might also possess other characteristics that are distinctive. Existing theory tends to deal with this situation in one of two ways. It can either consider the MNC as a single entity facing a common global environment, or treat it as a set of subunits, each operating in a distinct environment that is independent of the environments of all other units. Neither view is satisfactory, for the first ignores the differences across national borders, whereas the second ignores the similarities and interdependencies.

The problem of how to characterize the environment of MNCs, and the consequences of the diversity and interdependence of various national environments on different aspects of organization–environment relations in MNCs, lies at the core of the chapters by Westney (Chapter 3) and Ghoshal and Bartlett (Chapter 4). Westney focuses on institutional theory, which defines the environment as an "organizational field" of interacting organizations, which affect the structures and behaviors of the organizations operating in that field through processes of social influence: the

8

emulation of apparently successful patterns ("mimetic isomorphism") and compliance with the demands of more powerful organizations, or with the shared expectations of the many organized groups of social actors (such as professional groups). After an initial explication of this paradigm, she deals with two sets of questions. First, she asks how the study of MNCs might facilitate further development and enrichment of the paradigm. She believes that using institutional theory to study the MNC would force its advocates to deepen their treatment of three major issues: the analysis of the diversified organization that is a participant in several different organizational fields; changes in the boundaries of organizational fields; and the relationship between isomorphism and innovation. In turn, the analysis of certain key issues for the management of MNCs can be illuminated by the institutionalization paradigm, which views the MNC as an organization whose subunits are subject to potentially contradictory sets of isomorphic pulls from the parent-dominated multinational organization and from the local organizational field in each host country. She identifies three such key issues (the problem of standardization versus local tailoring in organizational structures and processes, the challenges of organizational learning across borders, and the relationship between host societies and the MNC) and suggests how institutional theory can facilitate a more theory-grounded analysis of current research questions, and raise interesting and important questions that have so far remained unaddressed.

In the next chapter, Ghoshal and Bartlett start with the same observation of diversity and interdependence among the national environments faced by MNC subunits to propose a model of the MNC as an internally differentiated inter-organization network. Their conceptualization of organization–environment interactions in the MNC is as a complex network of resource exchanges between MNC subunits and external actors, and across MNC subunits within and across the different national environments. They focus on resource exchange relationships as the defining characteristic of their model of the environment, although they too draw on an institutional theory base in considering these as social relationships rather than simply resource flows. Based on this conceptual model, they draw on developments in exchange theory and network analysis to propose a set of hypotheses that relate certain attributes of the MNC, such as resource configuration and internal distribution of power, to certain structural characteristics of the broader external network of all the key actors in the different national environments in which the MNC operates. Past research on MNCs, the authors claim, has at times been misleading because of its focus on dyadic exchange among specific actors—typically the headquarters and one subsidiary—while ignoring the structural effects of the broader network. They identify a variety of new research directions that they see as necessary to develop more fully the network theory approach.

The next chapter by Jacques Delacroix takes another influential paradigm

9

in organization theory, population ecology, and explores its relevance for the analysis of MNCs. This contribution challenges Doz and Prahalad's contention that the utility of the ecology model for the analysis of MNCs is limited to serving as a null hypothesis for studying organizational adaptation and change. Delacroix argues that important MNC-related phenomena can be both explained and predicted by using the very different conceptualization of environment–organization interactions in the ecology model: that change in the organizational landscape results from replacement of some organizational forms by others through the process of natural selection, rather than adaptation by existing organizations.

Delacroix, like Westney, provides a brief tutorial on the theory. He too presents a strong case for the potential synergies between the fields of organization theory and MNC-focused research. He argues that in order to identify the extent to which organizational change is shaped by selective elimination and replacement of organization forms versus the adaptation of individual organizations, survivor bias must be overcome through extended longitudinal studies of organizational populations. Cross-sectional research on one or a few chosen survivors will reveal adaptation as a self-fulfilling prophesy built into the research design. In arguing how MNC-related research can contribute to the development of the ecological approach, he suggests a theoretical extension that could have far-reaching consequences. For complex, multi-unit organizations such as MNCs, adaptation can be a selection process, in that selective elimination of parts out of a system may constitute a form of adaptation for the system as a whole. Thus, by letting specific underperforming subsidiaries "die," the MNC can evolve and adapt to changing environments. This proposition, stated as a speculation in Hannan and Freeman (1989: 42) and applied to the MNC by Delacroix, can provide a powerful extension of ecological theory. MNCs—offering the maximum heterogeneity in organizational change—can serve as a particularly attractive testing ground for this theoretical formulation.

In the fourth chapter on organization–environment interactions, Bruce Kogut begins with three of the most important and enduring questions in the field of international management: how firms internationalize, why they invest abroad, and what factors contribute to their competitiveness. Kogut suggests that the answers to these three questions are inseparably intertwined: firms develop out of the socioeconomic conditions of their home environment, and even as they internationalize, they remain imprinted by their early development in their domestic markets. With such a perspective, the analysis of the international expansion and competitiveness of firms becomes inseparable from the comparative analysis of organizations, which provides the basis for understanding the different imprints that firms from different countries carry into the international domain.

Starting from the empirical observation that competitive differences

10

among countries persist for long periods of time, Kogut argues that countries differ in their organizing principles and organizational capabilities, and that these capabilities diffuse more slowly across national boundaries than across firm boundaries. Companies within the national environment come to share these organizing principles because of their involvement in inter-industry networks within the country, which leads to learning from suppliers and customers: because of competition that leads to learning from competitors; because a shared societal knowledge base allows them to identify differences in the practices of other domestic firms and therefore to discern what is to be learned; and because of similarities in internal preferences and societal expectations which make such learning relatively more feasible. Diffusion of these organizing principles has been relatively slower and more difficult across national boundaries because inter-firm linkages have tended to be less dense internationally. The resulting differences in the organizing principles in different countries have led not only to different organizational capabilities of firms originating in those countries, but also to differences in their learning capabilities, since these capabilities are tied to the same organizing principles. These national organizing principles, rooted in the social and institutional structures of countries, therefore influence how firms internationalize and how competitive they are internationally. Kogut raises the fascinating question of the extent to which growing cross-country linkages and the growing internationalization of firms will erode country differences in organization and management, leading presumably to an erosion of the barriers to international organizational learning.

The seventh chapter, the new contribution by Mauro Guillén and Sandra Suárez, takes up one of the most striking theoretical developments of the past decade, the rise of the concept of "institution" to dominance in a wide range of disciplines and subfields, including political science, economics, the resurgent subfield of economic sociology, and comparative management. Where Westney's chapter focuses on the organization theory variant of institutional theory, Guillén and Suárez draw on a wider range of institutional paradigms to identify five approaches to understanding the institutional context of the MNC at the country level, thereby picking up on Kogut's challenge to bring more theory-based approaches to the understanding of country effects on the MNC. They identify and compare the five approaches (cross-cultural approaches, comparative authority and business systems, the political economy of foreign direct investment, the comparative analysis of corporate legal traditions, and the framing of the institutional environment in terms of political and contractual hazards). They assess the potential contributions of each approach to the analysis of MNC activities, and provide some recent examples of MNC research that adopts these perspectives, advocating the greater integration of these approaches into the study of MNCs in future. They assert the continued viability of the country level of analysis, which has so long been a touchstone of theory and research on the MNC.

ORGANIZATION STRUCTURE, GOVERNANCE, AND CULTURE

As issues of organization–environment interactions moved to the center stage of organization theory in the 1970s and 1980s, internal organizational issues in complex organizations received relatively less attention. In consequence, despite significant contributions by a few noted scholars, the concepts and tools of intra-organizational analysis perhaps failed to keep up with the significant changes that were occurring in practice.

For several of the dominant organization theories focused on structure and governance, including the transaction cost paradigm and agency theory, Chandler's description of the M-form organization still served as the model of complex organizations. In this model, a complex organization consists of a number of more or less self-contained, semi-autonomous divisions, grouped according to some set of criteria such as product lines, technologies, distribution channels, geography, or some combination of these under a corporate administrative structure. The distinguishing structural characteristics of the M-form, as described by Oliver Williamson, for example, are (1) the responsibility for all operating decisions is assigned to divisions, and (2) the staff attached to the general office are primarily concerned with monitoring division performance, allocating resources among divisions, and making strategic plans.

Nohria and Ghoshal (1989) argued that this stylized model of complex organizations did not provide an effective analytical framework for understanding the structural complexities of today's MNCs. One problem is that the model glosses over potential sources of variation in dispersed divisionalized firms. Allen (1978), for instance, has argued that a number of differences exist among firms that are ostensibly all M-form: differences in which of the firms' activities are centralized and which left to the divisions, as well as in modes of budgeting and control. Further, as Doz and Prahalad argue in their chapter, even within the same organization different divisions are often governed differently, with different levels of strategic and operational autonomy, according to variations in their environmental context and strategic focus. But by treating the divisions as independent of each other, the model also ignores a second key source of complexity in MNC structure and governance: inter-unit interdependence. As described by Doz and Prahalad, different national subsidiaries of an MNC share sequential, reciprocal, and pooled interdependencies with many other subsidiaries as well as with the headquarters. Assumptions that relationships must be either dependent or independent—common in theoretical analyses of centralization and control, for instance—are unrealistic in the MNC context.

These two limitations of the model contribute to a third: the model does not address a complicated issue concerning the level of analysis with which research on MNCs must cope. In the MNC, structural effects can arise from relational patterns at three different levels: the level of the subsidiary itself; that of the headquarters–subsidiary relationship; and the relational networks within the system as a whole, among the various organizational units, including the headquarters and all the national subsidiaries. These complexities of organization structure and governance in MNCs are the topic of the next four chapters.

Jean-François Hennart's chapter on control in MNCs suggests an alternative theoretical formulation using transaction cost and agency theory to analyze the issues of MNC structure and governance. Although he draws on these two well-established paradigms of organizational economics, his approach also represents a significant departure from how the two theories have generally been applied to MNC-related research. In contrast to a one-to-one correspondence between markets and price systems, on the one hand, and firms and hierarchies on the other, he distinguishes between methods of organization (the price system and hierarchy) and economic institutions (markets and firms). Both kinds of institution can and do employ both methods of organization, though with differing emphases. The objectives of organizing economic activities include facilitating both exchange and cooperation among actors. Under different conditions the two methods of organization incur different kinds and levels of costs for facilitating exchange and cooperation. The choice between the methods of organization within complex firms is governed by the desire to minimize these costs. With cost minimization as his guiding principle, Hennart presents a number of hypotheses regarding different aspects of MNC structure and modes of governance for different kinds of tasks and different subunit contexts.

In Chapter 9, William Egelhoff draws on contingency theory and, more specifically, on the information processing perspective developed by Galbraith (1977) and others to propose a broad research agenda that focuses on modeling "fit" between different aspects of the MNC's environmental and strategic context, and different attributes of its internal organization design. Drawing on his decade-long empirical research on this topic, Egelhoff puts forward a conceptual framework based on information processing as a means of guiding rigorous and theory-grounded research on structural and governance aspects of MNCs. Unlike some of the other theoretical proposals contained in this book, Egelhoff's model represents an established and relatively mature line of inquiry within the field of international management research. His focus, therefore, is on developing more rigorously defined constructs and on fine-grained operationalization that can move this approach forward to greater explanatory power and more multidimensional and differentiated analysis of microstructures for different subunits and tasks, as well as of the overall macrostructure of the corporation.

Whereas both Egelhoff and Hennart propose extensions and refinements in existing concepts of MNC structure and governance, Gunnar Hedlund suggests a more radical reconceptualization. Gunnar's tragically early death from a brain tumor in 1997 deprived the field of one its most original and playful minds, and both qualities are strongly evident in this chapter. His chapter challenges the often implicit and taken for granted belief in the hierarchy as an efficient and effective mechanism for social organization, and suggests that this belief is premised on assumptions of pre-specification and stability of input, throughput, and output processes; of preordained and unchanging relationships among different actors within the system and between the actors and the total system; and of universality and one-way ordering in the relationships between the parts and the whole. These assumptions, however valid in Simon's famous example of two watchmakers in his classic defense of hierarchy, are inappropriate in the context of complex social organizations in general and the MNC in particular. Instead of the hierarchy—a concept carried forward from the past and from another field—Hedlund proposes a new model for the modern corporation: "heterarchy." The heterarchy is not a stable ordering of jobs, roles, and transactions, nor is it a particular structure or governance mode; instead it is a mechanism for constantly selecting and adapting structure and governance mode. Hedlund reviews many well-known and well-documented characteristics of MNC organization to argue why his concept of the heterarchy is particularly suited for describing, understanding, and analyzing complex multinational organizations, and he formulates a set of distinguishing characteristics for heterarchies that can serve as reference points and define the points of departure for future research.

The next chapter also represents a significant departure from many popular research approaches to MNC governance. Chan Kim and Renée Mauborgne begin from the importance of decision-making processes for effective governance in complex and dispersed organizations such as MNCs, and draw on the fields of social psychology and law to explicate the importance of procedural justice in maintaining commitment, trust, and social harmony in such organizations. The authors share Hedlund's basic premise that hierarchical power has increasingly lost its effectiveness in mobilizing subsidiaries and in obtaining their cooperation in corporate goals and objectives. As the subunits have grown in size and complexity, and as dependence on the center and isolation from other subunits have been replaced by pervasive interdependence, procedural justice has become increasingly important in fostering a sense of community in the MNC's worldwide network of subsidiaries. Procedural justice, the authors claim, is what makes the difference between perfunctory and committed cooperation, and is therefore the key to effective worldwide management, which often requires a subsidiary to sacrifice its own immediate gains for system-level benefits.

In their chapter, Kim and Mauborgne provide a detailed review of procedural justice theory and the empirical support it has received in the field of legal studies, and define the various factors that contribute to the definition of fairness of process, as perceived by subsidiary managers. They present some empirical evidence to show the positive association and causal link between this perception of a just and fair process and higher-order attitudes of individuals, such as commitment and trust, and their overall satisfaction with outcomes. While emphasizing the potentially important and powerful contributions that this theoretical approach can make to the analysis of governance issues in MNCs, the authors also point out several limitations of this approach and suggest how they might be overcome in future research.

The 1980s witnessed a mushrooming of interest in organizational culture (Barley, Meyer, and Gash 1988). Some theorists saw culture as the middle ground between what they perceived as the overly deterministic models of behavior in and of organizations, set forth in functionalist macro-organization theory, and the overly voluntaristic models of individual behavior presented in micro-organization theory. Culture, in this model, serves as a bridge that offers at least a partial explanation of why people are in fact able to do things together in organizations. Organizations are socially constructed systems of meaning: they do not have cultures, they *are* cultures. As cultures, they help create the realities perceived by organization members, which in turn serve as the basis for organizational action.

Others, with a more normative orientation, have seen culture as the glue that holds organizations together, in spite of the centrifugal forces generated by multiple and conflicting objectives, pervasive uncertainty and ambiguity, and increasing diversity and interdependence. Rational strategies of organizing, including normal structures and systems, are incapable of organizing such complexity. Culture, in this view, is a powerful managerial tool for creating integration, cooperation, and alignment between individual and organizational interests.

From either of these perspectives the case of the multinational presents an interesting arena for concept building and empirical research. The multinational represents a theater of action at the intersection between two cultures: the culture or subcultures of the MNC organization and the culture or subcultures of the different countries in which the MNC operates. If culture is a socially defined meaning system that allows individuals to interpret organizational actions and to determine their own roles and beliefs with regard to those actions, individuals in MNCs must somehow reconcile the demands each of these two cultures places on the other. And the MNC, in turn, must take into account the processes and challenges of this reconciliation, as it attempts to develop and protect a broader organizational and administrative coherence amid the diversity that exists not only among its employees but also among its customers, suppliers, and others with whom it must interact in its operations around the world. The complex interactions among kinds and levels of culture in and around MNCs constitute the focus of the last two chapters in this volume.

In Chapter 12, Martin Kilduff emphasizes the importance of routine behavior in organizations, and argues that the MNC provides an interesting arena for research on the formation, diffusion, and unintended consequences of the reproduction of norms and routines in complex organizations. One view of organizational culture, he points out, is as a set of social constructs negotiated between knowledgeable actors to anticipate and control the motivational and cognitive diversity in organizations. These constructs, however, which serve as the rules of everyday life in organizations, are often tacit and opaque to the members, including top management. Because of this tacit nature of organizational routines, they are difficult to replicate, and their reproduction is accompanied by distortions and random variations. In the MNC, given the diversity of cultural premises of actors in different countries, these variations and distortions become particularly acute and difficult to control. As a result, when organizational routines are replicated in different parts of the MNC, perverse and unintended outcomes are as likely as the intended ones. Drawing primarily on micro-organizational theories of enactment and structuration, Kilduff suggests a set of theoretical anchors on which research on the micro-level behaviors of individuals and teams can lead to richer and more detailed understanding of the processes by which norms are formed and replicated to guide day-to-day actions in MNCs.

In the final chapter, John Van Maanen challenges much of the existing conceptualization of organization culture, which, he claims, either trivializes culture by reducing its relevance to something thought to be fully controllable or enshrines culture as something impenetrable and unique. Culture, he argues, deals with patterns of thought and not behavior; it is a model *for* behavior, not a model *of* behavior. The student of culture must recognize that it is both a socially organized process and a collectively validated product.

This view of culture focuses attention on the flow of cultural influence across nations, a process in which MNCs play a key role. In all such flows, even when a direct replication or transfer is attempted, the meaning of what is transferred is always adapted. The foreign and the indigenous are combined into a new idiom that is consistent with the socially validated distinctiveness of the host nation and its norms. In the original chapter, Van Maanen illustrated this process of adaptation through an analysis of the Disneylands in the United States and Japan; in this volume, he has added Disney's expansion into France and China. His fundamental conclusion remains the same: culture implies simultaneously both differences and similarities among people, and the concept of an organizational culture for large, complex, and internally differentiated organizations such as MNCs has limited meaning, except as a conscious managerial effort to describe to stakeholders how corporate officials would like their organization to be seen. Van Maanen instead argues for analyzing culture deeper within organizations, where it is a felt reality of smaller units and thereby can provide insights into the complicated, divisive, unpredictable but lively processes of daily social life. Accordingly he argues that research focusing on culture as the organization of diversity rather than as a structure of homogeneity is more likely to provide insights on how it is symbolically constructed, represented, and used by different organizational groups.

POSTSCRIPT

It is not our objective to present a balance sheet of what the chapters in this book have accomplished and how much progress, if any, they have made in the bridge-building enterprise. Our hope is that the book will continue to trigger reflection and debate in the organization theory and the international management communities; that perhaps it will generate more collaboration across the two fields; but above all else that it will stimulate mutual interest and further research that can benefit both fields.

Although the book is premised on the assumption that research on MNCs can enrich OT and that theory can, in turn, enrich research on MNCs, it would be overly optimistic to claim that the validity of this approach has been established unambiguously. Many key questions remain unanswered, not least of which is the speculation of Doz and Prahalad in this volume: that the phenomenon of the MNC may be changing so rapidly that any effort to build systematic and durable theory about this phenomenon may itself be premature.

Yet some assertions can perhaps be made. The MNC is an important social institution. Collectively, MNCs account for over 40 percent of the world's manufacturing output and almost a quarter of world trade. A major source of research and development resources, they are an important vehicle world-wide for technological innovation and its diffusion. Their catalytic role in the growing density of cross-border linkages among nations and firms make MNCs one of the major agents of organizational and social change in modern society, and one of the most important actors in the processes of globalization that are the focus of so much contemporary debate in the popular press and among social scientists. And yet in much of the popular and even the scholarly literature on globalization, MNCs are either demonized or "black-boxed": treated as unitary actors driven by over-simplified goals. For organization theorists, continuing indifference to this organizational form may well amount to staying away from one of the main arenas that is influencing and even defining the processes of social change that lie at the heart of their discipline.

The model of the "new" MNC implies that however important the organizational history of individual MNCs and the national pattern of their evolution, MNCs face an increasingly shared international environment which generates commonalities in the pressures for organizational change and the direction of that change; and they face challenges that are not encountered by comparable domestic firms. This model suggests, in other words, that at least in this regard MNCs constitute a distinct form or population of organizations, defined by their multinationality, and that in the new MNC, multinationality has implications for every subunit in the organization—including the home country organization—which cannot be ignored in organizational analysis. In broad terms, each subunit is influenced not just by its own environment but by the environments of other subunits. The very small number of studies of firms that explicitly analyze the effect of multinationality on organizational behavior (outside the international management field) suggests how radical an assertion this is.

But if organization theorists have something to get from research on MNCs, we remain equally convinced that they have much to give. Even if the chapters in this volume raise more questions than they are able to answer, they do demonstrate the wide range of MNC-related issues that organization theory can address and potentially illuminate. Further, representing perhaps the serendipitous process by which the contributors to this volume came together, the issues that are raised are a small and unsystematic sample of the vast array of questions about MNCs and their environments that can easily be generated, for which OT can provide a strong research anchor. For example, the insistence of some international management scholars and corporate managers on overcoming the inadequacies of the formal organizational structure by socializing managers to deal with the contradictions as they arise should generate some skepticism among organization theorists. The formal organization chart may no longer capture the key elements of structure, but the insistence on the importance of shared experience and socialization processes as the solution to the strains on the formal system suggests that the *social* structure of the emerging MNC is of critical importance. The contribution that organization theorists make in identifying crucial elements and indicators of social structure could be of critical importance in understanding the evolving form of the new MNC, if indeed it is as new as many in the international management field believe.

Another issue that has yet to be directly addressed in the international management literature on the new MNC is the extent to which the tighter coupling of organizational subunits, the growing density of interactions across the subsidiaries, and the postulated reliance on coordination through socialization of upper-level managers, will result in increasing structural and process similarity across subunits. If this occurs, one of the potential advantages of the MNC posited in the new model—the range of internal variation across subsidiaries that provides avenues for innovation and learning—will erode over time.

To turn to scholars in the field of international management, they too must confront some disturbing questions. In spite of over two decades of research, their efforts have not proved to be cumulative or consistent. Part of the resulting frustration may well be ascribed to the changing nature of the phenomenon, as suggested by Doz and Prahalad, and to the double hermeneutic to which Kilduff alludes. But at least in part, the ability to make satisfactory progress in building a coherent body of knowledge on the MNC may also be a result of the lack of theory grounding and theory building, as some international management scholars have themselves asserted (Egelhoff 1988b; Toyne and Nigh 1997). Irrespective of how far this book has advanced the claim of macro-organization theory to serve as an anchor of future research, the need for an anchor has, we hope, been made evident.

Note

1 The "integration/responsiveness" framework originated in C. K. Prahalad's Harvard dissertation, "The strategic processes in a multinational corporation" (1975) and was further developed by Yves Doz (1979) and Chris Bartlett (1979).

2 Managing MNCs: A Search for a New Paradigm

Yves L. Doz and C. K. Prahalad

The increasing intensity of global competition (Porter 1986), the develop-ment of multinational companies (Stopford, Dunning, and Haberich 1980; Dunning and Pearce 1985), and the attendant academic and managerial interest in the role of the diversified multinational corporation (Prahalad and Doz 1987; Ghoshal 1987; Bartlett and Ghoshal 1989) are too well docu-mented to merit repetition. Although there has been a lot of debate on the nature of global competition and of the diversified multinational corporation (hereafter referred to as the DMNC), very little attention has been paid to the conceptual and theoretical frameworks used to analyze DMNCs and their management. Many attempts have been make to analyze aspects of the MNC starting from an established theoretical base. For example, Buckley and Casson (1986) and Hennart (1982) have attempted to seek a rationale for the MNC using a transaction cost perspective. Others (e.g. Dunning 1980a, 1980b, 1981b) have emphasized the need for an "eclectic" theory explaining the DMNCs. We argue in this chapter that on the whole, schol-arly research on the functioning of the MNC has suffered both from the desire among some scholars to persist with existing paradigms, and from other scholars' ignorance of what existing theories could bring them. Since existing paradigms, by the very nature of their underlying simplifying assumptions, are not fully adequate to capture the complexity and richness of the DMNC, and since discipline-based researchers have seldom taken the DMNC as an object of research, this discrepancy is not surprising.

The development of a "process school" of research on the DMNC over the last 15 years led to the emergence of a new paradigm. This chapter positions this paradigm and existing "streams" of organization theory research in relation to each other, in an attempt to resolve the observed discrepancies between organization theorists and scholars of the DMNC. The argument is developed in three main steps. First, we describe some basic requirements that a paradigm used in the study of DMNCs must satisfy. Second, we analyze the dominant paradigms that have been used by researchers studying organizations (not necessarily DMNCs), and evaluate the adequacy as well as the adaptability of specific paradigms to the study of DMNCs. Finally, we outline the search for a new paradigm, and the contributions of a process school of research on multinational management.

THE NATURE OF THE DMNC AND THE
SPECIFICATION OF A PARADIGM FOR RESEARCH

In this section, we attempt to establish how the complexity of the DMNC, as an organizational firm, sets some distinctive requirements for any theory to be useful in analyzing, conceptualizing, and explaining management tasks in the DMNC. Our purpose here is not to explain why the DMNC exists as an organizational form. Various researchers, starting with Hymer (1960) and culminating in Dunning's eclectic theory, have explained the logic for internalization of transactions and firm-specific assets in the DMNC. Our purpose in this chapter is to analyze management processes in DMNCs, not to explain the boundaries of DMNCs compared with other forms of organization of international investment and trade.

We see the essential difference between DMNCs and simpler organizations as stemming from the combined consequences of multidimensionality and heterogeneity. Multidimensionality results from the very nature of DMNCs: they cover multiple geographical markets with multiple product lines in typically multifunction activities such as sales, manufacturing, service, and research and development. DMNCs therefore face the problem of structuring the interfaces between these multiple dimensions which are intrinsic to their activities. In turn, multidimensionality means that no simple, unidimensional, hierarchical solution to the issue of structuring the DMNC exists (Stopford and Wells 1972; Davis and Lawrence 1977; Beer and Davis 1976; Prahalad 1975; Doz 1976, 1979). Beyond the structural indeterminacy of DMNCs lies the need to handle multiple stakeholders, externally and by reflection internally, and multiple perspectives on choices and decisions. Simple concepts of centralized versus decentralized organizations break down in the face of strategic, structural, and political multidimensionality, calling for more complex, "multifocal" approaches that constantly reach trade-offs among priorities expressed in different dimensions (Doz 1979, 1986) and embodied in different management subgroups.

Heterogeneity results from the differences between the optimal trade-offs for different businesses, countries, functions, and tasks as a function of a whole range of economic and political characteristics that differ between countries and affect individual businesses and tasks in quite varied ways. DMNCs are therefore very heterogeneous organizations. Any theory of organization applied to DMNCs must incorporate this heterogeneity. In particular, some businesses and functions may be much more "global" than others, which are more "local." The advantages of globalization versus the needs for local responsiveness and adaptations are quite varied across businesses, countries, and functions. To be applied to DMNCs an organizational theory must therefore incorporate a differentiated approach to businesses, countries, and functions, and provide enough flexibility for different trade-offs among multiple dimensions to be made.

Except in advocating a matrix organization, which is another way to acknowledge structural indeterminacy, a structural theory of DMNCs has little to offer. One needs a theory that transcends the structural dimensions and focuses on underlying processes. Issues of information and control become essential. More than the formal structure, the informal flow of information matters. So do the processes of influence and power, how the trade-offs between multiple stakeholders and multiple perspectives are made.

If one considers the evolution of sources of competitiveness in global competition, the perception of the importance of information flows is reinforced. As competitors increasingly achieve parity in access to resources (including technology) in various parts of the world, sources of competitiveness shift from location-specific factors to firm-specific factors: that is, the overall organizational capability to coordinate the use of resources in order to respond to short-lived opportunities that may arise in many different parts of the world. The traditional stable international oligopolies, with a handful of "friendly" competitors, are replaced by a quick succession of potential shorter-term monopolies, which only the more agile and discerning forms identify and exploit. Although this shift takes place unevenly across global industries (with financial services and electronics leading the way, and more stable, traditional products such as tires being less affected), it does suggest that researchers need to shift their emphasis from the physical infrastructure and the resource deployment of DMNCs to their information processing networks and to resource mobilization (Doz and Prahalad 1988; Martinez and Jarillo 1989).

Adopting an information network and organizational capability perspective, however, is not enough. The size and complexity of the typical DMNCs, which often have hundreds of business units active in scores of countries, means that linkages and interdependencies can be neither planned nor centrally managed. Which linkages are going to be useful at a particular point in time for a specific task between two or more subunits is unpredictable, and probably needs to be self-adjusting. Management in the DMNC thus calls for providing decentralized, delegated decision contexts within which opportunities for linkages between subunits will arise at various points, levels in organization, and times. In that sense, an inter-organizational relation perspective may well be necessary to account for the polycentric MNCs (Ghoshal and Bartlett in this volume).

This raises an issue of fuzzy boundaries. Relational contracting within the DMNC and with external partners, customers, and suppliers has produced situations where the boundaries of the firm are no longer always clear-cut and well delineated. A theory of DMNC management has to take this fuzziness of boundaries into consideration as well. Here again an inter-organizational network perspective is appropriate.

The nature of this decentralized network management process creates a trade-off between repeatability and learning. For the DMNC organization to survive and keep its value to subunits, it must allow repeatability at a low cost: that is, it must provide for routines and organizational memory that allow interaction patterns to be repeated. Yet at the same time it has to invent, select, and retain new interaction patterns when external conditions require an innovative response. This combination involves a delicate balance between institutional continuity and change capability.

In summary, considering the multidimensionality and heterogeneity of the DMNC has led us to specify particular demands on the DMNC organization and on its management tasks that an organizational theory of the DMNC has to take into account:

1. **Structural indeterminacy.** Neither a single stable unidimensional structure nor simple concepts of structure such as centralization and decentralization are likely to be useful.
2. **Internal differentiation.** Management processes need to differentiate between various countries, products, and functions in the management process.
3. **Integrative optimization.** Management processes need to foster varied decision trade-offs among multiple priorities, expressed along different dimensions and represented by diverse groups of managers.
4. **Information intensity.** The importance of both formal and informal information flows as a source of competitive advantage and as an implicit structure in DMNCs is such that managing information becomes a central task of management.
5. **Latent linkages.** In a complex DMNC it is not possible to prespecify linkages and interdependencies, but only to facilitate the emergence of appropriate linkages, as the need for them arises, in a decentralized self-structuring process.
6. **Networked organization and fuzzy boundaries.** This structure creates a need explicitly to incorporate partners, customers, and suppliers' relationships, as well as networked relationships in the management tasks.
7. **Learning and continuity.** There is tension between the need for repeatability of interactions at a low cost and that for innovation and change.

These seven demands of DMNC organization and management, derived from the multidimensionality, complexity, and heterogeneity of the DMNC, provide a grid against which to review various strands of organizational theory, and to assess how and to what extent they may contribute to an understanding of DMNC management.

THE APPLICABILITY OF ORGANIZATION THEORY TO THE STUDY OF DMNCS

Organizational theorists have very seldom taken the DMNC as their focus of investigation. They have, however, dealt with many of the issues that are germane to the DMNC and some that are conceptually similar. We will examine the contributions that theorists can make to the study of DMNCs from two standpoints: Do contributions address the seven elements of the DMNC established above, and how useful are they to help conceptualize DMNC management processes?

The study of complex organizations has a long intellectual history, to which many illustrious scholars have contributed. Any attempt to summarize this field must therefore be approached with caution and humility. By its very nature, such an effort is likely to cluster different streams of intellectual effort, attempt to distill the basic premises behind the lines of inquiry, and make generalizations. Furthermore, our brief review is made from a very particular perspective: To what extent do these theories contribute to an understanding of the tasks involved in meeting the specific demands of DMNC management, as outlined above? We recognize that risk. But this attempt, with all its limitations, is an important part of building a new paradigm.

An implicit recognition of the complexity of the phenomenon under scrutiny—complex organizations—is the fact that there is no single dominant paradigm to study it. Over the last ten years, however, several streams have gained currency in the academic literature. These are summarized in Table 2.1, and discussed in detail below.

Economic theories of organization

The application of institutional economics theories to DMNCs has grown from two distinct but increasingly intertwined theories: transaction cost analysis and principal–agent theory (Arrow 1985; Williamson 1975; Williamson and Ouchi 1981; Williamson 1985). The former focuses on transaction costs in markets, and explains organizations as a consequence of market failure. The latter focuses on transaction costs within hierarchies, and the cost of control and compliance in organizations.

Transaction cost analysis provides a powerful point of departure for analyzing choices between institutional forms, and thus can be used to establish the efficient boundaries of a DMNC (Dunning 1980b; Buckley and Casson 1986; Hennart 1982; Teece 1985). The usefulness of transaction cost analysis for research on management processes is limited by the simplifying assumptions inherent in the "hierarchy" category and by its primary focus on single transactions as units of analysis. Thus, although transaction cost analysis does not formally violate the seven criteria established above, it is of limited usefulness for our purpose unless one adds to it reputational (Kreps 1984) and relational contracting (Dore 1983) dimensions.

Transaction cost analysis has proven useful in analyzing specific types of inter-organizational relationships in a North American context, such as relationships between US firms and their suppliers, vertical integration (Monteverde and Teece 1982; Stockey 1983), and joint ventures with rigorous constraints on the

24

nature of the joint venture (Hennart 1982). Transaction cost analysis, however, does not explain relationships between Japanese firms and their suppliers, a relationship built on mutual trust and on a belief that the joint benefits (in contrast to self-interest) are worth pursuing in a "win–win" framework over the long term (Dore 1983).

In fact, one of the most challenging management tasks in the DMNC is to make the assumptions of transaction cost analysis untrue: hence the emphasis on organizational culture, clan behavior, and control (Ouchi 1980), and on normative integration of managers in MNCs (Hedlund 1981). Transaction cost analysis, by its very assumptions about human beings and organizations, prevents itself from addressing managerial issues.

Agency theory, on the other hand, aims at analyzing management control issues in various forms of contractual relationships between principals and agents, and makes a useful contribution to the study of DMNC management. Agency theory does raise relevant managerial issues by casting issues of control in "outcome" or "behavioral" terms (Eisenhardt 1989). For example, the outcome-based model of control provides an interesting perspective in which to cast the problem of controlling subsidiaries, especially nationally responsive subsidiaries about which the headquarters may have very little information, whose behavior cannot be monitored easily and whose managers may not fully share headquarters' goals. Conversely, control over globally integrated subsidiaries may be a problem in behavior-based control, because the relationship between specialized and interdependent subsidiaries is based on the headquarters' substantive understanding of the tasks to be performed. In fact, headquarters may provide the skills needed at the subsidiaries. The task is to create greater goal convergence between headquarters and subsidiaries, which is often fostered by international mobility of managers, multidimensional measurement systems, and a desire to create a shared sense of purpose. The dichotomy between outcome-based and behavior-based control is not new, remains quite simplistic, and certainly under-emphasizes the non-economic dimensions of control. The simplicity of the binary choice it posits prevents it from exploring the more subtle blends of control and management approaches used in companies (Lawrence and Dyer 1983).

By emphasizing these non-economic dimensions, the literature on organizational culture and normative integration of MNCs challenges the simplifying assumptions of the agency theory approach in a much needed direction, to include psychological affiliation models of control and goal congruence often ignored by the economic theories of organization, thereby relaxing the assumptions of economic self-interest and rationality.

Further, agency theory implies a hierarchical relationship between principal and agent and assumes implicitly the centrality of headquarters. By treating the organization as a series of contracts, agency theory may not include the multitude of contingencies that arise in the management of

25

Table 2.1 The relevance of organization theories to DMNC management research

	Major streams of organization theory		
Criteria of relevance to DMNC management	**Transaction cost**	**Agency theory**	**Population ecology**
Structural indeterminacy	Yes	Implicitly hierarchical	No
Internal differentiation	Yes	Simplistic: outcome versus behavior control	No
Decision trade-offs between multiple priorities	Narrowly defined self-interest not compatible; extension needed to include relational contracting	No, mainly dyadic principal–agent relationships	No
Importance of information flows	Yes, but limited to uncertainty and asymmetry issues	Yes, but focused mainly on observability of behavior and measurability of results	No
Emergent rather than prescribed languages	Transaction patterns are not specified a priori. Hierarchies, however, are useful for interorganizational analysis	Yes, series of contracts but not encompassing multiplicity of linkages	No
Fuzzy boundaries	Yes, well suited to the analysis of boundaries, but needs to be complemented to incorporate relational contracting	Yes	No
Repeatability versus change			Change capabilities are very limited

Table 2.1 continued

Major streams of organization theory			
Institutional theory	Contingency theory	Power relationships and adaption	Organizational learning
Yes	No, structure "fits" the environment, except for matrix management	Yes, self-adjusting network of power relationships	Yes
Yes, depending on influences	Yes	Yes, depending on external uncertainties	Yes
Not explicitly, but compassed in multiple 'fields'	Yes, at least on the part of some embody researchers (Lawrence and Lorach)	Yes, power "games" embody multiple priorities	Yes, part of learning processes
Yes	Yes	Yes, information is a key determinant of influence	Yes
Yes	Possible, but not specified clearly, although consistent with theory	Yes	Yes, result of learning processes
Yes, "isomorphic" pressures to conform	Not explicitly	Yes, network of relationships in and out of the organization	Not explicitly, but not excluded
Yes	No	Yes, depends on network structure	Yes, central to theory

DMNCs. As one tries to extend the agency theory framework to include a complex web of networked relationships, the researcher's task becomes extremely complex as the one-to-one nature of relationships, the simplicity of contracts, and the clear identities of principals and agents tend to fade.

The increasingly related theories of transaction costs and principal–agent relationships both suffer too much from restrictive and culturally bound assumptions to allow them to do more than raise managerial issues. Although they provide useful starting points from which to consider firm boundaries and control issues, their formulation of the working of an organization is too simplified to be useful for management purposes.

Environmental adaptation theories

The issue of whether and how organizations adapt to their environment in order to succeed—or at least survive—has been central to organization theory for decades. Out of the very rich and diverse literature on organizational adaptation emerge the themes of proactive versus reactive or even random adaptation, and of the modes and processes of adaptation, which are studied at various levels of aggregation: populations of organization (population ecology), organizational fields (institutional theory), and individual organizations and their subunits (contingency theory). Since each of these levels is relevant to DMNC management research, as is the polarity between active and passive adaptation, we concentrate our analysis on these three main streams of environmental adaptation theories.

Population ecology

Population ecology provides the "null hypothesis" to strategic management of the DMNC. Population ecology assumes that environmental resources are unequally distributed between "niches" in the environment, and either an organization finds itself in a resource niche it can use or it does not, and it succeeds or falters accordingly (Hannan and Freeman 1977). Population ecology normally assumes strategic choices on the part of organizations to be infeasible (Aldrich 1979), although some recent developments now distinguish "core" unchanging features of organizations and "peripheral" ones, which can change, creating the possibility of proactive adaptation (e.g. Singh and Lumsden 1990). From the standpoint of research on the management of DMNCs, population ecology is most useful when it stresses the difficulties that limit the feasibility of successful strategic redirection in MNCs (Hannan and Freeman 1989). Population ecology reports findings similar to those of some researchers of DMNC management processes when it stresses how over-adaptation to specific environmental conditions makes reaction to changes in the environment particularly difficult (Aldrich 1979; Doz 1979; Prahalad and Doz 1987). However, the level of aggregation of the theory of population

ecology (populations of organizations) tells us little about why or how companies fail to adapt, as compared to the management process literature (Doz
1979; Doz and Prahalad 1984; Bartlett and Ghoshal 1989).

The very fact that population ecology does not consider managerial issues,
but questions their relevance, makes it a little unfair to apply our seven elements of appropriateness for DMNC analysis to population ecology:
population ecology fails on nearly all criteria (Table 2.1), but population
ecology never set out to analyze managerial behavior!

Perhaps, however, the population ecology theory can be made useful by
shifting the level of aggregation at which it is applied to the inside of large
complex firms, where it can provide a logic to selection and adaptation of
subunits within the DMNC network, the network itself being considered as
the population (Hannan and Freeman 1989; Delacroix, Chapter 5 in this
volume). Focusing on selection processes within the firm and on the relative
success of various geographical affiliates and product lines in different environments and over time under specific management processes and
management system settings can open an interesting avenue for research, and
can use population ecology reasoning to study the adaptation of subunits to
different environments under different management conditions.

Institutional theory

Institutional theory is most useful for DMNC research in considering
subunit adaptations to differentiated local environments and to corporate
management systems. The concept of organizational field (DiMaggio and
Powell 1983) allows us to consider interactions, mutual awareness, information and patterns of competitive and coalitional behavior between
organizations as determinants of their adaptation. This is clearly consistent in spirit with the early categorization work on MNC structures
(Fayerweather 1960; Perlmutter 1969) and more recent clinical studies
of organizational adaptation to diverse types of multinational environments (Prahalad 1975; Doz 1976, 1979; Bartlett and Ghoshal 1989). By
showing that some of the most interesting institutionalization processes
may occur in organizations that straddle several "fields" (Zucker 1987),
institutional theory is also consistent with the observation on the part of
DMNC scholars that "multifocal" (Doz 1979, 1986) or "transnational"
(Bartlett and Ghoshal 1989) management processes hold the most strategic promise and raise the most difficult managerial issues in the context
of DMNCs.

At a second level of analysis, that of adaptation within firms rather than
between institutions, institutional theory is also interesting. Both Meyer and
Rowan (1977) and Zucker (1983) stress that organizations are powerful entities providing meaning and encouraging conformity in individual behavior. The
fact that MNC managers are subject to both corporate and external influences

Yves L. Doz and C. K. Prahalad

(Westney, this volume) makes them a particularly rich territory in which to apply institutionalization theory.

Although the current development of institutional theory is not specific enough (in its analysis and conceptualization of institutionalization mechanisms) to make it directly applicable in the management of MNCs, it provides a most helpful theoretical base for researchers. For example, it allows the formulation of problems of headquarters–subsidiaries relationships and of the possible organizational implications of addressing national responsiveness and global integration demands at multiple levels of aggregation, from the individual to the interorganizational level (Scott 1987a).

In summary, institutional theory is very consistent in its approach to organizational phenomena with the criteria we established. The dearth of explicit use of institutional theory in the study of DMNCs may reflect more the youth of the theory, the lack of discipline base for many MNC scholars, and the methodological and epistemological differences between institutional theory researchers and the clinical researchers working on the management of DMNCs. It seems, however, that as institutional theory develops further it will holds much promise for the study of DMNC management issues and processes.

Contingency theory

Contingency theories of organization developed mainly in the 1960s (Woodward 1965; Thompson 1967; Lawrence and Lorsch 1967). Contingency theory clearly influenced research on MNCs. The early models of structural adaptation of MNCs to geographic and product diversity (Fouraker and Stopford 1968; Stopford and Wells 1972) are clearly examples of structural functionalist contingency theory applied to MNCs organizational forms. Research on patterns and modes of headquarters control over affiliates (Negandhi and Baliga 1981; Hedlund 1981; Doz and Prahalad 1984; Ghoshal and Nohria 1990) has also been clearly cast in a contingency model, although it considered both the adjustment of subsidiaries to their environment and to the culture and style of the parent company, thus raising issues of institutional isomorphism which are closer to the institutional school of organization theory. Researchers who focused on information flows and information processing capabilities of MNCs also clearly adopted a contingency framework (e.g. Egelhoff 1988a), drawing largely on the work of Lawrence and Lorsch and on that of Galbraith (1973). Subsequent research by Bartlett and Ghoshal (1986, 1989) also clearly draws on the contingency framework, although the interpretation of their detailed analysis of nine MNCs draws on many strands of theory and remains phenomenological in focus.

Although the contingency theory of organizations, with its emphasis on differentiated responses to diverse environments and integration of action across environments, has had the most direct impact of all strands of organization theory on MNC management research, it leaves the issues of change and adaptation to new environmental demands, and thus part of the challenge to management research from population ecology, unanswered. Empirical research on contingency theory has been mostly static, seldom researching change processes. The most notable exceptions are Prahalad (1975), Doz (1976, 1979), and Doz and Prahalad (1981, 1987). The primarily static and functionalist views taken by most contingency theory research do not easily allow the incorporation of change processes in their theory, except at the broadest level of assuming that system dynamics applies to organizational change processes. Issues of empowerment, decentralization, and the deliberate mismatch between organization and environment to create a state of tension that facilitates adaptation are all recent additions, and often challenges, to contingency theory (e.g., Norman 1976; Hamel and Prahalad 1989). A functionalist, top management-driven perspective, in which adaptation is primarily organization design and development, begs the issue of how top management perceives the need for adjusting the fit, or for responding to new environmental conditions.

Further, an explicit use of contingency theory may lead to simplistic dichotomous thinking in considering the management of DMNCs, and in particular to polarization of one's understanding of MNC management into an opposition between responsiveness and integration categories when, in fact, a fusion is needed: that is, how to achieve both integration and responsiveness and to build on the dualities that result (Evans and Doz 1989).

Despite possible criticisms that contingency theory is static and encourages dichotomous thinking, it does meet most of our criteria, at least to an extent. Although contingency theory does not encompass structural indeterminacy (except in its extension to matrix organizations by Davis and Lawrence 1977), it does provide for internal differentiation and multiple perspectives. It also stresses both the importance of information flows (for example, the interfunctional integration in Lawrence and Lorsch 1967) and the possibility of emergent linkages in the management of interdependencies, rather than the presumption of linkages a priori.

Beyond the obvious applicability of a differentiation–integration framework to the managerial dilemmas of the DMNC, the language in which contingency theory was developed provided the intermediate levels/conceptual constructs that allowed us to bridge theory and the phenomenological approach to MNC management. The analysis of management processes and systems by Lawrence and Lorsch (1967) provides a rich basis to study integration within complex organizations, and can readily be applied to DMNCs. In sum, contrary to the other, more abstract streams of organization theory, which seldom develop intermediate-level constructs, contingency theory went a good part of the way towards process research and provided a relatively firmer and easier framework for scholars of the

DMNC. In fact, one wonders whether contingency theory has not had an excessive influence on subsequent research and thus limited progress in research on the DMNC.

Power relationships and organizational adaptation

The work of Crozier (1964) and Crozier and Friedberg (1980) provides an insightful analysis of organizations as networks of relationships in which "actors" play self-interested and individually rational strategies in collective "games" mediated by collectively accepted "rules" and driven by the resources and constraints of the individual "actors". In particular, Crozier saw control over uncertainties affecting the performance of other members of the organization as a critical resource.

The network of relationships is thus never totally integrated or disintegrated. Organizations maintain a degree of cohesion, and consistency in relation to their environment, through the regulation of internal antagonism (Astley and Van de Ven 1983). The game in the system of relationships balances tensions between integration and fragmentation. Its rules must be followed for the mutually beneficial association to continue, but players follow different personal strategies in the game depending on their own objectives and the resources they control.

In this perspective, adaptation to the environment takes place as those players most directly able to mediate dependencies with the environment for other players become more influential in the network of power relationships. Uncertainty brought by control over information is a key dependency, but other sources of dependence are also important—for example, the ability to influence the environment's munificence. Structural inertia does exist, as in the population ecology view, but adaptation to changes in the environment may take place through an evolution in the game that reflects the changing relative criticality of various dependencies with the environment, and brings more power to players best able to face these dependencies successfully. The adaptive capability of the organization depends on the density of the network of relationships. Very hierarchical organizations, with star and spoke patterns of communication and dependence, are not adaptive because the games they allow comprise relatively few strategies and cannot be changed easily. Organizations with more diverse linkages in their networks, in particular more lateral and diagonal rather than vertical linkages, are more adaptive. The network of relationships can reconfigure itself as new environmental contingencies become important. A system of relationships is therefore more or less "blocked" or adaptive depending on whether its structure is narrowly hierarchical or not (Crozier 1964). This is congruent with earlier studies of the innovativeness and adaptativeness of organizations: for example, Burns and Stalker's (1961) contrast of "mechanistic" and "organic" organizations.

In this approach power accrues to players who control resources, irrespective of their hierarchical positions. The model posits no hierarchical system or collective goals, and thus escapes the criticisms leveled by population ecologists at the strategic choice and deliberate environment–organization adaptation models. Adaptation takes place, or not, as a function of the structure of the network of relationships and of the external constraints in the environment (and presumably of how fast they change). Although individual rationality is usually assumed, organizational rationality does not necessarily follow. Information asymmetry, misunderstanding of the strategies of other actors, and differences in goals among individuals allow for loose coupling and unstructured decision-making processes. Action can emerge and generate random variation in the system, which in turn helps its adaptation. Events can thus unfold and be incorporated into the relational system, which then in turn responds to them (March and Olsen 1980; Weick 1979).

By providing a very rich yet simple analytical theory of intra-organizational influence processes, the power dependence school addresses, albeit often implicitly, the seven elements of a relevant theory of the management of DMNCs. Beyond these elements, the power-and-dependence model holds a clear attraction for MNC management scholars, who have usually originated from a phenomenological rather than disciplinary perspective and have an applied rather than theoretical focus.

First, the power-and-dependence model's assumptions about human beings and the nature of organizations seem more realistic than those of other models, including the strategic choice model. The assumptions about human beings as purposively rational and self-interested but with differentiated personal goals and operating in a boundedly rational fashion are realistic to those familiar with organizational life. The assumption of an organization as a network of relationships among members of the organization, where uncertainty-reducing information is a resource and a source of influence, is also useful. In particular, it makes it possible to incorporate information-processing theories of MNCs (Egelhoff 1988a) into broader theory. That the network of relationships may extend outside the organization to key players in its environment is also realistic.[1]

Second, the power-and-dependence model is seductive to MNC management scholars because it clearly holds application potential. It is both a theoretical and an applied model: that is, it can easily drive action. Analyzing and understanding the network of relationships that constitute the organization, and discovering the strategies followed by participants in the games played in these relationships, allow the researcher to start considering how the stakes and perceptions of the players can be modified, and to simulate how changes in the rules of the game and in the active relationships in the network would affect outcomes (the overall behavior of the system of relationships). This is clearly a powerful set of tools for implementing actions in MNCs, in line with an applied perspective.

Gains in realism and applicability offered by the power-and-dependence theory, however, compared with the other strands of organization theory applied to DMNCs, come at a loss of simplicity and theoretical power. The detailed analysis of internal relationships, and the careful categorization of players (which do not easily match organizational lines) require clinical research of a very detailed variety not easily carried out by most organization researchers. Simpler models of power relationships in and between organizations (Dahl 1957; Pfeffer 1981), provide a less grounded argument than Crozier's but make the model's integration with other theories easier and more explicit. Pfeffer's work, for instance, introduces explicit contingency dimensions and can be seen as a detailed analytical approach to the solution of agency problems.

The influence of the resource dependence and power approach on scholars of MNC management is rather obvious. Early work on the responsiveness–integration dilemma in MNCs conceptualized the issue as one of relative power (Prahalad 1975), and discussed adaptation to contradictions in the environment as achieving a "power balance" between geographic and product-line executives (Doz 1976, 1979). Work on matrix organizations in DMNCs used a rather similar set of premises (Davis 1974; Davis and Lawrence 1977). Thus, the research on the MNC management process has drawn extensively on the power-and-dependence literature. Similarly, studies of strategic control of affiliates have used the power-and-dependency model extensively (Doz and Prahalad 1981; Negandhi and Baliga 1980).

Although less explicitly connected to process research on DMNCs, the research on external power and dependence, in particular Pfeffer and Salancik (1978), is also quite relevant to research on DMNCs. Models of external control and dependence are used, for example, by Prahalad and Doz (1980) in their study of different relational modes between headquarters and subsidiaries in DMNCs.

Organizational learning and the DMNC

Of the various major strands of organization theory, the organizational learning literature is the only one to focus primarily on change and development. Although the discussion of environment–organization adaptation is common to all, other strands of the literature usually start from a static perspective and do not empirically address learning, change, and development processes, with the exception of some institutionalization theorists (Scott 1987a).

This may be partly because most scholars of organizational learning take the view that learning and development are essentially individual, but take place in the context of an organization. Those theories that do focus on aggregate patterns stress that learning involves adaptive processes at all levels of the organization (Levitt and March 1987) and that the institutionalization of learning takes place through organizational routines in which inferences about past successes and failures are embedded (Nelson and Winter 1982). Organizational routines then guide behavior. Levitt and March (1987) also point out why and how the concept of organizational learning itself is fraught with problems. Learning along a wrong trajectory leads to "competency traps." Inductive learning from experience by individuals is often far from accurate, largely because real causality linkages may be much more complex and interdependent than those inferred by observers and participants in an organization. Satisficing behavior leads to superstitious learning, that is, the first plausible explanation of successful outcome is accepted as true. Further, the assessment of outcomes as successful or unsuccessful may be very idiosyncratic and personal. Also, the diffusion of results from learning in organizations is far from perfect, and learning results decay if they are not frequently used. Finally, the process of deepening the knowledge of an organization (from information to understanding) often conflicts with the process of sharing such knowledge within the organization (Chakravarthy and Lorange 1991).

Although the organizational learning literature, as opposed to the individual learning literature, is still in its infancy, it holds tantalizing promises for MNC management scholars. It has been loosely argued (e.g. Ghoshal 1987) that a key asset of MNCs is their opportunity to learn from multiple markets and multiple environments, in particular as they build differentiated networks to achieve such learning (Ghoshal and Nohria 1990). In our view, the applicability of the organizational learning literature is limited by its content-free nature: that is, the object of learning remains unspecified. In the context of the MNC the extent and process of learning may be quite different according to content. A lot of local autonomous learning may be vital to marketing success, whereas local experimentation and learning on safety of operations may be lethal if technical operations are invariant between countries. The blend of responsiveness and integration in various tasks drives the need for autonomous, localized learning and for sharing such learning in those tasks. Processes for learning may need to be different for geography-based learning, for learning about management systems and processes that need to reflect both integration and responsiveness needs, and for rather invariant disciplines, such as safety procedures. More research is needed on both organizational learning processes in general and their application to MNCs.

Overview

Although they differ deeply in their premises, as well as in the levels of analysis they cover (see Figure 2.1, on the vertical axis), most streams of organization theory share a few key characteristics that make their applications to the study of management in MNCs somewhat difficult (as the figure shows).

First, with the exception of contingency theory and of some recent developments of institutional theory, these theories fail to operationalize the theories into a model, or a framework, in terms other than the statistical. As a result they are relatively weak at the operational construct level: that is, the linkage between theory and empirical analysis (the horizontal axis on Figure 2.1). When the objects of study are homogeneous groups of organizations that are relatively similar (such as local administrative units and agencies in public administration) and not excessively complex, it is quite feasible to move between variable specification and measurement and theory directly, using simple statistical tests. This is clearly less feasible when dealing with heterogeneous groups of complex organizations, or when focusing on their management. Mid-range constructs are needed to conceptualize and model the behavior (both strategic and organizational) of complex organizations and to be managerially relevant (Bourgeois 1979). In summary, studying large numbers of relatively similar, simple

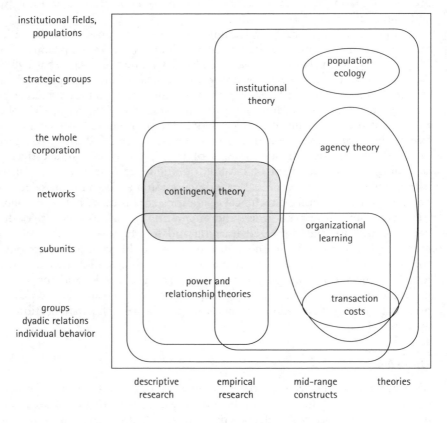

Figure 2.1 Levels of aggregation and theory development

organizations leads one to very generalizable theories, but these theories treat the organizations as a "black box" and do not develop detailed knowledge of how organizations really work. What is needed from a managerial research standpoint is a robust conceptual model of how the DMNC works, a model that researchers and managers can play with to simulate reality.

Although we did not review it here, much of the literature on multinational management suffers from an opposite but almost symmetrical problem. Although it is long on descriptive analysis, it is short on theories and even shorter on mid-range constructs. As a result, many clinical studies of MNCs amount to little more than compendia of descriptive case studies, and the few large sample studies focusing on the management of MNCs often suffer from lack of conceptual and theoretical integrity (e.g. Negandhi and Baliga 1980). What is required is a mid-range theory that bridges the gap between descriptive analysis and theories, and can span various levels of aggregation, from individuals and small groups within MNCs to clusters of MNCs following conceptually similar strategies.

Second, the streams of organization theory, although conceptually relevant, need a more detailed way to address process variables and process issues. Key managerial processes, such as resource allocation (both financial and human) or conflict resolution within organizations need to be captured by the theory. With the exception of the models based on power and relationship analysis, organization theories usually operate at too high a level of abstraction to capture such processes. Further, they do not, for the most part, focus on processes, with the exception of institutional, power, and learning theories.

Third, change and adaptation processes need more explicit attention. Organization theories are mostly static, geared to cross-sectional analysis rather than to longitudinal processes of change. Although it is possible to use these theories to analyze and conceptualize change processes, such use requires many intermediate steps of conceptualization, with the exception of the organizational learning and power/relationship streams.

Fourth, most theories of organization do not accommodate substantive variables: that is, they do not overcome the false dichotomy observed between context and process in the strategy literature. Context variables are captured, if at all, by abstract proxies.

Lastly, although the tests have seldom been made systematically, some aspects of organization theory may well be culture-bound. For example, the assumption of self-interest and opportunism, critically important to transaction cost theory, may be deeply rooted in an economic and legal tradition quite specific to the professions in the USA.

In summary, the review of the main strands of the organization theory literature suggests the need for a mid-range theory of the working of DMNCs, emphasizing constructs and frameworks and linking a potentially very useful set of theories with the often insufficiently conceptual and theoretical descriptive analyses performed by the observers and analysts of DMNCs. An effort at developing such a mid-range theory is summarized in the next section.

THE SEARCH FOR A PARADIGM

Our review of the various streams of organization theory research shows them to be implicitly suited to the study of the DMNC. Although none of them takes the DMNC as an object of study, they all address issues that can be transposed to the DMNC context—in particular, issues of part–whole relationships and of integration and differentiation in managing these relationships.

However, none of these theories allows a complete transfer to the study of DMNCs. We found these theories wanting on several key dimensions:

- importance of mid-range constructs to managerial understanding and action
- attention to management process issues
- attention to longitudinal change and adjustment processes
- incorporation of substantive strategic and environmental variables, not just abstract categories of environments; and
- need to avoid being culture-bound, which may apply both to theories based on US views of economics (such as transaction costs), and, for example, to French views of organizational power (e.g. Crozier).

The development of MNC management research: Towards a new paradigm

Although early scholars of the MNC phenomenon (e.g., Perlmutter 1969; Fayerweather 1960; Wilkins 1970) developed organizational process categories and identified the essential tension between fragmentation and unity in managing MNCs, the bulk of researchers' attention was focused on economic and competitive models of the MNC, building on the seminal works of Hymer (1960) and Vernon (1966). It was only later, following the development of contingency theory and the emergence of a process school of policy research (e.g. Bower 1970) that empirical research on the organization and management processes of MNCs started anew.

The line of research starting with the work of Prahalad (1975) is united on the common theme of organizational processes and organizational capabilities in MNCs, but focuses on various aspects of the general management task in MNCs. A full summary of the findings of this research is not the purpose of this chapter, but a few words putting the various contributions to that line of research in perspective may be useful. In particular, understanding the stream of process research on the management of DMNCs is complicated by the lack of discipline among researchers in the choice of labels to describe the concepts and in the language systems used. Further, the language systems used by individual researchers have also evolved over time as their understanding progressed. This can give a casual reader the impression of a lack of conceptual unity in the line of research.

Prahalad's research (1975) focused on the processes by which the management of a single business, not subject to intense host government constraints, perceived changing environment demands and responded to them by redirecting the attention of managers, refocusing the strategic direction, and realigning power and influence processes, consistent with the new environmental conditions. The early work of Doz (1976, 1979) analyzed, on a comparative basis, the management processes used in several companies, and in several businesses in each company, to manage the tension between economic and technological pressure for globalization and integration, and host government demands for responsiveness to national industrial policies. Doz (1979, 1980) then analyzed how differences in competitive positions between firms in the same industry affected their response to the tension outlined above. Bartlett (1979) compared the management systems and processes used in a sample of companies in industries differently affected by global integration and national responsiveness demands, and also analyzed how different functions were affected by these pressures, and further extended the understanding of redirection processes initiated by Prahalad (1975) and Doz (1978). Mathias (1978) compared redirection processes initiated by top management with processes emerging from tensions among middle managers in the organization without top management's playing an active role in the initiation of change processes. Bartlett went on to consider how what he called the "institutional heritage" of a firm constrains the development of new capabilities and constitutes a form of "organizational inertia" that top management has to take into consideration (Bartlett 1981).

Ghoshal (1986) added a detailed analysis of innovation processes, stressing the existence of different patterns of interactions in the innovation process between affiliates and headquarters and among affiliates. This led to a more general analysis of DMNCs as differentiated networks (Ghoshal and Nohria 1990), and to the discussion of network theory applied to DMNCs (Ghoshal and Bartlett 1990).

Finally, the research of Hamel and Prahalad (1990) led to reconceptualization of the basis for global competitiveness away from resource deployment to skill development and leverage, and both that work and that of Doz and Prahalad (1988) stress the importance of organizational capabilities in this process.

Simultaneously but largely independently, a rather similar line of process research developed in Sweden, based on the clinical analysis of the internationalization of major Swedish companies. Initially much of this work was concentrated on empirical tests of the validity of various propositions stemming from previous research (for instance, that a subsidiary's managerial autonomy would be inversely correlated to cross-shipments of goods between that subsidiary and other parts of the organization) or of grounded propositions stemming from detailed case studies of Swedish MNCs (e.g. Hedlund 1981). However, some interesting theoretical developments followed from the empirical research, in particular the concept of the "heterarchic" DMNC (Hedlund 1986; Hedlund in this volume), emphasizing the geographic diffusion of corporate functions, a wide range of "between market and hierarchy" governance modes, and an emphasis on action learning and on variation, selection, and retention processes in organizational adaptation.

Although this enumeration of issues, authors, and research work may look somewhat disjointed, it is important to understand its cumulative nature and underlying logic. The process of research has been to start initially with relatively discrete, researchable building blocks, bounding both the territory researched and the complexity of the concepts and constructs developed. Each step then constitutes an attempt to challenge, extend, and enrich the preceding steps by taking their findings to a broader, more complex set of issues, and adding to the existing concepts based on a richer understanding of their applicability.

Although each research piece illuminates only an aspect of the managerial task in DMNCs, taken together the work of Prahalad, Doz, Bartlett, Ghoshal, Hedlund, and Hamel provides us with a rich organizational theory of the DMNC, and with a detailed understanding of managerial tasks in DMNCs.

The emerging paradigm that results from this cumulative work has a few key characteristics. First, substance and process in a DMNC are captured using the same underlying framework. The underlying business characteristics can be mapped using the "global integration–local responsiveness" (I–R) framework (for a summary, see Prahalad and Doz 1987). All the elements that contribute to the pressures for global integration (I) needs, such as economies of scale, universal products, privileged access to raw materials, global customers, technology intensity, and presence of global competitors, are supported directly in the literature on competitive dynamics and strategy. *The framework considers all factors that contribute to the pressure for global integration simultaneously, rather than one element at a time, as is common in the literature.* Similarly, pressures for local responsiveness needs (such as distribution differences, local customs, differences in customer needs, market structure, and host government demands), also find support in the literature and are considered simultaneously. Further, the relative importance of the integration and responsiveness pressures can be used to map industry characteristics. The critical difference between this approach and traditional research approaches is that it explicitly recognizes the need for integrative optimization between multiple and often conflicting pressures in a business. *Studying the process of balance across apparently conflicting demands is seen as more important than studying the management demands created by one element of the business (such as technology intensity) at a time.*

40

Second, the same framework can be used to chart the changing nature of a business, by evaluating the shifts in the relative balance among the forces that contribute to the integration and responsiveness needs, and their impact on various key functions within a business. Furthermore, one can analyze management systems in a DMNC, and in its various countries of operation, functions, and businesses, and assess whether these management systems form a context consistent with the external demands, given business conditions and competitive positions.

The causes of enduring mismatches between external demands, strategic choices, and management systems, and the refocusing and realignment processes used to adapt to, or to anticipate, new environmental demands, have consistently been part of the emerging paradigm (Prahalad 1976; Doz 1978; Doz and Prahalad 1981; Doz, Bartlett, and Prahalad 1981; etc.). *In that sense the emerging paradigm can be used both cross-sectionally, to compare industries, business strategies and management systems and processes at one point in time, and longitudinally to map out, analyze, and understand change and adaptation processes.*

Third, the basic unit of analysis of the paradigm is the individual manager, rather than an abstraction at a higher level of aggregation. Thus the primary purpose of organizational processes—formal structure, administrative tools, decision-making culture—can be conceptualized as influencing the mindsets or cognitive orientations of managers, legitimizing a currently dominant coalition of managers representing a certain strategy that is pursued, and representing the authority structure and power to allocate resources. Organization can then be conceptualized as consisting of these three subprocesses. We can make the following generalizations.

1. Formal structure in an organization (organization structure) is nothing more than a shorthand way of capturing the underlying subprocesses: managers' mindsets (and the attendant information infrastructure in the firm), a consensus on strategy, and power to allocate resources consistent with strategy. As a result, managers consistently desire to have "pure organizations" (such as worldwide business or area organizations) because pure organizational forms describe the three orientations of managers unambiguously (Prahalad and Doz 1987).

2. Managers believe that a matrix organization is complex, because in a matrix the three subprocesses (cognitive orientations, strategic consensus, and power) are not aligned with the organization chart. Managers must understand the subprocesses in the matrix, independent of the formal structure. Irrespective of the formal structure, these three subprocesses continue and must be explicitly managed. Top managers must deal with the subprocesses and with individual managers, making a matrix complicated for managers who are not skilled at operating at this level of subtlety and detail.

41

3. Strategic change requires that managers change the cognitive orientations of a constellation of managers, gain a new consensus on strategy, and realign the relative power balance among the various groups involved in the interaction in the business.

4. Subprocesses in the organization can be managed effectively by the use of administrative tools such as planning, budgeting, information systems, rewards and punishments, training, career management, and socialization (Doz and Prahalad 1984). The implication is that major strategic redirection can take place without a formal structural change.

5. The nature of interaction and the intensity of information flows between subsidiary and head office, and across subsidiaries, reflect the strategic missions assigned to various units (Ghoshal and Nohria 1990). Even within a single business, all country organizations need not have the same strategic mission, and the differences will be manifest in the pattern and intensity of information flows. Patterns of information flow are predictors of the cognitive orientations of managers (which depends on the information infrastructure to which they have access), the strategic consensus process (that is, where are the sources of tension, and who is involved in resolving the tensions?), and the relative power balance to allocate resources.

Fourth, the whole paradigm is focused on mid-range constructs. It does not pretend to develop a universally applicable all-encompassing theory of organization, but aspires more modestly to provide a set of integrative constructs allowing the observation, analysis, understanding, and normative assessment of interaction processes between managers in DMNCs. As such it provides a mid-range theory, useful to link strategic issues with theoretical bases (Bourgeois 1979).

Finally, it is not possible to ensure that a theory is not culture-bound. It may be culture-bound in its observations or in its observers. Scholars of DMNC management belong to a wide range of nationalities and cultures, and have researched MNCs with a variety of home countries. Several research contributions (e.g. Bartlett and Ghoshal 1989) have built cultural variety into their research design by systematically comparing US, Europe, and Japan-based MNCs. Although this design does not offer a full guarantee against cultural bias, at the very least it decreases the odds of bias due to cultural boundaries.

CONCLUSION: MNC MANAGEMENT RESEARCH AND ORGANIZATION THEORY: A MISSED OPPORTUNITY FOR CROSS-FERTILIZATION?

In the second part of this chapter, we stressed that most organization theories were compatible with the characteristics that make the DMNC different from simpler organizations. It is not so much the features of the theories as the perspective adopted by their proponents that has made their application to DMNCs difficult. Researchers studying the management processes of MNCs have borrowed more from organization theories than they, or for that matter organization theorists, are likely to acknowledge. Why such a surreptitious rather than explicit convergence?

One reason can be described as the tension between theoretical dogma and a theoretical phenomenology. We believe that organization theorists have remained too involved with the development of their theories, whereas many, if not all, scholars of MNC management have under-exploited the theories available to them. The former have typically studied much simpler organizations than DMNCs, whereas the latter have often been engrossed in the complexity of what they studied, and have failed to develop or borrow a sufficiently powerful conceptual framework to shed light on the observed phenomenon. As a result, the bridge between the MNC phenomenon and organization theory was not built.

A second factor is the tension between managerial and institutional concerns. The difference in perspective between organizational theorists and scholars of the MNC extends to the purpose of their theories. MNC scholars have usually undertaken to "educate" practice: that is, they have put managerial relevance before theoretical elegance. The converse is true of most organizational theorists. This difference has made the dialogue more difficult.

A third factor is the tension between theory building and theory testing. By and large, scholars of MNC management have used data to develop their understanding of the phenomenon, and then to illustrate their concepts to facilitate their presentation. There was essentially no attempt to develop propositions and hypotheses. Theory development progressed by attempts at refutation and by tentative extensions. Some researchers were not concerned with testing hypotheses (their priority being to provide a useful, insightful perspective on the MNC phenomenon rather than to delimit its exact contours or specify all its characteristics). Most deemed the testing of hypotheses premature or too difficult given the complexity of MNCs and the large number of control variables. As a result, much research lacks rigor in measurement techniques. The work of Ghoshal (1987) constitutes a useful shift of emphasis towards measuring and testing. Overall, it is only more recently that researchers have undertaken to test systematically some of the key propositions from process research on DMNCs (Chapter 11 in this volume). More of this work can be done now, since the conceptual structure exists to enable scholars to understand the management processes in DMNCs.

Another factor is the tension between research complexity versus simplicity. Process research on the DMNC is complex, costly, and not always consistent with the funding and reward processes at many academic institutions. It is also demanding for the researcher, involving numerous interviews and process observations in many parts of the world, which only skilled field researchers can carry out effectively. As a result, management process research on MNCs has taken place only at a relatively few academic institutions with a tradition of field research, abundant funding, and a specific institutional interest in MNCs. The dearth of researchers has slowed down research progress.

Finally, the difficulty of bridge-building may well be the consequence of an elusive phenomenon. Observers have noticed that both the managerial cognitive maps and managerial tools within MNCs, and the focus of attention of MNC scholars, have shifted over time, without much clarity as to which influenced the other (or maybe they influenced each other over time). The underlying difficulty is the evolutionary nature of the MNC phenomenon itself. For example, the shift in MNCs from relatively long-term positions rooted in access to resources or in economies of scale to a succession of shorter-term positions built on intangible assets puts very different demands on management. The evolution of communication and information technologies may allow very different responses to existing problems and change management approaches. It is therefore not even clear that the search for a stable organization theory of the MNC is warranted. Perhaps researchers ought to satisfy themselves with addressing an evolving agenda of managerial issues created by changes in conditions for the success of MNCs and by the evolving technologies for their management.

Note

1 For example, researchers on MNC management have observed that headquarters–subsidiary relationships in the MNC could not be understood without an explicit analysis of the relationship with major customers and the governmental authorities of the countries in which the subsidiaries operate. Country managers may use their privileged relationships with the local subsidiary's environment to limit the influence that headquarters, or other affiliates, may exert on its operations. Since the relationship is not transparent, such opportunities to leverage external relationships internally lead managers to seek out their environment in ways that increase their own influence in the organization. In so doing, they contribute to making the organization more responsive to the constraints and opportunities in the environment. Strategic choice is not central, it results from individual strategic choices made by individual players in selecting and adapting to their relevant environment.

Part I
Environment and Organization–Environment Interactions

3 Institutional Theory and the Multinational Corporation[1]

D. Eleanor Westney

Among those who study multinational corporations (MNCs), growing recognition that it is easier to develop appropriate international business strategies than it is to build organizational systems to carry them out is increasing the awareness of the potential contribution of organizational theories that analyze constraints on organizational forms and processes. In addition, the widespread sense that we have entered an era of major shifts in organizational patterns in the highly industrialized societies, shifts fostered by growing international competition and interpenetration and by rapidly changing technology, has broadened both the interest of business scholars in macro-organizational paradigms and the interest of organizational theorists in analyzing large complex business firms.

This chapter presents a brief explication of the most recently developed of the macro-organizational paradigms, institutional theory, identifies some aspects of the paradigm where the study of the MNC and of international business environments suggests the need for further conceptual development in the theory, and sets out three international management issues to which the institutional paradigm can make a significant contribution: the problem of standardization versus local tailoring of the organizational structures of subsidiaries; learning across borders; and the relationship between the state and the multinational enterprise.

INSTITUTIONAL THEORY

Institutional theory begins with the premise that organizations are social as well as technical phenomena, and that their structures and processes are not shaped purely by technical rationality. But whereas earlier critics of technically deterministic approaches to organization tried to explain departures from technical rationality by looking inside the organization (to factors such as informal social structure or power relationships within the organization), institutional theory looks first to the social context and focuses on "isomorphism within the institutional environment" (Zucker 1987: 443), whereby organizations adopt patterns that are externally defined as appropriate to their environments, and that are reinforced in their interactions with other organizations.

As W. R. Scott has pointed out, the analysis of organizations as social

47

systems was considerably slower to move toward this kind of open-systems model than was the analysis of organizations as technical systems (Scott 1983). In the latter field, the early 1960s witnessed the development of "input–throughout–output" paradigms that analyzed the effects on organizational structures and processes of the organization's interdependence with its environment in terms of resource inputs and outputs. However, only in the late 1970s did a distinct paradigm emerge to address the social interdependence of organizations and environments.

One basic premise of institutional theory is that the "environment" is itself socially organized: that is, it is populated by organizations that have "relationships," not simply transactions, and it is the source of pressures and constraints on their consideration of alternative ways of organizing, thereby influencing organizations toward "isomorphism": the adoption of structures and processes prevailing in other organizations within the relevant environment (Zucker 1987). In the vivid metaphor developed by Meyer and Rowan in one of the seminal pieces in institutional theory, the environment provides "the building blocks for organizations" (1977: 345).

DiMaggio and Powell (1983: 150–154) have proposed three categories of institutional isomorphism: *coercive* isomorphism, where organizational patterns are imposed on organizations by a more powerful authority (often the state); *normative* isomorphism, where "appropriate" organizational patterns are championed by professional groups and organizations; and *mimetic* isomorphism, where organizations respond to uncertainty by adopting the patterns of other organizations defined as "successful" in that kind of environment.[2] Scott (1987b) expanded the categorization to seven isomorphic processes. Three are analogues of the DiMaggio and Powell categories: "*imposition* of organizational structure" is equivalent to coercive isomorphism, "*acquisition* of organizational structure" to mimetic isomorphism, and "*authorization* of organizational structure" to normative isomorphism. Scott adds the "*inducement* of organizational structure" (where an organization that lacks power to impose patterns on other organizations instead offers inducements such as funding or certification); "*incorporation*" (where "organizations come to mirror or replicate salient aspects of environmental differentiation in their own structures"); "*bypassing* of organizational structure" (where institutionalized and shared values can substitute for formal structure); and "*imprinting*" (period effects on an organization, where an organizational form retains some of the patterns institutionalized at the time its industry was founded). "Imprinting" has been explored at the industry level by Stinchcombe (1965) and at the country level by theorists of late development (Gerschenkron 1962; Dore 1973; Cole 1978) and by some more recent work in international management on country effects on the competitiveness of firms (Kogut 1988, 1993).

A formulation of institutional theory by Scott and Meyer (1989) provides a useful way of categorizing these seven processes. Scott and Meyer identify two major complementary strands of institutional theory, which are represented in these processes. One emphasizes the role of external "institutional agencies" in the organization's environment, which try to shape organizations. DiMaggio and Powell's concept of coercive isomorphism and three of Scott's seven processes (imposition, authorization, and inducement) share this focus. The other strand emphasizes the processes whereby those within organizations come to take certain externally validated organizational structures and processes for granted or to value them as ends in themselves. Normative and mimetic isomorphism and Scott's acquisition, incorporation, and bypassing processes share this emphasis on initiatives from within organizations, largely in response to sustained interactions with other organizations which share the same patterns and assumptions. Scott's seventh process, imprinting, encompasses elements of both strands of theory.

Both sets of processes are reinforced by the fact that, as institutional theorists point out, the environment is not only external to the organization; the environment *enters* the organization. As Scott has pointed out, "The beliefs, norms, rules, and understandings are not just 'out there' but additionally 'in here.' Participants, clients, constituents all participate in and are carriers of the culture" (1983: 16). Organizations and environments "interpenetrate"—to use the somewhat awkward phrase used particularly by those interested in the ideational components of institutionalization processes (Zucker 1988). This interpenetration is the key both to environmental constraints on organizational change and to environmental pressures for the diffusion of organizational structures and processes.

For institutional theorists, the appropriate level of analysis for the environment is neither the society as a whole nor the organization-set of any single "focal" organization, but some intermediate level. The term applied to this level varies. Scott (1983) has identified four in the relevant literature: "interorganizational field" (proposed by Aldrich 1972); "interorganizational network" (Benson 1975); "industry system" (Hirsch 1972); and "organizational field" (DiMaggio and Powell 1983)—and Scott and Meyer (1983) have proposed a fifth: "societal sector". Usage in the institutional literature seems to be converging on "organizational field," although the precise definition of this term has yet to be agreed. DiMaggio and Powell define it as:

> those organizations that, in the aggregate, constitute a recognized area of institutional life: key suppliers, resource and product consumers, regulatory agencies, and other organizations that produce similar service or products. The virtue of this unit of analysis is that it directs our attention not simply to competing firms, as does the population approach of Hannan

and Freeman (1977), or to networks of organizations that actually interact
... but to the totality of relevant actors.

(DiMaggio and Powell 1983: 148)

While this definition sounds very much like another term for industry, there
is one very important difference: the organizational field is a *social* structure
in that it involves mutual awareness of the activities participants have in
common (DiMaggio and Powell 1983). It is also, more problematically, a
cognitive structure, in which participants recognize other organizations as
referents and as sharing a similar set of activities.

Thus the organizational field may be coterminous with an industry, as in
DiMaggio and Powell's definition; on the other hand, it may be applied to a
more circumscribed field such as a regional economy or to a broader group
of organizations such as the Fortune 500. Therefore defining the boundaries
of an organizational field raises significant methodological problems. A key
element of the definition is mutual recognition of participants that they share
the same activity clusters. DiMaggio and Powell have suggested that this
process of institutional definition can occur through competition, regulation,
or professionalization; unfortunately, each of these three can produce different definitions of the field boundaries. Given this, identifying the
boundaries of the organizational field is, as yet, a time-consuming process,
and Powell has singled this out as a major methodological problem in the
institutional paradigm: he laments that "surely we need more expedient
methods [for determining the structure of an organizational field] than several years of field research" (1988: 131). It is a problem that is exacerbated
when the researcher begins to analyze an organizational field in which key
participants operate across national boundaries—as is the case for MNCs.

Another problem for the paradigm is the challenge of identification and
measurement: that is, whether institutionalization is a dichotomous variable—
institutionalized versus non-institutionalized—or a continuous variable, subject
to varying degrees of institutionalization, and how one knows when an organizational structure or process is in fact institutionalized. A cognitive approach
to institutionalization might suggest that it is dichotomous: after all, one either
takes a pattern as given or one does not. An emphasis on the normative
elements of institutionalization (patterns that are infused with value) would
favor the concept of a continuous variable. In either case, the measurement
problem is difficult, and institutional theorists of both stripes tend to avoid it
to some extent by implicitly regarding widespread prevalence of a pattern as an
indicator of institutionalization.

Institutional theory is increasingly portrayed as complementary to, rather
than antithetical to, paradigms of population ecology and resource dependency. As DiMaggio has pointed out, "most institutional theorists assume
that the interest of organizations in survival leads them to accede to the
demands of other actors (usually organizations) on which they depend for

resources and legitimacy" (1988: 8). Institutional theorists also generally expect that "isomorphism" will be particularly strong where organizations rely heavily on one organization within their field for key resources (DiMaggio and Powell 1983; Dobbin et al. 1988). Institutional theory can therefore be seen as sharing the population ecologists' concept of environmental selection, but expanding the criteria for selection to include legitimacy, and as sharing the interest of resource dependency in exchange relationships, but focusing on social exchange.

We should not, however, overstate the commonalities across the three paradigms. Although institutional theory shares with population ecology a strong interest in inertia in organizations, much of the empirical research using its framework examines the spread of organizational innovations within existing organizations. This is an area that many population ecologists consider uninteresting, because by definition such changes do not alter the core "organizational form" (Hannan and Freeman 1989: 79–80). And though resource dependency and institutional paradigms share an interest in the resource linkages across organizations, those working in the first field have been interested primarily in how organizations act to control dependencies and increase their decision-making autonomy, rather than in isomorphic or normative pulls across those organizations. Indeed, the institutional paradigm raises the question whether the basic assumption of resource dependency—that organizations are driven by efforts to reduce dependencies and increase autonomy—might not reflect the American environment in which it was developed.

The institutional paradigm has other integrating elements that are perhaps more important. Organization theory has long been marked by a tension between environmental determinism and voluntarism (Aldrich and Pfeffer 1976; Astley and Van de Ven 1983; Hrebiniak and Joyce 1985). While institutional theory leans to environmental determinism, the processes listed above clearly span a range from strongly deterministic (coercive isomorphism and imprinting) to voluntaristic (mimetic isomorphism). The paradigm also potentially spans the micro–macro divide that has long characterized organization theory. At the individual level it examines the "taken for granted" character of much of organizational structure and process; at the macro level it examines the overarching structures of legitimation and ongoing reinforcement ("structuration").

Finally, in asking the question "What causes similarity across organizations?" institutional theory deals with both organizational change ("Why do organizations adopt certain structures and processes?") and organizational stability ("Why are organizations slow to change their structures and processes?"). It is worth emphasizing that whereas previous paradigms have attributed the persistence of organizational patterns to "inertia" and resistance to change within the organization itself, institutional theory emphasizes the reinforcing role of the environment, particularly relationships with other organizations.[3]

In analyzing the adoption of organizational innovations, some institutional theorists (see Zucker 1988) focus on what has been called the "institutionalization project:" the efforts of organizations, subgroups within organizations, or external agencies to enhance the legitimacy of certain patterns by encouraging their dissemination throughout an organizational field.

Early formulations of institutional theory suggested that the paradigm did not apply to all organizations; that it was more powerful in explaining organizational structures and processes in some organizational fields than in others. In consequence, earlier work on institutionalization focused on state subsystems such as schools (Meyer, Scott, and Deal 1983) or on non-profit organizations, rather than on business firms where researchers expected that technical efficiency criteria would be clearer and more salient. However, institutional theorists have come to recognize that even those organizations in which technical rationality is presumed to be strongest are subject to significant institutional pressures (DiMaggio and Powell 1991). Some writers have pointed out that those subunits in business firms where it is difficult to draw clear causal linkages between the activities of the subunit and the overall performance of the firm, such as marketing departments and research and development laboratories, are more likely to be subject to institutional pressures than others, such as the factory (Meyer, Scott, and Deal 1983). Researchers working in the institutional paradigm have increasingly been turning their attention to functions of business firms in which productivity and efficiency are difficult to measure, such as due process procedures (Dobbin et al. 1988), on the grounds that these will be more subject to isomorphic pressures to emulate the structures and processes of leading organizations in the field than will functions in which there are clear performance indicators. Other analyses of business firms have focused on the role of state regulatory authorities or officially chartered agencies in endorsing or prohibiting certain organizational patterns. (See for example Neil Fligstein's 1990 study of the role of anti-trust regulations in the emergence of the finance-based model of the diversified firm and Stephen Mezias's 1990 analysis of the spread of certain accounting practices in the Fortune 200.)

The study of the MNC should be particularly fertile ground for developing institutional theory: the MNC operates in many institutional environments, and provides a context in which the nature and strength of isomorphic pulls within and across fields can be analyzed. Since the 1980s, scholars working on the MNC have shown a growing appreciation of the importance of the institutional context and of the patterns in the way MNCs respond to that context. The MNC as an organizational phenomenon provides a locus not only for enhancing and testing some of the better developed areas of the institutional paradigm, but also for confronting some of its relatively undeveloped areas, as the next section suggests.

THE MNC CHALLENGE TO THE INSTITUTIONAL PARADIGM

Turning the lenses of the institutional paradigm on the MNC brings into sharper focus several areas in which the paradigm itself needs further development. These include the analysis of organizations that straddle organizational fields, changes in the boundaries of organizational fields, and the relationship between isomorphism and innovation.

Organizations that straddle fields

The institutional paradigm has to date largely avoided the challenges of analyzing the diversified organization that is a participant in several different organizational fields, even within a single society. The study of the MNC, however, makes the investigation of the organizational consequences of straddling fields imperative, and provides an unparalleled venue for empirical research on the issue. Most large multinational enterprises span both countries and industries, as Doz and Prahalad emphasized in Chapter 2. As such, they are likely to be subject to a variety of different and potentially contradictory isomorphic pulls in the different environments in which they operate.

To date, the principal foundation that institutional theory provides for analyzing these contradictions is derived from the conceptual and empirical work on organizations operating within a fragmented or pluralistic field, in which a variety of institutional agencies advocate different patterns (Meyer and Rowan 1977; Meyer, Scott, and Deal 1983; Zucker 1987). The model so derived posits that organizations respond to incompatible or inconsistent isomorphic pulls by setting up formal structures to cope with or replicate the environmental pressures (for example, corporate legal departments that are isomorphic with the law firms with which they deal, or public affairs offices in Washington staffed and organized by former public officials). When the environmentally induced subunit or process is incompatible with other institutionalized patterns or with structures shaped by technical efficiency criteria, the organization responds by loose coupling across subunits. In some cases, the coupling is so loose that the isomorphic subunit is functionally isolated from the rest of the organization, a situation that Meyer and Rowan (1977) call "ritual conformity" and Hannan and Freeman describe as "the organizational equivalent of smoke and mirrors" (1989: 94). Where loose coupling is not possible, conflict results. Organizations turn for conflict resolution to informal structures and human relations: "The organization cannot formally coordinate activities because its formal rules, if applied, would generate inconsistencies. Therefore individuals are left to work out technical interdependencies informally" (Meyer and Rowan 1977: 258).

The relevance of this model to the "new" MNC described in the introduction to this volume is obviously considerable. The growing interdependence and coordination across MNC subsidiaries make less and less feasible the loose coupling that has hitherto characterized many MNCs, which made it possible for them to vary each subsidiary's structure to be isomorphic with the local environment. Yet the growing pressures to strengthen local linkages with customers, suppliers, and sources of technology raise the costs of rejecting local isomorphic pulls. As the institutional theorist would expect, the reaction of MNCs has been to eschew reliance on formal structures (Bartlett 1986: 384). The growing emphasis on "creating a matrix in managers' minds" (Bartlett and Ghoshal 1989: 176) suggests that MNCs are responding to the problems of competing isomorphic pulls just as the theory would predict: by relying on individuals to deal with the contradictions. On the other hand, MNCs are too large and complex to rely solely on individual-level solutions. In consequence, they are turning to intermediate-level mechanisms (task forces, systems of socialization, mandated networks) that themselves are becoming institutionalized (Martinez and Jarillo 1989). Another response seems to be to broaden the scope of mimetic isomorphism: that is, MNC managers are widening their search for systemic solutions beyond what they have conventionally defined as their organizational fields.

The analysis of how MNCs respond to these conflicting pulls provides a most promising venue for deepening the paradigm. It also raises the following questions for research. At what point do inconsistent isomorphic pressures generate forces for change within the field? And if a large number of powerful organizations suffer from inconsistent isomorphic pressures, is "de-institutionalization" an outcome, or are new patterns institutionalized that transcend or attempt to resolve the contradictions?

Changing field boundaries

If a single organization straddles two or more organizational fields, the researcher can focus on how the organization copes with different and potentially contradictory isomorphic pulls. But when a number of organizations cross the same organizational fields, do not the boundaries of the field begin to change? Under what conditions would we begin to redefine the key issue as organizational responses to and involvement in changing field boundaries, rather than responses to participation in multiple fields?

While the institutional paradigm has encouraged numerous longitudinal studies of organizations and of the emergence of organizational fields, it has generated relatively little analysis of changes over time in the boundaries of existing fields. But the study of the MNC makes such analysis essential. The changes most easily assimilated to the institutional paradigm are the cases of regional market integration, such as the European Community in 1992 and the North American Free Trade Pact. These involve the establishment of new formal regulatory agencies, the jurisdiction of which crosses national borders, and the creation of a new cognitive space: the unified market, the single competitive arena, the shared playing field.

More challenging than the cases of formal regional integration is the question of whether a "global industry" constitutes a case where the boundaries of an organizational field have changed and widened to cross national boundaries. The fact that in a global industry MNCs "spread activities among nations to serve the world market ... [and] coordinate among the dispersed activities" (Porter 1990: 54) means that subsidiaries in different countries are increasingly integrated across borders, either directly or through their parent organizations—not just in one company, but in those companies that aspire to be "major players" in the industry. A growing portfolio of business school cases analyzes how certain industries were "globalized" by the cross-border integration strategies of a major competitor (for example, Michelin in the tire industry). In the language of institutional theory, in such cases the behavior of one firm in straddling borders was emulated by other firms, resulting in a major redrawing of the boundaries of the organizational field.

Moreover, a global industry, to use what has become a standard definition in the international management field, is one "in which a firm's competitive position in one nation significantly affects (and is affected by) its position in other nations. Rivals compete against each other on a truly worldwide basis" (Porter 1990: 53). The shared recognition of competitors from several countries that they are, in fact, global competitors operating in the same space fulfils one condition of DiMaggio and Powell's definition (1983) of an organizational field. This shared recognition is both demonstrated and reinforced by the recent popularity of global competitive benchmarking, in which an MNC attempts to measure its own organization and allocation of resources against those of its major competitors, whatever their home country. This interaction is intensified by the fact that, in many industries, supporting organizations (suppliers, banks, advertising agencies) follow their customers abroad and emulate their strategies. (That is, in globalizing industries they attempt to offer standardized services worldwide.) In other words, institutional theory gives us reason to expect that a global industry constitutes an organizational field whose boundaries have come to transcend national borders, and in which there are strong isomorphic pulls on structures and processes not fully accounted for by efficiency criteria. Among the challenges this poses for institutional theory is the analysis of how such changes come about, and how the emerging isomorphic pulls relate to those in the older fields. It may be that the new fields affect only a small number of very large MNCs; on the other hand, they may constitute a fundamental realignment of isomorphic pressures in ways that have broad implications for most of the organizations in the older fields. The focus on the large MNCs in the international management field has perhaps obscured the issue of how changes in those MNCs affect the very large number of organizations with which they interact.

But there is an even more challenging question about the changing boundaries of an organizational field: do global industries *in toto* constitute a single organizational field? Clearly for many firms global competitive benchmarking has come to mean not only measuring the company against leading companies in the same industry, whatever their home country, but also against "excellent companies" in any industry. The institutional agencies of mimetic isomorphism—the business press, consulting firms, academic organizations—themselves increasingly span borders in a variety of ways and foster the spread of shared definitions and models of the international or global corporation. For example, the London Business School, INSEAD in France, Canada's Ivey School, and other leading US and European business schools offer very similar executive education programs in international management and often informally exchange teaching faculty to do so. Researchers in the international management role play a sensitive role in this process: the large MNCs grant them deep research access in exchange for insights into the company's problems. In their research roles, international managers cross industry lines in their desire for cases that will cover a variety of industries and business environments; in their roles as advisors to MNC managers they extrapolate problem definitions and apparently successful practices across those lines.

It is becoming increasingly evident that MNC managers are coming to share definitions of what is the most desirable model of a modern multinational, and the high value that they place on being seen as global, international, or transnational companies is one of the drivers behind "globalization." The challenge of analyzing the complexities of the emergence and the implications of global organizational fields is therefore an arena with particular promise both for the development of the institutional paradigm and for our understanding of the phenomenon.

Isomorphism and innovation

Scholars working in the institutional paradigm have focused their research on how innovations spread across organizations, rather than on how innovations emerge. The application of the paradigm to complex organizations that straddle fields and that play a major role in changing the boundaries of fields, however, indicates that the paradigm is also useful for explaining the emergence of certain kinds of organizational innovations. In particular, there are two types of innovations that fall within the purview of the paradigm: innovations produced when an organizational pattern institutionalized in one field is introduced into another, and innovations that emerge when conflicting isomorphic pulls produce new structures or processes that may, in turn, become more widely institutionalized through mimetic isomorphism.

One reason for the paradigm's lack of attention to the contribution of isomorphism to innovation is that its mimetic isomorphism is much more difficult to trace through a field if it produces variation rather than similarity. Mimetic processes, however, can produce variety. They offer considerable scope for formal departures from the organizational model being institutionalized. Some of the departures may be unintended and largely unrecognized: since direct access to the organizational model is often limited (especially when the model is a successful competitor), information is likely to be imperfect and even distorted. Information drawn from the model itself is likely to be idealized, as may information from mediating organizations such as consultants or the business press. Consultants or internal information gatherers are also likely to interpret the information on the model through the filter of their own organizational templates. Other departures from the model may be deliberate efforts to adapt a pattern originating in a different organizational field (another industry or another country) to the institutional landscape of its new setting. (See Westney 1987 for a more detailed discussion of the interplay between isomorphism and innovation.) Of course not all departures from the model will be innovations: some, if not most, may be the result of efforts to minimize change by adapting the new model to established organizational patterns. But even here, the established patterns cannot remain unchanged; some innovations are likely to emerge.

The Japanese MNCs establishing production and research facilities in the USA provide a set of contemporary examples. Despite strong efforts to institutionalize many aspects of their work organization, supplier relationships, and technologies in their US plants, the Japanese must adjust their practices to a different labor environment (which entails hiring and training women for heavy work on assembly line jobs in the auto industry, for example, and the creation of more formal evaluation and grievance procedures). They must also adapt their supplier relationships to greater geographic distances and a different legal environment (see Gelsanliter 1990; Fucini and Fucini 1990). It is more than likely that in turn, the Japanese firms may in future try to "learn from" and adapt some of the adjustments to their organizational patterns not only to their future plants in Europe but to their Japanese plants as well, as the Japanese institutional environment changes over time (with, for example, a shortage of skilled labor, which may necessitate the greater employment of women and the move to greater flexibility of rewards, and an increase in foreign component procurement). US firms, in turn, are learning from the Japanese transplants, a process which involves further adaptation of the patterns.

When organizational patterns cross fields, isomorphism produces innovation. The MNC provides an unparalleled venue for investigating this dynamic.

INSTITUTIONAL THEORY AND INTERNATIONAL MANAGEMENT ISSUES

Standardization versus local tailoring of organization

The debate over the globalization versus localization of MNC organization often takes places in murky conceptual terrain. "Localization" can mean adding more value locally (what gets done), using local rather than expatriate or third-country managers (who does it), or adopting local rather than parent company organizational patterns (how it gets done). There is no clear logical linkage among these three facets of localization, but the assumption is often made that the more value the subsidiary adds locally and the more dominant local managers are in the organization, the more likely the subsidiary is to adopt local rather than parent company patterns (see for example Rosenzweig and Singh 1991).

The extent to which MNCs adopt local organizational patterns in their subsidiaries is a continuing theme in the literature on managing the MNC. One long-standing framing of the issue is cultural (and highly normative): organizational structures and processes must allow for the distance between local national cultures and the cultural underpinnings of the parent MNC's organization (e.g. Hofstede 1980a, 1980b). Work in this tradition tends to focus on the need for adapting the parent company's organizational patterns to the national culture of the local environment. Another approach is political: organization becomes one of the arenas for the struggles between the desire of local managers for autonomy and the headquarters' desire for control (e.g. Doz and Prahalad 1981). In this latter formulation, local managers' resistance to the imposition of externally mandated patterns is general and undiscriminating. Both approaches, in the language of institutional theory, focus on "coercive isomorphism" or the imposition of parent company patterns on subsidiary organization, and on local resistance to such imposition. (This, in turn, raises for the institutional theorist the issue of levels of analysis within complex organizations: organizational isomorphism that, from the viewpoint of the top management of the organization, is mimetic—emulating successful organizations in the organizational field—can be seen by subunits, such as national subsidiaries, as coercive.)

This question of standardization versus local tailoring of an MNC organization might be better understood as the result of a larger range of potentially competing isomorphic pulls (Westney 1988; Rosenzweig and Singh 1991). The MNC organization is the source of strong isomorphic pulls towards similarity across the organizational structures and processes of subsidiaries, pulls that are not altogether a matter of conscious choice or imposition. In their classic study of the organization and strategy of multinational enterprise, Brooke and Remmers noted this phenomenon:

> The foreign subsidiary will naturally have a much simpler organization, but it is likely to mirror head office to some extent.... This mirror effect

may not be produced by instructions from head office, but by an almost unconscious development along the lines of communication.

(Brooke and Remmers 1970: 40, 41)

And yet each subsidiary is also operating within a local organizational field that exerts a range of isomorphic pulls on its organization.

Putting the standardization/local tailoring question into the framework of competing isomorphic pulls from the environment helps to draw attention to the fact that local tailoring may not necessarily mean adopting patterns that are dominant in local organizations, just as "standardization" may not necessarily mean adopting parent company patterns. A local organizational field may be populated largely by MNC subsidiaries, either because there are few major local competitors or because MNC subsidiaries define their field in terms of each other rather than local organizations.[4] In such a field, the "local" patterns that are exerting the strongest isomorphic pulls may be those institutionalized in the MNC subsidiaries, rather than those institutionalized in purely local firms.

On the other hand, the model of the "new" MNC tries to separate the issue of standardizing organizational patterns across the MNC system from the imposition of parent company patterns. To do so it draws on a stream of work on the MNC that follows Perlmutter's seminal model of the evolution of multinationals from ethnocentric (strongly shaped by home country patterns) to polycentric (each subsidiary shaped by local patterns) to geocentric (distinctive patterns that are shaped exclusively by neither home nor host country patterns, but develop overarching and emergent commonalities across the multinational's organizational system). These assumptions tend to be built into current thinking about "transnational" or "multifocal" firms (see Bartlett, Doz, and Hedlund 1990). The MNC that must respond to pressures simultaneously to localize its products and its value-adding activities and to achieve the technical and economic benefits of close cross-border coordination and division of labor is portrayed as "geocentric"—as one which must free itself from both home and host country patterns to create a distinctive "transnational" (Bartlett and Ghoshal 1989), "heterarchical" (Hedlund 1986 and this volume), or "multifocal" (Prahalad and Doz 1987) organization which is not subject either to strong home or host country effects. Since this perspective implicitly regards the primary loci of home and host country effects on MNC organization as the cultural socialization of managers and the kinds of behavior that are evaluated and rewarded in the MNC, the "geocentric" or "heterarchical" organization can counter both home and host country pulls through intensive shared socialization and training, and through appropriately designed evaluation and reward structures.

Home-country isomorphic pulls on the MNC organization, however, may not readily be visible to parent company managers. What to the home country manager is "the way things are done" (indicating a lack of awareness of genuine alternatives) or "the way we do things" (indicating a belief that the patterns are company-specific rather than country-specific) often appears to locals as the product of the parent's home country. An observation by John Harvey-Jones, former Chairman of the British-based ICI, provides an excellent illustration of this phenomenon:

> Any firm with an American subsidiary must have experienced on the one hand a continued suspicion at the British end that the Americans wish to have nothing whatsoever to do with the main group and are interested in unilateral independence—regardless of the cost to the rest of the group—which on the other hand is mirrored with equal intensity on the part of the Americans, who are convinced that the sole aim of everybody outside America is to force them to operate in a way which is inappropriate in their country. No matter how many times you tell them that you do not wish to introduce British management into the USA they are convinced that every move you make is a step in that direction.
>
> (Harvey-Jones 1988: 160–161)

What may seem to the home country manager to be cultural paranoia (or a "syndrome," as Harvey-Jones calls it) may actually be a more accurate perception of the institutional grounding of the parent company's organizational patterns than exists at headquarters.

Whatever the source of the standardization, however, it is possible to put the pulls for similarity across the MNC system into the context of isomorphism. In their article on MNC organization, Rosenzweig and Singh (1991) propose a two-dimensional typology of "pressures for consistency within the MNE" and "pressures for isomorphism with the local environment" which is analogous to the widely-used typology of integration and responsiveness (see Chapter 2 in this volume). Indeed they explicitly assimilate their typology to the earlier one by hypothesizing that isomorphism with local patterns will be stronger in multi-domestic industries than in global industries, because subsidiaries in the former are more dependent on the local environment. In global industries, they suggest, pressures for consistency within the MNC will mean that isomorphism with the patterns of the parent prevails over local pulls.

Underlying the Rosenzweig and Singh hypothesis identifying cross-border isomorphic pulls with global industries, and within-country pulls with multidomestic industries, is the assumption, drawn from institutional theory, that resource exchange between organizations generates isomorphic pulls on the dependent organization. The theoretical foundation for this assumption is the role of legitimation in interorganizational relationships: organizations that follow institutionalized patterns authorized by resource-providing organizations gain access (or perhaps preferential access) to those resources.

In subsidiaries that draw most of their resources from local organizations (presumably the case in multidomestic industries), adopting the patterns institutionalized in the local organizational field should contribute to the subsidiary's legitimacy and therefore to its ability to acquire the resources it needs in its local environment. Increasingly, however, managers in industries marked by global competition are being urged to foster the capacity of subsidiaries in key countries to become "insiders" in the local technology, information, market, and even political networks, regardless of the extent to which their activities are dominated by cross-border rather than local transactions (Ohmae 1990). Their success in doing so is dependent on "the skilful management of boundary relations and conformity to the normative codes of the relational networks in which it participates"—which is Powell's characterization of an organization operating in an environment subject to strong institutional effects (1988: 119). In other words, even MNCs in global industries can expect to encounter strong local isomorphic pulls. Moreover, as Brook and Remmers indicate, mimetic isomorphism with the home-country organization occurs even in multidomestic industries.

This is not to deny the premise that there are strong isomorphic pulls across MNC units engaged in a dense network of transactions with each other, but that premise can be made on efficiency or transaction cost grounds as well as institutional grounds: transactions are less costly in time and effort between organizations or subunits that are similar. (See for example Flaherty (1986) on the greater ease of coordinating production across borders when the subunits involved have similar organizational structures and processes.) Efficiency and institutional arguments would agree with the hypothesis that cross-border isomorphic pulls within the MNC increase with the density of interactions across subunits. Where efficiency and institutional arguments differ is on the appropriate level of analysis and on the scope of isomorphic pulls. Efficiency arguments would examine individual organizations and organizational subunits, in the expectation that isomorphism is strongly associated with the density of interactions in that particular organization or function, and would therefore vary greatly across the units of analysis. Institutionalists would advocate looking at patterns in the organizational field and across subunits, with the expectation that isomorphic pulls within the field would operate across organizations and across subunits and functions, to produce greater similarity across organizations than would be predicted from the variation in individual interaction density.

Learning across borders

The view of the MNC as a "learning network" in which successful innovations in management as well as in products can be transferred from one subsidiary to another (Bartlett and Ghoshal 1989) raises anew a long-standing issue in comparative organization theory: when is an organizational pattern that is established in one context transferable to another? The importance of this issue is increasing with the growing internationalization of service industries, especially financial services, in which such organizational technologies as task specialization, structures for communicating and adding value to information, and personnel development programs are the core technologies of the firm.

It is a truism that the greater the similarity of contexts, the greater the ease of transfer. In the MNC, where the transfers take place across societies, the definition of similarity of contexts has in the past focused on national culture. To the extent that institutional theory also emphasizes "the preconscious understandings that organizational actors share, independent of their interests" (DiMaggio 1988: 3), the institutional paradigm may at first seem to involve primarily a recasting of the existing literature on culture into new terminology, giving employment to numbers of graduate students but doing little to further our understanding of the multinational enterprise or its contexts.

The institutional paradigm, however, does make two important contributions to the discussions of learning across borders: an alternative way of defining and assessing "context" in terms of the organizational relationships affected by the pattern being transferred, and attention to the organizational field as a level of analysis. Here again the Japanese transplants in the auto industry provide a useful set of examples. Japanese auto firms are strongly committed to work organizations that institutionalize highly flexible work patterns and the involvement of workers in continuous improvements and quality control. The means taken by these firms to have their US organizations learn from the patterns of their Japanese operations have been described at length in the business press and by industrial relations scholars. Location is a key variable: Japanese firms tend to locate their plants in areas where the institutionalization of current US auto industry patterns is weak or non-existent, either areas where unionization rates are low and the labor force unaccustomed to assembly-line work (such as Tennessee and Kentucky), or areas where high unemployment and plant closures have de-institutionalized existing patterns (such as the California NUMMI plant). They have undertaken extensive pre-employment education and screening, intensive socialization in Japanese production organization (including experience in Japan for considerable numbers of blue-collar workers), and continuous reinforcement of the model through exhortation and ongoing training. The role of supplier networks has rarely been mentioned in this connection, but institutional theory suggests that Japanese assiduous cultivation of close supplier linkages either with Japanese subsidiaries or with US firms willing to undertake total quality control, J-I-T delivery, and close interaction on component development has a role beyond the assurance of quality that is usually adduced. The supplier network that the Japanese firms want is one that reinforces and institutionalizes the production organization of the branch plant, and they are willing to expend great effort to create such a network.

The experience of the Japanese auto transplants, interpreted through the lens of institutional theory, illustrates the major ways in which multinationals can reinforce the processes of learning across borders:

- recreation of the home country organization-set to provide local reinforcement of the transferred pattern
- countervailing legitimation: that is, highly visible bowing to other highly institutionalized local patterns on dimensions that are less critically important to the firm (such as Japanese firms' growing emphasis on "good citizenship," including contributions to local charities and amenities)
- challenge and delegitimation: a direct articulation of an alternative and generically "better" model of organization.

The case of the Japanese transplants, however, suggests the importance of examining field effects. All three of these modes of reinforcing cross-border learning are made much more feasible when the number of firms entering the local organizational field is significant enough to change the field itself. In the case of the auto industry, six Japanese companies have established production facilities in the USA, in an industry where there are only three local firms. A single organization entering a national organizational field overwhelmingly dominated by local firms will have a far more difficult time resisting adaptation to local isomorphic pressures.

The state and the multinational enterprise

The role of the state is a central focus of institutional theory (e.g. Meyer and Hannan 1979; DiMaggio and Powell 1983; Dobbin et al. 1988), as it has long been in work on the multinational enterprise. But the concerns of the two fields seem, at first glance, to be very different. Work in international management has focused on the role of the state in shaping what activities are carried out by the MNC within its borders; the influence of state policy on ownership strategy and industrial relations; and opportunities for MNCs to take advantage of their operating in multiple state jurisdictions by mobilizing one state (usually their home country government) to influence the policies of other states. In other words, international management has concentrated primarily on identifying the constraints on strategic decision making and the strategic opportunities that various state policies generate for the MNC. The paradigm has been overwhelmingly that of strategic choice.

Institutional theory, in contrast, has been focused on the isomorphic pulls exerted by the state on organizational structures, usually (although not exclusively) beyond the realm of conscious strategic choice, and it has made the implicit assumption that each organization operates in an organizational field bounded by a single state. The state-induced isomorphic pulls identified have been:

- pulls toward isomorphism with state structures
- pulls towards structures approved by the state but not necessarily incorporated into state structures
- "second-order" normative isomorphism induced by state-approved certification of professionals.

The strength of the first two kinds of isomorphic pulls is posited to match the salience of the state in the organizational field. For example, a study of the institutionalization of grievance procedures and affirmative action programs (a study that included both private and public sector organizations in the USA) found that "linkage to the federal government is a significant factor in the elaboration of due process rights for both public and private organizations." (Dobbin et al. 1988: 84). The "linkage" referred to is primarily a resource linkage, where the government is a source of contracts or subsidies or of monopoly power (for the utilities, for example).

Two critically important areas where both isomorphism toward state structures and state-mandated isomorphism operate are internal control structures and inter-organizational relations. Orru, Biggart, and Hamilton (1989) suggest that there are powerful state influences on inter-organizational relations (their own focus is on industrial groups in East Asia, but the argument has wider application). The state is the original "multi-divisional," multi-unit organization. Both its modes of coordination among its varied constituent parts and its modes of interacting with non-state organizations exert powerful isomorphic pulls on the modes of coordination in large, diversified non-government organizations, and on inter-organizational relations. This "mimetic isomorphism" is reinforced by "coercive isomorphism" imposed through laws and regulations. States that rely on arms-length, formal, and largely statutory modes of dealing with non-state organizations tend both to provide an important model for interorganizational relationships and to reinforce that model through regulation (as in US anti-trust law and regulation of collusive interactions across organizations). States that themselves rely heavily on non-formal, densely interactive modes of influencing the behavior of non-state organizations tend to have regulations and laws that mirror this mode of coordination (as in Japan).

One area of inquiry that would both increase our theory-based understanding of the organizational structure of MNEs and contribute to refining institutional theory is to explore under what conditions MNEs respond to such isomorphic pulls by engaging in one or more of the following:

- resistance to state-induced local isomorphic pulls in favor of isomorphic pulls from the MNE's internal system
- substantial differentiation of organizational structure in different state-induced institutional environments
- ritual conformity.

There is yet another area related to the relationship between the state and the MNC to which institutional theory could make a major contribution: the impact of MNCs on society. The analysis of MNC effects on society has primarily been focused on either the local or the home-country economies (exploitation versus multiplier effects, "hollowing out" versus returns on investment and the maintenance of globally competitive firms—see for example Dunning 1981b), or on political effects (Vernon 1971; Moran 1985). The organizational effects have been less systematically explored, largely because of the lack of a theoretical paradigm such as institutional theory can now provide.

There are two major dimensions of the potential impact of MNCs on organizational patterns within a society. The first is the MNC role in institutionalization. MNC subsidiaries in some countries can play a major role in establishing what Meyer and Rowan (1977) called "the building blocks of organization." To take just one example, Canada and Australia both have unusually low levels of investment of R&D in industry, compared with other highly industrialized countries. Economic nationalists have blamed the high level of foreign ownership of industry; their opponents have considered this charge to be refuted by the fact that local firms have rates of expenditure on R&D that are very little higher than those of the foreign firms (see for example Capon et al. 1987). The institutional perspective would suggest that the dominance of foreign-owned subsidiaries in both societies has been the major influence on the institutionalization of patterns of organization and expenditure in R&D, so that local firms are following patterns institutionalized by the MNC subsidiaries.

A second aspect of MNC influence on organizational patterns is "de-institutionalization." The introduction of new modes of organization in MNC subsidiaries can challenge the legitimacy of existing patterns—witness the role of US multinationals in Europe in the 1960s, or perhaps the current role of foreign-affiliated firms, such as US financial institutions, in Japan. The empirical investigation of the influence of MNC organizational patterns on the level and kind of institutionalization of organizational patterns within a society over time can both contribute to the debate over the impact of multinational presence, and provide a counterweight to the current emphasis on institutionalized patterns as externally imposed on organizations.

A related area of interest emerges from another issue that has been receiving increased attention in the international management field: the role of the state in the advanced industrial societies in the context of the growing concern with international competitiveness and with the future of the world economic system. In the USA, anxieties over competitiveness in comparison with Japan legitimized a newly cooperative relationship between government and business. In Japan, on the other hand, the gradually increasing movement of production offshore, government efforts to hold down public expenditure, and the fear of criticism of "Japan Inc." are reducing the leverage of the state over the business community. And in Europe, the movement toward greater regional integration has reduced the leverage of individual national governments over their business communities, as a regional regulatory structure slowly emerges.

One element of the increased concern over competitiveness in all three regions is the fear that institutionalized organizational patterns that served the business community (and by extension the nation) extremely well in previous years have now become handicaps in international competition, and that some kind of intervention by the state is necessary to speed up the deinstitutionalization of those patterns and their replacement by more effective ones. In Japan, for example, the lingering recession has led both Japanese and Western critics to question the continuing value of long-admired patterns such as the long-term commitment to employees, the close linkages across firms, and a decision-making process that is skewed toward the domestic market, and to call on the Japanese state to play an active role in forcing firms to re-structure. There are fascinating echoes in this discussion of the intense efforts in the 1980s to improve US competitiveness, when many aspects of the American business system came under fire and when many voices called for an American industrial policy. The institutional paradigm provides at least the rudiments of a framework for interpreting some of these change agendas, and the analysis of those efforts can provide an arena for deepening the paradigm's ability to deal with de-institutionalization.

POSTSCRIPT

Of the avenues for further work on the MNC opened by the institutional perspective outlined in this chapter, the one most traveled in the past decade has built on the insight that organizations seek legitimacy in the environments in which they operate, and institutional theory is invoked as a touchstone in a growing number of publications in the international business field. However, work that builds seriously on the organizational variant of institutional theory is not easily found (although the broader approaches to institutions covered in Chapter 7 are more common). One significant contribution is the influential work by Srilata Zaheer on the concept of the MNC's "liability of foreignness" and her research on how performance of MNCs is affected by adoption of internal practices versus local practices (Zaheer 1995; Zaheer and Mosakowski 1997; Kostova and Zaheer 1999). Two additional contributions of importance come from the comparative institutional community: the volume edited by Glenn Morgan, Peer Hull Kristensen, and Richard Whitley (2001) and the fascinating and detailed study by Peer Hull Kristensen and Jonathan Zeitlin (2005) of a process equipment manufacturing firm that expanded by acquisition during the 1970s and 1980s. An overview of the organizational approaches to the analysis of the MNC can be found in Westney and Zaheer (2001).

Notes

1 This chapter is based on a paper first presented at the Academy of International Business annual meeting in 1988. Its present form owed much to the discussions at the INSEAD workshop on Organization Theory and the Multinational Corporation in 1989, especially to the comments of Dick Scott, Chris Bartlett, Cathy Enz, Gunnar Hedlund, and Bruce Kogut. Woody Powell also made some extremely helpful suggestions.

2 The parallels with Amitai Etzioni's typology (1961) of organizational control systems—coercive, normative, and utilitarian—are striking, and not only in terminology. Etzioni focuses on the ways in which organizations induce compliance from their participants; DiMaggio and Powell on how environments induce compliance in structures and processes from participating organizations.

3 In fairness to the organizational ecology paradigm, we should note that Hannan and Freeman's discussion of organizational inertia also recognizes the constraining role of the environment (1989: 67).

4 There is some anecdotal evidence that this has tended to be the case in Japan: in some industries local subsidiary managers, Japanese and foreign alike, have tended to regard their major competitors in the markets and in recruitment as other MNCs, rather than large Japanese firms. In such cases, they tended (at least until recently) to collect market share information and engage in competitor analysis primarily on other MNCs in Japan. (Based on personal communications from MNC managers in the United States and Japan.)

4   The Multinational Corporation as an Inter-Organizational Network

Sumantra Ghoshal and Christopher A. Bartlett

The late 1980s witnessed a significant evolution of academic interest in the multinational corporation (MNC). The focus of research shifted away from the dyadic headquarters–subsidiary relationship in MNCs, or the specific decision of a company to invest in a foreign location, to the coordination tasks of managing a network of established foreign subsidiaries, and analysis of the competitive advantages that arise from the potential scope economies of such a network.

This research focus demanded new theoretical, conceptual, and methodological anchors. Analysis of international competition, for example, embraced a range of new theories, such as those of multi-plant production, multi-point competition, and valuation of options to explore the costs and benefits of the MNC's geographic scope of activities (e.g. Teece 1980; Ghemawat and Spence 1986; Kogut 1983). This chapter advocates a similar adoption of inter-organizational theory for future MNC-related research, albeit with some modifications to reflect the ownership-based intraorganizational ties that exist between the MNC headquarters and its different foreign subsidiaries. We believe that inter-organizational theory, properly adapted, can provide new insights on a complex and geographically dispersed organizational system like the MNC, and our main objective here is to propose an initial formulation on how the concepts and tools of inter-organizational analysis can be applied to fit this different but analogous case.

To frame the context of our discussions, it may be useful to begin with an illustration. Figure 4.1 shows the simplest possible representation of N.V. Philips, a multinational company headquartered in the Netherlands. The company has its own operating units in 60 countries as diverse as the USA, France, Japan, South Korea, Nigeria, Uruguay, and Bangladesh. Some of these units are large—fully integrated companies developing, manufacturing and marketing a diverse range of products from light bulbs to defense systems. Such subsidiaries might have 5000 or more employees and be among the largest companies in their host countries. Others are quite small, single-function operations responsible for only R&D, or manufacturing, or marketing for only one or a few of these different businesses, employing 50 or fewer people. In some cases the units have been in operation for more than 50 years; a few began their organizational lives less than ten years ago. Some of these units are tightly controlled from the headquarters; others

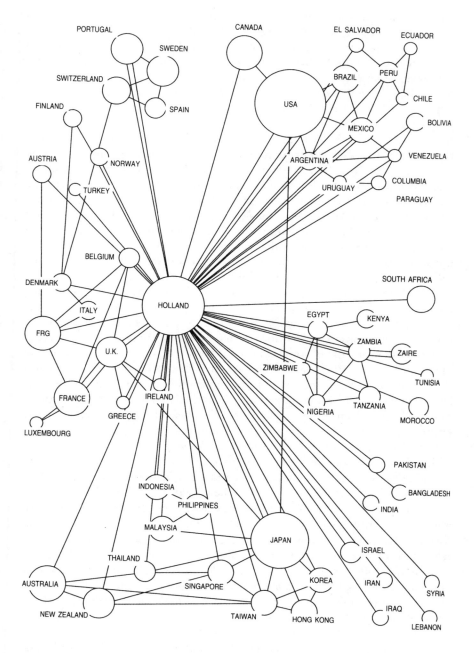

Figure 4.1 Organizational units and some of the interlinkages within N. V. Philips

enjoy relationships with the headquarters more akin to those between equal partners than those between parent and subsidiary.

With only minor alterations, Figure 4.1 could also be a representation of an American multinational such as Procter and Gamble, or another European company such as Unilever, or a Japanese company such as Matsushita Electric (see descriptions of these companies in Bartlett and Ghoshal 1986 and 1987). In many ways our description of Philips is a generic account that characterizes many large MNCs. As suggested by a number of authors, MNCs are physically dispersed in environmental settings that represent very different economic, social, and cultural milieus (Robock, Simmons, and Zwick 1977; Fayerweather 1978; Hofstede 1980a); they are internally differentiated in complex ways to respond to both environmental and organizational differences in different businesses, functions, and geographic locations (Bartlett and Ghoshal 1986; Prahalad and Doz 1987); and, as a result of such dispersal and differentiation, they possess internal linkages and coordination mechanisms that represent and respond to many different kinds and extents of dependence and interdependency in inter-unit exchange relationships (Ghoshal and Nohria 1990).

We believe that an entity like these large MNCs can be more appropriately conceptualized as an inter-organizational grouping rather than as a unitary "organization," and that valuable insights can be gained on the internal structures and operations of such entities from the concepts of organization sets and networks that are more commonly used for exploring inter-organizational phenomena (Evan 1967; Aldrich and Whetten 1981). In particular, we believe that the concept of a network, both as a metaphor and in terms of the tools and techniques of analysis it provides, reflects the nature and complexity of the multinational organization and can provide a useful lens through which to examine this entity. We propose here a framework that conceptualizes the multinational as a network of exchange relationships among different organizational units, including the headquarters and the different national subsidiaries, which are collectively embedded in what Homans (1974) described as a structured context. Further, following Tichy, Tushman, and Fombrun (1979), we visualize this context as an "external network" consisting of all the entities such as customers, suppliers, regulators, and competitors with which the different units of the MNC have to interact. The main hypothesis we develop in this chapter is that different attributes of a multinational, such as the configuration of its organizational resources and the nature of inter-unit exchange relations that lead to such a configuration, can be explained by selected attributes of the external network within which it is embedded and on which it depends for its survival.

A note of caution must, however, be sounded at this stage. Because network analysis is a rapidly emerging and highly complex field of study, and because of the considerable divergence on definitions and approaches that exists within this field, it is unlikely that this initial attempt to apply network concepts to the study of MNCs will be either complete or above reproach. In the penultimate section, we discuss some of the limitations of the present effort and suggest how future conceptual and empirical research might overcome them. This chapter must be viewed, therefore, as an initial attempt to identify the potential of developing a "network theory of the MNC," rather than as a rigorous presentation of such a theory.

While the attempt to apply the inter-organizational network perspective formally to the study of MNCs is relatively new, it should also be noted that the conceptual foundation for such an approach already exists in the international management literature. For example, Perlmutter's (1969) scheme for categorizing MNCs as ethnocentric, polycentric, and geocentric organizations is clearly consistent with a network theoretic view. Similarly, the stylized models of MNC organizations developed by Bartlett (1986) and Hedlund (1986), the concept of a "coordinated multinational system" proposed by Kogut (1983), and the application of the resource dependency model by Herbert (1984) for explicating strategy–structure configurations in MNCs have all been implicitly or explicitly grounded in the conceptualization of MNCs as inter-organizational systems. While building on this foundation, the present chapter also differs from these earlier pieces in two important ways.

First, most of these models see the structure and attributes of the MNC as rising from technical and economic rationality and constraints in resource allocation (Kogut 1983), or from the administrative heritage (Bartlett 1986) and cognitive orientation (Perlmutter 1969) of its managers. Our explanation focuses instead on the social and institutional structure of the environments in which the MNC operates. As institutional theorists have argued, the relational networks in the institutional environment play an important role in influencing the structure and behavior of organizations (Meyer and Scott 1983; Zucker 1988). The uniqueness of the MNC as an organizational form arises from the fact that its different constituent units are embedded in different national environments in which the structures of these relational networks can be, and often are, very different (Westney 1988). Further, in an era of expanding transnational linkages among individuals and organizations, these relational networks in the different countries are also increasingly interconnected among themselves in complex ways. These differences in national industry systems and the interconnections among them are central to our explanation of both economic action and administrative coordination within the dispersed system of the MNC.

Second, the concept of a network has so far been used in this literature mostly as a metaphor to describe and categorize MNC structures and to support normative arguments on the importance of lateral relationships, shared values, and reciprocal task interdependencies for effective management of MNCs. While we believe that such a metaphorical use of the term has been useful for descriptive and normative purposes, this chapter represents an effort to move to the next step of theory building by using network concepts to explain specific structural attributes of multinational organizations.

In the next section we discuss why, despite the intra-organizational ownership ties, a multinational can be legitimately conceived as an inter-organizational grouping, and draw on inter-organizational theory to develop a conceptualization of the MNC as a network that is embedded within an external network. We then illustrate how this conceptualization might be applied for analyzing the extent of dispersal and specialization in the configuration of the MNC's resources (section 2) and distribution of power in the internal exchange relationships among its different units (section 3). Our arguments suggest a general model of the MNC as a differentiated inter-organizational network, described below. We conclude by discussing some research implications which follow from our theoretical arguments, and by suggesting some ways in which this inter-organizational network perspective of MNCs can be improved and extended.

INTER-ORGANIZATIONAL THEORIES APPLIED TO THE MULTINATIONAL CORPORATION

Much of the existing theory and almost all empirical analyses of inter-organizational networks have focused on inter-organizational groupings that are not connected by ownership ties (e.g. Pfeffer and Salancik 1974; Bacharach and Aiken 1976; Van de Ven and Walker 1984). Before applying any of the concepts or empirical findings from such studies to the analysis of MNCs, it is first necessary to make a prima facie case that the ownership ties in the multinational do not necessarily preclude the discretionary behaviors possible among interacting organizations that are not so connected.

A number of authors have argued that the linkage between ownership and hierarchical power (fiat) in complex organizations is much weaker than is often assumed (see, for example, Granovetter 1985: 499). We believe that this link is particularly weak in the case of MNCs because of the large physical and cultural distances between the owned and the owning units. Case histories of extreme subsidiary autonomy have been well documented in the literature on multinationals: the refusal of North American Philips to sell the V2000 video cassette recorder developed by its Dutch parent, instead purchasing VHS machines from a Japanese arch-rival, is a good example. Even more dramatic, however, is the case of the British and German subsidiaries of Ruberoid which unilaterally severed all ties with the parent and, with the support of local financial institutions, ultimately secured complete legal independence. Such situations are relatively more common for MNCs headquartered in small countries, many foreign subsidiaries of which often control more resources and contribute more revenues than the parent company. However, many such cases have also been observed in companies such as ITT and Unilever, even though

72

the parents were headquartered in large countries such as the USA and the United Kingdom (Bartlett and Ghoshal 1989).

The efficacy of *fiat* is particularly limited in the case of multinationals, not only because some of the subsidiaries happen to be distant and resource-rich, but more so because they control critical linkages with key actors in their local environments—particularly the host government. To cite but one illustration, the Australian subsidiary of Ericsson, the Swedish telecommunications company, accumulated a very high level of R&D resources primarily because of a coalition between the local management and the Australian post and telegraph authorities, that had as its principal goal the creation of a major R&D center in Australia. Subsidiary-company links with local customers, suppliers, and investors also contribute to the local management's autonomy. For example, following deregulation of the US telecommunications industry, the influence of the American subsidiary of NEC expanded significantly within the company, despite its relatively small size and short organizational life. This was so because of its role in building the company's relationships with the Bell operating companies, which came to be viewed by NEC not only as major potential customers but also as contacts for joint development of new products.

We do not claim that the relationships among the parent company and the national subsidiaries in an MNC are identical to those among an interacting group of universities, or social service organizations, or regulatory agencies. Some anecdotal evidence of extreme subsidiary autonomy notwithstanding, the parent company of a multinational typically enjoys considerable hierarchical authority. However, we suggest that the existence of such hierarchical authority does not necessarily lead to hierarchical power as the dominant or even the "last resort" mechanism of control. Typically, in such large, dispersed and interdependent organizations, hierarchical authority coexists with significant local autonomy; and such a situation, we believe, is not inappropriate for the application of inter-organizational theories.

For example, in one of the seminal articles on the topic, Warren (1967) developed a typology of inter-organizational relationships that distinguished four ways in which members of an organizational field could interact: unitary (the classic hierarchy), federative, coalitional, and social choice. In our view the multinational organization lies somewhere between Warren's unitary and federative structures, both of which admit some level of hierarchical decision making at the top of the inclusive structure. Further, even though the formal structure of MNCs may often resemble the unitary form, or what has been described in the literature as "mandated networks" (Aldrich 1976; Hall et al. 1977), the actual relationships between the headquarters and the subsidiaries and among the subsidiaries themselves tend to be more federative because, contrary to the case of both unitary and mandated networks, issues of competency and power tend to be contested within the MNC, and interdependencies among the units tend to be reciprocal as well as sequential (Ghoshal and Nohria 1990). This claim is consistent with Provan's analysis of different kinds of federations and his observation that the network characteristics of divisionalized firms are generally similar to those of independent federations (see Table 1 in Provan 1983: 83). As demonstrated by Provan, Beyer, and Kruytbosch (1980), the inter-organizational approach can be particularly useful for analyzing such federated relationships among units when the participants have only limited option for discretionary behavior and no opportunity to terminate the relationship.

Despite the broad theoretical scope of the inter-organizational perspective as shown in Warren's classification of the field, empirical applications of this perspective have so far been limited to contexts that range from federative to social choice; interaction contexts that range from unitary to federative have been excluded from the domain of inter-organizational inquiry and placed in the domain of intra-organizational analysis (Cook 1977). As such, the relationships between the diverse units of a multi-divisional or a multinational corporation have rarely been examined from an inter-organizational perspective.

Meanwhile, the limitations of applying traditional intra-organizational theory to the analysis of such complex and dispersed business organizations have become increasingly clear. As summarized by Nohria and Venkatraman (1987), the most critical of these limitations stem from the need in such analysis to provide a relatively clear separation between the "organization" and its relevant "environment." As a result, "the environment is typically viewed as an exogenous entity and is reified as a sources of undefined uncertainties (e.g., volatility, resource scarcity, etc.) as opposed to being seen as a field of specific interacting organizations which locate the source of those contingencies" (Nohria and Venkatraman 1987: 2). The organization is seen as a well-defined collective and is assumed to be internally homogeneous, coherent, and consistent.

> Therefore, it is typically described in distributional (e.g., organization chart, division of responsibility, authority, etc.) and categorical (e.g., centralized versus decentralized, mechanistic versus organic, differentiated versus integrated, etc.) terms as opposed to relational terms that focus on the actual interaction patterns based on both internal and external flows of products, information, and authority.
>
> (Nohria and Venkatraman 1987, 2)

In contrast to these limitations of traditional intra-organizational analysis, a dominant construct in many inter-organizational theories is an exchange relation (e.g. Ax and By), defined as consisting of "transactions involving the transfer of resources (x,y) between two or more actors (A,B) for mutual benefit" (Cook 1977: 64). The term "resources" as used in this context includes "any valued activity, service or commodity" (Cook 1977: 64), and therefore includes the flows not only of finances and products but also of technology,

Table 4.1 Different contexts of interorganizational interactions

Dimension	Type of context			
	Unitary	Federative	Coalitional	Social choice
Relation of units to an inclusive goal	Units organized for achievement of inclusive goals	Units with disparate goals, but some formal organization for inclusive goals	Units with disparate goals, but informal collaboration for inclusive goals	No inclusive goals
Locus of inclusive decision making	At top of inclusive structure	At top of inclusive structure, subject to unit ratification	In interaction of units without a formal inclusive structure	Within units
Locus of authority	At top of hierarchy of inclusive structure	Primarily at unit level	Exclusively at unit level	Exclusively at unit level
Structural provision for division of labor	Units structured for division of labor within inclusive organization	Units structured autonomously; may agree to a division of labor, which may affect their structure	Units structured autonomously, may agree to *ad hoc* division of labor, without restructuring	No formally structured division of labor within an inclusive context
Commitment of a leadership subsystem	Norms of high commitment	Norms of moderate commitment	Commitment only to unit leaders	Commitment only to unit leaders
Prescribed collectivity-orientation of units	High	Moderate	Minimal	Little or none

people, and information. Furthermore, as Cook observes, "the term actor in the theory refers not only to individuals but also to collective actors or corporate groups [thus making] it uniquely appropriate when organizations or subunits of organizations are used as the primary unit of analysis" (1977: 63). It is this suggestion of Cook that we adopt and develop in this chapter.

The multinational as a network: constructs and terminology

Let us consider a multinational corporation M with operating units in countries A, B, C, D, E, and F, and a focal organization in the corporate headquarters H. For the purpose of analytical simplicity, let us assume that all the units of M are engaged in a single and common business: that is, M is a single-industry company. Note that H serves as a coordinating agency and plays the role that Provan (1983) described as belonging to the federation management organization (FMO), and therefore must be distinguished from the organizational unit, say A, that is responsible for operations in the home country of M, even though the two may be located in the same premises. By the term "multinational network" we shall refer to all the relationships and linkages that exist among the different units of M: that is, among A, B, C, D, E, F, and H.

Each of the national operating units of M is embedded in an unique context, and for any specific type of exchange relationship, has its unique organization set (Aldrich and Whetten 1981). For example, the unit A can have existing or potential exchange relationships with a specific set of suppliers $[s_A]$, buyers $[b_A]$, and regulatory agencies $[r_A]$, and it competes for resources with an identifiable set of competitors $[c_A]$. Collectively, the group consisting of $[s_A, b_A, r_A, c_A$, etc.] constitutes what we call the organization set of A and denote by the symbol $[OS_A]$.

Different members of the organization set $[OS_A]$ can be internally connected by exchange ties. Following Aldrich and Whetten (1981), we can define the density of $[OS_A]$ as the extensiveness of exchange ties within the elements of the organization set of A. "Density" measures the extent to which actors within the set are connected, on average, to one another: that is, the mean relation from any one actor to any other actor. As suggested by Aldrich and Whetten, density can be operationalized in different ways. For present purposes, we can choose the simplest of these ways and define it as the percentage of actual to potential ties among members of $[OS_A]$. The concluding section of this chapter includes a more detailed discussion on identification of boundaries and measurement of densities for the different local organization sets.

The density of such connections within the different local organization sets of A, B, C, and so on may vary. For example, it has been noted by many authors that the level of connectedness among different members of an industry group is significantly higher in Japan than in some Western countries (see, for example, discussions and the quotation from Lohr in Granovetter 1985: 497). Similarly, it has been shown in the literature that within the same national environment, the level of cohesiveness among customers, suppliers, competitors, and so on may be higher in certain businesses such as construction (Eccles 1981), publishing (Powell 1985), textiles (Sabel et al. 1987), and investment banking (Eccles and Crane 1987), compared with others.

The organization sets of the different units of M may themselves be interconnected through exchange ties. For example, one of the supplying organizations in the local environment of A might be an affiliated unit of another multinational company, and may have exchange linkages with its counterpart in the local environment of B. Similarly, the actions of regulatory agencies in one location (say, r_C) may influence the actions of their counterparts in other locations (say, r_D). Such influence may be manifest in actions such as retaliation by r_C to what is seen as protectionist action of r_D, or deregulation of r_D to reciprocate or just emulate similar action by r_C (Mahini and Wells 1986). Such linkages may also exist among suppliers and competitors. In fact, much of the literature on global strategy considers such cross-border linkages among customers, competitors, and other relevant organizations as a key factor that does or should influence the behaviors of MNCs (for example, this is a focal issue for a number of essays in Porter 1986).

Because of such linkages among the different local organization sets, all members of all the organization sets of the different units of M collectively constitute what we shall call the *external network* (Tichy, Tushman, and Fombrun 1979) within which the multinational network is embedded. In the same manner as we defined the construct of density for each of the different organization sets of the different units of M, we can also describe the density of this external network as the ratio of actual to potential ties among all its constituents. To differentiate between these two densities, we shall refer to the density of ties within each of the local organization sets as *within density,* and the density of ties within the total external network, that is, across the different organization sets, as *across density.*

Our main thesis in this chapter is that different attributes of the MNC can be explained in terms of selected attributes of the external network within which it is embedded. Following the arguments of Benson (1975), the interactions within the different organizational units of the MNC are best explained at the level of resource exchange. This suggests two attributes of the MNC as particularly relevant to our analysis: (1) the distribution of resources among its different affiliated units, and (2) the structural characteristics that mediate internal exchange relationships within the MNC and continually restructure the resource configuration (Zeitz 1980). These two characteristics of the MNC, and how they relate to within and across densities, will provide the focus of our attention for the remaining part of this chapter.

RESOURCE CONFIGURATION IN MNCs

Resources such as production equipment, finance, technology, marketing skills, and management capabilities may be located in any one or more of the different units of M. By the term "resource configuration" we refer to the way in which the resources of M are distributed among A, B, C, D, E, F, and H. We use the word "resource" in the sense of Cook (1977: 64) to refer to "any valuable activity, service, or commodity." In some companies, which Bartlett (1986) describes as "centralized hubs," most resources are concentrated in a single location, typically the parent company. For example, 90 percent of the manufacturing investments of Matsushita, the Japanese consumer electronics company, and 100 percent of its research facilities, are located in Japan. In contrast, in companies such as Philips, Matsushita's European competitor and one that Bartlett categorizes as a "decentralized federation," over 77 percent of total assets are located outside the company's home, which is in the Netherlands, and no single national subsidiary has more than 15 percent of the company's worldwide assets. This difference illustrates one aspect of resource configuration in MNCs that is of analytical interest, namely, dispersal, by which term we refer to the extent to which the company's resources are concentrated in one unit versus dispersed among the different units.

However, while both Philips and Electrolux (the Swedish home appliances company) have a relatively high level of dispersal in the sense that both companies have significant parts of their total assets distributed in a number of countries, the pattern of distribution of such assets is very different in the two cases. Let us consider their resources within Europe. For Electrolux, while the resources are dispersed, they are also very specialized: that is, the resources and associated activities located in any one country are of sufficient scale to meet the company's worldwide, or at least regional, requirements for that activity, thereby avoiding the need for carrying out the same activity or task in multiple locations. For example, Electrolux's washing machine factory in France produces only top-loading washing machines for all of Europe. Similarly, the washing machine factory in Italy produces only front-loading models to meet Europe-wide demand. Electrolux's research centers, product development laboratories, and component producing units are all similarly differentiated and specialized. By contrast, despite considerable recent efforts to increase such specialization, Philips has five factories in Europe that produce identical or near-identical models of television sets, each basically for its own local market. In other words, the resources of Philips are distributed on a local-for-local basis (Ghoshal 1986): they are dispersed but undifferentiated, with identical resources being used by each unit to carry out essentially similar tasks in and for its own local environment. We refer to this dimension of resource configuration as *specialization*, and it represents the extent to which the resources located in each unit are differentiated from those in others.

Resource configuration in MNCs has traditionally been analyzed from an economic perspective, typically under the assumption that resource location decisions are based on rational, self-interested considerations such as the need for increasing profitability, gaining access to new markets or desired factors of production, protecting competitive position, and minimizing costs and risks (for reviews, see Caves 1982; Buckley and Casson 1986; Dunning 1981a; Hennart 1982). Explanations of both dispersal and specialization have therefore focused on factors such as differences in costs of inputs (e.g. Stevens 1974), potential scale economies in different activities (e.g. Porter 1986), impacts of transportation and other "friction" costs (e.g. Hirsch 1976), imperfections in information and other intermediate product markets (e.g. Magee 1977; Rugman 1980), defense against opportunism (e.g. Teece 1986), and potential benefits of risk diversification (e.g. Lessard and Lightstone 1986).

Following Granovetter (1985), much of this analysis can be criticized as "undersocialized" or "oversocialized" conceptions that ignore the important and ongoing effects of surrounding social structures on economic behaviors of organizations. We present here an alternative framework that relates dispersal and specialization to the densities of interactions both within and across the different local organization sets of the company. As suggested in the introductory section, our conceptualization is strongly influenced by the work of institutional theorists who have argued that the structure and behavior of organizations are influenced by both technical and institutional factors (Meyer and Scott 1983), and that "organizations compete not just for resources and customers, but for political power and institutional legitimacy, for social as well as economic fitness" (DiMaggio and Powell 1983: 150).

While Meyer and Scott have been cautious in suggesting that business organizations belong to "technical sectors" in which the economic need for efficiency and effectiveness in controlling work processes dominates institutional need for legitimacy, they have also contended that "while the two dimensions (technical and institutional) tend to be negatively correlated, they are apparently not strongly so" (1983: 140). As suggested by Westney (1988), we believe that for MNCs, strong needs for legitimacy and local isomorphism in each host country environment coexist with a strong demand for efficiency within the worldwide system. Therefore the institutional structure of the environment (that is, the attributes of the local organization sets and the external network) plays an important role in moderating the influence of technical and economic considerations. While different from traditional economic analysis, our arguments are much more consistent with the work of economists such as Porter (1990) and Kogut (1988), both of whom have shown the importance of inter-institutional structure in determining the competitiveness of different countries and companies in different businesses.

79

Effects of within density in national organization sets

As Bower (1987) has shown through his in-depth study of American, European, and Japanese companies in the petrochemical industry, the density of linkages among key players in a national industrial context greatly influences industry performance and company strategy. For a variety of economic, legal, sociological, cultural, and historical reasons, some countries, such as Japan, are characterized by dense linkages among the suppliers, producers, regulators, customers, and others involved in a particular field of industrial activity (Westney and Sakakibara 1985). Such linkages among the different actors may involve different kinds of exchange, such as those involving funds, people, or information. They may be established and maintained through many different mechanisms, such as integrating governmental agencies, interlocking boards of directors, cross-holding of equity, institutionalized systems of personnel flows, long-term contracts and trust-based relationships, and mediating roles of organizations such as trade associations, banks, and consultants (see, for example, the collected essays in Evan 1976). Bower's study shows how Japanese petrochemical companies were able to capitalize on such linkages not only to build entry barriers in the local market, but also as a means of restructuring and rationalizing the industry.

In locations where the local organization sets are densely connected, the implications for local units of MNCs are clear. As Granovetter (1973) has argued, strong and multiplexed ties among the existing members of the national organization sets will lead to exclusion from the sets of those who cannot establish equally strong and multiplexed ties with each member. Westney and Sakakibara's (1985) study on the R&D activities of Japanese and American computer companies illustrates this effect of within density in the local organization sets. According to these authors, the Japanese R&D centers of some of the American computer companies could not tap into local skills and technologies because the absence of associated manufacturing and marketing activities prevented the isolated research establishments from building linkages with the local "knowledge networks" embedded in the dense interactions among different members of the Japanese organization set.

Where the linkages within the local organization sets are sparse, no such barriers are created, as shown in the US Department of Commerce's account of the television industry in the USA in the early 1970s (Paul 1984). Absence of ties among producers because of rivalry and anti-trust laws, and their arm's-length relationships with suppliers, labor, and government, created an environment that made it easy for Japanese producers to enter the US market, with local sales offices importing finished products from the parent companies. However, when the American companies responded in a unified manner through the Electronics Industry Association, with the support of labor unions and suppliers, they were able to obtain government support on anti-dumping suits. The resulting politically negotiated import quotas forced the Japanese companies to establish local manufacturing facilities.

We can, therefore, make the following propositions about the effects of within density on dispersal and specialization in the configuration of resources in a multinational. When interaction densities within the different national organization sets are low, the social context exerts limited influence, and intended economic rationality becomes dominant in resource configuration decisions. In this situation, therefore, the MNC will concentrate research, production, assembly, and other similar activities based on consideration of potential scale and scope economies, and locate them on the basis of "resource niches" (Aldrich 1979) that may exist in different countries as a result of their comparative advantages (for example, R&D in the USA or Japan, manufacturing in Singapore or Brazil). As a result, its overall resource configuration will show relatively low dispersal and high specialization. When within densities are high, however, the company will be forced to fragment its activities and locate more of the different kinds of resources in each market so as to provide the variety that is necessary to match the structures of the local organization sets. Consequently, in this case, dispersal will increase while specialization will decrease.

Effects of across density in the external network

When the linkages across the different national organization sets are sparse, the MNC's resource configuration follows the pattern we have described above, based on consideration of the within densities alone. With high interactions across members of the different national organization sets, however, this situation changes significantly.

Consider first the case of low within density and high across density. We have argued that low within density will lead to low dispersal and high specialization, and the company will locate its resources according to the resource niches in different countries. But, with high across densities, many of these national resource niches tend to be eliminated because of freer flows. If technologies developing in one location can be accessed instantaneously from another, or if excess capital available in one environment can be borrowed in markets located elsewhere, there is no longer any need to locate specific activities in specific locations to benefit from access to local resources. Therefore, with high across density, resource-seeking concentration will decline (though not necessarily be eliminated, since regulatory and other barriers may selectively prohibit certain flows of people and products).

Consider now the case of high within densities coupled with high across densities. We have suggested that high within density will lead to high dispersal and low specialization because of the need for matching the structures of the local environments. However, when across densities are high, it is no longer necessary to establish a comprehensive range of resources in each

81

market, since exchange linkages can now be established across borders, without the need for complementary facilities on a location-by-location basis. In other words, with high across density, the logic of resource allocation for both high and low within densities becomes inappropriate. Instead, a completely different set of criteria emerges: in this situation, resource configuration is greatly influenced by the nodal characteristics of the complex external network.

Consider, for example, the situation when customers in locations A, B, D, and E are strongly influenced by the standards and preferences of customers in location C. Bartlett and Ghoshal (1986) and Prahalad and Doz (1987) have described the existence of such "lead markets" in many businesses, and their existence is predicted by the "normative systems" that Laumann, Glaskiewicz, and Marsden (1978) proposed as one of the modalities that influence the behaviors of members in a network. In such a situation, the MNC will tend to locate a significant amount of resources in C so as to be able to sense the demands of local customers and respond to them in a fashion that attracts their patronage. The level of resources in C will exceed what is required to match the needs for membership of the local organization set $[OS_C]$ and will instead be targeted to benefit from the greater role of C as a central node in the larger external network that is created by the linkages among $[OS_A]$, $[OS_B]$, $[OS_C]$, and so on. Given that for different activities of the MNC, different locations might emerge as the nodes in the relevant external networks, and that even for the same activity there might be multiple nodes instead of a single one, the consequence of increasing across density for the resource configuration of the company will be one of moderate dispersal (that is, not as high as in the case of local-for-local distribution, but higher than concentration only in countries offering specific resource niches) coupled with increasing specialization. Tasks will be divided into finer and finer segments so that each can be located at the appropriate nodal locations, which however might well be different from those that would be predicted by the traditional considerations of comparative advantages or resource niches as applicable to those tasks.

Chandler (1986), among others, has documented that because of improvements in communication and transportation infrastructures around the world, increasing across densities have affected a wide range of industries in the recent past. The observed consequences of this trend are entirely consistent with our arguments. For example, until the late 1970s the telecommunications switching industry was characterized by high within and low across densities. Interactions among members of the industry were high within each country because of its status as a "strategic industry" and the resulting coordinating role of the national governments. However, until the advent of digital technology, the industry was highly regulated in most countries, and the need to synchronize the switching equipment with the idiosyncrasies of local terminal equipments constrained opportunities for cross-border linkages. As a result, the resources of most multinational companies were highly dispersed, with low levels of specialization. ITT provides a good illustration: each of its national subsidiaries in Europe had its own local facilities for product development, manufacturing, and marketing, and the corporate staff, including the top management of the company, consisted of less than 100 employees.

The context of this industry has changed significantly in the 1980s: while within densities remained high, across density increased substantially, due to the emergence of digital technology and the growing trends of standardization and deregulation, all of which facilitated cross-border integration among suppliers, customers, and other industry participants. As a result, resource configurations of the producers also changed. While the overall level of dispersal reduced to a limited extent, the level of specialization increased drastically. Ericsson, for example, closed only a few of its factories around the world, but converted many of them into focused manufacturing centers that produced a narrow range of components. Similarly, each of the laboratories of Alcatel, the company created by merging ITT and CIT-Alcatel, were given the mandate and resources to pursue a specific and well-defined technology or development task, in contrast to the earlier situation when most of them operated quite independently, developing the entire range of products for their local markets.

CENTRALITY AND POWER WITHIN THE MULTINATIONAL NETWORK

Our preceding arguments on resource configuration in MNCs were based on a notion of isomorphic fit with the characteristics of the external network; we did not address the question of how such a fit is achieved. An MNC's configuration of resources at any point in time is the outcome of previous resource flows, and as argued by Benson (1975), the flow of resources within an inter-organizational network is influenced by the distribution of power within the network. In this section we suggest that within and across densities in the different national organization sets of an MNC predicate the relative power of the headquarters and the national units, and that the nature of resource flows generated by the resulting distribution of power leads to the pattern of isomorphic fit we have described.

Effects of within density in national organization sets

Applying Zald's (1970) political economy approach to the analysis of inter-organizational relations, Benson (1975) suggested that an actor in such a network could enhance its power in dyadic relationships with other actors on the strength of its relationships with other organizational or social networks. Subsequently, Provan, Beyer, and Kruytbosch (1980) provided empirical support to this proposal when they demonstrated that power relations within the network of United Way organizations were significantly modified by the linkages between the individual agencies and other elements in their local communities upon which the United Way depended for its survival. The dependence of the United Way units on their local communities is in some ways akin to the dependence of the multinational on the local organization sets of its different national units. Just as dense linkages with the key elements of their communities enhanced the power of the United Way organizations, dense exchange relationships with the members of their local organization sets can be expected to enhance the powers of the national units of the multinational.

It is inappropriate, however, to draw a direct correspondence between the United Way and an MNC, because the central management organization of the United Way lacks the hierarchical power of the headquarters of the MNC. To incorporate this difference in our analysis, it is necessary to consider how hierarchical power might modify the inter-unit exchange patterns proposed by Benson.

We suggest that the efficacy of the hierarchical power of the headquarters to counteract the linkage-based power of the subsidiary is contingent on the density of interactions among members of the subsidiary's organization set. When this within density is low, the potential power of the subsidiary is derived from its individual dyadic relationships. In this situation, the headquarters is more effective in counteracting the power of the subsidiary, because it is potentially easier to have a "direct control" over such relationships through mechanisms such as periodic visits by the headquarters staff. However, such direct control becomes more difficult in a situation of high within density in the subsidiary's organization set. In this case, the subsidiary's power is derived not from an individual dyadic relationship, but from the web of exchange relations in the local organization set of which it is a part. Remote control loses efficacy when "localness," by itself, is the key requirement for maintaining the relationships. For example, in the case of the Australian subsidiary of Ericsson which we referred to earlier, extensive cross-licensing arrangements among all the producers, and the resulting close relationships among equipment suppliers, customers, and regulators were the main factors (other than distance) that impeded closer control of the local subsidiary from Stockholm and allowed the subsidiary to build up the high level of research and other resources.

Therefore, the positive relationship between "environmental linkages" and power of the local unit of an inter-organizational network proposed by Benson (1975) will remain operational in the context of an MNC under the condition of high within density. Following the arguments of Emerson (1962) and Cook (1977), the local unit will use this power to reduce its dependence on the other units of the network. Therefore, it will bargain for and obtain a full range of resources so as to be able to carry out autonomously as many of its functions as possible. If all or most of the units of the MNC are located in environments of high within density, the consequence of this process will be a high level of dispersal of its resources on a local-for-local basis.

Effects of across density in the external network

The literature on the distribution of power in social networks reveals two main sources of power in such collectivities (Fombrun 1983). First, power is an antipode of dependency in exchange relations (Emerson 1962), and accrues to those members of the network that control critical resources required by others, but do not depend on others for resources (Aldrich 1979; Pfeffer and Salancik 1978). Following Cook (1977), this might be called "exchange power" to distinguish it from the second source of power, which arises from structural rather than exchange dependencies. "Structural power" emanates from the position of a member within the network: as shown by Lazarsfeld and Menzel (1961), it is an attribute induced by a member's context.

Our preceding discussions on power-dependency relationships within an MNC were based only on consideration of dyadic exchange between the headquarters and the national units. The situation changes when consideration of structural power is brought into the analysis. The structure of the external network now enters the calculation as an important variable, since different members of the multinational network can potentially develop different levels of structural power based on their positions within the larger network of interactions among customers, suppliers, and so on across different countries.

Ignoring for present purposes the exceptions to the rule pointed out by Cook et al. (1983), the structural power of actors in a network can be assumed to arise from their centrality within the network (Lehman 1975; Laumann and Pappi 1976). As pointed out by Freeman (1979), the term "centrality" has been defined and used in the literature in many different ways. For present purposes, we can limit our attention to what Freeman describes as point centrality of the different actors within the multinational network, and also define the point centrality of each actor as a function of its degree, that is, the number of other actors within the multinational network with which it has direct exchange relations. Following the arguments of Freeman, the headquarters enjoys the highest levels of point centrality when linkages among the subsidiaries are minimal. In a situation of extensive interactions among the subsidiaries, the centrality of the headquarters declines relative to those of the subsidiaries, and the centrality of the different members of the network becomes dependent on the actual structure of such linkages.

High across density typically implies a high level of interactions among the subsidiaries of a multinational. As an illustration, consider the case of a manufacturer of automotive tires such as Italy's Pirelli. The company produces and markets car and truck tires in a number of countries, including the USA, Italy, and Germany. It also supplies tires to the Ford Motor Company in each of these countries.

When Ford's local units in these countries operated relatively autonomously, with minimal coordination, there was little need for Pirelli's local units to coordinate their own activities with regard to their supply to Ford. But as the interactions and coordination among Ford's operations in these countries increased, leading to internal comparisons of the prices, quality, and support provided by common vendors (thereby enhancing across density, as relevant to Pirelli), Pirelli's subsidiaries also needed to enhance their internal coordination and communication, on issues of quality levels, pricing, service, and so on to prevent customer dissatisfaction (see Terpstra 1982). In other words, as a general principle, it can be stated that as across density increases, intersubsidiary linkages become more extensive and the centrality of the headquarters declines, relative to other units.

More interestingly, however, under this condition, multiple points can emerge within the MNC with the same or a similar degree of point centrality. In a hub-and-spoke structure, the headquarters has a very high level of point centrality, whereas in a configuration where each unit is connected to every other unit, the headquarters and the subsidiaries would all have the same point centrality. In a growing number of MNCs, however, some key subsidiaries have the same point centrality as the headquarters, whereas other subsidiaries have less. For Pirelli, for example, the USA, Italy, and Germany may emerge as external nodes since these countries may be the headquarters locations for its major customers in these and other markets. Further, only one of these external nodes (Italy) may coincide with the location of the company's own headquarters. Normative hierarchy in customer tastes and preferences (such as adoption by customers in other countries of a perfume or wine that is popular in France), and the advanced states of certain technologies in certain countries (such as ceramic technology in Japan, and computer software technology in the USA and the United Kingdom) are some other examples of external nodes that can affect the point centralities of different units within the MNC. For the different activities of the MNC, different locations can emerge as the nodes of the external network; for any one particular activity, a number of different locations can possess such nodal characteristics. Consequently, following the arguments of Burt (1978), the multinational network will typically develop multiple centers with different internal coalitions and nodes corresponding to the different coalitions and nodes that may exist in the external network.

Therefore, in such a situation, the nodal units of the multinational will develop structural power and use this power to attract resources from within the MNC network. As a result, the level of dispersal in the MNC's resources will be moderate—lower than local-for-local dispersal (since not all units will emerge as nodes) but higher than in the case of concentration in locations of specific resource niches (except for businesses where a specific country enjoys a dominant position in all activities). Further, a high level of specialization will also develop in the resource configuration, since nodal positions within the MNC network can be expected to vary by activities and tasks as a reflection of similar variance in the external network. Note that both the process and outcome aspects of this conclusion resonate with empirical findings such as those of subsidiaries being given "world product mandates" (Poynter and Rugman 1982) and "global leader" or "contributor" roles (Bartlett and Ghoshal 1986) for specific activities and tasks.

LARGE MNCs AS DIFFERENTIATED NETWORKS

Several highly simplifying assumptions were made in the foregoing discussions on resource configuration in MNCs under different conditions of local and global interlinkages. The enormous complexity of several disparate country-level organization sets and the diversity of the heterogeneous international business environment were dichotomized into high–low categories of within and across densities. In reality, the levels of connectedness within and across the national organization sets can be expected to vary across countries and groups of countries. The density of interactions across the national organization sets might be high for the developed countries, or among regional groupings, but low in developing countries, particularly the more regulated and autarkic. Similarly, interactions among members within the national organization sets might be high in homogeneous societies with a tradition of strong inter-institutional linkages, and low in countries where such linkages are discouraged through legislation, impeded because of societal heterogeneity, or rendered ineffective because of poor communication infrastructures or the absence of linking institutions.

Therefore, the configuration of resources in multinationals engaged in such businesses will be influenced by multiple criteria. In some locations internal interactions within the local organization set might be high, but external linkages with other organization sets might be low. In such locations, the MNC may provide all required resources in appropriate measures so that its local unit can build and maintain linkages with key members of its own community. The organization sets in some other countries might be sparsely connected internally, but different elements of the local environment might be strongly connected with their counterparts in other countries. For these locations the MNC may create a resource structure that is concentrated and specialized, and in some cases the location of the specialized resources might reflect the desire to gain access to special resource niches, while in other cases the location choice may be motivated by the modalities in the external network. Finally, the organization sets in a third group of countries might be characterized by high within and across linkages. In these locations, the MNC may establish all the complementary resources for integrated operating, but link these locations with others so as to leverage the resources and achieve economies of concentration and specialization.

The overall resource configuration for a company like Philips, then, will reflect a mix of some resources that are dispersed among some units on a purely local-for-local basis (such as product development, manufacturing, marketing, and other resources for the lighting business in India); some that are concentrated in different countries to access specialized local resource pools (such as the global-scale audio factory in Singapore), and others that are concentrated in lead markets (such as development and manufacturing facilities for teletext television sets in the United Kingdom). Elsewhere we have described such a structure as the "differentiated network," and have shown that a number of large multinational companies such as Procter and Gamble, Unilever, Ericsson, NEC, and Matsushita are increasingly converging to this structural form despite the differences in their businesses and parent company nationalities (Bartlett and Ghoshal 1989).

Such a convergence is consistent with the theoretical arguments we have presented here. Following the arguments of Chandler (1986), one effect of worldwide improvements in communication and transportation infrastructures is the increasing interlinkages among actors, both within and across national boundaries. When such linkages are low, the influence of structural embeddedness is low, and MNCs have a greater degree of freedom to locate their activities and resources to benefit from local resource niches, and in line with the economic and technological characteristics of their businesses. Thus, in such situations, the resource configurations of different MNCs can be expected to differ as a reflection of those differences in their businesses and as a result of their freedom to exercise strategic choices. However, in the context of high within and across densities, such freedom is reduced because of the network influences. Both dispersal and specialization now become essential, at least for the very large companies that have been the focus of our attention in this chapter. If within density is a country trait and across density is a world-system trait, the pattern of linkages in the overall structure of the external network is going to be increasingly similar for large multinational companies, irrespective of their businesses. In other words, mimetic and normative forces of isomorphism (DiMaggio and Powell 1983) may be getting stronger as the world jolts along to Levitt's (1983) "global village," and the observed trend of convergence to the differentiated network structure may be an outcome of these broader societal changes.

IMPLICATIONS FOR RESEARCH

In this chapter we have proposed a reconceptualization of the MNC as an inter-organizational system rather than as an organization. This reconceptualization creates the possibility of applying exchange theory and network methodologies to the study of MNCs, and has some important implications for future research on MNC-related issues.

First, at the aggregate level of macrostructural differences among MNCs, traditional analysis has tended to assume internal homogeneity within such companies. This has resulted in generalized conclusions at the level of the overall company, based on empirical studies that have focused on individual actors or specific dyadic links. For example, American MNCs are widely believed to be more centralized than their Japanese and European counterparts, based on analyses of parent companies' relationships with their subsidiaries, often in a single region (e.g. Hulbert and Brandt 1980). However, as we have argued in this chapter, headquarters–subsidiary relations within an MNC can vary widely from subsidiary to subsidiary. The inter-organizational network conceptualization can provide new concepts such as graph centrality (Freeman 1979) or hierarchy (Coleman 1966), which appear to be theoretically more appropriate for such macrostructural comparisons among internally differentiated and heterogeneous organizational systems like MNCs.

Second, given such heterogeneity, macrostructural analysis alone might not be enough, and might need to be complemented with micro-structural analyses of these internal differences so as to build a more complete theoretical understanding of the ways in which an MNC functions. For example, in the differentiated network MNC, there is no formal macrostructure that "fits" all parts of the company's heterogeneous environments. Yet the MNC has to choose a formal departmental structure, and might quite arbitrarily choose one that appears to be simple and consistent with its own administrative heritage (Bartlett 1983, 1986). Therefore, not only might macrostructure be more difficult to predict theoretically—as seems true, given the significant empirically-induced modifications to the Stopford and Wells (1972) contingency model proposed by subsequent studies of MNC macrostructures, such as those by Daniels, Pitts, and Tretter (1985) and Egelhoff (1988a)—but it might also have become a less interesting attribute to study precisely because of such indeterminacy. For example, contrary to the predictions of structural contingency, NEC, P&G and Unilever did not change their macrostructures in over two decades despite some very significant changes in their business conditions. What changed in these companies were the internal management processes: subsidiaries assumed new and specific roles to respond to changing local conditions, and the headquarters' control mechanisms evolved from ubiquitous "company ways" to multidimensional gestalts that were applied differently to different parts of the organization so as to respond to shifting global contexts (Bartlett and Ghoshal 1989). The network perspective is particularly suited for investigation of such differences in internal roles, relations, and tasks of different affiliated units (for example, through block modeling and analysis of functional equivalence), and of how internal coordination mechanisms might be differentiated to match the variety of subunit contexts (see, for example, the papers by Burt in Burt, Minor, and Associates (1983) on "distinguishing relational contents" and "studying status/role-sets using mass surveys").

The same argument we made for structure can also be made for strategy. Discussions of company or even business-level generic strategies and how they "fit" generic types of competitive structures are too far removed from the reality of highly differentiated strategic approaches that can be expected in different parts of the differentiated network organization. Instead, it may be more useful to explore the actual content of strategy in such complex organizational systems: network theoretic analysis of internal flows of resources, products, people, and information might be more relevant for developing middle-range theories on resource commitment, decision making, strategic control, normative integration, and creation and diffusion of innovations in such companies. (See, for example, the application of network analysis in Carley (1986), Burt (1987), and Walker (1985).) In this chapter we have focused primarily on the hierarchical network relationships between the headquarters and the national subsidiaries of an MNC. Investigation of the lateral network relations among the different subsidiaries can open up avenues for similar fine-grained analysis of both the causes and consequences of horizontal interdependencies and synergy.

Finally, as has been shown in some recent contributions, the interorganizational approach can be particularly useful for the study of another MNC-related phenomenon that is assuming increasing importance: that is, their formation of complex webs of alliances and joint ventures with customers, suppliers, and competitors (Ohmae 1985; Harrigan 1985). By focusing on relations among actors, the network analysis approach can provide both appropriate concepts and methodological tools for rigorous and theory-grounded investigation of the strategic and organizational aspects of such alliances. (See, for example, the contributions by Walker, Westney, and Hakenson and Johanson in Contractor and Lorange (1988).)

Building a network theory of the MNC

The concepts and arguments presented here suffer from a number of shortcomings which need to be overcome before the network conceptualization can yield a useful and testable theory of the MNC. The necessary improvement and extension of these preliminary ideas will require both deductive theory building with more sophisticated use of network theory than has been achieved here, and also empirical studies to induce and test more fine-grained propositions and hypotheses.

First, our definitions of constructs such as within and across densities are too coarse since, as we point out in the concluding section, these densities differ for different parts of the total external network of any company. Such differences can be expected along both geographic and functional dimensions. For example, the external organizations relevant for the R&D department of a company might be far more interconnected across national borders than those that are relevant for the service department. Similarly, while within density, on average, might be higher in Japan than in the USA, there might be significant differences between the two contexts for different parts of the local organization sets. One of the main attractions of the network perspective is that the implications of such differences can be explicitly included in both theoretical and empirical analyses, and the elaboration of these distinctions must be a priority for future research on this topic.

Second, we have considered exchange very broadly to include many different kinds of transaction involving products, information, affect, and so on, without distinguishing among these different flows. As follows from the general arguments of Mitchell (1973) and Kadushin (1978), each of these different kinds of exchanges can have some very different implications for the strategy, organization, and management of an MNC. Further, those effects are also likely to be interactive. The next phase of theory development, therefore, must explicate the separate and joint effects of these different kinds of exchanges.

Third, we have focused on density as the key parameter of the external network, since density appeared to relate most closely to the implications of social embeddedness described by Granovetter (1985). It is also a relatively simple construct that is easy to conceptualize and to measure once the relevant organization sets and external network are identified. Density, however, is not a complete description of a network, and it is possible that some other characteristics of the external network can significantly influence specific attributes of the MNC. Therefore, for more complete development of theory, it would be desirable to identify a set of parameters that completely and unambiguously define the external network, and then to explore the impact of each of these parameters on selected attributes of the multinational. Krackhardt (1989) proposed four parameters—connectedness, hierarchy, least-upper-boundedness, and graph efficiency—as necessary and sufficient descriptors of a network, and his work provides some interesting opportunities for modifying and extending our theoretical arguments.

Finally, it might also be necessary to improve the specificity and precision in our definition of some of the constructs so as to facilitate their operationalization in empirical research. One key issue concerns delineation of the boundaries of the different national organization sets, which is a general and widespread problem in network research (Laumann et al. 1983). As suggested by Aldrich and Whetten (1981), the relevant organization sets may well differ according to different kinds of exchange, and definition of the boundaries might therefore depend on the kind of exchange that is the focus of inquiry. In presenting our ideas here, we have been guided by the belief that these boundaries can be identified either through the naturalistic approach of a priori commonsense definition, or empirically, through measurement of structural cohesion (DiMaggio 1986). In the former approach, for example, all relevant suppliers, customers, regulators, and competitors in any country can be prespecified based on expert knowledge of the local structure of the business. In the latter approach, a broader population of potentially relevant members of the local organization set may be identified through a repeated process of snowball sampling till sufficient convergence is achieved, and the organization set can then be identified empirically from this population as the group of organizations that interact maximally with one another and minimally with other members of the population. Once all the relevant local organization sets are identified by one method or another, the external network can be defined as the collectivity of all these local organization sets.

Clearly the former method for identifying the national organization sets is the more convenient, and it is our belief that experienced researchers should usually be able to prespecify most of the relevant actors with sufficient accuracy. Some researchers, however, may prefer the latter approach for it avoids the arbitrariness of a priori selection. However, as Laumann et al. (1983) have argued, neither approach is fully satisfactory, and some better way for delineation of the boundaries remains as another important topic for further reflection.

POSTSCRIPT
By D. Eleanor Westney

When Sumantra and I first discussed this second edition two years ago, I asked Sumantra what he considered to be the most significant publications over the past decade that followed the network approach that he and Chris Bartlett laid out in this chapter. He named three contributions. The first was the book that he and Nitin Nohria had published in 1997, based in part on the network data that Sumantra had collected in the course of his dissertation research for his Harvard Business School doctorate (Nohria and Ghoshal 1997). He was justifiably proud of a book that advanced both the theory and the empirical analysis of a network model of MNCs and that had received the Academy of Management's book award in 1998. The second contribution he mentioned was the work by Anil Gupta and Vijay Govindarajan on internal knowledge networks in MNCs (Gupta and Govindarajan 1991, 2000). The third was Julian Birkenshaw's research on how subsidiary roles in an MNC change over time through the actions of subsidiary managers which leverage the subunit's external networks and internal capabilities (Birkenshaw 1997, 1998). Sumantra observed that although Julian's work focuses on the individual subsidiary rather than the entire MNC network and does not draw explicitly on network theory, it provides a very useful insight into the evolution of MNC subsidiary networks over time.

Sumantra did note, however, that the agenda set out in this chapter for rigorous, theory-based, empirical analysis combining internal and external MNC network mapping was an aspiration yet to be realized.

5   Ecological Analysis of MNCs[1]

Jacques Delacroix

Portentous and abrupt changes in the world economic order have recently rekindled public interest in the globalization of business. Students of international business thus face with renewed urgency the challenge of explaining the interaction between business organizations and their environment. This challenge is also an opportunity: large-scale environmental transformations provide many occasions to observe organizational reactions and proactions.

In this chapter, I explain how organizational ecology, a leading paradigm in organizational theory, can be put to work to explore organizational responses to multinational environmental change. I try to show how the organizational ecology style of research lends itself to the testing of eclectic theoretical models of multinational organization and feeds research intuition.

THE MULTINATIONAL COMPANY AS A PUZZLE

The existence of multinational companies (MNCs) once puzzled conventional neoclassical economics. Why should the functions served by organizations headquartered in one country but with subsidiaries or other dependent subparts in other countries not be served as well by trade? Any organization operating in environments that are initially unfamiliar is expected to suffer learning and stumbling costs not imposed on indigenous organizations. Thus MNCs and all organizations of their kind are chronically at a competitive disadvantage. Consequently, manufacturing and other producing subsidiaries appear as poor substitutes for arm's length imports and sourcing subsidiaries for exports.

The question asked by Anderson and Gatignon (1986), "Why should true and tried mechanisms be replaced by comparatively clumsy organizational attempts to reach across national boundaries?", has received two broad kinds of answers from economics-oriented scholars. Some scholars, following Hymer (1970) and Kindleberger (1969), have argued that MNCs constitute organizational endeavors designed to pursue a firm-specific monopolistic advantage (Teece 1980) which would be dissipated if market mechanisms were relied on. "Beachhead" and "headstart" (Kolde 1985: 300–304) explanations fall more or less into the same conceptual category.

A second type of explanation shows that markets are the most efficient economic mechanisms only under certain conditions pertaining to perfect competition. Scholars belonging to this school of thought, traceable to

93

Williamson (1975) and to McManus (1972), study the theoretical effects of relaxing certain assumptions on the likelihood that organizational solutions may be more efficient than markets (Hennart 1982, 1988, 1989). Transaction cost theory thus argues that some specific costs of trade, and of international trade in particular, are sometimes high enough to compensate for the costs of control and monitoring associated with organizational (or "hierarchical") solutions. (See Hennart, this volume, 1989, and his 1988 case study of one industry; Klein, Crawford, and Alchian 1978; Hill and Kim 1988; Klein, Frazier, and Roth 1990; for a different organization of the field see Kogut, this volume).

The conceptual rigor that transaction cost theorists bring to bear on the question of why MNCs exist is great enough, and their empirical results are persuasive enough, for contending schools of thought to appear on the verge of extinction. (For a more skeptical account, see Buckley 1988.) Even firm monopoly arguments are in the process of being integrated into transaction cost theory.

Organizational ecology within organization theory

Until the 1980s, organization theory had little to say about MNCs, in part because its conceptual tradition is largely blind to the special character of national boundaries (Carroll, Delacroix, and Goodstein 1988). However, the evolution of this field since then points to the possibility that significant contributions will emerge. As recounted in Scott's thorough survey of the field (1987a), the older "closed system" and "open system" approaches, which focused on the internal structure and behavior of organizations, have been vigorously challenged by a revised "open system" perspective that assigns priority to the relationship between organizations and their environments.

The "open system" perspective has a special affinity with the study of MNCs, and it can complement the dominant transaction cost approach to the study of MNCs. Organizational theory, in turn, would benefit from paying attention to MNCs and to the work of students of international business. Institutional theory (see Westney, this volume) and organizational ecology are two important schools of thought within the open system perspective. Institutional theory, as its name indicates, emphasizes the importance of the institutional environments within which organizations must exist. Roughly, according to this view, organizations' structures and strategies are conditioned by their need to be viewed as legitimate, because illegitimate organizations are not ordinarily given the means to succeed. Institutions granting legitimacy include political institutions but are not limited to them. One central argument of institutional theory, which may be pertinent to the study of MNCs, is that organizational structures reflect a great deal of mimetic behavior: Why invent new organizational forms that may be judged strange when there are plenty of models to emulate that are already taken for granted? An underlying assumption developed in Meyer and Zucker (1989) is that many organizations are subjected either weakly or not at all to the vigorous market trials envisaged by economic theory. Not surprisingly, much (but not all) of the empirical evidence in support of the institutional perspective has come from studies of commonweal, non-business organizations (Aldrich and Marsden 1988: 381).

Organizational ecology is the other major open system school of thought. Organizational ecology (sometimes called "population ecology" in textbooks) is built around the concept of structural inertia. In the ecological view, organizations in general have little latitude for effective structural change (Hannan and Freeman 1989: 67–69; Aldrich and Marsden 1988: 380; see Stinchcombe 1965 for a seminal substantive discussion; and Kilduff, this volume). Indeed, according to some ecologists (see, for example, Carroll 1987), important structural reforms are often recipes for disaster, and are more likely to lead to organizational demise than to organizational adaptation, as managerial schools of thought assume.[2] Hannan and Freeman propose further that structural inertia and its attendant vulnerability are not organizational pathologies. Instead, they argue, structural inertia is the expectable and mostly sound consequence of the role organizations are supposed to play in society (Hannan and Freeman 1989: 72–77). Compared with both markets and other forms of social collectivities,[3] organizations are specifically expected to provide reliability of performance. This mandate in turn is served by permanence of structure. If organizations are supposed to be recognizably themselves from day to day in terms of their demeanor, clearly they should not be able to modify their structure frequently or rapidly.

The concept of structural inertia has important consequences for the way one goes about studying organizations. Given that today's organizations are different from yesterday's, it is necessary to explain change in the organizational panorama. Managerial schools explain this change as the aggregate result of individual organizations' efforts to cope with an environment that is both changeable and encumbered by competing organizations. To the extent that structural inertia is granted, this form of individual adaptation must be rare, and contribute but little to organizational change. Instead, ecologists argue, organizational change occurs largely through the replacement of organizational forms by other organizational forms that may be either slight variants of the forms being replaced or completely different from them. Thus, for example, vacuum tube makers were replaced by transistor manufacturers with very little direct filiation between the two forms (Golding 1971). The efficient mechanism of change invoked by organizational ecologists is therefore not adaptation but selective elimination, or simply "selection."[4] A selection viewpoint, in turn, necessarily requires a research interest in organizational dissolution. Correspondingly, the organizational ecology perspective is supported by a large and growing number of empirical studies of dissolutions or "disbandings" pertaining to a wide variety of organizations. (For reviews, see Baum and Amburgey 2002; Carroll 1988; Hannan and Freeman 1989; see also Carroll and Hannan 2000.)

The counterintuitive logic of organizational ecology demands that a high replacement rate prevail within categories of organizations. If organizations seldom dissolve or if they are not replaced by new organizations, selection cannot account for the observable organizational change. Several studies place this replacement rate at about 10 percent annually (Aldrich and Marsden 1988: 378). To detect the effects of such moderately high rates in turn requires reasonably long periods of observation, and deep longitudinal studies rather than cross-sectional ones. Consequently, organizational ecologists tend to study, over long periods, broad categories of organizations of the same kind. (See Hannan and Freeman 1989, and Carroll and Delacroix 1982, for studies extending over about 120 years and 175 years, respectively.) They call the latter "populations." In most cases, ecological populations are phenomenologically defined saturation samples covering every organization of the same kind which ever existed in a given locale.[5]

Recently, ecologists have begun to integrate arguments from institutional theory into both their theoretical models and their estimation models (Hannan and Freeman 1989: 131, for example), a move not necessarily applauded by institutional theorists (Zucker 1989). Some organizational ecologists argue that it is especially important to incorporate into ecological models variables capturing changes in the political environment (Carroll, Delacroix, and Goodstein 1988).

Doing international management research with an organizational ecology framework

Transaction cost scholars are sometimes perceived as adaptationists (Aldrich and Marsden 1988: 377) because they often write prescriptively, a habit imported from mainstream economic theory, which tends to view organizations more or less as substitutes for *homo economicus* (for a constructive departure, see Hennart, this volume). Hence it appears as if they view the substitution of hierarchical, organizational solutions (such as the MNC) for cross-boundary market operations (imports and exports) as the result of conscious calculations by well-informed administrators (e.g. Kimura 1989: 297). This style of presentation seems in contradiction with what is known of market entry decisions. According to Robinson's (1978: 374–375) survey, such decisions are seldom made with careful considerations. Kobrin, Basek, Blank, and La Palombara (1980) show that entry decisions are seldom preceded by an adequate examination of the non-economic aspects of the host country environment.

Yet it appears that the extent to which conscious choice presides over the choice of entry solutions, including foreign direct investment (FDI), is not central to the logic of transaction cost analysis. A selection perspective is just as compatible. In this view, firms that choose FDI when they should select other modes of entry, from a transaction cost standpoint, will suffer in the long run through inferior performance. Inferior performance in turn should lead to elimination under certain conditions; however, this scenario lends itself to a realistic research strategy only if a long run is available for observation. Arpan and Ricks (1986) show that there is great stability in the pattern of FDI in the USA between 1974 and 1984; Kobrin (1976) observes a similar pattern for American FDI in less developed countries. Organizational ecologists have accumulated a wealth of experience in the manipulation of deep longitudinal data bases. Hence, empirical inquiry into international management matters may have something to gain from adopting some of the methodological practices pioneered in the social sciences by organizational ecology.

Scholars in all fields frequently call for more and better longitudinal studies (see, for example, Buckley 1988: 183; Egelhoff, this volume). Ecologists have brought a particular urgency to this call by drawing attention to the possibility that cross-sectional studies may lead not only to imperfect results but to thoroughly fallacious ones. This theme, developed by Carroll (1984), Freeman and Boeker (1984), and Hannan and Freeman (1989: 42–43, 92–93), among others, pertains in large part to survivor bias.

In spite of vigorous but usually merely ritualistic denials that any generalization is intended, many studies of business organizations generalize on the basis of cross-sectional convenience samples (e.g. Cvar 1986) or on the basis of shallow longitudinal samples.[6] With this practice all organizations existing at the time of the study constitute the statistical population being sampled. The problem arises when scholars generalize unwittingly or implicitly from this sample to an undefined but much larger population extending far back in time. The population in existence at the time of the study is, in fact, itself a sample of the larger, chronologically undefined population. The former is a very biased sample of the latter. Ecological studies have shown (Aldrich and Marsden 1988: 382) that survival is systematically linked to both organizational age and organizational size. Older and larger organizations are more likely to survive into the next time period than are younger and smaller organizations. The two effects are additive. Since the population in existence at the time of the study is composed in part of organizations that have survived from an earlier period, it is loaded with entities that are larger and older than the base population, at least. Thus users of cross-sectional samples are in danger of proffering generalizations about business organizations that are systematically biased because they do not take into account the effects of size and age on whatever they are studying. Note that drawing a perfectly random sample from the population in existence at the time of the study does not solve this problem of survivor bias.

In general, survivor bias violates the fundamental logic of scientific inquiry, which requires that we compare the effect of initial conditions presumed to be causal on systematically arrayed different outcomes. In many cases, the outcomes of substantive interest are various conceptualizations of business success. Hence, one wishes to compare a fair sample of successful organizations with a fair sample of unsuccessful ones. Keeping from consideration the many organizations that were so unsuccessful that they did not survive in effect may eliminate the most important fraction of the test or treatment group.[7] Only a longitudinal study based on all organizations of the relevant type that ever existed (or a random sample thereof) can completely eliminate survivor bias. Every effort in that direction will at least attenuate the effect of this bias and minimize the gravity of the fallacious inferences it implies.

A simplistic but not unrealistic example can help illustrate the seriousness of the problem. Suppose that we use a sample of 80 contemporary MNCs to assess the effect of giving intercultural training to CEOs on some specified measure of market share. We find that 60 of the CEOs have received such training. We find further that of these, 50 preside over firms that have increased their market share over a given period of observation, while of the 20 CEOs who have received no such training, only eight manage firms that have experienced market share growth. The overall picture is expressed in terms of percentages of the total sample in the table below.

	Training	No training
Success	62%	10%
Failure	12%	15%

With such results it would be tempting to state that intercultural training has a positive effect on, or at least is positively associated with, performance as measured.

If we had opted for a more inclusive longitudinal study and collected the corresponding data, however, we might have found that the 80 firms in our sample were survivors from a cohort of 800 similar MNCs, all founded at about the same time. We might also have discovered that of the 720 MNCs that were disbanded before the period of the study of 80, 650 had had CEOs who had received intercultural training. Keeping in mind that being disbanded is a genuine barrier to gaining market share, the relationship between cultural training and success would now appear as follows:

	Training	No training
Success	6%	1%
Failure	82%	10%

With these more inclusive results one would hesitate to assign any role to cultural training in achieving the form of success captured by market share gain.

Aside from reducing the probability of this kind of error, longitudinal designs give us a chance to build historical events explicitly into our models. This has both substantive and methodological advantages. As institutional theorists insist, and as international management research seeks to demonstrate, contextual events, especially those of a political nature (see Doz 1986), may affect the fates of business organizations. Delacroix and Carroll (1983), for example, show that political turbulence has a positive effect on the propensity to found newspapers, while Carroll and Delacroix (1982) show that newspapers founded under such conditions tend to be short-lived. In general, business organizations exist within a legal framework that is frequently modified in obvious or in subtle ways (see Carroll, Delacroix, and Goodstein 1988) by political developments. Thus, it is not very useful to deploy treasures of ingenuity to uncover the economic causes of massive failure in an industry that was largely disenfranchised by parliamentary fiat, such as the wine industry in the USA with Prohibition. Instead, such a political variable should be explicitly incorporated into the estimation model so that it will compete with all other covariates for the variance available in the dependent variable. Historical and other macrosocietal effects can easily be incorporated into longitudinal estimation models through the use of dummy variables. It is also relatively easy to study the combined effects of political and other factors by creating interactive variables around the dummy political variables. (For an illustration of these methods, see Delacroix and Carroll 1983, or Hannan and Freeman 1989: 209–210 and tables 9.1 and 9.3.)

Aside from helping answer substantive questions, longitudinal designs can contribute to theory building by palliating one of the built-in weaknesses of international management research. Such research is often also cross-national research: that is, it makes use of the variability occurring naturally across nation states because nation states are especially bounded environments. In the attempt to establish cause and effect relationships on the basis of this variability, research runs against an absolute limitation: there are fewer than 200 nation states, and the number for which reliable data are routinely available is much smaller. Hence, it is important to make maximum use of those country cases for which there are data. One way to achieve this result is more extensive exploitation of information about those countries that are well documented (see Ragin 1987 for techniques especially appropriate for small-number cross-sectional investigations). An alternative strategy is to make better use of changes occurring within those same well-documented countries. What is unobtainable through width of observation can often be reached through depth. It is possible to treat the history of individual countries as a ready-made laboratory offering variability in addition to that found across countries.

Thus, if we are interested in the effects of tariff barriers on the propensity to establish subsidiaries in the countries within the tariff barrier, for example (a central question naturally derived from transaction cost theory), two research strategies are available. First, we can examine the frequency of subsidiary foundings in different countries with different levels of tariff barriers. Second, we can locate tariff changes within the history of a given country or region, and ascertain to what extent such changes are accompanied by spells of subsidiary foundings, or conversely by a slowing down of such foundings. ("Accompanied," because in this case, the effect may not follow the proximate cause; it may precede it, since the efficient mechanism might be anticipated rather than realized tariff changes.)

Note finally that it is possible to combine in the same research design cross-country and cross-time variability through recourse to pooled, cross-sectional time series techniques for maximum power. (For an introduction to such techniques, see Stimson (1985) and Sayrs (1989).) Thus, in addition to helping us use historical events to account for concrete phenomena, longitudinal approaches contribute to the construction of theories or systematic explanations about a class of phenomena.

The particular kinds of longitudinal design models pioneered by organizational ecologists are known collectively as "event history analysis." This is too technical a topic to be treated here. To summarize the advantages of such methods for international management research, it is enough to say that with this mode of analysis, a case is one organization in existence for a given time period. This longitudinal approach improves upon more familiar panel models by placing at the researcher's disposal all the overlapping sub-time periods available within the total period of observation of the study. Thus, the period 1950 to 1980 includes 1950 to 1951, 1950 to 1952, but also 1951 to 1953, and so on. Any of these subperiods can be used, though not in the same estimation models. For a clear introduction to event history analysis, see Allison (1984) and Carroll (1983); for a more advanced treatment, see Tuma and Hannan (1984); for examples of applications, see Hannan and Freeman (1989).

How the study of international management can benefit organization theory

One of the central problems of organizational theory is as follows: How do organizational parts that have the potential to act independently of one another, unlike the parts of a watch, for example (see Hedlund, this volume), come to behave sufficiently in concert to benefit the whole organization? The word "benefit" here is to be taken broadly; one weak interpretation of it is that organizations simply continue to exist as such, in spite of their great potential for dissolution, because of the centrifugal forces to which they are subjected. Organizational theorists have sought answers to this question by studying the mechanisms by which organizations cope with their diverse and diversely varying environments without falling apart (Aldrich and Marsden 1988). Curiously, organizational theorists' long-standing interest in environmental diversity is usually operationalized in terms of industrial sectors or institutional-political contexts, and more rarely in terms of organizational fields of relevance to the focal organization. When diversity of operating conditions is examined from a spatial standpoint, inquiries tend to be limited to a domestic context (Aldrich and Marsden 1988: 369–370). This is curious because for many purposes the greatest diversity of conditions encountered by a single organization has to be that faced by the MNC, an organization existing in a plurinational context. This must be so because of the special nature of nation-state boundaries (Hennart 1982: 2; Kogut, this volume).

The degree of difficulty encountered by complex organizations in coping with a heterogeneous environment (or in remaining organizations) is a dynamic function of the degree of heterogeneity of the relevant environment. Let's simplify the problem by ignoring the term "dynamic" in the above statement (for a rigorous examination of this matter by organizational ecologists, see Freeman and Hannan 1983). What is left is the extent to which different subparts of the relevant environments exert different pressures on the organization. Relevant environments can be defined in terms of resource dependence or in terms of their capability to award legitimacy. Both angles matter to international management scholars. The simplest case might be that of a dyad on an island, abundantly furnished with creature comforts but facing lions inland and sharks in the sea. At the other extreme might be a complex organization facing different sets of constraints in a wide variety of locales, with each constraint taking on different values in those different locales. A multinational environment is one where an organization (the MNC) faces the same basic sets of constraints in multiple locales where the constraints all take on different values.

A multinational environment comes very close to offering maximum heterogeneity because of the particular nature of national boundaries. National boundaries perform two functions which insure that each national environment will be different from any other, from a business standpoint. First, the boundaries constitute obstacles to the free movement of goods, of capital, of persons, and to a remarkable extent of informations—the latter through their monopoly over the attribution of hertzian space and occasionally through jamming communications from without, and through censorship. Unlike all other kinds of social boundaries, the boundaries of nation states are backed by force, ensuring that these obstacles are more sturdy than any others. Second, nation states intervene actively in social processes, contributing to the homogenization of conditions within, and therefore to heterogeneity across, nation states. They do this by erecting judicial systems, which are the umbrellas under which most business transactions take place, by setting up more or less directly educational standards and programs, and by supplying a large fraction of the information on which the mass media has come to rely (when they do not exercise a monopoly over such media). The process of state-directed homogenization may have been more transparent in earlier times because it involved such dramatic practices as universal military draft, intended to mix recruits from different regions, but the strength of current processes may be no less. In addition many nation states, as the term indicates, were founded on the basis of preexisting national, that is cultural, groups: Italy, for example, is the state of people speaking closely related languages. States usually do nothing to dilute the cultural singularity of their population, and often act to strengthen it. Thus, Japanese children are exposed primarily to Japanese history and French children to French history, which is probably not a random phenomenon.

The two sets of processes pertaining to the unique nature of national boundaries tend to reinforce each other to ensure that the operating conditions an organization will encounter on one side of a national border will differ markedly from the conditions it will face on the other side. Thus, organizational theorists should not fail to take advantage of the natural laboratory that the division of the world into nation states offers to their inquiry, and of the wealth of empirical findings accumulated by students of international business.

The multinationalism of the world environment supplies organizational ecologists in particular with opportunities to test a variant of their central conceptual model. We saw how organizational ecology favors a selection mechanism of organizational change over the adaptationist perspective implicit in all managerial, voluntaristic schools of thought. Organizational ecology focuses on selection mechanisms; however, the distinction between processes of selection and processes of adaptation does not have to be absolute. Hannan and Freeman (1989: 42) discuss the possibility that the selection of parts out of a system may constitute a form of adaptation for the system as a whole. Multinational companies give us a superior opportunity to test this formulation. Every subsidiary is a part of a larger organizational system that is subjected to the pressure of an environment that tends to be significantly different from the environments to which other subsidiaries in the same system are subjected. This is, again, because national boundaries, unlike most other kinds of social boundaries, circumscribe quite discrete environmental processes. Consequently, the configuration of organizationally relevant forces operating within one country is likely to be quite different, at any one time, from the corresponding configuration in another country.

Hence, the MNC as a whole is subject to a degree of environmental variation unlikely to be duplicated within a purely domestic environment. The proximate target of this environmental variation is each subsidiary in each individual country. The local (national) environment selects for or against the arrangement of parts this subsidiary constitutes by allowing it to be more or less successful, in conventional terms. "Success" is defined in this context as simply the ability to make sufficient contributions to the whole MNC to be allowed to continue to exist as a subsidiary of the same MNC. It matters little whether the subsidiary goes bankrupt in a conventional business sense or whether its contribution is judged insufficient by the management of the parent company.[8] In either case, below this sufficiency threshold, the subsidiary is eliminated as a subsidiary. This act of selection may constitute an effective form of adaptation for the MNC as a whole in the sense that it achieves a better fit with the global environment than it would without the elimination of this particular subsidiary in its particular (national) local environment. This process of global adaptation through elimination of local subsidiaries, repeated many times for many MNCs, may also begin to explain the evolution of MNC structure over time, which has been the subject of much inquiry in the international business disciplines.

DISCUSSION

Bringing the style of research and the techniques of one field to bear on the concerns of the other, one might, for example, use archival data to explore the effects of substantively heterogeneous variables on the likelihood that a foreign subsidiary will be disbanded. One could include in longitudinal logistic regression models such disparate variables as whether the subsidiary is an acquisition or a greenfield operation, the international experience of the parent company (measured as number of other foreign subsidiaries previously owned, for example), the favorableness of the business or of the political climate in the host country (using whatever measures are available from the host countries concerned, or a ready-made index), the fact of the subsidiary or the parent company having been in existence during a given period considered as a critical for any reason. (This can be treated as a dummy variable.) Similarly, one can include in such models critical events, such as fiscal events occurring in the country of the parent company. Other facts of central importance to international business scholarship such as a country being a member of the European Union can also be incorporated into the same logistic models, contemporaneously, or during some past period selected on theoretical or historical grounds. With this approach, one can estimate the joint effects of complex sets of variables simultaneously and in competition with one another. Finally, the relative adequacy of competing models comprising diverse sets of causal variables can be tested comparatively through chi-square methods.

Estimations performed in this ecological manner often fall short of resolving any important theoretical issues with finality. Considered together, however, this approach constitutes an economical way to select certain research directions over others. This style of modeling can be viewed as a quick method to feed the research intuition. In particular, event history analysis gives the researcher a convenient but fairly rigorous means to question received wisdom. This is true, whether one has any interest in selection processes as such or not.

The evolutive nature of this mode of analysis allows the researcher conveniently to assess the likelihood that hypotheses derived from quite disparate bodies of theories may complement one another, or conversely be incompatible with one another. Hence, this style of research holds two kinds of promises. First, it promises to help free us from the habit, firmly implanted in the social sciences, of talking past one another. Second, this style of research contributes to the realization of the dream of making theory truly incremental via the accumulation of legitimate empirical results.

Common wisdom has it that large multi-case studies belong in research that already benefits by a high level of rigor. This seems a corollary to the view that case studies are a good approach to phenomenological understanding. The first idea may be shortsighted, however. An organizational entity taken in isolation might be quite different from the same entity considered in its large numbers. Hence, the observation of many organizations of the same kind, even if it is done over time, might be necessary to the acquisition of an intuitive understanding of the category of entities that is both concrete and realistic. Large-scale studies of whole populations may thus play a role similar to that traditionally advocated for case studies.

One might raise a reasonable objection to this research strategy prescription: it is very onerous, in money and in time, to collect the kind of large data set used by organizational ecologists. However, the latter's universal experience seems to be "Seek and ye shall find." Moreover, large detailed longitudinal data sets can usually be used repeatedly or by numerous scholars, each with his/her own theoretical interests. The collecting, beating into shape, and exploitation of such data sets even foster cooperative research endeavors with long-term career benefits for the participants.

Students of international business reared in a managerial, voluntaristic atmosphere may find the working assumption of ecologists regarding selection absurd, repugnant, immoral, or "too horrible to behold" (as one of my colleagues puts it). Kogut's extensive and detailed discussion (this volume), shows that there may be little fundamental philosophical incompatibility between these approaches. Actually, it is easy to view strategic management as the application of managerial skill within the area of freedom left by non-managerial processes, or by processes not under the control of managers. There is no reason why this rudimentary model of reality cannot be tested with the methods presented in this paper. At any rate, it seldom makes sense to expel history from the study of social phenomena (Kogut 1988), from either a theoretical or a policy viewpoint. Rather, it is sensible to incorporate it explicitly in empirical models, through the use of simple dummy variables, for example.

In general, it is useful to keep in mind that event history analysis models can be used very eclectically on both sides of the equation. Thus in principle, and given data availability, one could incorporate into such an analysis factors designed to capture Ghoshal and Bartlett's (1988) propositions on the innovations subsidiaries contribute to parent companies. (Perhaps they thereby stave off their own or the parents' selection out of the relevant population.) On the other side of the causal arrow, event history analysis and organizational ecology research strategies in general lend themselves well to the study of transition processes that have captured the attention of international business scholars, such as the transition from purely domestic expansion to the several modes of foreign expansion that are the subjects of transaction cost theory.

Notes

1 This paper is an extension of an earlier empirical analysis with John H. Freeman to whom I am thankful for a solid push-start. I am also grateful to Mark Makiewicz for cool, collected, and competent research assistance.
2 The seemingly more common-sense managerial schools of thought which favor an adaptation stance tend to rest on few hard findings. This is especially true of adaptationist perspectives applied to business organizations. Thus, Boyd and McSween's exhaustive (1988) survey of published, multi-case empirical studies shows a "weak" link between the practice of strategic planning and measure performance.
3 Note that this explanation of the role of organizations differs markedly from the explanation embedded in transaction cost theory. Nevertheless, the two conceptualizations are not incompatible.
4 It is essential to remember that selection, which applies to groups of organizations, is different, and even conceptually incompatible with individual adaptation, although the two mechanisms for change may exist side by side in the real world.
5 For an example of such a population, see Delacroix and Carroll (1983). For a discussion of the delineation of organizational populations, see Hannan and Freeman (1989: 48–65). Aldrich (1979) constitutes a good introduction to organizational ecology thinking. See Carroll (1988) for a collection of empirical studies in organizational ecology.
6 Although this way of doing things is most noticeable in practitioner-oriented works (e.g. Peters and Waterman 1982), it is not difficult to find instances in scholarly journals.
7 It is true that success as well as failure may lead to elimination, as with many acquisitions. This poses a technical problem, discussed by Freeman, Carroll, and Hannan (1983), without impairing the soundness of this reasoning.
8 There is some indication, see Li and Guisinger (1990) who cite Stobaugh's 1970 study, that American MNCs are quite reluctant to save their subsidiaries from business failure.

6 Learning, or the Importance of Being Inert: Country Imprinting and International Competition[1]

Bruce Kogut

An unfortunate development in the study of multinational corporations has been the separation of comparative management from the theory of foreign direct investment (FDI). The narrow effect of this separation has been to neglect the development of an understanding of how the country of origin influences the capabilities of firms and their domestic and international competitiveness. In fact, this chapter argues that FDI is the expression of the differential organizing capabilities of firms across countries.

The wider effect has been to impoverish organizational theory as well as the theory of the multinational corporation (MNC). To a surprising degree theoretical efforts have been directed to sustaining an argument that the blandest international comparison would falsify. At the same time, an unfortunate amount of effort has been invested in developing a theory of the MNC that duplicates, with varying degrees of success, well-established principles in organizational theory.

It is a common complaint of outsiders to a field that they cannot make sense of its research program, or paradigm. Indeed, the panoply of theories in macro-organizational studies is often bewildering, ranging from resource dependency, to organizational ecology, to institutionalism. Curiously, the field of international management has generated over 30 years a rather well worked-out research program based on the Dunning (1981b) trinity of ownership, location, and internalization (OLI) advantages. Yet research on the economics of the MNC has, perhaps by the very force of its success, not been matched by corresponding gains in developing a predominant view of the organization of firms that span borders.

One of the most promising areas of dialogue between the fields of international management and organization theory concerns the pivotal question of the bias of the country of origin on the capabilities of firms, or populations of firms, to learn and adapt. This question lies at the foundation of three major areas of study in international management: how a firm internationalizes, the effect of the home market on firm-specific advantages leading to foreign direct investment, and the transfer of new practices across borders. All three areas share a common assumption that the firm develops, much as Bendix (1956) and Stinchcombe (1965) stressed, out of the socioeconomic

106

conditions of its home environment.[2] Even as the firm internationalizes, it remains imprinted by its early developmental history and domestic environment. In this light, the tendency to separate the study of the international firm from comparative management is in fundamental contradiction to the implicit recognition of the conceptual interdependence of the two fields.

The common assumption of the significance of the early bias of the home environment presents a thorny patch of issues when the assumption itself becomes the focus of inquiry, for to what extent does the institutional context influence the creation of organizational forms and capabilities? And if different national contexts generate organizational forms that differ in performance, why is there such slow convergence to best practice? In this process of convergence, what are the relative weights assigned to selection (through firm entry and exit) and to learning?

These questions are clearly also central to the organizational literature on learning, population ecology, and institutionalism. In the following pages, I seek to show the benefits of establishing a broader dialogue between organization theory and the theory of the MNC by establishing the elements required to address these questions. Ultimately, a theory of organizational learning, whether within or across countries, is the study of firm's knowledge and its inertia. The central problem analyzed below is the extent to which a portion of this knowledge is contingent on the country of origin.

The first section identifies three problems of long-standing interest in international management, and argues that their analysis requires a comparative management perspective. The next section sets out the view of the firm as competing on organizing principles, that is, how it organizes its activities, and argues that these principles are influenced by the prevailing templates of organization in a society. We put forth the view that foreign direct investment is the extension of organizing principles across borders. The subsequent section then turns the table and asks what organization theory can learn from this definition of the problems in international management. Finally, the implications for the study of the MNC are examined.

PROBLEM ONE: GENESIS

Without question one of the most troubling areas of analysis in the field of international management is explaining the origins of institutions and their differences across countries. This problem has not gone unnoticed in the relatively ahistorical literature on the theory of foreign direct investment. Hymer (1960), for example, wrote:

> Why do firms of different countries have unequal ability? In part, it is due to the fact there is an unequal distribution of skills among people. The population of every country is a sample of the universe, and the particular distribution of skills will vary from country to country for no

107

other reason than this. In part it is also due to the chance discovery of a gold mine, a valuable formula, or Scotch Whiskey.

Hymer's explanation has deep similarities with the notion of random genetic drift, or what we can call technological drift. By technological drift, I mean that the historical accident of an innovation behaves like a mutation in a small community, leading to a potential increase in frequency by a process of path-dependent diffusion. As outlandish as this seems, it should be recalled what a powerful effect the wheel had on Indo-European civilization following its discovery in Sumeria; however, the Aztec and Mayan civilizations did not apparently adopt it. Indeed, Hymer seems to have understood well the implication of his reflections, as he writes, "This consideration of historical accident comes into play whenever it is true that a firm's ability in a given year depends on its past activity" (Hymer 1960: 76).

Of course, no matter how intellectually engaging an explanation resting on path-dependent drift may be, it is, sociologically, an inadequate and unsatisfactory theory. After all, the Aztec toys used wheels; it was not lack of discovery, but of the social process of adoption. An economic speculation might be that the use of slave labor reduced the attractiveness of adopting the wheel. Indeed, the relative factor bias explanation is the cornerstone of Vernon's (1966) theory of the product lifecycle of international trade and investment.[3] However, it would seem that, whatever the relative factor costs in Mexico, adoption of the wheel would have had substantial benefits. In fact, the Samuelson objection to the bias-induced theory of innovation is, by the principles of rational choice, devastating: why should a firm care about relative costs, he argued, when the objective function is to minimize total costs, and thus the costs of any factor of production? Moreover, to return to our earlier example of the wheel, the demand for its discovery would surely be phenomenal in any civilization. Demand alone does not seem to be sufficient. In short, the Vernon notion of biased innovation is a convenient but unexplained assumption.

This perspective is also explicit in the influential ideas of Burenstam Linder (1961). In Burenstam Linder's original identification of the importance of intra-industry trade, exports are the extension of the home market network overseas. The multinational enterprise arises out of the initial variation in country environments that influences entrepreneurial endeavors and cumulative investments. Although Burenstam Linder sketches an explication of the firm as consisting of cumulative capabilities molded by the home environment, it is not grounded in a general theory of organizational capabilities.

PROBLEM TWO: LOCATION AND OWNERSHIP ADVANTAGES

It should be recalled that the traditional explanation for the rise of the MNC and its international expansion has emphasized the importance of intangible assets (such as technology and product differentiation). These assets must provide a sufficient advantage to the firm to offset its disadvantage in competing against local firms in their home markets. At the same time, the intangibility of these assets discourages arm's-length contracting for the familiar reasons of market failure. This traditional argument does not, however, suggest an explanation why certain countries should own a substantially larger share of FDI than indicated by their share of the world's income. We have thus come full circle back to the problem of genesis.

Another way to approach the question of genesis is to eschew direct explanation, but rather to develop a taxonomy of location factors that influence the ownership advantages of the firm. Such an approach is given in Dunning (1981b, 1993). He argues that comparative advantage encompasses a broader spectrum than simply factor costs of labor and capital, since location influences the economics of the resident firms. Analytically the task is to link "the type of ownership advantages particular countries are most likely to generate and sustain, and then relate these to the resource and market requirements of particular industries" (Dunning 1980b: 280). For example, Dunning speculates that large and standardized markets will lead to larger firms due to the reaping of scale economies and product diversification. Furthermore, technological advantages are likely to be created in countries where governments sponsor innovation and research.

This argument is appealing and sound. It is possible, of course, to come to other conclusions while accepting the overall logic: for example, to suggest that firms from small countries must concentrate on fewer standardized products in order to compete effectively on world markets. Whether the handicap of a small national market or the abundance of a large home market leads to standardization and larger firm size are two conflicting predictions which, prima facie, seem equally plausible.

The empirical evidence on this question is mixed, as the variance in size distributions across countries indicates. If we compare, for example, the upper percentages of the distribution, the variation is remarkable.[4] The USA and the United Kingdom have substantially larger corporations than Japan or Germany, a pattern going back to the earlier part of the twentieth century. Even within the same industries, the differences are striking. According to Fruin's (1989) calculations, there is considerable disparity in the size of leading American and Japanese firms in the auto, electronic, and chemical industries. In 1987, General Motors had 813,400 employees compared with Toyota's 64,329; IBM, 389,348 to Hitachi's 76,210; and DuPont, 140,145 to Asahi Chemicals' 15,595.

A good deal of the explanation for the United States and Japan difference lies in the prevalence of subcontracting practices in Japan (e.g. Nishiguchi 1989). It is not compelling to attribute these differences to size differences of the economy, especially when we consider the extent of the export market that Japanese corporations serve. Rather, these differences in the size distribution appear to be the result of long-term historical developments in the two countries.

An understanding of the differential performance of US and Japanese corporations cannot be derived by comparing individual corporations. The degree of vertical integration in the USA stands in stark contrast to the role of inter-firm relationships in Japan. One suspects, as the study of Westney and Sakakibara (1985) has shown, that a comparison of Japan and the USA would also reveal strikingly different institutions regarding science-based ties to universities and research centers, internal and external labor markets, and organizing principles. The concept of ownership advantage is difficult, in many respects, to separate from the wider institutional linkages binding firms into national industrial networks.

PROBLEM THREE: INTERNALIZATION

As noted earlier, theories of foreign direct investment frequently rely on the notion of intangible assets which are easier to transfer through the firm than across markets. The intangibility assumption is critical, as it suggests that the firm has a cost advantage in transferring this knowledge within its ownership as opposed to within a contractual or market context. A misleading form of the argument states that this transfer has the characteristics of a public good, and it is the public good characteristic, according to the well-known argument of Arrow, that leads to market failure. A more plausible rendition is simply that the marginal costs of internal transfer are lower than of the market, and the incremental saving is greater than the incremental costs of doing business abroad. One avenue by which to explain why the internal marginal costs are lower is to appeal to the differential incentive properties of organizations and firms. As this perspective is well laid out elsewhere in this volume (see Hennart, Chapter 8), we do not need to repeat the argument. Let us turn instead to a discussion of the effects of the country of origin on contracting.

In this regard, one of the striking results of an international comparison is the high variance in institutions across countries, ranging from differences in the degree of subcontracting to union activity to the internal organization of the firm. This variance is at odds with the ahistorical abstraction of the transaction costs or internalization approach. For why should economic institutions not evolve similarly to resolve the problems of opportunism under uncertainty?

A simple but elusive answer is that the degree of opportunism differs across countries. I am reminded of a lecture by the anthropologist Clifford Geertz in which he described an island culture where the prevailing practice was to conceal one's purpose and to respond to questions deceptively. A country filled with liars is likely to develop institutional mechanisms by which veracity might be tested, or be forever stalemated. Similarly, Ronald Dore

(1983) has argued that the conventions of trust in Japan, backed by an extensive social network, lead to lower degrees of opportunism, and hence a greater willingness to rely on long-term relationships among partners.

A more detailed institutional analysis would point to a comparison not only of the dilemmas of market exchange among countries, but also of the internal characteristics of firms. We have, in fact, come far in understanding these issues better. The studies of Lincoln, Hanada, and McBride (1986) point to different authority and decision characteristics between Japanese and American firms. Interestingly, commitment levels in the firms from both countries were relatively high, despite different incentive systems. (One suspects, in passing, that Hennart's polar attributes of shirking and cheating may not fully capture the affiliation needs of the individual to engage in purposeful activities within an organized and stable context.)

The literature on internalization and transaction costs may, with sufficient fine tuning, be able to explain differential performance of countries on the basis of national variations in contractual and organizational incentives; the works of Aoki (1988) and North (1981) are impressive examples of such efforts. This fine tuning, however, should not obscure the fundamental point that these differences exist because of historical developments and social characteristics unique to the country of origin. Nor should we fail to observe that such practices, even though they are widely believed to be causally responsible for differential performance, diffuse slowly, if at all.

A COMMENT

It seems surprising that studies of the MNC should have neglected so markedly the implications of the country of origin for the analysis of the central problems listed above. Part of the explanation is that studies of foreign direct investment and, though less so, the MNC have rarely been comparative. Since Hymer, the question to be answered has been why foreign direct investment flows vary across industries, not the question of what the country patterns are in FDI. The nature of the answer has been, except for occasional outlier studies such as that by Aharoni (1966), to treat firms as largely homogeneous, but responding differentially to the market and demand conditions of their home countries.

Let us briefly follow a different avenue, suggested by Nelson and Winter (1982), which begins with the view of the firm as consisting of a set of capabilities, or competences, as embodied in a stock of knowledge that is developed cumulatively. Because of differences in their experiential histories, the cumulative learning of firms displays considerable heterogeneity. From this simple description, the lower marginal costs of internal transfer of intangible assets across borders reflect the accumulation, or sunk investment, in a specific set of capabilities within a firm. Organizations, however, are social communities in which individual and social expertise is transformed into economically useful

111

products and services by the application of a set of higher-order organizing principles. Firms exist because they provide a social community of voluntaristic action supported by a set of organizational capabilities which are not reducible to individuals (Kogut and Zander, 1992).

For the sake of exposition, consider the implications of this view for a firm that seeks to maximize its value through costly and bounded search under uncertainty. This costliness is a function of the distance of the new technology from the current technology being employed by the firm. Because knowledge of current technologies can be used to increase the probability of success in searching in related technologies, it pays to search in the local neighborhood. Clearly, the above behavioral description provides a better match for the argument of Vernon and Burenstam Linder than the inconsistent story of relative factor bias.[5]

From this perspective arises a central claim: that is, direct investment is simply the extension of the organizing principles and capabilities of the firm across countries. The drawback of the inherited schema of the OLI approach has been the failure to spell out exactly the ownership advantages of the firm. Intangible assets represent the accumulated capability of a firm to advertise, to adapt products, or to produce cheaply. The theoretical challenge facing the theory of the firm is to understand the abilities of organizations to carry out these activities. Before determining boundaries, such as whether a technology should be licensed or not, it seems logical that we first need to understand why this technology would be better created and exploited in one organization as opposed to another.

These are large issues that cannot be addressed here, other than to note that the type of capabilities will vary across countries. This variance will in part be attributable to the effects of a common history and environment (what Westney calls "isomorphic pulls") on firms. But it is also because part of the capabilities a firm enjoys consists of its relationships with other firms and institutions. In the early history of firms, the predominant factor in these relationships is that they are usually contained within the borders of a single country. In the remaining pages, I trace out the implications of this perspective.

INSTITUTIONALISM AND IMPRINTING

When Robert Solow received the Nobel Prize in economics for his seminal work in growth theory, the Swedish economist Assar Lindbeck posed the question of whether the real sources of growth are less proximate than costs of inputs and the productivity in the process of transformation. Solow answered that clearly the institutions of education, government services, and so on are critical; nevertheless, the consequences of these less proximate economic activities could be best analyzed by the principles of economics.

The heroism of the economic assumptions required to explain the variety of institutional arrangements among countries, however, is hard to imagine.

An aggregation of firms' heterogeneous productive capabilities to a generic production function is itself an assumption that has not been without its critics (see for example Nelson and Winter 1982). Similarly, we can assume, without more discussion, that the heterogeneity of institutional arrangements—why countries do not adopt optimal institutional structures—would prove a troubling issue.

Part of the problem is that bias toward the status quo is strongly underestimated. Most people do not ponder whether they could trade their parents, or their children, if only markets were to exist. Rather they become attached to their idiosyncratic characteristics; a "charming rascal" is the oxymoron which consoles many parents. Norman O. Brown (1947) noticed that in mythology, cultures tend to impose their world on the heavens. The Greeks saw the gods fighting among themselves as if they were city states; the Persians imposed a royal hierarchy on their stories of divinity. Divine order is the projection of the human polity on the heavens.

That individuals have templates of how activities are organized is a powerful force in the replication of social structure.[6] Unquestionably other mechanisms of institutionalization (as described by Westney in this book) play significant, perhaps at times, dominating roles. The coercive role of the state is well documented, from Kemal Ataturk to Peter the Great, and the state's ability to induce change by incentives is exemplified in the policies of Meiji Japan and Bismarck's Germany. Indeed Weber, who clearly emphasized the role of ideas as becoming "common to whole groups" of individuals (as he stated in the Protestant Ethic) also stressed the importance of the government as an agent of change from "on high" (see Weber 1946).

But coercion, and even imitation, would not be needed in the absence of normative obstacles to change. While some of these obstacles may reflect the rational resistance of agents who would suffer by change, it would be hard to explain mass movements on the basis of economic self-interest. We should not forget Marx's frustration over the false consciousness of workers and inability to see their "true" interests. There is no optimal arrangement of human affairs or organized economic activity that can serve as a template, because social knowledge is evolutionary and embedded in the social relationships that prevail. The history of Utopian movements shows that contrarian ideas enacted in a hostile or indifferent social setting do not take hold. Capitalism grows, Eisenstadt noted (1966), when commercial elites are not isolated—as the overseas Chinese in Indonesia are—from the larger community.

That organizational forms reflect the social context of the times of their founding is a widely held but understudied contention. The frequency of organizational births is certainly influenced by economic conditions and/or the munificence of critical agencies, be they governments or charitable organizations. Where new industries such as biotechnology are born, new firms invariably take the structure of incumbent organizations in their environment as their template. The recipes by which activities are organized are likely to be far more persistent than technologies per se, because they are expressions of enduring social relations.

There is a frequent confusion in the writings on the ecology of organizations regarding new technologies and new organizational forms.[7] Foundings may represent the inducement of new entrants into an industry due to the arrival of new technologies, and the rate of entry will be influenced by such factors as the degree of competition and the availability of resources. But these foundings, though competing on new technologies and for resources, are likely to share the organizing principles prevailing in the wider society (see Kimberly 1975). Indeed, once a start-up firm begins to grow, its reliance on the collection of technological skills of individuals shifts to the important task of creating organizing recipes. These recipes, such as bookkeeping, divisionalization, hiring, and promoting, are adopted from the current agreement on what constitutes best practice.

It is not so much that firms are inert than that social structure is enduring. Firms learn, but in the context of what they can know. The disposition of the availability of knowledge is shaped by the structure of social relations. What firms know is determined by their position in an industrial network.[8] Whether a firm has a tie (either directly or via intermediaries) to a set of university research units conditions its information and its potential to learn of new scientific discoveries. Localized search and learning is an activity that does not occur in some abstract plan of theoretical possibilities, but is embedded, in the sense of Granovetter (1985), in the available information set: that is, in the structure of a firm's environment.

A critical question, then, is the extent to which the vicinity surrounding a firm's position in a social network is largely national or international. In order to learn, there must be first new lessons to be taught. International competition is interesting exactly for the reason that it presents new templates of organizing principles. Although these templates have national origins, the growth of cooperative and competitive relationships in an international network of firms and institutions changes the content of information available to firms, permitting the diffusion of national practices across borders.

As a result, we come to a conclusion that differs from a narrow ecological perspective. We do not see firms as strictly inert, but rather as learning within a prevailing social structure. Some structures promote relatively rapid learning; others are less receptive. Let us examine how an international comparison throws light on the perennial, and falsely stylized, debate on adaptation versus selection.

LEARNING AND ORGANIZATIONAL ECOLOGY

It is easy to underestimate the importance of learning if firms tend to be born with similar templates. What appears as inertia reflects the similarity of organizational forms at birth and of developmental histories within fairly homogeneous (national) environments. This similarity is clearly violated in environments characterized by international competition, and hence we should expect to find more striking examples and trends of learning among a population of firms of diverse national origins. But before turning to the international aspects, we consider first the abstract argument.

The link between learning and inertia is, to varying degrees of explicitness, central to most theories on organizational learning. Levitt and March (1987) identified most theories of organizational learning as falling under either adaptive or imitative behavior.[9] These theories generally share the property of being cybernetic: that is, they formulate the problem as bounded search with feedback.[10] It is easy to see this principle in operation in the formulation commonly used by March for trial and error learning,

$$Ft = Ft - 1 + \alpha(F^* - Ft - 1)$$

where learning is described as gradual convergence of the current state F to some goal F^* at a learning rate α.[11]

Though Levitt and March focused only at the organizational level, this cybernetic view, as Steinbruner (1974) has noted, also fits learning at the population level, where the learning dynamic is Darwinian selection. In the population ecology literature, convergence is to a hypothetical number of homogeneous firms that can be supported by the environment. It is important to realize that the learning and hazard rates are roughly symmetric, with the former representing convergence to an optimum from below (that is, the number of firms learning best practices grows to approach some limit) and the latter, representing convergence from above (that is, the number of entrants is in excess of the surviving number, with the total population declining to the same hypothetical limit).[12] The population ecology literature usually specifies the convergent number of firms empirically, such as the estimate of the asymptotic limit in the Makeham specification of the hazard models or as estimated solutions to the Lotka–Volterra equations.

Both the adaptive and selection view of change ignore, in their crudest formulations, the role of guided learning—that is, learning from others—whether by imitation, by consultancy, or by cultural institutions (such as schools). Given the existence of large consulting firms, guided learning seems to be, to say the least, significant. While the earlier equation of adaptation appears to include these wider considerations, the mechanisms by which guided learning occurs are not characterized by a simple feedback loop of trial and error (or trial and selection in the ecological description).

It is not hard, however, to relate the models to each other. In the adaptation model, α, the rate of adaptation, can itself be a function of how many other firms are engaged in a similar activity (see Herriot, Levinthal, and March, 1985; Stiglitz 1987). Thus, the rate of adaptation is influenced by the possibilities of externalities through an undefined mechanism of imitation. Or, to

115

use the cybernetic language of Argyris and Schon, if attention is switched from loop one (learning to do a task better) to loop two (learning to choose which tasks), F* may also be set by an adaptive formulation tending to best practice among a firm's plants or among the firms in an industry (Herriot et al. 1985). Imitation, therefore, can affect not only the rate of adaptation, but also the selection of the goal.

It is in fact difficult to reconcile the extreme assumption of limited trial and error learning with the results of most studies on the diffusion of innovations. As the studies of Rogers (1971) and many others have shown, communication plays a critical role in the diffusion of new innovations. Imitative channels are also created through the interchange of buyers and suppliers (von Hippel 1988). Firms which are sufficiently endowed with the ability to recognize shortfalls in performance are arguably also capable of comparing their performance against competitors in the industry.

Even though the population ecology models are seemingly remote from adaptive and imitative theories, a selection model is not necessarily incompatible. There is no intrinsic reason that selection can itself not be influenced by the varying learning abilities of the individual firms. The variation of the hazard rates faced by individual firms may well be a function of their differential abilities to learn from each other, just as size, generalism or specialism, and other covariates are allowed to shift the hazard rates.[13] A population of firms may be driven to homogeneity by selection pressures, but these pressures are not inconsistent with heterogeneous capabilities of learning and imitation.[14]

To date, population ecology models have considered externalities among firms largely in the context of competitive effects created by density dependence. Whereas some kinds of externalities may arise through communication and cooperation and promote group survival, density dependence is usually interpreted to represent competitive pressures forcing a population to some finite number of firms. But it may also arise, somewhat intriguingly, by firms inferring best practice from observations on firm survival. Through subsequent trials, stochasticity can be separated from differential capabilities, and the reduction in the noise to signal ratio leads to more accurate appraisals of the true causality between firm characteristics and survival chances.[15]

The importance of learning by imitation or by instruction has tended to be neglected in the literature on ecology and adaptation. It is possible that learning is underestimated because firms within the same nation are more similar at birth and hence have less to learn from each other. At the same time, the sources of differences in their efficiencies are easier to identify and adopt, as there is less noise (because of their similarity) to confound the search for best practice. To take a much-cited industry as an example of learning, the inertia of large corporations to change is frequently illustrated by noting the failure of firms such as General Electric and RCA to succeed in semiconductors. But a simple international comparison raises challenges to this claim: in Japan it is the large companies, such as NEC, Mitsubishi, and Hitachi, that dominate Japanese (and world) production. Though not innovators in the original technologies, these companies showed strikingly capabilities for imitating major breakthroughs from the very start of the industry (Tilton 1971).

The international setting is interesting in another regard, for it illustrates also the difficulty of learning when the requisite institutional mechanisms are not well developed. This difficulty is greater when new organizing practices must be learned, as opposed to the imitation of technologies, because these practices are likely to be embedded in the social network and values of individual countries. In this sense, learning of new organizing principles is both more transparent, and yet more difficult, across the borders of a country than a firm (see Kogut 1992 for a more extended discussion). It is because learning across borders is difficult, and because country differences in capabilities pose survival threats at the community level (that is, the ability of national firms as a group to survive), that the process by which foreign practices are adopted often becomes institutionalized by governments. A recent example is the US Malcolm Baldridge Award for quality, a clear response to Japan's Deming Prize. In the next section, we turn to examine one important mechanism by which best practice is transferred internationally, namely the MNC.

MULTINATIONAL CORPORATIONS

Theories of organizational learning are applicable to many issues important to international management in addition to competition among countries. Certainly, one of the most promising topics is the MNC and "learning how to learn." In this case, the MNC is no longer seen, as in the theories of Vernon and Burenstam Linder, as a repository of its national imprint. Rather, it is an instrument whereby learning is transferred across subsidiaries that are responding and adapting to different environment pressures.

In this regard, Westney has identified the interesting question, what happens when an organization, isomorphic to its origins, extends into new environments? It is interesting to note how the failure to frame the question in this manner detracted from the study of the receding importance of the country bias on the organization of the MNC. From the studies in the tradition of Stopford and Wells (1972), we know that organizational change occurs when thresholds, such as the proportion of international sales to total sales, are broached. Moreover, the type of structure adopted appears to reflect a firm's "strategy." Global product divisions tend to accompany technology-driven firms; area divisions, marketing-driven firms in mature industries. But these structural changes still reflect adaptations of organizational structures molded by the home bias. The adaptive

117

response for the American multinational was how to adjust the organizing principle of profit accountability for business in international markets. The solution was simply to enlarge the heuristic of divisionalizing the company to include international responsibilities.

This adaptive response, as has been often noted (see Hedlund in this volume), was less prominent among European MNCs. European corporations tended to be organized along informal ("mother–daughter") lines, with far looser accountability. In fact, to the extent that international divisional structures were adopted, their adoption reflects an imitation of American practices rather than an outgrowth of indigent European organizing principles. Whether this imitation was greater among European MNCs than among European firms in general is an important question for the understanding of the process by which practices diffuse among countries. But the relevant point here is that unquestionably European firms first grew internationally on the extension of European organizing practices across borders. Organizational change reflected a searching for a solution in the neighborhood of established best practice.

This stylized contrast of the American MNC operating on tight measures of accountability and the European company relying on decentralized informal control has been confirmed in many studies (see Chandler 1962, Chandler and Daems 1980, Channon 1973, Dyas and Thanheiser 1976, Franko 1976, Pavan 1972). It points to the importance of the home market conditions in imprinting the early developmental structures of resident firms. Some of these conditions reflect the technological requirements of different countries, as best expressed in the studies of Chandler and his students. But other conditions, such as the role of the state and educational institutions, have not been well studied, possibly because so few scholars have been willing to tackle comparative studies of business firms across borders.[16]

Whereas we have well-documented histories of how firms learned to do business internationally, there are a number of other, more subtle, issues that have not been examined. One issue is explored in Westney's chapter: how a foreign subsidiary integrates itself and is integrated into the local social structure, while remaining integrated within the multinational structure of its parent. From the perspective of a firm as engaging in search activities within an embedded social structure, the MNC presents an unusual case of belonging, with varying degrees of membership, to multiple national networks.

A second issue is the operating flexibility of the MNC. As a normative statement, it is logical that a firm competing on the extension of home market practices to foreign countries could subsequently enjoy the advantages of exploiting its network of subsidiaries on a multinational basis. This argument, given in Kogut (1983), was meant largely as a corrective to the prevailing view that FDI should be understood as a problem facing a firm investing overseas for the first time, even though the data showed that most investments were made by existing MNCs. Instead the network of subsidiaries provides a firm with incremental learning (inclusive of foreign practices) and the option to coordinate operations flexibly in response to difficult-to-forecast events, such as exchange rate changes, innovations, or government policies.

An emerging argument is that country advantages also serve to pull foreign direct investment. The traditional view has been that firms may choose to source raw materials or cheap labor in foreign markets. But due to the work of Cantwell (1989) and others, there is also recognition that the technological leadership of certain countries can attract FDI. Empirical evidence is also provided by Kogut and Chang (1991) in their study of the pulling of Japanese investment into the USA.

Over time, this perspective has broadened into more ambitious claims about the capabilities of firms to capitalize on best "organizational" practice, no matter where it occurs. I am not convinced that this constitutes a third issue—it may be a variation on the themes of flexibility and variation in national types—but it has received considerable attention in its own right. In this form of the argument, the MNC is a conduit of best practices resident in diverse countries. It had long been noted that multinational practices influence local environments. An outstanding example is Dunning (1986), where he finds that practices of Japanese MNCs in the United Kingdom diffused more rapidly by the threat of competition than by isomorphic pulls among suppliers and Japanese buyers, a finding that underlines the significance of the joint presence of competition and learning.

The novelty of the more recent contentions in the organizational literature is that the international firm itself is influenced by the local environment, an influence not limited to the subsidiary but potentially extended to the whole corporation. There is little question that there are important cases whereby, say, the practices of quality control were transferred from Japan to other countries by non-Japanese MNCs. There is also growing evidence that a set of organizing principles has evolved that allows for cross-border flexibility, an evolution empirically in support of the idea of operating flexibility. But the organizational implications of how subsidiaries can constitute an integrated entity when regulated by organizing principles influenced by the local environments are still murky.

In this volume, Hedlund suggests that national variations can be accommodated by a system where subsidiaries are given free rein to develop unique resources, as long as they are harnessed to a coordinated international strategy. He clearly has in mind how the European mother–daughter structure has been coupled with greater degrees of integration to exploit national variations under a system of global coordination. In their contribution to this volume, Bartlett and Ghoshal (Chapter 4) have a vision of a firm as a set of subsidiaries that are nested in their national networks and yet form an integrated network internal to a firm.

It is hard to evaluate the success of these early efforts in characterizing the organization of firms whose early imprinting has dimmed in importance. I suspect that part of the problem is that organizational theories in general have downplayed the capabilities of organizations to design themselves and to respond positively and flexibly to uncertainty (but see Starbuck 1983 for an important exception). It is not surprising, though, given the complex demands of operating across national borders, that questions of organizational design have been of paramount importance in international management. (See Doz and Prahalad, Chapter 2 in this volume.) More coordination across these differentiated fields might shed light, in both directions.

CONCLUSIONS

A review meant to bridge organizational theory and international management should be able to arrive at a formula that will please everyone: that is, that comparative country studies can shed important light on the robustness of organizational theory. Questions such as the effects of density dependence in Japanese industries can, for example, lead to the rethinking of our theories. The opportunity to do such studies is slipping away, however, because the world economy is so much more integrated. Immanuel Wallerstein's (1979) comment that the dilemma of the world system is that economies are integrated, but the political order is not, represents an incisive, but until recently a misleading, observation. Economies have been historically integrated largely through transactions, monetary and physical. Until the 1970s, the transnational linkages of organizations and institutions, though often of substantial economic value, were dwarfed by the predominance of national, if not regional and local, institutions.

Yet the major changes in the 30 years to 1990 point in the direction of Wallerstein's observation. Even in one of the most autarkic of countries, the USA, foreign trade (including both imports and exports) is over 20 percent of the gross national product. The share of manufacturing total domestic sales by foreign affiliates domiciled in the USA in 1986 was over 10 percent (Graham and Krugman 1989). When we turn our attention to smaller countries, the share of sales by foreign affiliates in the national economies of France, the United Kingdom, and Germany for 1986 were 27 percent, 20 percent, and 18 percent respectively (Graham and Krugman 1989). In industries where spatial competition is important, American restaurants can be analyzed independent of German establishments—even those of Van Nuys, California, independently of those in New York. If the industries, however, are semiconductors, computers, biotechnology, financial services, and autos, the time is already past where industry borders can be safely assumed to be coterminous with those of countries.

If our focus is only on counting things, then it is easier to miss the importance of the international dimension. If we compare the number of new

120

entrants in American industry with the number of foreign entrants, clearly the foreign entry count is insignificant (less than 0.01 percent in the late 1980s according to Department of Commence data). But it should be kept in mind that foreign entries tend to be of an entirely different magnitude. Partly, this difference is due to the simple fact that MNCs are very much larger than the average American firm; their entries are therefore large on average. For example, foreign direct investment in US assets amounted to US$40.3 billion in 1987. As total entries for that year were estimated at 1219, the average size was over US$33 million. The primary explanation for the large size of foreign entry is that acquisitions accounted for US$33.9 billion of total investment, a striking figure when it is considered that the share of entries by acquisition represents less than 50 percent of the total.

Yet the challenge is far greater than widening the scope of data collection. The studies on the MNC have already made some contributions to the organizational literature, from internalization theory to the effects of the country environment—inclusive of governments—on organizational development as well as on the behavior of MNCs. Yet there is far more to be done. The apples are hanging in the orchard. The outcome is guaranteed to be less eventful than the first transgression, but consequential nonetheless.

POSTSCRIPT
By D. Eleanor Westney

Bruce Kogut himself continued to pursue the ideas presented here, exploring the effect of national organizing patterns on the behavior of firms (Kogut 1993) and developing an influential organizational capabilities-based theory of the MNC (Kogut and Zander 1993, 1995). In addition to the related literature cited in the next chapter, those who study comparative business systems have recently begun to train their sights on the MNC: a conference at Warwick organized by Europe's leading scholar of comparative business systems, Richard Whitley, and two of his colleagues (Glenn Morgan and Peer Hull Kristensen) led to the publication in 2001 of an edited volume entitled *The Multinational Firm: Organizing across Institutional and National Divides.*

Notes

1 I would like to acknowledge the comments of Jacques Delacroix on the draft, the roundtable discussion chaired by Sidney Winter, and the patience of the editors, Sumantra Ghoshal and Eleanor Westney.
2 See Kogut and Singh (1988) for a discussion of environmental imprinting and traditional theories of foreign direct investment.
3 This theory states that firms innovate in response to relative costs (for instance to substitute expensive labor with new capital equipment) and to demand characteristics (such as a liking for luxury goods). (See Davidson (1976) for the

cross-country evidence.) As these innovations saturate the home market, the myopic bias of the firm to serve only the home market erodes, first by exporting and later by investing overseas.

4　See the listings in Chandler (1990) and Fruin (1989).

5　For a formal model of bounded search consistent with relative factor bias, see Winter (1981).

6　This idea of a template is related to Meyer and Rowan's (1977) description of the cultural foundations to institutionalism. See also Scott (1987b).

7　See Scott (1987a) on the distinction between administrative and technological cores.

8　See Kogut, Shan, and Walker (1990) for an examination of the consequences of this claim on the recreation of cooperative patterns in the biotechnology industry.

9　As the following discussion is not meant as a review, the reader is referred to Levitt and March (1987) for citations to the relevant literature.

10　In fact, the schema used by Levitt and March (that is, learning mechanisms, interpretation, memory, and intelligence) is strongly reminiscent of Deutsch's adaptation of cybernetics to political organizations.

11　In studies in the organizational literature on learning, an error term is usually neglected, as it is also neglected in the population ecology specifications of the hazard model.

12　Of course, the exact dynamic by which selection may vary from this account, but essentially this described symmetry between learning and selection provides the right intuition. Note that the proper analog to the equation describing adaptation is the standard variation on evolutionary fitness.

13　Similarly, transaction cost considerations can be subsumed in this perspective, whereby firms are viewed as differing in their abilities to manage contractual dilemmas.

14　These issues are carefully worked out in the sociobiology literature. See Boyd and Richerson (1985) for a summary and analysis. The models of Nelson and Winter (1982) also explicitly allow for a mixed dynamic of learning and selection.

15　See Bohn (1988) for a model of noise to signal in the context of learning in factories.

16　Of course, Chandler's *Scale and Scope* (1990) stands out as a remarkable exception, but in many ways, succeeds most in showing the need for a better understanding of the institutional histories across countries.

7 The Institutional Context of Multinational Activity

Mauro F. Guillén and Sandra L. Suárez

The comparative theory of institutions is based on the premise that the underlying assumptions guiding economic behavior vary across time and space. As an economic actor, the multinational enterprise (MNE) is exposed to a variety of institutional contexts (Westney, Chapter 3 this volume), which create the need for it to diagnose their peculiarities, and decide whether to adapt its strategy and organizational structure accordingly. This chapter reviews the main ways in which scholars have looked at cross-national variations that are relevant to the study of foreign direct investment (FDI) and the MNE. Five main cross-national approaches are identified: cross-cultural, comparative authority and business systems, political economy of foreign investment, comparative corporate legal traditions, and political hazards. The theoretical, methodological, and empirical accomplishments of each approach are systematically compared.

INSTITUTIONS AND INSTITUTIONAL CONTEXT

Most social scientists today agree that institutions and institutional context matter when it comes to understanding economic, political, or social behavior by individual actors and organizations. Organizations—including MNEs—are constrained and supported by institutional forces (Scott 1995: 55). MNEs are born into a specific institutional context in their home country, and they carry its features with them when expanding abroad (Doremus et al. 1998). And the institutional context in the *host* country is relevant to understanding the level of FDI, the choice of entry mode, and the way in which the MNE is organized and managed. Although institutions are relevant to the study of multinational activity, however, no attempt has been made to review the various ways in which scholars have defined the institutional context.

The study of institutions has a long history in the social sciences, going back to at least the second half of the nineteenth century (Scott 1995). Institutions are sense-making frames that (1) constitute actors as such, and (2) guide their action in appropriate and effective ways towards legitimate and meaningful ends. Institutions refract motives and behavior, goals and means, into meaningful action. Institutions come under many different guises. Laws and other "rules of the game" are highly formalized institutions, imposed by legitimate actors like the state or other powerful organizations. Institutions, however, also refer to taken-for-granted assumptions, developed through habit and rooted in collective understandings. Formal and informal institutions have the same effect: providing for stability and meaning to economic, political, and social life (Scott 1995: 33). Whether formally sanctioned or not, institutions are historically developed and relatively resilient to change.

There are three key aspects of institutions that deserve careful attention. First, it is important to underline that *institutions are simultaneously constraining and enabling.* They constitute actors, guide action, and pose limits on behavior. Choice is informed as well as constrained by the way knowledge is institutionally constructed (Scott 1995: 51). The sociological concept of institutions as constituting actors as well as shaping action stands in contrast with the economic view of institutions. Economists tend to see institutions as constraints on behavior, as "the rules of the game in a society ... the *constraints* that shape human interaction" (North 1990: 3; emphasis added). Given human tendencies to cheat one another, institutions become mechanisms to overcome anomalies, such as market failure because of the costliness of measurement and enforcement (North 1990; Williamson 1985). Institutions, however, are more than just constraints on behavior. They constitute and enable actors to engage in socially meaningful action by making them legitimate and knowledgeable in a given situation. Thus, local law or culture may view foreign firms as intruders whose activities need to be curtailed, or they may see them as contributors to local prosperity. As a result, MNE behavior will differ depending on the nature of the institutions in the host country.

Second, institutions shape not only the means of social action but also the ends: that is, *preferences are endogenous to the institutional understanding of the world* (Scott 1995: 51). Institutions affect to what extent organizations— including MNEs—pursue profitability, growth, technological advancement, or employee well-being as their primary goals. It is important to note that an MNE may be started up in a country in which profitability is the overriding goal of firms, and expand into countries in which technological development and employee welfare are also relevant considerations.

Third, *institutions are embedded in carriers or repositories,* which facilitate their continuity over time. Scott (1995: 52–55) distinguishes between three main institutional carriers, namely cultures, social structures, and routines. Cultures are symbolic representations of the world, of problematic social reality (Geertz 1973: 220), and they provide not only values and beliefs, but also strategies of action (Swidler 1985). Social structures consist of constellations of roles and positions in which actors operate. They create channels for the articulation and deployment of institutions because actors tend to behave according to the institutions recognized as such in the social structure in which they are embedded (Granovetter 2001). Routines are learned, non-reflective patterns of behavior that provide for continuity, stability, and predictability. Unlike other organizations, MNEs are by definition exposed to two or more cultures, social structures, or sets of routines, one in the home country, and one or more in the host countries in which they operate. Thus MNEs are exposed to possibly different and potentially conflicting institutional demands (Westney, Chapter 3). In organizational terms, the demands of the home-country environment stem from the "imprinting effect" (Stinchcombe 1965), while the institutional conditions in the host country may be conceptualized according to the resource-dependence, neo-institutional, or transaction-cost perspectives (see Scott 1998; Perrow 1986).

When it comes to the study of FDI and the MNE, institutional contexts tend to be defined at the country level of analysis. Rare is the country, however, that contains only one relevant institution. Thus, institutional contexts are more likely systems of somewhat mutually consistent and coherent institutions that have co-evolved over a relatively long period of time. The different approaches that scholars have used to characterize cross-national institutional contexts adopt one of two strategies to accommodate this complexity. Some of them make simplifying assumptions and focus on a relatively narrow type of institution. Others deal head on with the complexity of institutional systems. The former strategy generally is in a better position to provide testable propositions and quantitative indicators, while the latter is best equipped to offer a more complete, nuanced, and historically meaningful understanding of the phenomenon under examination. The next section compares examples of the two different strategies for characterizing institutional contexts.

FIVE APPROACHES

While there are many approaches to the comparative study of institutional contexts, only a few have been pioneered by, or have influenced, students of FDI and the MNE. Table 7.1 summarizes the main features of the five approaches considered here: cross-cultural, comparative authority and business systems, political economy of foreign investment, comparative corporate legal traditions, and political hazards. We compare each approach systematically to the others in terms of its main line of argument, basic concepts, methodology, resulting classification or measurement of different institutional contexts, main research questions related to FDI or the MNE, and leading proponents.

The cross-cultural approach

Perhaps the most influential way of capturing cross-national institutional differences relevant to the study of FDI and the MNE is the one pioneered by Geert Hofstede, a Dutch social psychologist and organizational consultant (see Werner 2002). His 1980 book, *Culture's Consequences*, is one of the

Table 7.1 Main approaches to the study of the institutional context of multinational activity

Approach	Cross-cultural	Comparative authority and business systems	Political economy of foreign direct investment	Comparative corporate legal traditions	Political and contractual hazards
Main argument:	Culture predisposes thinking and action.	Country institutions shape organizational structure and action.	Paths to economic development shape role of MNEs.	Corporate law traditions affect firm ownership, governance, and financing.	Contractual and political hazards interact to shape governance mechanisms of FDI.
Main empirical concepts, categories, or variables:	Individualism, uncertainty avoidance, power distance, masculinity.	Culture; authority system; business system.	Model of economic development, ideologies and policies towards MNEs.	Protection of investor and creditor rights; legal enforcement.	Governance mechanisms, contractual hazards, political hazards.
Resulting classification or measurement of institutional contexts:	Continuous measures; distances between pairs of countries; country clusters.	Cohesiveness and distinctiveness; horizontal and vertical relationships.	Cross-classification of development orientation and policies towards foreign MNEs; asymmetry indexes.	Legal traditions; shareholder and debtholder rights indexes; enforcement indicators.	Time-varying, continuous measures of political hazards.
Applicable research questions:	Level of inward FDI; mode and sequence of entry; longevity of foreign ventures; HRM in the MNE.	Level of outward FDI; organization of the MNE; HRM in the MNE; local adaptation of the MNE.	Goals & levels of inward & outward FDI; mode of entry; bargaining power between local government and the MNE.	Mode of entry; level of inward FDI.	Level of inward FDI; mode of entry.

Table 7.1 continued

Approach	Cross-cultural	Comparative authority and business systems	Political economy of foreign direct investment	Comparative corporate legal traditions	Political and contractual hazards
Theoretical antecedents:	Tönnies 1887; Pareto 1976; Weber 1922; Herzberg et al. 1959.	Weber 1922; Bendix 1956; Dore 1973.	Polanyi 1944.	Watson 1974; Reynolds & Flores 1989; Glendon et al. 1994.	North & Thomas 1973; Williamson 1985; North 1990.
Main proponents:	Hofstede 1980a, 1991.	Hamilton & Biggart 1988; Whitley 1992.	Gilpin 1987; Gereffi 1989, 1990; Haggard 1990; Stallings 1990.	La Porta, Lopez-de-Silanes, Shleifer & Vishny 1998, 1999.	Henisz & Williamson 1999; Henisz 2000a.
Examples of empirical studies of FDI or MNEs:	Kogut & Singh 1988; Barkema et al. 1996; Zaheer & Zaheer 1997; Lubatkin et al. 1998.	Iyer 1997; Guillén 2000a, 2001b; Yeung 1997; Zaheer & Zaheer 1997.	Gereffi 1978; Bennett and Sharpe 1979; Doner 1991; Guillén 2000a, 2001b.	Rueda-Sabater 2000.	Gastanaga et al. 1998; Delios & Henisz 2000, 2003; Henisz & Delios 2001; Henisz 2000b.

most widely cited monographs in the management literature. Its empirical analysis is based on 117,000 individual responses from 88,000 IBM employees in 66 countries obtained through surveys at two points in time, 1968 and 1972. His initial data analysis focused on 40 countries; a later book (Hofstede 1991) expanded the analysis to cover 50 countries.

Hofstede sees culture as the "collective programming of the mind" (1980a: 13). His main argument is that culture shapes thinking and action. "People carry 'mental programs' which are developed in the family in early childhood and reinforced in schools and organizations, and ... these mental programs contain a component of national culture" (1980a: 11). Since people from different nationalities have different values and perceive things in different ways, designing and managing an organization that spans different countries—like IBM—requires gaining an understanding of cross-national cultural differences. Hofstede's approach to characterizing institutional context is indebted to several key sociological concepts—including power and authority (Weber 1922; Pareto 1976), and community and society (Tönnies 1887)—as well as psychological ones like the distinction between intrinsic and extrinsic work goals (Herzberg, Mausner, and Snyderman 1959).

Methodologically, Hofstede (1980a: 14, 17) argues that mental programs cannot be observed directly, so one needs to rely on observable and measurable verbal and non-verbal behavior, or on answers elicited by well-crafted questions. He uses a questionnaire whose items capture different values and attitudes towards work and management, and finds that differences in responses across national groups of interviewees are statistically significant. It is important to keep in mind that the responses are also statistically different across occupation, gender, and age groups (1980a: 71–72). Hofstede then uses these responses to calculate aggregate scores denoting certain key cultural characteristics or dimensions. He focuses on four: power distance, uncertainty avoidance, individualism, and masculinity.

Power distance is defined as the extent to which a boss can determine the behavior of a subordinate. Hofstede argues that power distance is accepted by both boss and subordinate, and shaped to a large degree by national culture (1980a: 99). The power distance index is a composite measure combining responses to questions about subordinates' fear of disagreeing with their manager, and subordinates' preferred and perceived types of decision-making behavior by their manager. Similarly, he measures attitudes towards organizational rules, employment stability, and stress to calculate an index of uncertainty avoidance. The index of individualism focuses on the relationship between the employee and the organization, that is, the individual and the collectivity, and is measured in terms of perceptions whether the job provides the respondent with personal time, freedom, challenge, use of skills, adequate physical conditions, and training. Finally, the masculinity [sic] index attempts to capture the extent to which the respondent emphasizes job content and rewards at the expense of interpersonal relations, security, and the company (Hofstede 1980a: 99–103, 153–164, 214–222). He also classified countries into groups based on a cluster analysis of the data: Anglo, Germanic, Nordic, Near Eastern, More developed Asian, Less developed Asian, More developed Latin, and Less developed Latin (Hofstede 1980a: 332–339).

Students of FDI and the MNE have adopted Hofstede's cross-cultural concepts and measures to provide answers to several important questions. They have used his cross-national cultural indexes and clusters to address several questions about the foreign expansion of the firm. In a frequently cited paper, Kogut and Singh (1988) found joint ventures preferred to wholly owned subsidiaries, the greater the cultural distance between the host and the home country. They calculated distances between pairs of countries based on Hofstede's four cultural dimensions, an indicator that has been used subsequently by other scholars. In addition, they found that companies prefer greenfield entry over acquisitions when uncertainty avoidance in their home country is high. Barkema, Bell, and Pennings (1996) predict and show empirically that the longevity of foreign ventures decreases with cultural distance between the home and the host country, especially in the cases of joint ventures and acquisitions. Finally, myriad researchers have used Hofstede's approach and measures to explore how the MNE is structured (e.g. Lubatkin et al. 1998) and how it uses its human resources across different institutional contexts (Liberman and Torbiörn 2000).

Scholars have been using Hofstede's measures of individualism, power distance, and uncertainty avoidance for nearly two decades, although the data were originally collected between 1968 and 1972. While cultural attitudes and values are supposed to be relatively stable, it is hard to deny that there is cultural change in the world, especially as countries develop economically. Drawing on comprehensive surveys of the general population in 38 countries between 1981 and 1997, Inglehart and Baker (2000) document that national cultures and values change over time. Somewhat consistent with Hofstede's general approach, however, they find that most cultural change is "path-dependent" rather than convergent. Thus, cultural change does not seem to erase cultural differences across countries. Hofstede (1980a: 342–371) himself looked into this issue and found that his indexes evolved somewhat between 1968 and 1972, but, like Inglehart and Baker, found no convergence across countries.

Hofstede's cross-cultural approach suffers from a number of shortcomings. First, his approach is overly deterministic, and he "oversocializes" actors (Granovetter 1985), as is evident in his definition of culture as a mental program. Second, many social scientists are uncomfortable with the idea of aggregating individual responses to characterize a culture or a national institutional setting, and would rather take history and institutions into account. In other words, Hofstede's approach suffers from reductionism in that he assumes that any given entity (the national culture in his case) is a collection or combination of several simpler entities (individuals). Third, Hofstede uncritically assumes that there is only one culture within the boundaries of a given nation state, a heroic assumption indeed in these times of postmodern globalization (Guillén 2001a). And fourth, the question remains whether one can characterize national cultures with the responses of employees of a single organization. Research in this area would benefit from using the more representative data collected by the World Values Survey (Inglehart and Baker 2000). The comparative authority and business systems tradition attempts to correct for some of these problems by adopting a historical approach.

Comparative authority and business systems

The second approach to characterizing national institutional context descends directly from the work of Max Weber (1922), as reinterpreted by scholars such as Bendix (1956) and Dore (1973). It argues that institutions shape organizational structure and action. It uses the ideal type as the basic analytical tool to compare systematically different configurations of institutional factors that are found to be empirically stable. Detailed historical description lies at the core of the theory-building process by comparative scholars. Within this approach, the work of comparative sociologists Gary Hamilton and Nicole Biggart (1988), and Richard Whitley (1992) has attracted the attention of students of FDI and the MNE, although it was not initially intended to appeal to them.

Hamilton and Biggart (1988) seek to explain why the three most successful East Asian economies—Japan, South Korea, and Taiwan—evolved into different structural configurations in terms of state–business relations, principal corporate actors, intra-firm managerial decision making, and market strategies. Japan is dominated by inter-market business groups (*keiretsu*) engaged in a cooperative partnership with the state. Company ideologies emphasize consensus building, and management seeks to make and sell new, technologically advanced products. In South Korea, by contrast, the economy is dominated by diversified conglomerates (*chaebol*) engaged in an intimate relationship of reciprocal dependence and fear with the state. Managers and the state rely on centralized controls and repression to discipline a restless workforce while investing in capital-intensive production of relatively mature goods. The Taiwanese economy is comprised of family firms populating a sphere separate from that of the state, which dominates the production of intermediate inputs. Family firms rely on control through personal ties, and make capital-light durable and expendable goods.

True to their Weberian credentials, Hamilton and Biggart assess the effects of economic, cultural, and authority variables. They point out that economic explanations based on economies of scale and technology cannot explain the observed cross-national differences. Next, they explore a cultural explanation.

They associate culture with "norms, values, shared meanings, and cognitive structures" (1988: S71), and argue that organizational patterns are the expression of the larger societal culture. They make distinctions between individualist and communitarian cultures, in a way strikingly similar to Hofstede's. They also point to belief systems such as Confucianism, Catholicism, or Protestantism as potentially relevant (see also Dore 1973; Guillén 1994). They find, however, that Japan, South Korea, and Taiwan have relatively similar cultures but vastly different organizational patterns.

Finally, Hamilton and Biggart turn to authority structures as an explanatory variable. In this view, organization is an expression of patterns of domination in the larger society (Bendix 1956; Dore 1973; Guillén 1994). They discuss the authority relations between managers and workers, the state and business, and banks and business. In particular, they distinguish among the cooperative state–business relations in Japan, the subordination of business to the state in South Korea, and the Taiwanese state's "benign neglect" of business. They also examine differences in family structures and inheritance practices, which privilege the eldest son in Korea but equally benefit all sons in Taiwan. Hamilton and Biggart see the authority explanation as the key to understanding why business structures look so different in the three societies. They conclude that "organizational structure is not inevitable; it results from neither cultural predispositions nor specific economic tasks and technologies. Instead, organizational structure is institutionally determined, and, therefore, the most appropriate form of analysis is one that taps the historical dimension" (1988: S87).

Also based on a detailed comparison of East Asian countries, sociologist Richard Whitley has proposed the concept of "business systems," that is, "particular arrangements of hierarchy–market relations becoming institutionalized and relatively successful in particular contexts" (1992: 10). This definition is admittedly vague but serves as a useful starting point. Whitley characterizes business systems in terms of three characteristics: market structure, firm organization, and authority systems within the firm (1992: 242). Market structure refers to the number, size, degree of interdependence, and scope of interaction between firms. The nature of the relationships (frequency, duration, level of commitment) and the degree of vertical integration are also relevant. Firm organization has to do with the extent of internalization of economic activities, the level of managerial discretion from owners, and the interplay between specialization and integration of activities. Finally, intra-firm authority systems have to do with the degrees of specialization of tasks, centralization, power distance, impersonality, delegation, autonomy, and commitment, as well as with the characteristics of the recruitment, training, and reward systems.

Like Hamilton and Biggart (1988), Whitley (1992: 231) follows in the tradition of comparative organizational studies (Weber 1922; Bendix 1974; Dore 1973; Westney 1987) to argue that business systems are the developmental result of such societal factors as pre-industrial legacies (bases of legitimacy, family organization), the state's structure and role in development, the nature of the financial system (market versus credit-based), the type of educational and training systems (state versus employer centered), and the characteristics of the labor system (basis and strength of unionization, pattern of bargaining, union–party relationships, reward systems, segmentation; see also Dore 1973).

Whitley (1992: 256–257) forcibly argues that differences across business systems are likely to persist because there is no such thing as the one most effective way of organizing markets and firms. Business systems are effective under a particular set of institutional arrangements. Accordingly, no single business system existing in the world today can claim total superiority under all circumstances. Moreover, the potential variety in business systems is virtually endless, although some combinations of system characteristics are unlikely.

As far as MNEs are concerned, business systems may be characterized in terms of their internal cohesion and external distinctiveness. Holding external distinctiveness constant, the more internally cohesive a business system, the harder it will be to reproduce it somewhere else, given that cohesion is based on a unique configuration of institutional factors specific to a society. Multinational firms may be faced with the need to become deeply embedded in business systems that are very different from their home country's. Therefore, the organization of their international operations will be shaped by the cohesion and distinctiveness of the various national business systems in which they operate.

While it is influential in sociology and organizational studies, few students of the MNE have embraced the comparative authority and business systems approach. Perhaps the main reason is that no readily usable quantitative cross-national indicators have been proposed or calculated. Still, comparative scholars offer a theory and a way of doing research that appeals to some students of the MNE. They have used the comparative authority and business systems approach to address the level of outward FDI from a given home country, the organizational structure and human resource practices of the MNE, and the issue of local adaptation by the MNE. In a study of 111 MNEs headquartered in Hong Kong, Yeung (1997) finds intra-firm, extra-firm, and inter-firm networks to shape the patterns of international expansion observed. Guillén (2001b) finds systematic differences in the level of outward FDI in Argentina, South Korea, and Spain depending on the dominant relationships among business actors in the home country. Marketing researchers have proposed to use the comparative authority and business systems approach to conceptualize the extent to which the MNE needs to adapt to local circumstances (Iyer 1997).

Scholars have also attempted to combine elements of the cross-cultural and authority approaches. For instance, Zaheer and Zaheer (1997) explore country effects on information seeking in response to market volatility by 3266 banks located in 25 countries. They find strong country effects even after controlling for relevant variables, including Hofstede's uncertainty avoidance index. Guillén (2000a) seeks to explain cross-national differences in the importance of diversified business groups. He measured Hamilton and Biggart's (1988) concept of social hierarchy with Hofstede's power distance index, but the results contradict the hypothesis that greater power distance encourages a greater presence of business groups in the economy.

Perhaps the most significant way in which the comparative authority and business systems approach is limited in its application to the study of FDI and the MNE lies in its neglect of certain variables that are key to understanding cross-border investment. The best example is the issue of national techno-logical capabilities, an institutional feature of countries that other scholars have developed recently (Nelson 1993). Empirical researchers have found ways to measure national technological institutions and use them to explain patterns of FDI (e.g. Anand and Kogut 1997).

Political economy of foreign direct investment

The third approach to characterizing national institutional contexts for FDI draws from the literature on political economy. The main argument is that different paths to economic development generate distinct patterns of inward and outward FDI. Scholars have typically characterized different paths to development by means of pairs of opposed concepts such as export-led growth versus import substitution, modernizing versus populist, nationalist versus pragmatic, or protectionist versus liberal (Bresser Pereira 1993; Haggard 1990; Gereffi 1990; Gilpin 1987; Stallings 1990).

There are only two factors, however, that are relevant to understanding the level and operational mode of multinational activity in host countries. One is the orientation of development efforts: that is, whether the strategy is to accel-erate growth by substituting local production for imports (the import substitu-tion model) or by increasing exports (the export-oriented model). The other is whether policies toward foreign MNEs are permissive or restrictive. For exam-ple, host governments might impose certain levels of domestic ownership, limit profit repatriation, demand minimum local product content and technological transfers, or require production to be exported (Gereffi 1989; Haggard 1990; Stallings 1990). Table 7.2 lays out the four contexts that result from cross-classifying these two dimensions, each associated with a different view, image or ideology about the MNE (see Guillén 2001b). Table 7.2 also notes which development theories, kinds of investment strategies, and labor requirements are consistent with each image.

Import-substitution industrialization can be accompanied by permissive or liberal foreign investment policies (cell 1 in Table 7.2). In this situation, multinationals gain access to a protected domestic market in exchange for

Table 7.2 Economic development and foreign direct investment

Policies towards MNEs	Strategy of economic development	
	Export-oriented	**Import substitution**
Permissive	*Inward FDI:* Foreign MNEs seen as partners in outward-oriented economic development. Acquisitions in mature industries. Wholly owned in growth industries. MNE labor requirements: Flexibility, skill formation, stability. *Outward FDI:* High. Large oligopolistic firms; SMEs.　　　1	*Inward FDI:* Foreign MNEs seen as necessary evils in the effort to sustain and deepen import substitution. JVs in mature industries. Wholly owned or JVs in growth industries. MNE labor requirements: Enhanced purchasing power, stability. *Outward FDI:* Low. Business groups; some SMEs. 2
Restrictive	3 *Inward FDI:* Foreign MNEs seen as arm's length collaborators to obtain the technology and marketing skill needed to increase exports. XPZs Manufacturing contracts (OEM); Minority JVs. MNE labor requirements: Low wages, docility, union avoidance. *Outward FDI:* High. Business groups; SOEs.	4 *Inward FDI:* Foreign MNEs seen as villains to be avoided so as to preserve national sovereignty and independence. Exodus of MNEs in the face of hostile incentives, expropriations or nationalizations. *Outward FDI:* Low. SOEs; large oligopolistic firms.

FDI: Foreign direct investment.   JVs: Joint ventures.
MNEs: Multinational enterprises.   OEM: Original equipment manufacturing.
SMEs: Small and medium enterprises. SOEs: State-owned enterprises.
XPZs: Export processing zones.

Source: Adapted from Guillén (2001b).

import-substituting investments that create jobs and save hard currency. The arrival of foreign multinationals to invest jointly with local businesses as "necessary evils" is justified because import substitution in growth or new industries—such as automobiles or electronics—usually requires technology and capital that the average developing country lacks. The cases of Indonesia and Spain during the 1940s and 1950s or of India, Brazil, Argentina, and Mexico until the early 1980s illustrate this situation (Evans 1979; Gereffi 1989; Haggard 1990). In this context, given that exports of local production are not encouraged, multinationals expect an industrial relations system that promotes adequate levels of purchasing power inside the protected domestic market. The literature, however, has observed that the multinationals attracted to an import-substitution environment will rarely make the most innovative products, transfer the most sophisticated technology, or spend large sums on worker training, given that trade protection allows them to sell at high prices and thus obtain large profit margins even with mature or plainly obsolete products (Haggard 1990). The multinationals' readiness to enter into coalitions with other inward-looking interest groups to preserve protectionist measures or even to perpetuate friendly governments in power regardless of their legitimacy may also cause tensions with labor unions that feel excluded from the political process.

Countries pursuing an import-substitution strategy sometimes give way to nationalist sentiment and prevent multinationals from operating in the country. They justify such policies by reference to autarkical versions of dependency and world-system theories. This is the situation captured by cell 2 of Table 7.2. Countries as diverse in their resource endowments as Argentina, Venezuela, Mexico, and India periodically adopted utterly restrictive policies towards the multinationals. In this situation, multinationals are depicted as "villains" that plunder the country's riches, thwarting its economic potential and limiting its national sovereignty. Typical policy initiatives are expropriations of the subsidiaries of foreign multinationals, especially in such highly visible industries as oil, mining, and public utilities. At least in the short run, workers and their unions have often celebrated the wage increases and enhanced job security afforded by state ownership, especially when compared with the shortsighted attitude of multinationals under import-substitution conditions.

Like import substitution, the export-oriented strategy can also be accompanied by either permissive or restrictive policies towards the multinationals. Export-led growth with restricted FDI (cell 3) typically takes the form of export processing zones, original equipment manufacturing (OEM) contracts, and minority joint ventures.[1] These special arrangements allow multinationals to take advantage of the natural resources or cheap labor so plentiful in developing economies, but impose on them a number of limitations on the production process and the sale of the output, as proposed by late-industrialization theory. Under such restrictive export-oriented conditions multinationals become "arm's length collaborators," precisely because the state prefers to follow a strategy of "indebted" industrialization rather than one based on the attraction of equity capital—that is, foreign MNEs (Suárez 2001). Multinationals are attracted to this situation by low wages, labor docility, and the absence of unions (Guillén 2001b). The cases of South Korea and Indonesia stand out as instances of this strategy (Haggard 1990). The emphasis on exporting products manufactured with cheap labor will often lead to friction between workers and multinationals over wages and working conditions, which can escalate into serious political conflict, especially under repressive authoritarian regimes (Guillén 2000c).

An export-led strategy accompanied by permissive policies towards foreign multinationals results in the "partner" image (cell 4). This context is only feasible in countries that are willing to ignore or downplay ownership issues, and to pursue full integration with the global economy or trade blocs in exchange for economic growth and job creation, as preached by modernization and neoclassical theories of development. The cases of Singapore, Puerto Rico, Ireland, Spain, and more recently Mexico, illustrate the image of multinationals as partners (Haggard 1990). Multinationals will stay in an export-oriented country only if they can develop a long-term labor strategy geared towards flexibility, skill formation, and stability: that is, they can invest in a workforce capable of adapting to changes in the global economy (UNCTAD 1994: 168–173, 204–206, 215–236). Tensions may also arise in this context. The government, labor unions, and other interest groups may feel that multinationals are not fulfilling their part of the partnership contract if they decide to cut jobs or divest altogether. Another area of friction might be acquisitions of domestic firms by multinationals, which could restrict competition in the host industry.

The ideal-typical scheme of Table 7.2 conceptualizes the level and mode of multinational activity under different development contexts. The same conceptual scheme can be applied to outward FDI. Guillén (2001b) argues that different kinds of firms will become outward investors depending on the development orientation and the extent to which foreign MNEs are kept at bay. Under import substitution with permissive policies, local diversified business groups and small and medium enterprises (SMEs) tend to become the most important outward foreign investors, although the overall level of outward FDI is not high. Under import substitution with restrictive inward FDI policies, state-owned enterprises (SOEs) and large oligopolistic firms dominate the little outward FDI that typically characterizes this context. Argentina is a good illustration of these two contexts, as policy making shifted back and forth between permissive and restrictive policies during the post-war period.

Under export-led growth and restrictive inward FDI policies, local diversified business groups—and the occasional SOE—dominate the economy (as in South Korea) and eventually become large foreign investors. Finally, under export-led growth with permissive policies, large oligopolistic firms and SMEs are the key outward investors, as in Spain during the 1980s and 1990s (Guillén 2001b). The overall level of outward FDI in the two export-led contexts tends to be higher than in the two import-substitution ones (see Table 7.2). Besides comparative-historical analysis of inward and outward FDI based on the scheme in Table 7.2, Guillén (2000a) has proposed a continuous measure of development contexts based on the concept of asymmetry between inward and outward trade flows, or between inward and outward FDI flows (or stocks). These indexes explain the proliferation of different organizational forms—business groups, SMEs, foreign MNEs, and so on—in the four cells of Table 7.2.

The international political economy approach can also be used to elucidate the issue of bargaining power between a local government and the MNE. This area of research has a long pedigree. Early dependency theory concentrated on the structural constraints faced by host country governments (Cardoso and Faleto 1979). The state was seen as subordinate to international capital, which in turn contributed to the continued underdevelopment of the Third World. A revisionist approach to dependency theory proposed a more reciprocal relationship between multinationals and the host country. In his study of Brazil, Evans (1979) argued that the economic development of Brazil was shaped by a "triple alliance" among multinationals, the state, and local capital. This approach—which is a variant of the bargaining model—promotes the notion that the relationship between MNEs and host country governments is a dynamic one (Doner 1991: 7).

The bargaining literature did not make inroads until scholars recognized that the relationship between the local government and the MNE differed depending on the economic development model. Different factors determine the balance of bargaining power between host countries and multinational over time. Doner (1991: 7) noted that "for foreign investors, firm-specific assets such as technology, management skills, capital, and access to overseas markets yield leverage to the extent that they are critical to an investment project's success but not accessible to the host country." The host country has leverage over the foreign MNE to the extent that it possesses resources desired by the foreign investor, including a large domestic market, inexpensive and/or skilled labor, and natural resources. The host's bargaining power also increases with the degree of competition among foreign firms for access to these resources, and "the host country's ability to develop resources such as technological capacities and overseas market links capable of substituting for those controlled by foreign firms" (Doner 1991: 7).

In extractive industries the bargaining model argues that the interests of MNEs and home countries are inherently in conflict, but there is still the possibility of mutual benefit. Bargaining occurs over the distribution of the benefits. Once the initial fixed investment is made by the MNE, however, the balance of power shifts in favor of the host-country government (Kobrin 1987). When the foreign investment is in manufacturing, however, a shift in balance of power towards the host country is less likely, or occurs more slowly than in the case of extractive industries (Bennett and Sharpe 1979; Gereffi 1978). Hence, while there is an argument for a bargaining approach to relations between the host country and the MNE, and it can be accepted that MNEs may contribute to economic development, when it comes to manufacturing, especially in high-technology industries, the relationship is still one of dependency of host governments on foreign investors.

With the economic success of the Asian tigers, a "strong state" model of development gained sway, only to be challenged by society-centered approaches. Once again, the bargaining model between the local government and the MNE has become relevant. An example of this revival is Doner's (1991) analysis of the patterns of bargaining of the Japanese automobile industry in Thailand, Indonesia, and the Philippines. He finds that the cross-national variation in the distribution of bargaining power between Japanese multinationals and host governments is a factor of the level of collaboration between public officials and private domestic actors.

Haggard's (1989) critique of the bargaining model in the literature is that it fails to take into consideration that different national development strategies—import substitution versus export-oriented—call for a particular relationship between MNEs and the host country. He agrees that investments in extractive industries are unique, and that the balance of power shifts in favor of the host government after the investment is made. He argues that, by contrast, in the case of manufacturing investments that seek to substitute local production for imports, the balance of power shifts in favor of the MNE after the investment is made because "networks of suppliers, distributors, consumers, joint-venture partners, and labor provide a political base of support" for the MNE. In the case of export-oriented manufacturing investments, the balance of power favors the MNE throughout the investment cycle because such investments tend to be relatively small, and the assets involved mobile (Haggard 1990: 221–222).

The political economy approach to institutional context strikes a balance between the cross-cultural approach—entirely based on quantitative indicators—and the comparative authority and business systems approach, which emphasizes historical processes. A second strength is that it allows for a comparison of different organizational forms: state-owned firms, family firms, business groups, MNEs, and so on. Still, it contains certain limitations. First, it focuses perhaps too narrowly on government policy as a determinant of FDI and MNE activity. And second, most of the empirical applications of this approach relegate the study of the MNE to the background, with perhaps the exception of the bargaining literature.

Comparative corporate legal traditions

Like the political economy approach, the comparative legal traditions approach focuses explicitly on a concrete institution that has a direct impact on organizational structure and processes: corporate law. The most influential categorization of countries according to corporate legislation has been proposed by economists La Porta, Lopez-de-Silanes, Shleifer, and Vishny (1998). They argue that the degrees of investor and creditor protection in a country generate distinct patterns of ownership, governance, and financing of business firms. They analyze each country's corporate legal provisions to identify the extent to which the rights of equity capital providers (shareholders) are protected. The greater the degree of protection, the more likely it is that new firms will be founded, their ownership will become eventually dispersed over a large number of shareholders, and their financing will be tilted towards equity rather than debt. These predictions have been supported empirically (Guillén 2000b; La Porta, Lopez-de-Silanes, Shleifer, and Vishny 1999).

Drawing on comparative legal scholarship (Watson 1974; Reynolds and Flores 1989; Glendon, Gordon, and Osakwe 1994), La Porta, Lopez-de-Silanes, Shleifer, and Vishny (1998, 1999) classify countries into five main corporate legal traditions: English, French, German, Scandinavian, and formerly socialist. English or common law is shaped by the decisions of judges ruling on specific issues. By contrast, French and German law emerged from Roman civil law, which "uses statuses and comprehensive codes as a primary means of ordering legal material" (La Porta, Lopez-de-Silanes, Shleifer, and Vishny 1998: 1118). Scandinavian legal systems are in part based on civil law, but are not as derivative from it as the French and German are. Lastly, the former socialist countries need to be treated as a separate category because their legal systems, while in many cases influenced by either French or German law, have been in flux since the end of the Cold War in 1989 and generally failed to provide a sound foundation for entrepreneurial activity (Spicer, McDermott, and Kogut 2000). A comparative analysis of corporate legal traditions reveals that English (common) law affords the best protection of investors, followed by German and Scandinavian law. French law provides the worst protection (La Porta, Lopez-de-Silanes, Shleifer, and Vishny 1998, 1999).

English, French, and German corporate law diffused widely throughout the world following patterns of imperial, economic, or cultural influence. Former British colonies— the USA, Canada, Australia, Ireland, Singapore, and many others—adopted English law. French law spread not only to colonies in the Near East, Northern and sub-Saharan Africa, Indochina, Oceania, and the Caribbean, but also to Portugal, Spain, Italy, and those countries colonized by the latter countries. The German legal tradition has been most influential in Austria, Switzerland, Greece, Hungary, Yugoslavia, Japan, Korea, Taiwan, and China, among others.

In addition to clustering countries into different legal families, La Porta, Lopez-de-Silanes, Shleifer, and Vishny (1999) calculate three important measures for 49 countries: shareholder rights index, debt-holder rights index, and various indicators of legal enforcement. The shareholder rights index, also called "anti-director rights," is calculated by determining whether or not certain provisions that generally protect the rights of shareholders are present in corporate law, including the following six rules: one share equals one vote, proxy by mail, non-blocking of shares before the shareholders' meeting, cumulative voting or proportional representation, oppressed minority protection, preemptive right to new issues, and a percentage of shareholders necessary to call an extraordinary meeting of no more than the world median of 10 percent. This additive index can oscillate between 0 and 6. Empirically, it ranges between 0 for Belgium (French legal tradition), and 5 for Canada and the USA (English tradition). Tests of means across legal traditions confirm that the English tradition awards the best investor protection (mean of 4.0), followed by the Scandinavian (3.0), German (2.33), and French (2.33) traditions. Conveniently, the shareholder rights index is uncorrelated with per capita income.

A similar index of creditor rights is calculated by adding the scores for whether corporate law protects debt-holders along four dimensions (no automatic stay on assets, secured creditors first paid, restrictions for going into reorganization, and management does not stay in reorganization). Again, differences across legal traditions are significant: English (mean of 3.11), German (2.33), Scandinavian (2.0), and French (1.58). Shareholder and debt-holder rights are correlated with each other. Finally, La Porta et al. calculate several measures of enforcement, or the extent to which the courts can step in and uphold the rights of shareholders even when the rules protecting their interests are weak. The measures are continuous indicators of the efficiency of the judicial system, rule of law, corruption, risk of expropriation, risk of contract repudiation, and rating on accounting standards. Enforcement is strongest in the Scandinavian tradition, followed by the German, English, and French. Unlike shareholder and debt-holder rights, enforcement is correlated with the level of development.

Given that the corporate legal tradition approach was formulated only recently, it has yet to exert a major influence on published empirical studies of FDI, although Rueda-Sabater (2000) has suggested that corporate legal traditions may affect the level of inward FDI in developing countries. It would also be interesting to test empirically whether differences in corporate legal tradition between the home and the host country might affect entry mode choice.

The corporate legal tradition approach offers both qualitative and quantitative ways of addressing empirical issues related to FDI. Its main strength is that it conceptualizes, analyzes, and measures a well-defined set of aspects related to corporate governance. Naturally, its narrow focus on a limited set of institutions is its biggest limitation.

Political hazards

Political hazards or risks have long been on the research agenda of students of the MNE. Perhaps the best treatment of this subject from an organizational perspective is Stephen Kobrin's *Managing Political Risk Assessment* (1982). He proposed to study country risk as a feature of the organizational environment in the host country. Building on the open systems perspective in organizational theory, Kobrin argues that political risk should be distinguished from the contingencies arising from the normal functioning of market processes, and from sheer political instability. Rather, political risk has to do with "potentially significant managerial contingencies generated by political events and processes" (1982: 48). He further argues that political risk arises from the interface between the political environment and the firm's operations, with government policy usually mediating between the two. He notes that political risk most frequently arises from the routine functioning of the political process: that is, "contingencies are likely to be firm- or even project-specific and are likely to result from the interaction of organizational strategy and structure with the environment, rather than from political events that affect all foreign firms in a given country" (Kobrin 1982: 49).

Kobrin's approach calls for a detailed, firm-level analysis of risks. He collected quantitative and qualitative data on 193 large American firms with international operations in order to identify how they scanned the political environment and engaged in risk containment strategies. Unfortunately, firm-level studies like this are not common in the literature. A recent exception uses organizational learning theories to explain the changing political strategies of US multinationals aimed at preventing the repeal of an important tax break that greatly enhances the profitability of their international operations (Suárez 2000). Instead of in-depth case studies, scholars have tended to focus on the country level of analysis. Several agencies or consultancies routinely produce political risk indicators, such as the *International Country Risk Guide* and *Business Environmental Risk Intelligence*.

Recent scholarship has improved the conceptual approach to the study of political hazards at the country level by drawing from key contemporary organizational theory–transaction-cost economics. Witold Henisz and Oliver Williamson (1999) have proposed a theoretically coherent and empirically operational way of assessing the impact of host-country institutional context on the level and mode of FDI. Transaction-cost economics focuses on the question of what is the most efficient governance mechanism—market, hybrid, or hierarchy—to undertake a specific transaction, depending on the contractual hazards associated with it. Contractual hazards arise because the other party to the transaction may behave opportunistically, especially under conditions of uncertainty or asset specificity (Williamson 1985). This framework—initially formulated with no mention of the cross-national dimension—can readily be extended to the problem of cross-border investment by taking political hazards into consideration. Political hazards arise when the government's commitment to a set of rules for doing business in the host country (regulation, taxation, property rights regime) can easily change. This unpredictability may be caused by opportunistic behavior on the part of the government itself when it tries to expropriate the MNE (direct political hazards), or on the part of a local partner or competitor lobbying the government in a way that is detrimental to the interests of the MNE (indirect political hazards).

Henisz and Williamson (1999) assess the effects of political hazards on the choice of entry mode (partnering versus wholly owned) by noting that contractual and political hazards are not simply additive. Political and contractual hazards interact in a complex way because the MNE expands internationally on the basis of intangible assets that provide it with a competitive advantage but that are difficult to protect contractually, especially if political hazards are high. They note that "the impact of variation in property rights regimes either across countries or over time on the relative costs of governance of partnership and [whole] ownership will depend crucially on the level of contractual hazards posed by the individual transaction" (1999: 272). When political hazards are high—for example, property rights are not well protected—the probability that a cross-border transaction by an MNE "will be organized under partnership increases for transactions with low contractual hazards... while it decreases for transactions with high contractual hazards" (1999: 273).

Henisz (2000a, 2000c) proposes a way to measure political hazards as a structural attribute of countries that may change over time. His indicator of "political constraints" attempts to capture "a government's ability to credibly commit not to interfere with private property rights," a concept first advanced as relevant to the study of long-term capital investments by North and Thomas (1973; see also North 1990). Henisz's political constraints index is based on positive political theory, and incorporates information on the number of independent branches of government with veto power (executive, higher legislature, lower legislature, judiciary, sub-national government), and the distribution of preferences across and within those branches. He gathered data on 157 countries for each year between 1960 and 1994, characterizing the political system in terms of the number of branches of government, the partisan alignments across each of them, and the party composition of legislatures. Under certain simplifying assumptions, one can calculate an index of political constraints that ranges between zero (no constraints) and unity (totally constrained). The index increases with the number of de jure veto points in the political system, the degree to which veto points are controlled by different parties (that is, when branches of government are not aligned), and the extent to which preferences of the decision maker who can potentially change the conditions for FDI are aligned with party preferences within the legislature or the judiciary, tempered by the fact that party preferences may be more or less fractionalized.

This political constraint index is highly correlated with the risk indexes included in the *International Country Risk Guide* (ICRG 1996), and with the seven-point index of executive constraints of the Polity Database (Gurr and Jaggers 2000). Unlike these other indicators, however, the political constraint index is forward-looking in that it assesses the probability that policy will be constrained rather than the government's historical record of doing so.

The political hazards approach has been applied empirically to the questions of the level of FDI in a host country and the choice of entry mode. Using a sample of Japanese direct foreign investments over time, Henisz and Delios (2001) found that MNEs prefer to establish plants in countries with a high index of political constraints: that is, with lower political hazards. In an earlier article using data from the *Business Environmental Risk Intelligence*, Gastanaga, Nugent, and Pashamova (1998) found that inflows of FDI into 49 developing countries were inversely proportional to the level of corruption, the enforceability of contracts, the degree of bureaucratic delay, and the risk of nationalization. Following Kobrin's (1982) emphasis on firm-level strategies for risk containment, Delios and Henisz (2000, 2003) also find that MNEs mitigate the effect of political hazards by accumulating international experience, and by taking into account the FDI decisions made by competitors and other firms in their same business group. When contractual hazards are low, political hazards have been found to increase the likelihood of joint venturing, as opposed to whole ownership, in samples of Japanese (Delios and Henisz 2000) and American multinational corporations (Henisz 2000b).

The political hazards approach offers a conceptually and empirically useful way of characterizing host-country environments for FDI. Its main weakness lies in that it is perhaps too narrowly focused on political constraints, especially when compared with the comparative business systems approach. Unlike the latter, though, it offers testable propositions, and time-varying empirical indicators.

UNRESOLVED THEORETICAL AND EMPIRICAL ISSUES

Students of FDI and the MNE can draw from a variety of approaches and research traditions when it comes to conceptualizing and operationalizing empirically the institutional context in the home and host countries of the firm. The five approaches considered in this chapter differ substantially from one another in terms of their focus, style of theorizing, methodological tools, handling of some of the key issues in institutional analysis, and actual impact on the field (see Werner 2002 for a recent review).

The cross-cultural, corporate legal tradition, and political hazards approaches tend to provide relatively narrow definitions of institutional context. Only a few variables are analyzed in depth. By contrast, the comparative authority and business systems approach embraces a whole range of political, cultural, economic, and social variables that are assumed to co-evolve over time. The political economy approach lies somewhere in between the two extremes. Differences in focus result in different styles of theorizing and doing empirical research. The cross-cultural, corporate legal tradition, and political hazards approaches offer relatively well-defined theoretical predictions, and invite researchers to use quantitative indicators of the main underlying concepts. By contrast, the comparative authority and business systems approach proposes to use the comparative-historical method to arrive at a meaningful interpretation—in the Weberian sense—of observed historical events and processes of change. The political economy approach combines deductive and inductive reasoning, and proposes to combine quantitative and qualitative research strategies.

The theory of comparative institutions has long been afflicted by an uneasy relationship with other social and economic theories that emphasize conflict, power, and discontinuous change. The five approaches considered in this chapter differ sharply in their ability to address these issues. The cross-cultural and corporate legal tradition approaches relegate conflict, power, and discontinuous change to the background. These aspects lie, however, at the core of the comparative authority and business systems, political economy, and political hazards approaches.

The five approaches also differ in how effectively they can accommodate change and de-institutionalization. At one extreme, the cross-cultural and corporate legal traditions approaches are miserably inept at dealing with change. At the other, the comparative authority and business systems, and the political economy approaches are especially well suited to exploring how institutions change over time. In this respect, the political hazards approach, while narrow in focus, strikes a balance between concise theoretical prediction and empirical quantification, on the one hand, and sensitivity towards discontinuity and change, on the other.

This review of the theoretical, methodological, and empirical merits of five main approaches to the institutional context of multinational activity reveals that no one perspective is superior to all others under all circumstances. While researchers may decide to opt for one or the other depending on the nature of the question being explored or the data at hand, the study of FDI and the MNE would benefit immensely from a judicious combination of two or more of these perspectives in answering any one research question. The foreign expansion of the firm is a very complicated phenomenon, driven by a great number of variables, both quantitative and qualitative. Moreover, it is a phenomenon that is prone to the effects of power, conflict, and discontinuous change because of its distinctive cross-border character. The goal of this chapter was not to determine the best approach, but rather to expose the strengths and weaknesses of each, and to provide some guidelines as to how researchers might effectively combine approaches to arrive at a better understanding of FDI and the MNE.

Note

1 Foreign firms in export processing zones hire local workers to assemble components of foreign origin for re-export. By contrast, in an original equipment manufacturing (OEM) contract a foreign firm supplies a local company with the technology and most sophisticated components so that it can manufacture goods that the foreign firm will market under its own brand in international markets.

Part II
Organization Structure, Governance, and Culture

8   Control in Multinational Firms: The Role of Price and Hierarchy[1]

Jean-François Hennart

How do firms manage to perform their functions efficiently? How do they constrain individual behavior to make it compatible with the overall goals of the firm? These age-old questions take on new significance in the context of the multinational corporation (MNC), where the problem of control is particularly acute. Geographical and cultural distance increase the cost of establishing control, and make it difficult for MNCs to secure the cooperation of their foreign affiliates. Over-centralization of decisions leads to paralysis, while excessive decentralization results in chaos (Doz and Prahalad 1981).

The issue of control in MNCs has elicited a considerable volume of empirical research. A survey of coordination mechanisms in MNCs lists 85 empirical studies undertaken since 1953 (Martinez and Jarillo 1989). Yet in spite of this significant effort, our knowledge of control mechanisms in firms remains fragmentary. For example, Gates and Egelhoff (1986: 72) report that "researchers have generated inconsistent hypotheses ... and reported inconsistent results" concerning one of the most salient issues, that of the determinants of centralization (the extent to which decisions are taken at the headquarters of the MNC).

The goal of this chapter is threefold. First, it will sketch a theoretical structure that will clarify some of the concepts used in the study of coordination mechanisms in firms. One of the main building blocks of this framework is the distinction between methods of organization (the price system and hierarchy) and economic institutions (markets and firms) that use those methods. A second building block is the argument that the price system and hierarchy can be regarded as substitutes. The price system can be used in firms to overcome the basic flaws of hierarchy, while hierarchy can alleviate the most glaring defects of the price system. This theoretical framework will then be applied to some of the control issues studied in the organization theory literature of the MNC, such as the relationship between the degree of centralization and the extent of interdependencies between the parent and its foreign affiliates. I shall show how the framework developed here explains some of the paradoxical results found in previous studies.

A THEORY OF ECONOMIC ORGANIZATION

The framework developed here, based on Hennart (1982), draws from transaction cost and agency theory, but differs from both to some extent. It posits that organizations are designed to minimize the cost of organizing exchange and cooperation, and that competition in the product and factor markets leads individuals to organize themselves under the form of organization that minimizes these costs.

The major insight of transaction cost theory is that firms and markets are alternative institutions devised to organize economic activities. If one accepts this premise, then to understand the nature of organizational processes within firms one must ask two separate questions. First, what must be done to organize economic activities: that is, what are the tasks that both firms and markets must perform? Second, how do firms differ from markets in the way they perform these tasks?

What is involved in organizing economic activities?

Economic institutions (such as firms and markets) exist to organize cooperation. Cooperation between individuals can be productive for two reasons. First, some tasks require more capabilities than can be provided by a single individual, and consequently can only be achieved by pooling the efforts of two or more people. Individuals also have differing abilities, and cooperation through trade allows individuals to exploit those differences by making it possible for each to specialize in tasks for which he/she has a comparative advantage. In both cases the utility that individuals receive from cooperating exceeds what they could achieve through their solitary efforts.

Although cooperation is productive, achieving it involves organizing costs, which arise from people's "bounded rationality" and from their "opportunism" (that is, their self-seeking behavior). Three tasks must be undertaken to achieve cooperation.

- Individuals must be told that their interaction will be profitable.
- The benefits from cooperation must be shared among the cooperating parties. Cooperators can be expected to invest resources to increase their share, an activity which might be rational from the individual's point of view, but which is wasteful in the aggregate because it reduces the benefits to be shared. The gains of cooperation must therefore be divided between the parties in a way that discourages bargaining.
- The division of the gains of cooperation (the sharing rule) must be enforced. Failing this, cooperation could not take place or would not last. Achieving cooperation therefore requires carefully devised techniques that reduce information, bargaining, and enforcement costs.

In contrast to this view, neoclassical economics assumes that these three tasks are performed costlessly by both firms and markets. What economists call "the theory of the firm" starts by assuming that this problem is solved (Alchian and Demsetz 1972). In reality, all economic institutions experience costs in performing these three tasks. At any point in time, some potential gains of cooperation will be forgone because the gains from such cooperation are too small to warrant the establishment of institutions to organize it. Individuals will have to give up the gains of trade and specialization, and we will observe subsistence farming, self-insurance, and home production of clothing and food. The greater the potential gains from trade, the larger the amount of resources expended to achieve cooperation.

Prices and hierarchy are two alternative methods of organization

It is important at the outset to distinguish between "method of organization" and "economic institution." The price system and hierarchy are alternative methods that can be used to organize economic activities. They are alternatives in the sense that they use different coordinating mechanisms that result in different biases. Consequently, for a given interaction (transaction), they entail different levels of organizing costs. Each mode will therefore have a comparative cost advantage in organizing a particular set of transactions.[2] Firms and markets are economic institutions. These institutions generally use a mix of both price and hierarchy, although the mix in firms is heavily biased towards hierarchy, while markets predominantly use the price system. As we shall show, the choice between organizing a transaction within the firm or having it organized through the market (the make-or-buy decision) can be represented as a choice between using the price system and using hierarchy. Furthermore, the same analysis can be used to decide whether to organize an activity within a firm through prices or through hierarchy.

Let us first consider how the price system and hierarchy are viable ways of organizing cooperation. To simplify the exposition, assume that there are no transaction costs. This makes it possible to distinguish between the method of organization used and the actual performance of these methods of organization when organizing costs are positive.

We have seen that organizing exchange and cooperation requires that individuals be informed of their interdependence, rewarded for cooperating, and discouraged from bargaining. Prices can perform these three tasks. Prices inform individuals about opportunities for cooperation. The information structure of a market is fully decentralized, with prices conveying to all participants information on every one else's needs and desires, allowing them to act in a way that maximizes social (and individual) utility.[3] Prices also act as sharing rules that allocate the gains from cooperation. When markets function perfectly (that is, when there is a large number of buyers and sellers),

151

these sharing rules become exogenous. Individuals do not have the power to change them, and bargaining is discouraged. For example, the gains obtained by having farmers specialize in food production and workers in the construction of farm machinery are divided between these two groups through food and agricultural machinery prices. Prices also meter and reward perfectly an agent's behavior. The gross rewards that individuals receive are a direct function of their output multiplied by market prices.

In the absence of organizing costs, a hierarchy would also perfectly organize economic activities. We define hierarchy as a method of organization, and hence "hierarchy" is not synonymous with "firm" or with "upper managers" as popular usage would imply. Hierarchy as defined here is characterized by centralized information and the use of behavior constraints. Information is decentralized with prices, but it is centralized with hierarchy. The hierarchical method of organization channels all the information possessed by individuals (employees) to a central party (the boss) who assimilates all this information, draws up consistent plans, and retransmits information to employees in the form of directives. If individuals have "unbounded rationality," this method is as efficient in making optimal joint decisions as the decentralized system of market prices.

In a price system individuals collect their own information, make their own productive decisions, and are rewarded by their output measured at market prices. By contrast, under hierarchy the individual relinquishes to a central party, the boss, his or her right to make decisions concerning the allocation of his or her own resources (such as his or her labor time and effort), and instead agrees to do as told, within the constraints established by social custom. The answer to the question "Why do employees agree to have their behavior directed by the boss?" is that their reward under hierarchy is independent of their output. They are therefore less concerned about being ordered to perform tasks that do not seem to maximize their income than in a price system where their income is directly related to the tasks they perform. A hierarchical system does not reward employees by their output measured at market prices, but by their obedience to managerial directives. In other words, firms use behavior constraints to organize cooperation; employees are paid a fixed amount for following orders. Employees will be less concerned about the tasks they are ordered to perform than they would be under a price system because they will not bear the full monetary consequences of poor decisions.[4] Consequently, it will be possible for the boss to assign tasks by fiat.

Markets and firms in the presence of positive organizing costs

In the real world, both the price system and hierarchy will experience costs in informing parties, curbing bargaining, and enforcing sharing rules. However, because these two methods are fundamentally different, they will experience different levels of organizing costs for a given transaction. Let us first consider the costs incurred by a price system in informing parties, before turning to those involved in enforcing the terms of transactions.

Information

The price system communicates information to all interacting parties. That information must by necessity be condensed, for otherwise the information needs of the system would be overwhelming. In a society consisting of n independent parties, organizing activities through prices requires $1/2(n^2-n)$ two-way communication channels, as every individual must communicate with all others. By contrast, hierarchy only requires n two-way channels, since all messages are channeled through a central party (Williamson 1970: 20). Whenever price information has to be supplemented by complex descriptions, transferring information to all parties rises dramatically with an increase in n. As Arrow (1974) pointed out, prices are concentrated information: one number expresses all that is needed for parties to make the appropriate production and consumption decisions. But this presupposes that the characteristics of the goods are known to all. Knowing that grade A butter sells for $4 a pound or that virgin aluminium grade P1020A costs 65 cents a pound is useful to guide behavior; knowing that cars are 50 cents a pound or that Old Master paintings are $5 per square inch is of little use because the latter two goods have an infinite variety of attributes. With bounded rationality, individuals will not have a perfect knowledge of the characteristics of goods transacted. Prices will no longer perfectly describe all of their relevant dimensions. In some cases, they may provide "wrong" signals that will mislead economic individuals, leading them to over-consume (under-produce) underpriced goods and under-consume (over-produce) overpriced ones.

When prices fail to act as efficient guides to behavior, a centralized system may efficiently replace a decentralized one. A decentralized system requires individuals to gather all the information they need. If the compact information provided by prices needs to be supplemented by extensive additional information, then centralizing information is efficient. It may be desirable for each individual to specialize in collecting a limited type of information and to transfer the information to a central party, the "boss." The boss can then synthesize that information, make decisions, and send directives for execution. This is the essence of the hierarchical solution.

The benefits of hierarchy are especially noticeable in rapidly changing environments. Since information and decision making are concentrated in the boss, a single person can make decisions. Decisions can be imposed on employees by fiat, because their income does not depend on what they are asked to do. The price system, on the other hand, rewards parties in proportion to their output. When the price system works perfectly, prices are exogenous and bargaining is impossible. In conditions of imperfect competition, however, prices are no longer exogenous, and parties to the exchange will resist changes detrimental to their interest unless they are fully compensated. Hence, when the environment is changing rapidly, a real-world price system is at a disadvantage relative to a hierarchical system. The time spent communicating the information to all concerned and resolving disputes may be such as to make adjustment to new conditions impossible: by the time an agreement is reached, further adjustment may be needed. By contrast, hierarchy allows the boss to respecify the system quickly through fiat (Williamson 1975).

There are, however, two major problems with the hierarchical solution. First, information collection and decision making are dissociated. In a price system individuals can be expected to use the idiosyncratic information they have acquired in the course of their activities to increase their income (Hayek 1945: 521). Under hierarchy employees have less incentive to become informed and to transmit to the boss information on how to maximize the employer's income because they will not be directly rewarded for doing so.[5] Even if employees faithfully transmit everything they observe, information can be lost as it moves across hierarchical levels. The information loss may be voluntary or involuntary. Involuntary distortion results from encoding/decoding gaps (Williamson 1970), and occurs because employees can be expected to distort information in ways that benefit themselves. With a constant span of control, an increase in the size of the firm will result in more hierarchical levels, and the larger that number, the higher the information losses incurred by hierarchy.

Enforcement

Prices provide appropriate signals to guide behavior if they reflect the social value of goods and services. In reality, bounded rationality makes it costly to measure outputs. It will not pay for market traders to measure outputs perfectly because better measurement incurs increasing costs. Traders will invest in measurement up to the point where its marginal cost is equal to its marginal benefit. Consequently market participants will be able to alter the terms of trade to their advantage without a corresponding loss of revenues.

Consider a farmer who contracts for a fixed price to have fertilizer spread on a field. One important dimension of performance is the uniformity of application. If the fertilizer has not been uniformly applied, the crop in some parts of the field might suffer burns while in others it might fail to grow. Since an even application of fertilizer takes more time and effort than an uneven one, a subcontractor paid a fixed amount for the job will be incited, if detection is costly, to apply fertilizer in a quick, and therefore uneven, way (Roumasset and Uy 1980). To protect against this eventuality the farmer could carefully measure performance, by sampling parts of the field after application and calculating the weight of fertilizer per square yard. This, however, is likely to be very costly since the fertilizer might dissolve quickly into the ground.[6] In this case, the cost of using the price system is the cost of measuring performance plus the cost of cheating (the cost to the farmer of a reduced crop because of uneven application). More generally, high measurement costs will make it possible for individuals to cheat: that is, they will supply too little of what is desired and too much of what is not. Hence the costs of a price system (from the viewpoint of the reward function) will be the cost of measuring output plus the cost of cheating that will result from imperfect measurement. We call these "cheating" costs.

Where the cost of measuring output and the consequences of doing it imperfectly are substantial, as in the case above, it may be cheaper for both parties to use a different method of organization: hierarchy. Rather than expend resources to measure output in all of its dimensions, it may be desirable to change the behavior of individuals by reducing their incentives to cheat, by breaking the connection between output and rewards. In our case, the farmer can hire the subcontractor who applies fertilizer and promise him or her a fixed sum of money per unit of time, on condition that he or she follows orders. Since the salary no longer depends on output per unit of time, the farm hand has less incentive to spread fertilizer unevenly.

One unavoidable consequence of this decoupling of output and reward is that, although it reduces cheating, it also reduces incentives to work. Self-employed individuals who slack or decide to take the day off pay the full cost of their behavior in the form of reduced income. Since their rewards are no longer tied to performance, employees will have incentives to shirk: that is, to break the promises they made to obey managerial directives. How much they shirk depends on the extent to which the employees' objectives differ from those of the boss. If effort is painful, employees have incentives to reduce the effort they devote to their tasks. Note that shirking does not necessarily mean loafing: it can involve doing the work too well. Bosses therefore have to expend resources to direct and monitor behavior. In our example, the farm hand has fewer incentives to exercise effort to get the job done as quickly as possible if he or she is paid on a time basis than if he or she is paid by the task. Because of diminishing returns to monitoring, it is not profitable for the farmer to eliminate shirking completely, and some residual amount remains. As a result, "shirking costs" are the sum of the costs of monitoring behavior and of those of bearing the residual amount of shirking.

From method of organization to economic institutions

The argument so far is that prices and hierarchy are two different methods of organizing economic activities. Their solutions to the problem of information, bargaining, and enforcement are radically opposed. Hierarchy centralizes information; the price system decentralizes it. A decentralized information structure avoids the losses caused by information transfer, but it experiences the problem of suboptimization if prices do not provide the "right" information. Hierarchy's solution is to centralize information, but this reduces the incentives individuals have to collect information and can also lead to information loss.

The price system's solution to the problem of rewarding useful behavior differs substantially from hierarchy's. The price system motivates individuals to maximize output, but the system's efficiency is limited by the cost of measuring output in all of its dimensions: individuals can be expected to cheat, under-producing those dimensions of output that use positively priced inputs. Hierarchy solves the problem of cheating by decoupling reward from (market-measured) output, but this solution requires control of behavior. Since such control is costly, it generally will not pay to monitor perfectly, and employees will relax their effort (they will shirk).

Since the price system and hierarchy provide different methods of organizing economic activities, they tend to result in different levels of organizing costs for a given transaction. In our previous example, measuring the quality of the output (the evenness of fertilizer application) costs more than specifying and monitoring behavior (how the fertilizer should be and is applied). In that case, the farmer will hire an employee to spread the fertilizer rather than use the market to contract for that task. Inversely, the price system will be used when output is relatively easy to measure, but behavior is difficult to direct and monitor. Such would be the case for home workers, who toil in dispersed locations and are therefore costly to supervise.

Note that this example shows that the choice between using the price system (contracting to have fertilizer applied) or hierarchy (hiring someone to do it) is not only based on costs, and that it is not necessary to complement this "transaction cost-based" analysis with one based on "transactional value," as argued by Zajac and Olsen (1993). It should be clear that the preceding analysis incorporates both value and costs. Choosing the wrong method of organization (in this case using contractors to spread fertilizer) leads to lower revenues (lower transactional value) because some of the crop will be burned and some will be insufficiently fertilized. This negative effect can be controlled through more complex (and hence more costly) contracting, resulting in more even spreading of fertilizer by the contractor, and hence in a better crop (higher revenues), but the cost of drafting and negotiating this more complex contract will have to be deducted from the higher revenues. Alternatively, hiring employees to spread the fertilizer might, given incentives to shirk, end up costing more than hiring a contractor, but the more even application of the fertilizer will result in a better crop (higher value). The method that will be chosen is the one for which revenues net of costs are the highest. Hence hiring employees may be chosen in spite of higher costs if the additional revenues that result from this method of organization are more than enough to cover these costs. In other words, the criterion that parties in our model use to organize their interdependence is the maximization of rents (the difference between revenues and the costs that result from the use of a particular method of organization), not the narrow minimization of contracting costs, as has been argued by some (for example, Madhok 1996).

So far we have described two methods of organization: the price system and hierarchy. What is the relationship between these two methods of organization and the economic institutions of firms and markets? A simplistic answer is that firms are institutions that use hierarchy, while markets use price signals. In fact, both firms and markets use a mix of both methods of organization, for reasons shown below. However, the example of fertilizer application shows that the essence of firms is the employment relationship (that is, the imposition of behavior constraints). It is by imposing behavior constraints (and simultaneously relaxing price constraints) that the cost of uneven application of fertilizer is reduced. Hence the use of hierarchy (behavior constraints) is the distinguishing mark of firms. The use of pure employment contracts, in which the employee is rewarded entirely in relation to his or her obedience to managerial directives, is widespread in firms.

The level of shirking may grow in some activities more than proportionally as behavior constraints replace price constraints, so the firm may then introduce price constraints alongside behavior constraints within the employment relationship. Consider the sales function. Commercial success requires coordination between the manufacturer and the sales force. There are two main ways to achieve this coordination: the firm can either use the price system (contract with sales representatives to be paid on the value of sales made) or use hierarchy (hire employees who are paid on a time basis). The choice between those two options depends on the comparison of two types of cost: sales representatives will maximize effort to "move the goods," but may also fail to supply outputs that manufacturers find costly to measure, such as customer service (Anderson and Oliver 1987). When the latter is important, firms rely on employees to do the selling. Because their salary is now independent of performance, these employees will probably be less energetic in making calls. If the cost of curbing shirking is very high, paying employees in part through commissions can increase their incentives to make sales calls and may provide a cheaper method of control than hiring additional supervisors to monitor their behavior. Hence a mix of both modes of organization may be, in some instances, the least costly way of organizing the sales function. Firms generally use a mix of price and behavior constraints that varies with the nature of the tasks involved. What defines the firm is a relatively heavy emphasis on behavior constraints; markets, on the other hand, are characterized by the predominant use of price constraints.

CONTROL PROCESSES WITHIN FIRMS

This section describes in more detail the control processes used in firms. The discussion focuses on the relationship between the employer and the employee, first at the task level, then at that of the subsidiary.

Control of employees

In the hierarchical method of organization, the boss tells employees what to do and rewards them in relation to their obedience to orders. Since employees are paid a fixed amount, the information they collect in the course of their work no longer benefits them directly. Because of this reward structure, employees can be expected to be less motivated than self-employed individuals to gather and to make use of relevant information. Hence in order to be able to voice or draft clear directives to guide their behavior, the boss needs to know what the employees must do to generate the desired output. In other words, bosses must know the employees' production functions. In some cases bosses can acquire this knowledge if they spend the necessary resources. In others, directives for the effective execution of tasks cannot be drafted in advance, for efficient production requires situation-specific decisions. In Ouchi's (1979) terminology, tasks are not "programmable."

The extent to which the boss knows (or can know) the employees' production functions, together with information on the relative level of shirking costs versus cheating costs, can be used to categorize the various types of control mechanisms used in firms. Table 8.1, adapted from Ouchi (1979), summarizes the argument. Firms can use three types of control, depending on the degree to which management has an information advantage over employees, and on the level of shirking costs relative to cheating costs.

Cells 1 and 2 correspond to behavior control. As argued above, this method of control is useful when all dimensions of performance cannot be easily specified ex ante and measured ex post, so that rewards based on outputs would generate high cheating costs. It may then be cheaper to control behavior. There are, however, two ways of imposing behavior control. The first one is hierarchical control (cell 1), which consists of explicitly telling

Table 8.1 Employee control modes used in firms

Cheating costs/ shirking costs	Management knowledge of the worker's production function	
	Higher than workers	Lower than workers
High cheating, low shirking	1. hierarchy	2. selection and/or socialization
Low cheating, high shirking	4. no interaction within the firm	3. price control (e.g. piece work)

Source: Adapted from Ouchi (1979)

employees what to do, and of observing their behavior to ascertain that they are following orders. This control can be exerted personally by the boss, or impersonally through bureaucratic rules and regulations: what Child (1973) has called a "centralizing" and a "bureaucratic" strategy of control. In a fundamental sense, those two modes of control are similar: they aim at specifying behavior (how employees must act). Hierarchical control will be used when two conditions are met: the employer knows well the employee's production function, and the cost of shirking is less than that of cheating. For example, machine-paced processes, such as assembly lines, make monitoring easier because the productivity of employees is indicated by their behavior. Using piece rates on assembly lines would be dysfunctional because workers would fail to cooperate and would abuse the machinery. Additionally, assembly-line processes make it difficult to separate the productivity of one employee from that of the others. Firms tend therefore to use hierarchical control for such processes.[7] The costs of using hierarchical control are likely to rise dramatically with geographical dispersion (which raises monitoring costs) and with idiosyncratic tasks, because it is impossible to specify how to perform these tasks in advance.

In some cases, workers have an information advantage over management, and output is difficult to measure and price in all of its dimensions (cell 2, a situation characteristic of "professional" work). Efficiency requires that employees be left free to make production decisions, yet output is difficult to measure. The solution then consists of aligning the objectives of the employee and those of the employer. This can be accomplished by (1) selecting employees who have the same goals as management, or (2) investing resources in persuading employees who may have different goals to internalize the employer's values so that they act without external constraint in the employer's best interest (Ouchi 1981a: 414–415).[8] These two strategies are often combined.

The first of these two strategies makes direction and monitoring unnecessary, since employees will perform as required out of their own self-interest. An example is to hire student athletes to do maintenance work; they would exercise anyway, but now they are paid for it (Pratt and Zeckhauser 1985). Firms can also attempt to persuade employees with divergent goals, through indoctrination and socialization, that "what they want to do is the same as what they have to do" (Kanter 1972: 1; see also Van Maanen 1975). If the firm is successful, employees will voluntarily choose not to shirk. This method, which Baliga and Jaeger (1984) call "cultural control," economizes on information and monitoring costs. Socialized employees need not be monitored, and they do not have to be given specific answers to specific problems; they only need to be inculcated with the goals or philosophies of the organization. They can deduce from these the rule appropriate for any situation (Ouchi 1981a: 421). Because employees are given a general rule to guide their behavior, they have no need to seek orders from their superiors in unexpected circumstances. Hence the system is much more flexible than hierarchical control. Because employees now espouse management's goals, few resources need be invested to measure performance or to monitor behavior. Rewards can be tied to the dedication of the individual to the group and to his or her length of service, facilitating further socialization.

Worker selection and indoctrination involve very substantial up-front costs. Compared to hierarchical or price control, more resources must be devoted to selection, to training, to communication and to social interactions so as to impart the philosophy of the firm to the new recruits. Socialization strategies can be cheaper to implement if employees are recruited from a culturally homogeneous society. Investment in selection and socialization will pay off only if the employee remains with the firm for an extended period. This, and socialization in general, tend to create an inbred group of employees, intolerant of differences, and unreceptive to outside ideas, increasing the risk of "groupthink" (Janis 1972). Creative types do not do well in organizations with strong socialization strategies, as shown, for example, by the difficulties experienced by IBM in developing in-house software (Depke 1989).

In both cells 1 and 2, the employer exercises behavior control (explicitly in the case of hierarchical control, implicitly through internalization in the case of socialization). The third type of control (cell 3) is output-based in the sense that the reward of the employees directly relates to their individual output, but not to the way they have achieved it. We call this price control. This mode of control is efficient when the employee's knowledge of his or her production function is better than that of the boss, and when all dimensions of employee performance are easily measurable. Directing the behavior of the employees and rewarding them for following orders, would be inefficient in that case, since the employees know better than the boss how to achieve management's goals. The employees will be more productive if left free to choose the best course of action and if their shirking is curbed by reintroducing a market mechanism linking rewards to outputs. This type of control takes the form of bonuses, piecework and commissions.

The benefit of using price controls within firms is that, given positive monitoring costs, they elicit greater effort.[9] They also harness the capabilities and the knowledge of the employees, and make control possible without the need for management to know the production function and to monitor employees closely. Output-based rewards thus save on managerial capabilities. Unfortunately, unless all dimensions of performance are measured and priced (or constrained), maximization of effort may also lead to maximization of unwanted side-effects:[10] for example, paying piece rates for picking crabs (for extracting their meat) will incite workers to extract only the easy-to-remove back meat and to leave claw meat in the shells. This tendency is easily checked by weighing the picked shells and deducting from the picker's earnings a penalty proportional to the weight of the shells. This discourages pickers from leaving too much meat in shells. In this case, the ability to control suboptimal behavior makes it possible to use piece rates. On the other hand, application of fertilizers on fields is done on a time-wage basis under hierarchical control because it is difficult to determine whether or not the chemicals have been applied uniformly, and because the consequences of uneven concentration can be substantial (Roumasset and Uy 1980).

Finally, it should be noted that the relative cost of using each form of control varies across transactions within a given firm, and not just across firms, as the characteristics of tasks change. Thus employees in some departments of a store may be paid through commissions (price control) while others receive a straight salary (hierarchy).

Control of subsidiaries

The analysis just presented can explain not only the pattern of control over individuals, but also control at the level of the firm's subsidiaries (Table 8.2). If the performance of the subsidiary is difficult to gauge, and headquarters (HQ) knows better than the subsidiary what has to be done, then hierarchical control will be implemented (cell 1). Decisions will be made by HQ and the subsidiary will be told what to do. If HQ goals can be internalized by the management of the subsidiary, then control can be achieved through socialization (cell 2). Bartlett and Ghoshal (1989:163–164) describe how Unilever, like many Japanese MNCs, uses socialization as its main control mechanism.

As an alternative, control can be achieved through prices by setting up the subsidiary as an independent profit center (cell 3). By choosing appropriate internal transfer prices, the firm can elicit the same behavior as it would through direct behavior control. If output is measurable, and HQ has less knowledge than the subsidiary manager about how to achieve the desired outcome, then leaving subsidiary managers free to maximize the subsidiary's profits (and rewarding them as a function of those profits) will achieve better results than specifically directing their behavior from HQ. Then local managers will be induced to make use of their specialized knowledge for the benefit of their subsidiary, and thus for that of the firm. In addition to control advantages, establishing the affiliate as a profit center also has informational advantages over hierarchical control, since it relieves HQ of having to learn how to operate locally and economizes on the amount of information that has to be sent to and received from affiliates. Transfer prices take the place of frequent complex directives, and the profits achieved by the subsidiary serve as the single, yet all-encompassing, measure of performance and the basis of the manager's rewards.

The practical problems and limitations involved in setting up price controls provide a good illustration of their costs and benefits, and show why their use in firms is necessarily limited. To maximize their personal income, managers will maximize the profits made by their units. In the process, they will maximize the

Table 8.2 Subunit control modes used in firms

Cheating costs/ shirking costs	Headquarters' knowledge of the unit production function	
	Higher than local management	**Lower than local management**
High cheating, Low shirking	1. hierarchy "centralization"	2. selection and/or socialization
Low cheating, High shirking	4. no interaction within the firm	3. profit centers

use of underpriced inputs or the generation of underpriced outputs (as was discussed above). For example, if the impact of the subsidiary's reputation on that of the firm cannot be quantified by HQ and if the rewards of subsidiary managers depend only on the annual profits made by the unit, then they can be expected to engage in activities that maximize yearly profits even if those activities damage the firm's reputation. To make a price system an efficient method of control, all inputs and outputs used and produced by the profit center (including intangibles such as reputation and experience) would have to be correctly priced to reflect their cost and benefit to the firm as a whole.

Our model has shown that perfect pricing is an impossible task. If all interactions between the firm's subsidiaries could be priced, there would be no benefits to intra-firm organization. Activities are internalized within firms because market prices fail to organize at least one of the interdependencies. In consequence, not all intra-firm interdependencies can be priced correctly. Incorrect pricing of inputs and outputs will induce managers to suboptimize. Suboptimization is equivalent to "cheating" as defined above; it means that employees will take advantage of the imperfection of the system used to measure their output. To reduce unwanted side-effects and to encourage the production of desirable ones, HQ will supplement transfer prices with hierarchical constraints designed to organize unpriceable interdependencies. A subsidiary manager may be told to maximize profits, but he or she will have to follow specific rules concerning ethical behavior, worker safety, pollution control, employee turnover, and so on. However, as more and more hierarchical constraints are introduced, the advantages of profit centers will decline. HQ will have to expend costly resources to send more directives to the subsidiary and to collect more information on compliance. Subsidiary managers will see their autonomy decline, decreasing their incentive to work hard and show initiative. They will shirk more. Both the informational simplicity and the motivating virtues of profit centers will be lost.

We would expect the relationships between HQ and subsidiaries to be a mix of the three control techniques described above, and to vary with headquarters' knowledge of the subunit's environment and the degree to which interdependences between the parent and the subsidiary can be measured and constrained through prices. Non-priceable interdependencies organized through price controls will lead to cheating (suboptimization). On the other hand, imposing hierarchical constraints lowers the incentives that subsidiary managers have to show initiative. The optimum control system should balance those two sources of cost, shirking and cheating (suboptimization).

SOME OBSERVATIONS ON THE MODEL

How does the model developed above compare with agency theory and with organization theory approaches to the problem? In contrast with some agency models (Eisenhardt 1985), the model presented here makes no assumptions about differences in risk aversion between the employer and the employee, and consequently does not address the risk-bearing consequences of control strategies. The model also diverges from agency theory in specifying the cost of control as the sum of the resources spent to impose a particular method of control plus the cost of the unwanted side-effects that result from using this method.

In contrast to standard organization theory (OT), which emphasizes the information aspects of control (Galbraith 1973; Egelhoff 1988a), the model emphasizes its reward aspects. This difference in emphasis is particularly important in the case of "price control," an important component of our model that is downplayed in the OT literature.[11] Martinez and Jarillo's (1989) review of the OT literature on control lists the eight most common mechanisms of intra-firm coordination identified by OT researchers. Price control, as defined here, is not cited.

The neglect of price control is surprising, given its extensive use in firms. About one-quarter of all workers in US manufacturing industries in the mid-1970s (and 23 percent of all farm labor in 1959) worked under some type of price controls (Seiler 1984). Even at upper management levels, price controls in the form of bonuses made up 31 percent of the total compensation received by executive vice-presidents in 1986 (Reibstein 1987). Many firms also see in price controls the remedy for "bureaucratic failures": that is, shirking. The recent trend has been towards increased use of price controls in the form of intrapreneurship schemes and of a generalized commission schemes in department stores (Dunkin 1989).

Although Martinez and Jarillo do not mention price control, they do list output control, which they define as being based on the evaluation of files, records, and reports submitted to corporate management, and which they equate to "bureaucratic control" (Child 1973). Output control may resemble price control, although there are important but subtle differences between the two. Egelhoff (1988b), in a very thorough study of control mechanisms in MNCs, determined the extent of output control by measuring the frequency with which a number of performance measures (such as sales to specific accounts or inventory levels) had to be sent to HQ. This concept differs significantly from price controls. Although price controls are a form of output controls, since a price system rewards output, not all output controls are price controls. Price controls establish a clear link between rewards and output, insuring that the agents will not shirk and will use their privileged knowledge to the employer's advantage. They are informationally economical because they save the employer from having to collect extensive information on the employee's production function.

Output controls can differ from price controls for two reasons. First, some organizations collect output measures that have no direct influence on rewards, and hence on employee motivation. Second, the term "output control" is sometimes applied to intermediate outputs. Observing the levels of many intermediate outputs approximates to monitoring behavior. For example, HQ may ask a subsidiary manager to report the level of salaries for its sales department, and may intervene if the manager fails to cut the overall wage bill by 10 percent by the time of the next report. This is tantamount to telling him outright to cut the wage bill by 10 percent (the straight behavior control method). Thus the way organization theorists have defined output controls leads some to consider behavior control and output control as complements, while in our model (and in agency models) they are substitutes (Eisenhardt 1985).[12]

One important limitation of the model developed in this chapter is the lack of a time dimension. The model is implicitly a one-period model. No consideration is given to experience rating in firms and in markets. For example, repeated observation of the behavior of employees increases the employer's ability to control shirking. Similarly, market traders who expect continuation of the relationship may refrain from cheating so as not to jeopardize future dealings.

APPLICATION TO MULTINATIONAL CORPORATIONS

The three control techniques of hierarchy, socialization, and price control are used in varying proportions by MNCs to control their foreign subsidiaries. Hierarchical control over subsidiaries is exercised through visits from HQ personnel to the subsidiary and/or from subsidiary managers to HQ, written and oral directives sent to the subsidiary, and requests for information. When communication costs are high, socialization strategies may be the only way to control far-flung subsidiaries. In earlier days, family members were sent abroad with full authority to manage the foreign arm of the business. Later, these family members were replaced by a small corps of trusted home-country managers (such as the 'Dutch Mafia' of Philips), who ran the

164

subsidiaries. Increasingly, socialization is being used to develop a corps of both home-country and foreign country nationals (Edstrom and Galbraith 1979). Bartlett and Ghoshal (1989, Chapter 10) document the efforts of some MNCs to create such a cadre through extensive training and job rotation. Lastly, MNCs often set up subsidiaries as profit centers and reward their managers on the basis of the profits of their subsidiaries.

Cost and mix of methods of control for foreign subsidiaries

Extending our model to the MNC raises two main questions. First, how does doing business across national boundaries affect the level of organizing costs? Second, how does it affect the mix of control mechanisms used? Each of the three control modes will be more costly to implement in an international than in a domestic setting. Consequently, the lowest-cost mix of modes used to control foreign affiliates will be more costly than those used for domestic subunits.

Hierarchical control will be more expensive to implement internationally than domestically because geographical distance makes behavior more difficult to observe. Cultural differences make communication more costly, because the need to be explicit and the chances of distortion are greater. Furthermore, foreign environments are likely to be substantially different from their domestic counterpart, so that employees posted to foreign countries will have a substantial information advantage over HQ, making centralized direction less efficient. In fact, up until recently, the length of time it took to refer decisions to HQ and receive an answer made centralization an extremely costly proposition, and led MNCs to rely heavily on "on the spot" decisions.[13]

Operating internationally also increases the cost of socialization. Hofstede (1980a) has documented the presence of significant national differences in beliefs, behaviors, and attitudes concerning work that must be bridged when doing business abroad. The cross-cultural interface can be set at various levels. If locally hired managers run the foreign subsidiary, the cultural barrier lies between HQ and subsidiary managers. The cultural homogeneity of the management corps can be kept intact by sending expatriates to run the foreign subsidiary. This shifts the cross-cultural interface from the parent–subsidiary level to within the subsidiary. Using expatriate managers makes it possible to socialize the management corps, but using expatriates tends to damage relationships with local suppliers, customers, and host-country governments. Local employees may resent expatriates because they receive higher pay and fill positions to which locals could otherwise be promoted. Running the subsidiary with local managers, on the other hand, will automatically raise the costs of socialization by diluting the homogeneity of the employee pool. Imposing explicit or implicit behavior constraints thus costs more internationally than domestically.

The costs of using price constraints would seem to be less affected by distance. As argued earlier, prices are very condensed signals. The cost of communicating prices is not much greater across countries than within a country. Ouchi's finding (1978), that quantitative measures of output are less subject to distortion than qualitative measures of behavior when transmitted across hierarchical levels, supports this view.

If it is true that internationalization increases the cost of imposing behavior constraints more than that of setting price constraints, then interactions that would be organized within firms in a domestic context will be handled through the market (or not at all) when they involve agents located in more than one country. Although this proposition has not been tested empirically, there is some evidence that the use of market processes to exploit knowledge is much more common internationally than domestically. In their study of licensing contracts, Caves, Crookell, and Killing (1982) noted that licensing was much more frequent internationally than domestically.

Our assumptions about control costs also imply that the mix of techniques used to control foreign subsidiaries should be biased towards greater use of price control than that used for domestic subsidiaries. One testable implication is that a greater proportion of foreign subunits than domestic subunits should be run as profit centers. This, too, is an area in need of empirical verification.

Centralization and interdependencies

The explicit consideration of the full menu of methods of control used in firms could help explain some of the conflicting results found in the study of organization processes in MNCs. Consider first centralization and its determinants. Centralization is one of the fundamental dimensions of the design of large organizations. It refers to the extent to which HQ makes decisions (we have called this hierarchical control). Organization theorists have argued that interdependency among the subunits of the organization constitutes an important determinant of centralization (Van de Ven, Delbecq, and Koenig 1976; Tushman and Nadler 1978). According to Egelhoff, interdependencies increase the need for information processing. Centralizing decisions at HQ is one way to tackle this increased information load, as "centralization provides coordination and integration across the interdependency" (Egelhoff 1988a: 131); hence the extent of centralization in MNCs should be correlated with the degree of interdependence between the subsidiary and the rest of the organization.

Egelhoff tests this hypothesis by calculating the degree of centralization of decisions in marketing, manufacturing, and finance, and correlating centralization with nine measures of interdependency. As shown in Table 8.3, the results are mixed. Of the potential 27 correlations between the degree of centralization and the extent of interdependencies, only six are significant at 0.05 (one-tailed test) and have the right sign (two are significant, but are incorrectly signed).

Table 8.3 Correlations between centralization scales and strategic and environmental conditions

Measures of interdependency	Centralization in		
	marketing	manufacturing	finance
Marketing information dependence	.21*	.24*	.10
New manufacturing information dependency	.01	.14	−.19
Day to day manufacturing information dependency	.11	.15	−.06
New product design dependency	−.10	.16	−.25**
Product design change dependency	.10	.27**	0.00
Intracompany purchases by subsidiary	.08	.14	−.24*
Intracompany sales by subsidiary	.27**	−.01	.24*
Sales dependence	.11	.03	.19*
Size of subsidiary (sub size/parent size)	.19	−.19	0.00

* $p < 0.05$ (one-tailed test)
** $p < 0.01$

Source: Egelhoff, 1988a, Table 7.2

The theory proposed in this chapter suggests some explanations for these results. Egelhoff argues that efficiency requires that all types of interdependencies be organized through centralization of decision making at HQ. The model we have sketched suggests, however, that not all interdependencies require coordination through hierarchical control. Exercising behavior control from HQ requires collecting a tremendous amount of information on local conditions, and on the extent to which managers of foreign subsidiaries follow orders. If some interdependencies can be mediated through prices, HQ will economize on the need to gather information and to monitor behavior. HQ needs only to specify appropriate prices to govern inter-firm interdependencies, and let the subsidiary operate as a profit center. Centralization will be low even though controls may remain high. Only interdependencies that HQ cannot easily price will be organized through direct behavior control. For example, HQ is unlikely to make operating decisions for the subsidiary, such as how to price its products, unless it purchases these products from the affiliate (creating interdependencies) and there are no existing market prices to guide the transfers (that is, the interdependencies are not priceable). Dependencies that

167

are priceable include intra-company transfers of commodity materials and of standard technical knowledge. On the other hand, a subsidiary's use of a parent's trademark or of its guarantee in borrowing funds is difficult to price; hence the parent will find it desirable to establish procedures to be followed by the subsidiary in order to maintain the quality associated with that trademark, and to specify the uses to which borrowed funds must be committed. That is, HQ will impose behavior constraints on the subsidiary manager.

Another factor weakens the link between centralization and interdependencies. As argued above, behavior control can be explicit (hierarchical control) or implicit (socialization). An MNC faced with interdependencies that cannot be organized by prices need not resort to hierarchical control (centralization): it can instead socialize subsidiary managers so that their decisions align with those that would be made by HQ. Hence the connection between interdependencies and centralization is not as direct as hypothesized by Egelhoff. Price control and socialization can act as substitutes to centralization. That Egelhoff found few correlations between centralization and measures of interdependency may reflect reliance by the MNCs he studied on these methods of non-hierarchical control.[14]

Autonomy of affiliates

Our theory of MNC control also throws light on the concept of autonomy of foreign affiliates. Researchers typically measure autonomy as the locus of decision making: if HQ makes the decisions, the subsidiary is said to have little autonomy (Hedlund 1981; Welge 1987). The concept is clear, but its interpretation is more ambiguous. Decisions made by a perfectly socialized manager may be indistinguishable from those made at HQ. This will also be true for those made by an autonomous manager responding to a correctly specified system of transfer prices. Autonomy measures the relative use of hierarchical control (Table 8.2, cell 1) as opposed to socialization (cell 2) and price control (cell 3), but it does not necessarily reflect the subunit manager's degree of responsiveness to local conditions and to the needs of local stakeholders.

Is decentralization desirable?

The explicit consideration of price controls in firms also suggests new ways of looking at modern management methods. Consider the following parallel between profit centers and piece-work schemes. Both have the same goal: to motivate the employee to apply effort and initiative when output is relatively easy to measure and the employee has an information advantage over management. Yet although decentralizing management to subsidiaries and rewarding their managers on the basis of subsidiary profits (setting up a multidivisional structure) has generally been considered a major advance in management (Chandler 1962; Williamson 1975, 1985), the piece-rate system has been seen in a very different light. Piece-rate schemes have been said to "absolve managers of the responsibility and costs of exploring, designing and supervising craft labor processes, which are typically complex and arcane" (Brown and Philips 1986). This was certainly the point of view of Taylor and his Scientific Management schemes aimed at replacing price controls by behavior controls. This required management to invest in knowing the worker's production function (through time and motion studies), but the payoff was a significant increase in productivity (Edwards 1979). This suggests that decentralization, especially if it consists in having locals run the MNCs' foreign subsidiaries, may be a way to avoid learning how to operate in foreign countries: a way to avoid management, in fact. If so, the recent decline in the use of expatriates by US MNCs, a decline which has been attributed to the inability of US managers and of their families to adapt to conditions abroad (Kobrin 1988), may reflect the inability or the unwillingness of American MNCs to compete in increasingly global industries.

CONCLUSION

Organizing economic activities to capture the gains from joint effort and/or from specialization constitutes the main task of all economic institutions. Firms and markets are two broad types of institutions devised to perform these tasks, and they therefore face similar problems in achieving their goals. Because in liberal societies individuals are free to choose the institution that will organize their interdependence, the use of firms to organize economic activities will hinge on their relative efficiency in relation to markets. A theory of the methods of control used in firms must therefore be able to explain why firms are more efficient than markets. It must be a general theory of organization.

This chapter develops such a theory. The theory explains both the advantages and the drawbacks of firms as ways to organize economic activities. The same factors that explain why firms are chosen over markets also account for the relative mix of mechanisms of control used in firms. Framing the study of the control processes used in firms in this broader perspective has two main advantages. First, it allows us to consider the full range of control mechanisms used in firms (including price controls, which have been curiously downplayed in organization theory). Second, it explains how and why these mechanisms are combined in firms so as to minimize organization costs. The theory helps explain some of the paradoxical results found by researchers studying control processes in MNCs and advances a number of testable propositions.

POSTSCRIPT
By D. Eleanor Westney

Jean-François Hennart has continued to build the transaction-cost theory-based analysis of the MNC, and interested readers can find a more recent exposition of his approach in his chapter on "Theories of the multinational enterprise" in the *Oxford Handbook of International Business* (Rugman and Brewer 2001).

Notes

1 An earlier version of this paper was presented at the workshop on Organizational Theory and the Multinational Corporation at INSEAD on September 1–2 1989. I thank Yves Doz, Gunnar Hedlund, John Kimberly, Steve Kobrin, Guido Krickx, Andy Van de Ven, Keith Weigelt, Sidney Winter, and especially Kathleen Saul for their helpful comments.

2 If one assumes some degree of competition, one can expect the most efficient mode to dominate the less efficient one, and thus the mode actually chosen to organize the transaction should match that predicted by this theory. The model is thus applicable to those cases where institutions are not sheltered from competition by collusion or government intervention. It has, therefore greater applicability in competitive industries than in government offices.

3 Note that they do it "in complete disregard of the decisions of others, or even the existence of others" (Demsetz 1988). This is because prices reflect perfectly the social consequences of each agent's decisions.

4 Since poor decisions may result in the disappearance of the firm, employees will bear some of the consequences if they have firm-specific skills and if the costs of moving to another firm are high.

5 Indeed, in some firms they may be punished for bearing bad news.

6 To simplify, I am abstracting here from reputation effects. With bounded rationality, the probability of losing reputation due to dishonest behavior will never be 1, and can in fact be remarkably low. In some cases, however, reputation effects may be high enough to discourage dishonesty.

7 For a fascinating example, see Brown and Philips (1986).

8 We are considering here strategies of control within the firm. An alternative strategy, of course, is to subcontract the activity (to let it be organized through the price system).

9 Clark (1984) quotes the results of a number of studies comparing the hourly rates of pieceworkers with time workers in a number of occupations. Pieceworkers earned between 13 and 15 percent more than time workers. This cannot be due to self-selection, since firms using time rates have the possibility of firing the least efficient workers and of keeping the most efficient.

10 A typical example of this is the recent case of a tax employee who received bonuses linked to the percentage of taxpayers' queries answered. He maximized the bonus by systematically throwing out any query left unanswered by evaluation time. In terms of our model, the externalities generated by failing to constrain all aspects of behavior were probably greater than the reduction in shirking due to the use of market processes.

11 An exception is the work of Ouchi (1979, 1981a). Ouchi pointed out that firms could monitor the performance of employees on the basis of either behavior or output. His explanation of the choice between these modes differs, however, from

the one here. For him, "a bureaucratic form of organization succeeds because it replaces complete forms of contracting with a single incomplete contract, which is the employment contract" (Ouchi 1981a: 416). He does not link cheating and shirking (see for example 1979: 836).

12 Eisenhardt (1985) found commission payments and straight salary to be substitute forms of compensating salesclerks.

13 In the 1890s, for example, when steamship travel from the United Kingdom to Australia took a month, the chief executive of the Australian subsidiary of the London-based Bank of Australasia ran his business with full autonomy. He was not asked to visit the London head office, nor did he receive visits from London directors (Blainey 1984).

14 Egelhoff finds a significantly positive correlation between output control and centralization, and no significant correlation between the extent to which subsidiaries are staffed with expatriates and both centralization and output control. The first set of results may be explained by the way output control is measured. The second set of findings may come from the difficulty of keeping the desired level of control constant when observing the mix of methods used to control foreign subsidiaries.

9 Information-Processing Theory and the Multinational Corporation[1]

William G. Egelhoff

The multinational corporation (MNC) is probably the most complex form of organization in widespread existence today. Operating across products and markets, nations and cultures, it faces a far more diverse array of problems and situations than even the largest domestic firm. With the increasing globalization of business, a rapidly growing level of economic activity now depends upon this form of organization. Thus, the MNC is an important entity for scholarly study both because its influence is growing and because it presents organizational problems that lie at the forefront of organization theory and challenge the capacities of existing theory.

MNC research of an organizational nature has focused on two primary topics:

1. What kinds of organizational design contribute to effective MNC performance and under what strategic and environmental conditions is one form of design preferable to another?
2. How have MNC organizational designs changed and evolved over time, and what factors cause or explain this evolution?

The principal concept associated with the first type of research has been the concept of fit (between organizational design and strategy or environment). Work has centered on how to measure fit and how to relate such fit to performance (Stopford and Wells 1972; Franko 1976; Daniels, Pitts, and Tretter 1984). Most MNC research has used some form of correlation technique to relate organizational design to a variety of strategic and environmental variables. Generally, little attention has been given to developing an abstract theoretical framework that could explain or support hypothesizing the relationships. A noteworthy exception is Herbert's (1984) proposed set of relationships between four types of strategy and a variety of organizational characteristics, based on resource flow considerations. While research studies frequently discuss why certain fits might contribute to effective MNC performance, fit in MNC research has tended to be expressed more in empirical generalizations than in theoretical terms. That is, the primary reason for anticipating certain fits in MNCs is not that any abstract theoretical framework can explain why and when they should exist but that they have been found in the past. This paper will argue that information-processing theory is an attractive candidate for extending MNC research to include such a theoretical framework.

The second type of MNC research effort, how MNC organizational designs change and evolve, has largely produced a documentation, rather than a theory, of the evolution of MNC structure over time (Pavan 1972; Stopford and Wells 1972; Dyas and Thanheiser 1976). Contingency relationships developed with cross-sectional data have not been tested longitudinally. Evolution has generally been measured only with a limited number of case studies. Existing notions about what has caused MNC structure to change and evolve over time are relatively simple and tend to lack empirical support. The basic evolution of international business form or strategy has generally been explained in economic terms (Vernon 1971; Kindleberger 1973; Stevens 1974; Hymer 1976). As evidenced in the various stage models of organizational growth (Stopford and Wells 1972; Dyas and Thanheiser 1976), it is generally presumed that organizational structure has followed the evolution of MNC strategy and environment.

This brief overview of organizational research on the multinational enterprise has identified where the frontiers of such research might lie today. Throughout the present paper, which will develop and discuss an information-processing perspective of MNCs, we will evaluate how such a perspective might support future research on these issues.

THE CONCEPTUAL FOUNDATIONS FOR AN INFORMATION-PROCESSING PERSPECTIVE OF ORGANIZATIONS

A number of theorists have sought to understand organizations by describing them as communications systems, decision-making systems, or systems that have to cope with uncertainty. Although definitions of these concepts vary, and for certain purposes the distinctions may be important, they can all be subsumed under the broader notion of information processing. Information processing in organizations is generally defined as including the gathering of data, the transformation of data into information, and the communication and storage of information in the organization (Galbraith 1973; Tushman and Nadler 1978).

Theorists interested in viewing the organization from an information-processing perspective have taken environmental uncertainty as the key contingency concept. Thompson presents the conceptual argument for the importance of uncertainty:

> We will conceive of complex organizations as open systems, hence, inde-
> terminate and faced with uncertainty, but at the same time as subject to
> criteria of rationality and hence needing determinateness and certainty. ...

> With this conception the central problem for complex organizations is one of coping with uncertainty. As a point of departure, we suggest that organizations cope with uncertainty by creating certain parts specifically to deal with it, specializing other parts in operating under conditions of certainty or near certainty.
>
> (Thompson 1967: 10, 13)

Thus he suggests that uncertainty arises from certain characteristics in the environment and the technology facing an organization, and that differences in uncertainty somehow lead to differences in the organization's design.

Galbraith (1969, 1973, 1977) added further conceptualization to Thompson's general framework, and developed a much more operational framework and model that has generally been referred to as an information-processing approach to organizational design. He rigorously defined the concept of uncertainty in terms of information processing: "Uncertainty is the difference between the amount of information required to perform the task and the amount of information already possessed by the organization" (Galbraith 1977: 36). Thus, there is a relationship between the amount of uncertainty faced by an organization and the amount of information processing that must go on in an organization. Effective organizations are those that fit their information-processing capacities (for gathering, transforming, storing, and communicating information) to the amount of uncertainty they face.

Galbraith also specified the relative information-processing capacities of different organizational design features. These features are listed below, in order of increasing information-processing capacity (Galbraith 1973: 15):

1. Rules and programs.
2. Hierarchical referral.
3. Goal setting.
4. Vertical information systems.
5. Lateral relations.

Where conditions are routine and simple, rules and programs can be used to absorb the relatively small amount of uncertainty facing the organization. For example, how foreign subsidiaries will set up their accounting systems is usually specified in a set of rules from the parent headquarters (HQ) describing the chart of accounts and various closing and reporting dates. Such rules absorb a good deal of uncertainty, and eliminate the need for other forms of parent–subsidiary information processing. When uncertainty increases, exceptions must be referred up the hierarchical authority structure for decision making. When information-processing requirements threaten to overload the management structure, goal setting and planning allow more decisions to be made at lower levels in the organization as long as they are within the plan. This relieves the information-processing load on the hierarchical structure.

When such steps are no longer adequate, various vertical information-processing systems that increase the organization's information-processing capacity can be attached to the hierarchical structure. These systems frequently include computer-based information systems and staff groups, and tend to increase the capacity for centralized information processing. When uncertainty and information-processing requirements are very great, the use of lateral relations allows more information processing to be decentralized so that the more limited capacity at higher levels of the organization is not overloaded. Lateral relations mechanisms include direct contact between individuals, liaison roles, task forces, teams, and matrix designs. Thus, Galbraith's model suggests a more operational framework for linking quite a number of organizational design features to the level of uncertainty or information-processing requirements facing an organization.

Uncertainty and information-processing concepts have served as the basis for a substantial number of empirical studies (Burns and Stalker 1961; Lawrence and Lorsch 1967; Galbraith 1970; Duncan 1973; Van de Ven, Delbecq, and Koenig 1976; Tushman 1978; Egelhoff 1982; Kmetz 1984). It will be helpful to summarize these views in what might be called "the general information-processing approach to organizational design." As shown in Figure 9.1, this general approach or model is a summary of the Galbraith (1973) and Tushman and Nadler (1978) models. It is also consistent with the conceptual approaches used in the empirical studies mentioned above.

On the one hand, the impact on an organization of its strategy and the environmental factors with which it chooses to deal can be expressed in terms of the *information-processing requirements* they create. On the other hand, the potential of the organization to cope with these requirements can be expressed in terms of the *information-processing capacities* furnished by its organizational design.

The strategic and environmental conditions include all those factors external to the organization's design that influence the information-processing requirements of the organization. These include technology,

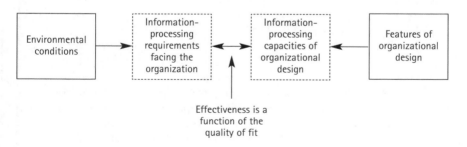

Figure 9.1 The general information-processing approach to organizational design

size, environmental change, environmental complexity, subunit inter-dependency, and goals. Similarly, the features of an organization's design (such as structure, degree of centralization, planning and control systems, interpersonal communication patterns) must also be measured or expressed in terms of the information-processing capacity they provide.

Measuring fit between such dissimilar phenomena as strategic and environmental conditions on the one hand, and features of organizational design on the other, has troubled organization theory ever since the emergence of contingency theory. Aldrich has stated that "we know the physics of air, water, and light to which flying, swimming, and seeing creatures must conform. We need much better knowledge of organizational types and appropriate environments before we can do as well in understanding organizational change" (1979: 45). Information-processing theory suggests that information processing may be the missing "physics" that can help us to understand better the critical conformities between organizational types and environments, and the impact of such conformities on organizational survival and change. The information-processing perspective calls for translating strategic and environmental conditions and organizational design features into their respective information-processing implications. Then it will be easier to measure fit between information-processing requirements and information-processing capacities, which are more comparable phenomena.

An important assumption underlying the information-processing perspective is that the quality of information-processing fit constrains organizational performance and survival. This assumption is more likely to be valid for large, complex organizations operating in difficult environments (competitive, heterogeneous, changing) than it is for small organizations operating in benign environments (low competition, homogeneous, stable). If information-processing fit is not constraining on performance, it makes more sense to organize around some other principle that might be constraining. An alternative example might be how to fit or satisfy the desires of local governments (a political perspective) or how to best motivate employees (a motivation perspective). Obviously it is desirable that the basis for evaluating organizational fit be stable over an extended period of time. It seems reasonable to assume that for large, complex organizations such as MNCs, the limits of information-processing capacity are frequently reached or exceeded by information-processing requirements, and that the difficulty in realizing information-processing fit consistently constrains performance in such organizations.

Before proceeding, it is useful to compare the proposed framework with more cognitive views of organizational information processing, which have recently become prominent. Cognitive theory views organizations as systems that learn (Fiol and Lyles 1985; Ginsberg 1990) and interpret their environments (Daft and Weick 1984). Information processing is primarily represented in terms of the cognitive abilities of organizational members (either individually or collectively) to learn, make sense out of, and make decisions for an organization, when influenced by a variety of factors such as values, beliefs, culture, and differences in power (Wood and Bandura 1989). Environmental conditions may still be the stimulus for information processing, but the emphasis is on explaining how information processing is influenced by what goes on in the heads of individuals (psychological determinants) and between individuals (social-psychological determinants).

By contrast, the proposed perspective, which has sometimes been referred to as a logistical view of organizational information processing (Huber 1982), views organizations as systems that need to balance the organization's information-processing capacities against the information-processing requirements inherent in its strategy and environment. Fit is equated with good organizational performance and survival, and misfit with poor performance and failure. Information processing is largely represented in terms of the capacities of different kinds of organizational structures and processes to transfer information within an organization, to move it across the boundaries of an organization, and to access specific kinds of knowledge and decision-making capabilities needed to transform data or information. This view focuses primarily on how information processing is influenced by organizational characteristics, independent of the individual characteristics of the organization's members.

The two perspectives should be viewed as complementary, and not contradictory, explanations of organizational information processing. The cognitive perspective largely addresses the question of how strategic decisions are made. It argues that much of the input or influence is cognitive, and that strategic decisions are not merely, or even primarily, determined by organizational and environmental considerations. The unit of analysis tends to be the strategic decision or strategic issue (Dutton and Jackson 1987). From a population ecology perspective, such strategic decisions become a source of variation and change in an organization and its position in its environment. The logistical perspective of information processing, on the other hand, does not attempt to explain the source of organizational or strategic variation or change. It tries to explain the information-processing capacities inherent in an organization's design, and generally evaluates these against requirements for information processing inherent in an organization's strategy or environment, and explains change not in terms of strategic decisions, but in terms of differential selection by competitive forces in firms' environments. Thus, the two perspectives have different arguments and a different purpose.

Information processing as an abstract intervening concept

With the exception of some of Galbraith's case studies (1970, 1977), the information-processing perspective has been used primarily in more micro-level studies, where the units of analysis are either individuals or small groups. Such studies have managed to measure directly such aspects of information processing as the frequency of oral communications between work groups (Tushman 1978), the extent to which policies and procedures, work plans, personal contact, and meetings are used to coordinate members of work teams (Van de Ven, Delbecq, and Koenig 1976), and the structure of groups during decision making (Duncan 1973). For more macro-level studies, such as those focusing on the parent HQ–foreign subsidiary relationship in MNCs, the difficulty of directly measuring such detailed information-processing phenomena between very large subunits of an organization necessitates a different approach to operationalizing the information-processing perspective.

Instead of attempting to measure information processing directly, macro-level studies must use information processing as an abstract intervening concept to aid in positing relationships between directly measured characteristics of an organization's design and its strategy and environment, both of which have identifiable information-processing implications. This approach is already reflected in the general information-processing approach to organizational design shown in Figure 9.1. The solid lines indicate that strategic and environmental conditions and organizational design features are directly measured variables, while the broken lines indicate that information-processing requirements and information-processing capacities are abstract variables that can only be derived from measured variables.

For the information-processing approach to advance, what is needed is a more precise translation of the measured contextual and design variables into the abstract information-processing concepts that are so useful for general theory building. This translation should be easier to accomplish if one first identifies the dimensions of information processing that are important to the type and level of organization being modeled, and then constructs decision rules for mapping measured contextual and design variables onto these dimensions.

Multidimensional measures of information processing

Most existing research that has sought to use an information-processing perspective to link organizational design to various strategic and environmental conditions does not rigorously specify the dimensions that are being used to measure and evaluate information-processing capacities and requirements. For example, consider the case of a bank that as a result of a growth strategy faces a sharp increase in the number of checks it must clear. Obviously such a strategy has led to increased requirements for information processing. Galbraith (1973) has indicated that increased information-processing requirements frequently need to be met by the addition of lateral information-processing systems to an organization, such as more face-to-face communications, cross-functional committees and task forces, and matrix structures. Yet it is doubtful that these information-processing mechanisms address the requirements associated with the increased load of check clearing. Instead, an expanded computer system, which Galbraith regards as a vertical information-processing system, seems better able to provide the kind of information-processing capacity needed to cope with the increased requirements for check clearing.

The bank's growth strategy may also call for the development of new financial products and services. This also increases requirements for information processing within the organization, and this time the kind of information-processing capacity provided by cross-functional teams and matrix designs seems more appropriate than that provided by an expanded computer system. Both strategies lead to increased information-processing requirements for the bank, but the required kinds of information-processing capacities differ.

There are a number of empirical studies that generally match suitable information-processing mechanisms to the different information-processing requirements, and discuss a number of reasons for the suitability of the match (for example, Galbraith's (1977) analysis of the information-processing requirements associated with Boeing's development of the 747, Van de Ven, Delbecq, and Koenig's (1976) analysis of the differing task requirements found in an unemployment agency, and Tushman's (1978) analysis of the differing information-processing requirements facing research versus development groups in an R&D laboratory). Most studies, however, do not directly address the issue of whether one, two, three, or four dimensions are needed to distinguish one information-processing requirement from another (or the capacity of one information-processing mechanism from another).

An important exception to this complaint can be found in the work of Daft and Lengel (1986) and Daft and Macintosh (1981). These studies distinguish between equivocality reduction and uncertainty reduction in information processing, and attempt to define the relative capacities of a variety of information-processing mechanisms for handling both types of information-processing requirements.

Our view is that at the macro level of large, complex organizations, other dimensions of information processing may also be useful—perhaps even more useful than uncertainty and equivocality—for measuring and evaluating information-processing requirements and capacities. At the macro level, information processing can readily vary in terms of subject and in terms of organizational purpose and perspective (Egelhoff 1982). It can also vary in terms of being relatively routine or non-routine within an organization, and in terms of the nature of the interdependency shared by organizational subunits involved in an information-processing event. Following this view, the next section will illustrate how existing organization theory and research in a number of areas provides useful guidance for constructing explicit multidimensional frameworks for measuring information processing.

DEVELOPING AN INFORMATION-PROCESSING PERSPECTIVE OF MNCs

This section will use the information-processing concepts already discussed to develop an explicit framework for analyzing and understanding organizational design in MNCs. Deciding along which dimensions to measure information processing requires some judgment, but the general criterion should be to select dimensions that best reflect the information-processing limitations of the various features of organizational design for the strategic and environmental context in which they must operate (in this case, the complex and dynamic environment faced by most large MNCs).

Structural dimensions

The first set of dimensions reflects the purpose and perspective of information processing (whether it is strategic or tactical) and the subject or content of information processing (whether it deals with product matters or company and country matters). Both require some explanation and conceptual development.

The *purpose* and *perspective* of information processing can be defined in terms of whether it is primarily strategic or primarily tactical, a conceptual distinction that comes from the strategic management literature (e.g. Ansoff 1965). Tactical information processing deals with the large volume of relatively routine day-to-day problems and situations confronting an organization. The decision-making perspective required to handle these situations tends to be relatively narrow, and it usually exists at the middle and lower levels of management. Strategic information processing attempts to deal with a much smaller volume of relatively non-routine, and usually more important, problems and situations. These problems deal with the fundamental position of the organization in its environment, and usually involve changing this position. Thus, strategic information processing has a different purpose and requires a different perspective from tactical information processing. It addresses higher level organizational goals, is broader in scope, and usually has a longer time horizon.

Research suggests that different levels of an organization's hierarchy tend to process different kinds of information and have different purposes for processing information (Landsberger 1961; Thomason 1966). Mintzberg (1979: 54) states that "the issues each level addresses are fundamentally different" and notes that strategic decisions generally involve members of the "strategic apex" or top management of an organization. Since the majority of tactical decisions do not involve members of the strategic apex, tactical and strategic information processing tend to occur at different levels of an organization.

The framework also reflects the subject or content of information processing, and distinguishes between information processing for product matters (product and process technology, market information) and information processing for company and country matters (finance, tax, legal, government relations, human resources). Subject knowledge or specialization tends to vary horizontally across organizations, and different organizational structures tend to cluster it into different subunits. Using these distinctions, four types of information processing are developed, as shown in Figure 9.2.[2] The four types are generally not substitutes for each other, since they tend to address different problem areas that require different types of knowledge and different perspectives of the organization and its goals.

This set of information-processing dimensions distinguishes the organizational locus of different kinds of knowledge and different kinds of decision-making capabilities. It helps to identify which parts of an organization need to be linked together in order to solve a given problem or address a specific decision-making situation. In other words, these dimensions are useful for measuring the structural aspects of organizations and understanding their implications for information processing.

Process dimensions

Another set of dimensions is needed, however, to measure and distinguish differences in the process by which information is gathered, processed, stored,

SUBJECT OF INFORMATION PROCESSING

	Company and country matters	Product matters
Tactical	Tactical information processing for company and country matters Example: Evaluating how and when to raise money in international money markets	Tactical information processing for product matters Example: Deciding on a routine change in the price of a product
Strategic	Strategic information processing for company and country matters Example: Deciding on the company's position *vis-a-vis* foreign government pressures for local ownership in foreign subsidiaries	Strategic information processing for product matters Example: Deciding on the long-range level of R&D support for a major product line

PURPOSE AND PERSPECTIVE OF INFORMATION PROCESSING

Figure 9.2 The structural dimensions of information processing

and exchanged. Such information processing occurs within and between the organizational subunits and levels that have already been identified. Here we will distinguish between routine and non-routine information processing, and sequential and reciprocal information processing.

There is a substantial literature supporting and describing the distinction between routine and non-routine information processing (Simon 1977; Daft and Macintosh 1981; Daft and Weick 1984). Routine information processing deals with inputs that are frequent and homogeneous. It transforms them under conditions of high certainty, and assumes that goals and means–ends relationships are well known. Information-processing mechanisms that most efficiently provide routine information-processing capacity are rules and programs (including organizational policies, standard operating procedures, and standard methods), formal single-cycle planning systems (where there is no feedback from a later stage of the process to an earlier stage), post-action control systems (where feedback occurs after the controlled activity or time period is completed) (Newman 1975), and most computer-based information systems. Non-routine information processing deals with inputs that are either unique or infrequent and heterogeneous. It transforms them under varying degrees of uncertainty about goals and/or means–ends relationships. Information-processing mechanisms that provide non-routine information-processing capacity include hierarchical referral; some vertical information systems such as planning staffs; multi-cycle, interactive planning systems (where information developed in later stages of a planning process can feed back to earlier stages); steering control systems (where feedback occurs before an event is completed) (Newman 1975); and most horizontal or lateral information systems (direct contact, task forces and teams, integrating roles, and matrix designs).

The distinction between *sequential* and *reciprocal* information processing reflects the kind of interdependency that exists between the parties to an information-processing event. This distinction is based on Thompson's (1967) typology of the three different forms of interdependence that can exist between organizational subunits (pooled, sequential, and reciprocal). Information processing is sequential to the extent that information flows in a predetermined direction across parties to an information-processing event. Information processing is reciprocal to the extent that information flows back and forth between parties in a kind of give-and-take manner that has not been previously determined.

Figure 9.3 shows the four types of information processing that emerge when the routine–non-routine and sequential–reciprocal axes are combined. A specific information-processing event is also provided to illustrate each type. In order to understand better the logic employed, we will further discuss one of these events.

Consider an event where it is necessary to decide on a routine change in the price of a subsidiary's product. Since this event occurs frequently, and

INTERDEPENDENCY BETWEEN PARTIES TO
AN INFORMATION-PROCESSING EVENT

	Sequential	Reciprocal
Routine	**Routine-sequential information processing** Example: Deciding on a routine change in the price of a product	**Routine-reciprocal information processing** Example: Deciding how to handle an expatriate manager's request for reassignment back to the parent company
Non-routine	**Non-routine-sequential information processing** Example: Exploring the possibility of selling a customer products not available in the local subsidiary, but available in another subsidiary	**Non-routine-reciprocal information processing** Example: Deciding on the long-range level of R&D support for a major product line

ROUTINISM OF AN INFORMATION-PROCESSING EVENT

Figure 9.3 The process dimensions of MNC information processing

the kinds of things that need to be considered (such as effect on volume and gross profit, and relationship to competitors' prices) are well known, information processing is routine. And since the information inputs of the various parties to this event (subsidiary marketing manager, subsidiary CEO, HQ marketing manager) can be combined serially in order to arrive at an informed and responsible decision, information processing will tend to be sequential (probably represented by a flow of memos between the concerned parties). In process terms this is simple hierarchical referral (or information processing through the chain of command), which is a commonly used routine-sequential information-processing mechanism in organizations.

In order to describe this event more fully, however, we need also to consider its structural dimensions. Recalling the previous set of information-processing dimensions described in Figure 9.2, it is obvious that this event deals largely with product-related knowledge as opposed to company-related and country-related knowledge. (If host government approval for the price increase were required, the latter might also be involved.) In this case, the subsidiary marketing manager provides information about the increase and its relationship to competitors' prices as well as the anticipated impact on margins and sales volume. The subsidiary CEO merely checks the proposal for broad consistency with his or her budgeted sales and profit targets, and goals concerning the subsidiary's competitive position. The proposal is approved at a relatively low level in the HQ marketing group, where it is again checked for consistency with broad goals for the product line, and more specifically checked against the price in other subsidiaries whose markets might interact with this particular subsidiary's. Since this kind of decision is not expected to alter significantly the position of the product line in its competitive environment, the perspective that these managers tend to apply is tactical rather than strategic. This event requires tactical information processing for product matters.

This identification or measurement has largely structural implications. It pinpoints which subunits or individuals in the organization need to be involved in the information-processing event (those that can contribute the right kinds of knowledge and capabilities). The previous identification or measurement, however, has primarily process implications. It helps to identify which information-processing mechanisms (processes) are most suitable for linking together the specific subunits or individuals that possess the necessary knowledge and capabilities.

The information-processing capacities of structure

The organizational location of specific kinds of knowledge and capabilities is strongly influenced by the organization's formal structure. Research on MNC structure (Brooke and Remmers 1970; Stopford and Wells 1972; Franko 1976; Hulbert and Brandt 1980; Egelhoff 1982) has helped to identify where different kinds of knowledge and capabilities tend to be located in the four elementary structures used to organize international operations. Table 9.1 provides a summary of the location of information-processing capacities in each structure.

In a worldwide functional division structure, the functional activities in a foreign subsidiary report directly to their respective functional divisions in the parent. Tactical information-processing capacity for company and country matters tends to lie in such functional divisions as finance, human resources, and government affairs, at both the parent HQ and foreign subsidiary levels. Similarly, tactical product-related information-processing capacity tends to lie in the R&D, manufacturing, and marketing divisions found at both levels. This structure should facilitate tactical information processing between the parent and foreign subsidiaries as long as the processing can take place within a functional area. Tactical information processing across functions, however, will be difficult (and will require non-hierarchical processes), since the structure does not facilitate communication between divisions at either the subsidiary level or the tactical levels of the parent.

Since the formulation of business strategy requires a cross-functional perspective, strategic information processing cannot readily occur within a foreign subsidiary or even at lower levels of the parent HQ. Only at the CEO and executive committee level does a cross-functional or general management perspective exist, and only at this level does the structure facilitate multifunctional information coming together. While non-hierarchical information processes might be employed to bring such information together at lower levels of the organization, a general management perspective is lacking at such levels, and therefore subunits in foreign subsidiaries cannot generally participate in or make direct inputs to the strategy-formulation process. This centralization of strategic information processing means that processing capacity is limited (only a few people at one level of the parent are involved) and it is difficult for new information about the environment to enter the process.

With an international division structure, all foreign subsidiaries report to an international division that is separate from the domestic operations. Brooke and Remmers (1970) found that this structure tends to facilitate information processing between the parent and foreign subsidiaries, while at the same time it hinders information processing at the parent level between the international division and the domestic operations. Product knowledge tends to be centered in the domestic divisions, while knowledge about such company and country matters as international finance and foreign political conditions is centered in the international division. Consequently, parent–subsidiary information-processing capacity is relatively high for company and country matters and relatively low for product matters. There is a general management or strategic apex at both the subsidiary and international division levels. Thus, strategic as well as tactical information processing can take place between a subsidiary and the international division, but it will center on company and country matters rather than product matters. Connecting foreign subsidiaries to the centers of product knowledge in the domestic product divisions requires non-hierarchical information processes.

A geographic regional structure divides the world into regions, each with its own headquarters. Each HQ is responsible for all of the company's products and business within its geographical area. The regional HQ is the center of the company's knowledge about company and country matters within the region. Most regional HQs also contain either product or functional staffs to provide coordination for product matters across subsidiaries in the region (Williams 1967). There is a general management or strategic apex at both the subsidiary and regional HQ levels. As a result, this structure facilitates a high level of all four types of information processing between a subsidiary and its regional HQ. The information-processing capacity between a foreign subsidiary and domestic operations or a subsidiary in another region is low. The only structural mechanism for coordinating across regions is the corporate HQ, and most regional companies tend to have relatively small corporate managements and staffs (Egelhoff 1982). Thus, coordinating product technologies and strategies between regions requires non-structural or non-hierarchical information processing.

A worldwide product division structure extends the responsibilities of the domestic product divisions to cover their product lines on a worldwide basis.

Table 9.1 Location of information-processing capacity in the four elementary MNC structures

Type of structure	Types of information-processing capacity			
	Tactical information-processing capacity for company and country matters	Strategic information-processing capacity for company and country matters	Tactical information-processing capacity for product matters	Strategic information-processing capacity for product matters
Worldwide functional divisions	Company and country-related functional divisions of parent HQ (e.g., finance, human resources) Similar functional divisions of foreign subsidiaries	CEO and executive committee of parent HQ	Product-related functional divisions of parent (e.g, R & D, manufacturing, marketing) Similar functional divisions of foreign subsidiaries	CEO and executive divisions of parent HQ
International division	International division HQ Foreign subsidiary HQs	Higher management of international division HQ Higher management of foreign subsidiary HQs	Domestic product divisions (outside of international structure) Product divisions of foreign subsidiaries	Higher management of domestic product divisions (outside of international structure) Higher management of product divisions of foreign subsidiaries

Table 9.1 continued

	Types of information-processing capacity			
Type of structure	Tactical information-processing capacity for company and country matters	Strategic information-processing capacity for company and country matters	Tactical information-processing capacity for product matters	Strategic information-processing capacity for product matters
Geographical regions	Company and country-related management and staff of regional HQs	Higher management of parent corporate HQ	Product-related management and staff of regional HQs	Higher product-related management of regional HQs
	Domestic and foreign subsidiary HQs	Higher management of regional HQs	Product divisions and domestic and foreign subsidiaries	Higher management of product divisions of domestic and foreign subsidiaries
		Higher management of domestic and foreign subsidiaries		
Worldwide product divisions	Foreign subsidiary HQs	Higher management of foreign subsidiary HQs	Parent product division HQs and domestic product operations	Higher management of product division HQs
			Product divisions of foreign subsidiaries	Higher management of product divisions of foreign subsidiaries

Under this structure, there is a tendency to centralize product-related knowledge and decision-making capability in the parent product groups, and to decentralize non-product knowledge and decision making to the foreign subsidiaries (Brooke and Remmers 1970). Consequently, the capacity for processing information on company and country matters tends to be concentrated in the foreign subsidiaries, while the parent HQ tends to have a product orientation. Product-related tactical and strategic information-processing capacities, on the other hand, tend to be highly developed at both the foreign subsidiary and parent product division levels. The product divisions in the foreign subsidiaries are directly connected through the hierarchy to the centers of product knowledge in the parent. For each product line, there is a strategic apex at both the subsidiary and parent product division levels, which facilitates strategic information processing at both levels for product matters.

Formal structure significantly influences where specific types of knowledge and decision-making capability reside in large organizations. The four dimensions of information processing employed in Table 9.1 seem a useful framework for describing these differences in MNCs. The author used a similar framework to develop hypotheses about strategy–structure relationships in MNCs which were empirically tested using a sample of 34 elementary structure MNCs and 15 matrix and mixed structure MNCs, representing both US and European firms (Egelhoff 1988a: 61–128). The testing tended to support the framework. Thus, research to date seems (1) strongly to support the assumption that formal organizational structure has a major influence on the location of knowledge and decision-making capability in organizations, and (2) to provide reasonable support for the logic used in developing the specific framework shown in Table 9.1. Formal structure is not the only determinant of the location of knowledge and decision-making capability, however, and there can be significant variation between companies with the same structure.

The capacities of information-processing mechanisms

Having created a kind of directory of where knowledge and capability tend to lie in an MNC, we need to produce an analogous directory of the kinds of information-processing mechanisms that can be used to access and connect the various sources of knowledge and capability. Figure 9.4 provides such a directory by showing the different information-processing capacities of Galbraith's information-processing mechanisms, as well as others that are frequently used at the parent-foreign subsidiary level of analysis in MNCs.

The routinism and interdependency axes are Gutman-like scales. Thus, mechanisms capable of providing non-routine information processing can also provide routine information processing; mechanisms capable of providing reciprocal information processing can also provide sequential information processing, but usually at a lower volume and/or at a greater

	Sequential information-processing capacity		Reciprocal information-processing capacity
Routine information-processing capacity	Rules & programs (H) Single-cycle planning (H) Post-action control (H) Stand-alone computer systems (H)		Integrated database computer systems (H)
	Vertical info. systems (M) Assistants, clerical staff & planning staff (M)	Steering control (M) Multi-cycle, interactive planning systems (M)	
Non-routine information-processing capacity	Hierarchical referral (L)		Horizontal information systems: Direct contact (L) Task forces (M) Teams (M) Integrating roles (L) Matrix designs (M)

Note: The letters in parentheses indicate the relative volumes of information-processing capacity: H = High, M = Medium, and L = Low.

Figure 9.4 The capacities of information-processing mechanisms

cost than mechanisms specifically designed to cope with more routine or sequential information-processing requirements.

Mechanisms that are specifically designed to provide routine-sequential information processing include rules and programs, single-cycle planning processes, post-action control systems, and stand-alone computer systems. As Figure 9.4 indicates, these mechanisms provide relatively high volumes of information processing, and do this at low cost compared with other mechanisms. Other forms of vertical information systems, such as assistants, clerical staffs, and planning staffs (Galbraith 1973), can usually handle more non-routine information processing than the preceding mechanisms, but also tend to provide largely sequential information processing. Hierarchical referral, such as the referral of an exception or non-routine event up the hierarchy and the transmission of a decision back down, provides a two-way flow of information that also tends to be sequential. Since managerial hierarchies can easily become overloaded, this mechanism provides a relatively low volume of information-processing capacity, and usually does so at a relatively high cost.

Computer systems with integrated databases (such as airline reservation systems) that can be simultaneously shared by many users provide more reciprocal information processing, but largely for predetermined, routine events. Galbraith (1973) identified a number of mechanisms that tend to provide horizontal or lateral information processing across subunits or individuals: direct contact between individuals, task forces, and teams, integrating roles, and matrix designs. These mechanisms facilitate information inputs being made in a flexible, give-and-take manner among all parties to the information-processing event, and consequently the mechanisms are the primary providers of non-routine-reciprocal information processing in organizations.

Several mechanisms are shown at the midway point of both axes in Figure 9.4, indicating that they fall between the two extremes already presented. Steering control systems (such as interim reviews by parent HQ of a foreign plant's start-up) clearly provide more reciprocal information processing and can handle more non-routine situations than post-action control systems, such as annual reviews of a subsidiary's sales and profits (Newman 1975). Multi-cycle, interactive planning systems also provide more non-routine and reciprocal information processing than single-cycle planning systems. Obviously, all locations in Figure 9.4 are approximations. Information-processing capacities can vary considerably depending on the exact design of a mechanism, its implementation, and its interactions with other aspects of an organization. Yet the generalizations expressed in Figure 9.4 are both useful and necessary for building a more systematic theory about information processing in organizations.

The reader will probably have noticed that there may be some positive correlation between the routine–non-routine dimension and the sequential–reciprocal dimension when the two are used to measure actual information-processing mechanisms. Thus, many mechanisms seem to fall along a single dimension (the 45-degree diagonal in Figure 9.4). Mechanisms that provide reciprocal information-processing capacity seem to be able to handle non-routine situations, and mechanisms that only provide sequential information-processing capacity seem to be confined most frequently to handling routine situations. It is useful here to recall that Galbraith (1973) originally ranked his information-processing mechanisms along a single dimension, in an order that is roughly similar to that which occurs along the diagonal in Figure 9.4. Galbraith did not explicitly identify the routine–non-routine or the sequential–reciprocal dimensions as underlying his ordering, but simply referred to information-processing mechanisms as varying from low to high. At a minimum, Figure 9.4 clarifies the differences that underlie Galbraith's general ordering of information-processing mechanisms. Daft and Lengel (1986) developed a similar ordering of information-processing mechanisms based upon the relative amounts of equivocality reduction and uncertainty reduction capacity a mechanism can provide.

The multidimensional framework in Figure 9.4 represents a significant extension of Galbraith's one-dimensional ordering, however, and even if information processing in organizations frequently reveals some correlation between them, both the routine–non-routine and the sequential–reciprocal dimensions need to be retained as conceptually distinct, for three reasons. First, some important mechanisms do seem to lie off the diagonal and thus to contradict a one-dimensional ordering. Second, new information-processing mechanisms may be developed that will increasingly lie off the diagonal, especially in the computer-based information systems area (Huber 1990). And third, many of the indicated mechanisms can be altered to vary along one dimension without necessarily varying along the other. For example, rules and programs can be altered to fit different contingencies or even turned into guidelines (which leaves the implementer with greater flexibility in responding to an information-processing event). Both alternatives increase the non-routine information-processing capacity of this mechanism without changing the fact that it provides only sequential information processing between the creator and the implementers of the rule or guideline.

The conceptual framework developed in this section defines four structural dimensions and four process dimensions to measure information processing in MNCs, and provides a more explicit way to define and measure information processing at the macro level. The following section will apply the framework to a currently important subject in international management: transnationalism. The purpose is to illustrate how the framework can be applied, and also to demonstrate that it can provide a meaningful new insight into complex organizational issues.

APPLIED EXAMPLE: THE INFORMATION-PROCESSING IMPLICATIONS OF TRANSNATIONALISM

Interest in new ways to organize and manage MNCs has been growing (Hedlund 1986; Perlmutter and Trist 1986; Prahalad and Doz 1987; Bartlett and Ghoshal 1989). Although details and terminology may vary, most of these proposals have at their core more multidimensional organizational designs and a wider variety of integrating and coordinating mechanisms than can usually be found in traditional designs. The new designs are responses to the need to compete with new strategies in an international business environment that is increasingly complex and competitive. Bartlett and Ghoshal (1989) call this new trend in strategy and organizational design "transnationalism."

Transnational strategies attempt simultaneously to realize (1) efficiency and economy through global-scale operations and global integration, (2) responsiveness to national and local differences through local differentiation, and (3) a high level of innovation worldwide through extensive learning and transfer of knowledge. Traditional strategies primarily emphasize only one of these. It is obvious, therefore, that transnational strategies generate much greater requirements for information processing between parent HQ and foreign subsidiaries and among foreign subsidiaries than is the case under more traditional strategies. Depending on the specifics of the strategy and the company's organizational structure, a variety of information-processing mechanisms (taken from Figure 9.4) can be employed to link together the relevant sources of knowledge and capability with the appropriate information-processing capacity (such as non-routine-reciprocal information processing). This is an information-processing picture of the flexible way that organizations will need to be designed in order to implement transnational strategies.

Bartlett and Ghoshal (1989) describe the key characteristics of transnational design, as revealed by their research on companies that are moving in this direction:

- Assets and capabilities are dispersed, interdependent, and specialized.
- There are differentiated contributions by national units to integrated worldwide operations.
- Knowledge is developed jointly and shared worldwide.

Other characteristics include flexibility, dropping the need for symmetry and consistency in designing HQ–subsidiary relationships, self-regulating systems, and a heavy dependence on company culture and shared values in facilitating coordination.

The information-processing framework developed in the previous section seems uniquely suited to analyze the new transnational designs that are now emerging in firms and provide useful insights into them. Four information-processing implications are particularly important to the future of transnational design.

1. The role and function of formal organizational structure may be changed

Formal structure is important because it provides a basis for locating, maintaining, and accessing different kinds of knowledge and decision-making capabilities. This is especially important in MNCs, where the range of knowledge and decision-making capabilities is extremely wide. A key function of formal MNC structure is that managers across the company know where specific sources of knowledge and capability lie: the locations tend to be fairly stable, and managers are generally familiar with how to access them.

Compared to traditional designs, transnational designs will tend to locate knowledge and decision-making capability in a more eclectic manner that is at the same time more dynamic and subject to change. For example, the Australian subsidiary may replace the parent's R&D laboratory as the center of knowledge for a new generation of product technology. The company's foreign subsidiaries are familiar with monitoring and transferring new technology from the parent's R&D laboratory (several existing information-processing mechanisms already provide the necessary linkage) but not from the Australian subsidiary. New, non-hierarchical information-processing mechanisms will have to be developed. Several years later, industry trends in some countries may favor yet another version of product technology that has

192

been developed in the company's German subsidiary for use in the local market. Again, sources of knowledge and information flows will have to change. As the situation in this example becomes widespread, formal structure begins to lose its value as an accurate and stable directory of where knowledge and capability reside and how they can be accessed.

The design logic that underlies formal structure is hierarchical and symmetrical. Transnational design gives up this logic in order to gain more flexibility. In the process, the organization loses some of its ability to locate and access knowledge and capability, because of the diminished role of formal structure. Thus, transnational designs need to provide new information-processing capabilities that address this loss.

2. The amount of strategic information-processing capacity for product matters must be greatly expanded

Of the four types of information processing identified in Figure 9.2, strategic information processing for product matters should increase the most under a transnational strategy. Under traditional strategies and structures, strategic knowledge and decision-making capability tend to be centralized at the upper levels of product division HQs and geographical region HQs. Only with a multi-domestic or polycentric strategy does the locus of this information-processing capacity move to the subsidiary level and become diffused. Thus, most strategic decision making for product matters tends to take place either through hierarchical referral or within hierarchically structured strategic planning processes. As a result, there tends to be great similarity in strategic product planning across product lines and subsidiaries within a company.

An important characteristic of transnationalism is that it disperses product knowledge across foreign subsidiaries and reduces the concentration of such knowledge at the parent HQ and in home country operations. This should result in a much more complex, heterogeneous, and less hierarchical strategic planning process in transnational firms. For some product matters, strategic information processing should occur directly between concerned foreign subsidiaries, with little or no involvement from parent HQ. Other matters will need to be coordinated globally through the parent HQ. And still other matters, those that primarily respond to local conditions, will be left to each subsidiary. Since these three information-processing events tend to supplement rather than replace each other, the amount and variety of strategic information-processing capacity for product matters will need to be greatly expanded in transnational as opposed to traditional MNCs.

These first two implications primarily stem from the impact of transnationalism on the location of knowledge and decision-making capabilities in MNC structures. They are the structural implications of transnationalism for information processing. The next issue deals with the primary process implication of transnationalism for information processing.

3. The use of non-routine-reciprocal information-processing mechanisms will need to be expanded significantly

Transnational designs require high flexibility in the way they link different parts of the MNC organization together. Bartlett and Ghoshal (1989: 2) state that "companies see that they can gain competitive advantage by sensing needs in one country, responding with capabilities located in a second, and diffusing the resulting innovation to markets around the globe." Thus, a transnational firm needs unusually high amounts of non-routine-reciprocal information-processing capacity in order to respond to the variety of changing opportunities this strategy seeks to exploit. Figure 9.4 shows the various horizontal information-processing mechanisms that provide this kind of capacity. All are people-intensive, in the sense that they employ large amounts of managers' and key employees' time. They are costly and difficult to control compared with more routine and sequential information-processing mechanisms. MNCs will have to be prepared to provide large amounts of non-routine-reciprocal information-processing capacity as they begin to embrace transnational strategies.

It is interesting to recall that matrix structures were once heralded as the inevitable design for coordinating more multidimensional international strategies (Stopford and Wells 1972; Davis and Lawrence 1977). Many MNCs were forced to abandon matrix structures, however, when they could not successfully implement them (Bartlett and Ghoshal 1990). Matrix structures (such as transnational designs) also require large amounts of non-routine-reciprocal information-processing capacity to coordinate and resolve conflict between the two formal hierarchies that constitute the matrix. Many MNCs adopted matrix structures without recognizing this fact or providing the required non-routine-reciprocal information-processing capacity. As a result, conflict was frequently not resolved through lateral information processing at lower levels (as it was supposed to be) but pushed vertically up the hierarchies to be resolved at the top by hierarchical referral. In some firms that abandoned matrix structures, such as Dow Chemical, the costs of duplication and conflict resolution seem to have outweighed the benefits. In others, such as Texas Instruments, the matrix structure resulted in more severe problems: the breakdown of information processing, the over-centralization of decision making because of the organization's inability to resolve conflict at lower levels, and serious delays in making critical decisions.

MNCs face a similar problem if they adopt transnational strategies and designs but fail to develop the necessary non-routine-reciprocal information-processing capacities to make them work. Here the problem is not conflict resolution between two formal hierarchies, as it was with matrix structures. Instead, it is (1) conflict resolution between some non-hierarchically organized transnational activity and the traditional hierarchy that still exists and interfaces with the transnational parts of a company, and (2) the need continually to redesign and alter transnational relationships within a company. Both of these activities will be commonplace in transnational firms, and will require an increased use of such non-routine-reciprocal information-processing mechanisms as direct contact and meetings, task forces and work teams, and liaison and integrator roles.

Bartlett and Ghoshal (1989) state that transnational firms need to rely primarily upon informal matrixing accompanied by high levels of commitment and shared values to achieve the necessary coordination. These qualities facilitate the kind of lateral, non-routine-reciprocal information processing we have been discussing, but do not automatically ensure it will occur. Many firms may require significant changes to their culture and large-scale organizational development (OD) interventions (team building, survey feedback, process consultation, grid OD) in order to develop the potential for high levels of non-routine-reciprocal information-processing capacity. The costs of these changes may be extremely high (in some cases even prohibitive), and clearly need to be weighed against the benefits of a transnational approach.

4. There will be a much greater need for design rules at all levels of the organization

A fourth implication of transnationalism is that the process of design itself is going to be a major problem. It must be flexible, emergent from the individual situation, and fitted to the opportunities and problems posed by a firm's technology and environment. Instead of largely imitating a well-known prototype, managers at various levels will require some kind of guidance on how to design transnational relationships, how to interface them with more traditional, hierarchical, and symmetrical parts of the organization, and when to convert emergent and informal coordination to more formal and traditional coordinating mechanisms. In short, the transnational organization requires a widely understood set of design rules that can be used to implement the various complexities of a transnational strategy by helping to create suitable flexible designs. Organizing itself becomes a new technology that almost all managers in a transnational firm must master. Such is not the case in a traditional firm, where organizing is done infrequently by relatively few people.

At present, implementing transnational designs in MNCs appears to rely too much on the simple notions of informal matrixing, and heavy doses of commitment and shared values among organizational members. More technical knowledge will be required to activate and maintain effective transnational designs. The information-processing model developed in the previous section provides both a design logic and a preliminary set of design rules that address this problem. While other conceptual frameworks for design might also be useful, information processing is one of the primary characteristics that differentiates a transnational approach from more traditional approaches to strategy and organizational design. More traditional approaches to change have typically called for structural change, which only indirectly leads to information-processing change. Transnational design generally bypasses structural change but calls for more direct changes in information-processing capacities both within and outside the existing formal structure of a firm. Thus, there is a need for a more comprehensive design approach and a model based on an information-processing perspective on the organization.

Applying the information-processing framework and model to transnationalism produces new insight and understanding. At the present time, transnational design is explained primarily by discussing examples of firms that are employing it. This section has demonstrated that the information-processing framework and model can provide a more conceptual and general understanding of transnationalism: one that is useful to practitioners and that can serve as a base for further research and theory building.

CONCLUSION

The information-processing perspective of organizational design developed in this paper can be used when studying large, complex organizations, such as MNCs. To date, most rigorous attempts to build theory with an information-processing perspective have taken place in micro-level studies, where the unit of analysis has been the individual or work group. By using information processing as an abstract, intervening concept to relate organizational design to the strategic and environmental conditions facing an organization, researchers can better evaluate fit between these two dissimilar and hard-to-compare sets of variables. The use of more explicitly defined multidimensional frameworks (such as the one developed in this chapter for MNCs) to measure both the information-processing capacities of organizational design and the information-processing requirements inherent in an organization's strategy and environment will add rigor to the measurement and evaluation of such fit.

It is probable that the information-processing perspective will be of greatest interest to researchers studying what organizational designs contribute to effective MNC performance, and under what strategic and environmental conditions one form is preferable to another. In order to develop and extend further the information-processing model presented in this paper, systematic empirical research is needed on the structural dimensions framework and the process dimensions framework described respectively in Table 9.1 and Figure 9.4. As indicated, some empirical research has already been done in MNCs on the structural dimensions of information processing, although support for the process dimensions framework rests largely on conceptualization intended more for use at the micro levels of organizations, and supported by research in settings quite different from the MNC. Research in MNCs also needs to identify and understand the capacities of new information-processing mechanisms, which Bartlett and Ghoshal (1989), Prahalad and Doz (1987), and others report are currently evolving in MNCs. It is reasonable to expect much more dynamism on the process side than on the structural side of MNCs; however, it is important for theory that new forms of information processing be identified and understood in terms of some conceptual framework, such as the one suggested here.

Although the study of how MNC organizational designs change and evolve may seem a less likely candidate for the information-processing perspective, the framework developed above might be useful to the extent that evolutionary change involves the maintenance of organizational fit during transition. At the other extreme, serious organizational (information-processing) misfit might be equally interesting, as it should lead to failure and a more revolutionary pattern of change. Thus, the information-processing perspective would appear to be potentially applicable to theories about change and evolution as well.

Theory and science are increasingly lagging behind the advancement of art when it comes to the management of MNCs. Recent books and articles report on many new trends and management approaches that seem to be currently developing within MNCs, yet the identification as well as our understanding of these phenomena lies largely outside of existing theory. Consequently, there is a pressing need for theory to catch up with practice. Otherwise, practice will increasingly be operating without theory. Only theory and science—not practice and art—provide the kind of abstract and generalized understanding that can be moved, with some reliability, from one situation to another and integrated with other theories of understanding.

POSTSCRIPT
By D. Eleanor Westney

In my opinion, the concepts and arguments of this chapter are as relevant today as they were when this book was initially published. The context for reading and understanding this chapter, however, has evolved. A major trend in organizational research over the past decade has been the growth in studies that employ some kind of knowledge-based perspective, especially in analyses of the MNC. Few of these studies analyze the underlying organizational processes that actually develop and transfer knowledge in organizations. Such studies could benefit greatly from using the dimensions, concepts, and variables of existing information-processing theory specified in this chapter.

Notes

1 An earlier version of this paper was presented at the workshop on Organizational Theory and the Multinational Corporation at INSEAD on September 1–2 1989. The author wishes to thank David Whetten, John Daniels, Andrew Van de Ven, Michael Gerlach, and Susan Schneider for their helpful comments. A later version appeared in the *Journal of International Business Studies* 22 (September 1991). This chapter is the third version.
2 The discussion about the framework shown in Figure 9.2 is excerpted from Egelhoff (1982).

10 Assumptions of Hierarchy and Heterarchy, With Applications to the Management of the Multinational Corporation[1]

Gunnar Hedlund

The virtues of hierarchical organization—of matter, of life, of information, of human institutions—are mostly taken for granted. Analysts invoke the supposed virtues of hierarchy without much specification. An example is Galbraith's (1973) synthesis of the information processing theory of organization design: the discussion is very detailed on most aspects of design dimensions, but hierarchy is left curiously anonymous. Hierarchical structuring is introduced as one of the first and most fundamental ways of improving the handling of information, but why it is so is left unexplained.

Other authors go into greater detail, but hierarchy is not really fundamentally questioned. For example, in a 1968 article discussing "the hierarchy of authority in organizations," Peter Blau focuses primarily on the number of levels in the hierarchy and related factors. He mentions but does not pursue a more ambitious project: to "explain why organizations develop various characteristics, such as a multilevel hierarchy or decentralized authority" (Blau 1968: 454). A somewhat later article (Blau 1970), however, analyzes the relationships between differentiation, size of the organization, and size of administrative functions, and thus approaches the more basic question of why there is hierarchy in the first place.

The importance of formal structuring of tasks and managerial hierarchy as a way to coordinate work is, of course, treated in great detail in the contributions of the contingency school (e.g. Burns and Stalker 1961; Woodward 1965; Lawrence and Lorsch 1967) and by the Aston group. Although these works often use the word "hierarchy," it is not sharply defined, nor are its opposite(s) or negations clearly stated, even when its functional equivalents are analyzed. Sometimes hierarchy figures as part of a more encompassing term, as in Weber's bureaucracy. Hierarchy is an element of a totality, and "each element operates not in isolation but as part of a system of elements that, in combination, are expected to provide more effective and efficient administration" (Scott's discussion of Weber, 1987a: 42). Thus although the concept is often used, most organization theorists seem to regard hierarchy as a primitive concept not requiring much further definition. Few authors

198

have grappled explicitly with the fundamental issues of the nature of hierarchy (Simon 1962; Koestler 1978; Pattee 1970; Herbst 1974; Camacho and Persky 1988 are examples).

The first aim of this chapter is to contribute to a discussion of the fundamental assumptions underlying a non-tautological concept of hierarchy, thereby making it possible to suggest basic alternatives to it. The second aim is to apply one such alternative, which I will term *heterarchy*, to the structure of multinational corporations (MNCs).

The chapter discusses some theoretical justifications for hierarchy and the historical roots of the concept. It argues that Simon's (1962) widely quoted defense of hierarchy is of less relevance to human organization than we might think at first glance, or infer from its acceptance among social scientists. The conceptions of the original inventor of the term, Dionysius the Areopagite, still serve as a guide to its meaning. If some of the assumptions in these two authors' arguments are challenged, hierarchy appears as less all-pervasive, and alternative structures become conceivable.

This rather abstract discussion will be preceded and followed by a discussion of the modern MNC, which constitutes a crucial arena for testing the viability of hierarchy. The complexity and size of such firms challenge hierarchical forms to deliver their promise of being efficient mechanisms for handling complex tasks. In the business strategy literature, the MNC is often seen as the latest, most complex stage in an evolution of structures logically related to the strategy of the firm. (See the important line of research initiated by Chandler (1962); significant contributions on MNCs are those by Stopford and Wells (1972); Franko (1976); Galbraith and Nathanson (1978); Teece (1983); and Chandler (1986).) Moreover, some lines of research originating in economics take the view that the MNC is the general case that a theory of the firm should discuss, and that simpler types of companies should be treated as special cases (see Casson 1987).

Three initial caveats have to be mentioned. First, this chapter does not discuss all uses of hierarchy and does not pretend to be a comprehensive review of the relevant literature. I argue for a restricted meaning of the word, indicating a breakdown of a totality into parts, and the establishment of clear notions of levels of units, with "upper" levels in some way being superordinate to others. Hierarchy is thus seen as one of many potential mechanisms to ensure the integrity of a totality; the mere existence of a totality does not in itself make it a hierarchy. This narrower definition conforms both to lay use of the term and to what organization theorists usually mean by it. However, it excludes some broader conceptions. Simon (1962: 88) explicitly includes systems "in which there is no relation of subordination among subsystems," and he reserves the term "formal hierarchy" for systems with subordination between levels of subsystems. Another broader view of hierarchy, transaction cost theory, will not be discussed in detail here. In that tradition, hierarchy is the alternative to market, and a firm is by definition a hierarchy.[2] I am more interested in the nature of the internal working of a system, where hierarchy is only one aspect, and where alternatives to hierarchy are conceivable within the firm. Therefore, although relevant and important discussions akin to my own appear in the debate on transaction cost theory (e.g. Ouchi 1980), this stream of thought will be ignored, for the most part.

The second caveat is that I focus on arguments for and against hierarchy that are couched in terms of efficiency rather than legitimacy or power. This does not mean that I think the latter are unimportant. On the contrary, unmasking some of the unjustified claims for the universality of hierarchy's efficiency will direct attention to those other sources for it.

Third, I have elected to treat one classical defense of hierarchy (Simon 1962) in depth rather than enumerate a number of contributions. The reasons are that Simon's paper is so widely quoted and yet so rarely discussed in detail, and that it goes into greater depth than most other contributions. My hope is that Simon's assumptions concerning hierarchy will prove to apply in other uses of the concept. The focus on this single paper should be seen as a heuristic device to clarify existing concepts and generate new ones. The critical tone of the following discussion should be read in this light. The paper is selected not because of its weaknesses but because of its strengths: it is important, well argued, and consistent.

A consequence of the concentration on Simon's work is that the discussion will have to mirror his use of examples and parables, although these may seem remote from the world of MNCs to some readers. In addition, Simon's focus is on establishing general principles for the structuring and behavior of systems, whereas mine is more restricted. In this sense, the discussion will be broader than justified by the nature of conclusions I seek, but I hope it will still be of some interest.

STRAINS ON HIERARCHY IN THE MULTINATIONAL CORPORATION

Four observations from the practice of MNC management seem pertinent. Together, they suggest that alternatives to hierarchy are emerging.

First, firms are finding that clean, streamlined organization structures are difficult to design and particularly difficult to make work. The debate in theory as well as practice is mostly phrased in terms of choosing the primary dimension of structure—function, geography, or product being the most common candidates. More and more MNCs are frustrated by such discussions. They need to coordinate along functional lines and geographical lines and product lines simultaneously.

The matrix structure, which is a way of institutionalizing ambiguity, was tried as a remedy for such ills. The summary judgment after a good deal of experience is fairly negative. The response in MNCs has been an increasing willingness to live with messy organization structures, happily blending dimensions and tolerating inconsistencies, overlaps, and non-institutionalized ambiguities. The organization chart—a favorite example for most theoreticians of hierarchy—becomes distinctly unwieldy and non-hierarchical. Some important MNCs even refuse to publish an organization chart; several regard their lack of one with pride.

Second, and partly as a consequence of the demise of pure structures, control systems other than the formal structure of the firm gain in importance. Two aspects stand out: the design of systems for information flows; and mechanisms to encourage shared goals, consensus on strategies, and generally a strong corporate culture. Organizational memory and capacity for rapid transfer of information between units is helped by long careers within the same firm and systematic rotation of personnel. Information technology increasingly allows access to information that is direct, rather than mediated through hierarchy. A metaphor for this type of information processing is the holographic corporation, in which information about the totality is shared in each and every part of the firm.[3]

Third, as is obvious from the first two points, lateral communication becomes much more important than heretofore. Subsidiaries talk directly to subsidiaries, divisions to divisions, and so on. Increasingly, the national subsidiaries are given *global* roles and are put in charge of supranational projects. The temporary international project team becomes a basic building block of the MNC. An interesting structural parallel to laterality is the tendency to use interlocking directorates as a means of coordination. The head of the German subsidiary may be on the board of the US company or perhaps even of the French parent company.

Fourth, the very *raison d'être* of the MNC seems to be shifting. Theories of the MNC emphasize monopolistic, firm-specific advantages (Hymer 1960; Kindleberger 1969; Dunning 1977) and the necessity of internalizing the exploitation of such advantages (Magee 1977; Teece 1983; Rugman 1980; Buckley and Casson 1976; Casson 1987). The modern, established MNC is better described in terms of "new" advantages having to do with scale and scope, learning, and operational flexibility (Vernon 1979; Kogut 1983). Thus, international reach itself and the organization's competence in exploiting it become the sources of competitiveness, rather than any narrowly conceived product/market position. The point about the MNC is its flexibility in mobilizing resources, and it becomes impossible to prespecify the crucial interdependencies. The information processing view of organization design, like transaction cost theory (Williamson 1975), assumes a given task or transaction with given processing needs. The modern MNC lives in the absence of these givens. Both Galbraith's and Williamson's hierarchies therefore do not really fit the bill.

Now, if hierarchy is starting to be modified or to become less relevant in the world of practice, how is it holding up in a theoretical analysis? Are the

201

deviations from an ideal hierarchical model either exceptions or mechanisms complementing hierarchy in situations of particular kinds, as Galbraith, Thompson (1967), and the contingency theorists would argue? Or do they signify more basic problems with the model?

THE THEORETICAL JUSTIFICATION OF HIERARCHY: WAS TEMPUS REALLY SO STUPID?

Interestingly, all writers seem to experience considerable difficulty in defining hierarchy in terms of more primitive concepts. Simon (1962) says that a hierarchy is a system that is composed of subsystems, each of which is in turn hierarchically organized. This is obviously a circular definition, and Simon seems to perceive the need for further delimitation. Rather than providing an abstract definition, he gives a number of examples: human authority structures, the composition of matter, computer programs, and so on. Later, he goes one step further in definition:

> "Hierarchy" simply means a set of Chinese boxes of a particular kind.... Opening any given box in a hierarchy discloses not just one box within, but a whole small set of boxes; and opening any one of these compound boxes discloses a new set in turn.... A hierarchy is a partial ordering—specifically, a tree.
>
> (Simon 1973: 5)

The reference to boxes and trees is significant. It is as if the author feels that more formal definitions lack meaning. Simon is very conscious of the possibility that hierarchy is partly a reflection of the mind of the analyst, and may be almost an a priori category through which we see the world. In the discussion of "nearly decomposable systems,"[4] he notes:

> The fact, then, that many complex systems have a nearly decomposable, hierarchic structure is a major facilitating factor enabling us to understand, to describe, and even to 'see' such systems and their parts. Or perhaps the proposition should be put the other way around. *If there are important systems in the world that are complex without being hierarchic, they may to a considerable extent escape our observation and understanding.*
>
> (Simon 1962: 108, emphasis added)[4]

Koestler (1978) also introduces the idea that hierarchy may be in the eye of the beholder rather than in the object beheld, but like Simon, he finds support for a less solipsistic view. I find this hesitation in drawing more far-reaching conclusions from the insight into the epistemological problems of hierarchy somewhat disappointing. Indeed, one could argue that Simon himself implicitly acknowledges the lack of meaning in his definition of hierarchy. He characterizes "complex systems" in general as those "made up of a large number of parts that interact in a nonsimple way" (1962: 86). "Hierarchic systems, or hierarchy" are systems "composed of interrelated subsystems, each of the latter being, in turn, hierarchic in structure ..." (1962: 87). Apparently, if we assume that the "parts" in the first definitions can also be complex, this means that all complex systems are hierarchic. Any discussion of the usefulness, or probability, of hierarchic as opposed to non-hierarchic systems thereby becomes irrelevant. As I will try to show, much of Simon's discussion does indeed implicitly assume a more restrictive conception of hierarchy, where there is subordination between components and levels.

Simon's important argument is that hierarchy is dominant in the architecture of complexity because hierarchical systems have an advantage in evolution due to their construction from stable subsystems. The conclusion is reached and illustrated through an example of two watchmakers, Hora and Tempus:

> There were two watchmakers, named Hora and Tempus, who manufactured very fine watches. Both of them were highly remarkable, and the phones in their workshops rang frequently—new customers were constantly calling them. However, Hora prospered, while Tempus become poorer and poorer. What was the reason?
>
> The watches the men made consisted of about 1,000 parts each. Tempus had so constructed this that if he had one partly assembled and had to put it down—to answer the phone, say—it immediately fell to pieces and had to be reassembled from the elements. The better the customers liked his watches, the more they phoned him and the more difficult it became for him to find enough uninterrupted time to finish a watch.
>
> The watches that Hora made were no less complex than those of Tempus. But he had designed them so that he could put together subassemblies of about ten elements each. Ten of these subassemblies, again, could be put together into a larger subassembly; and a system of ten of the latter subassemblies constituted a whole watch. Hence, when Hora had to put down a partly assembled watch in order to answer the phone, he lost only a small part of his work, and he assembled his watches in only a fraction of the man-hours it took Tempus.
>
> (Simon, 1962: 90–91)

After the parable follows a mathematical demonstration of the fact that Tempus practically never managed to produce a watch. Now, I would like to discuss the assumptions made in the example and the consequences for understanding complex social or social/physical systems. In turn, I shall consider the *nature of the system*, its *input*, its *throughput process*, its *output*, its *environment*, and the *relations between the parts*. The discussion proceeds from the watchmaker example but also relates to Simon's wider analysis.

203

First, let me consider *the system (the watch is a mechanical system)*. The parts have no meaning outside the watch, no projects or goals of their own. Another characteristic of the watch is that its behavior is completely and uniquely determined by the structure and configuration of the parts. The former can be derived from the latter. There is no "novelty through combination." These two characteristics hint at different classes of systems, for which hierarchy has different meanings.[5]

Second, *the parts—the inputs to the production process—do not change and are viable over time*. A watch consists of certain parts. As the Swiss watchmakers were saying when the Japanese were introducing batteries into watches, "That is not a watch—*eine Uhr ist eine Uhr*." Hierarchical breakdown of a process into "stable intermediate forms" tends to conserve the original system, make it resistant to change. (This would be more obvious if the example included a watchmaking factory with many people rather than one single master; however, there are also advantages in terms of flexibility if subsystems can be 'sealed off' from each other and independently improved, as Simon asserts. This assumes, of course, that the sealing off does not compromise the quality of linkage between subsystems.)

Third, *there are no problems of coordination between parts and between processes of manufacturing the parts: the throughput process is given and stable*. In fact, all parts are assumed to fit together perfectly. Also, it is possible to store components and have them around waiting for assembly without deterioration. If Hora were a cook rather than a watchmaker, he would have to contemplate issues such as sour milk and fermentation.[6]

Systems that evolve without mutual coordination tend not to fit together easily. Thus, there is a big jump from Simon's example—which assumes perfect fit—and the conclusion that the evolution and viability of complex systems is due to hierarchies built on independently originated building blocks. If we assume that contiguity in space and time facilitates mutual accommodation, which certainly is the case in social systems, the architecture of complexity involves *un*stable, *jointly developed* components.

Simon, in my view, implicitly assumes a kind of foreknowledge of the total system on the part of the components, which have to know, as it were, to stop developing when they are designed so as to fit well into a totality. Thus, the teleological "overtones of the watchmaker parable" (Simon 1962: 93) seem to be more than overtones. Hierarchy *is* important when there are partial results that *"represent recognizable progress towards the goal"* (Simon 1962: 96, emphasis added).

Fourth, *the product—the output of the process—is given: a watch*. Compare the situation in which exactly what to produce has to be discovered or invented. When the final product is known, it is possible to break it down into parts. This will, however, unavoidably create obstacles to later change, if we assume some inertia in the system of clustering tasks. Hora would probably never have figured out how to make a watch if he had started by making a series of parts.

This means that, at least for the kind of system the example is about, the stable intermediate forms *follow*, not precede, the more complex system.[7]

Fifth, *environment is interruption, which destroys only the system currently worked on, and then completely.* The first point about the influence of the environment is that, in the parable, it is a discrete interruption, not a continuous buzz of challenges (like a wind). The example also depicts a distinct rather than fuzzy intrusion, the appropriate locus of reception of which is problematic. Finally, the environment is seen as exactly an intrusion, not a source of livelihood and opportunity.

By changing the assumptions about the environment, one can easily imagine situations where Tempus would do better than Hora. A slightly crazy example may be forgiven, I hope:

> Imagine a crisis in the Swiss watch industry, which forces our two heroes to diversify into building houses of cards instead, in the traditional, elaborate Swiss style, for the enjoyment of tourists, on top of windy Alps. Hora follows his tried method of building the parts first, leaving ten chimneys, ten balconies, ten roofs, and so on, for later assembly. To his disappointment, he finds that by the time he has finished going through all components, the unpredictable gusts of wind on the mountain top have destroyed almost all his previous work.
>
> Tempus, on the other hand, finds that he can protect his gradually evolving creation through reinforcing each and every part's stability by combining them in the more solid structure of the entire house of cards. The creation stays up long enough to collect money from admiring Japanese with digital watches and cameras. Thus, Tempus thrives whereas Hora gradually becomes crazy, not understanding why houses of cards are different from watches.

Sixth, concerning *relations between parts, and between parts and the whole,* three different aspects are of interest: the temporal ordering of development, the degree of coupling between parts and levels in the hierarchy, and the nature of order and ordering.

As for *temporality,* is it empirically true that the hierarchies we observe are the effects of experiments with concoctions of previously existing components? An absurd counterexample is the human body. Was there a soup of organs—hands, feet, livers, brains, eyes, and so on—that luckily got combined into the first human being, miraculously also supplied with the capacity for procreation? Obviously not. If Simon's view of evolution is correct, we should observe many *independent* components floating about: protons without neutrons, brains without heads, accounting departments outside of firms. The theory may explain the existence of complex systems, but it does not explain the relative absence of independent intermediate forms. In this context, it may be worth noting that Chandler's (1962, 1977) work depicts the evolution of managerial hierarchies as much in terms of the breakdown and reorganization of complex into simpler forms as the other way around. The evolution of the multidivisional form in particular took the former shape.

Even if Simon's argument were to hold for biology and physics, in human systems *forethought can dramatically increase the speed of evolution* and decrease the need for hierarchy, as Simon notes in his discussion of the safe example (1962: 96). Sets of subsystems can be conceived simultaneously, and previous arrangements of components can be drastically altered as a result of learning. New complex systems often require new components. Big projects like the Apollo mission or a war effort can lead to advances in technology at a lower level. A stable superordinate form (a drawing or an objective) in these cases gives rise to intermediate ones, rather than the other way around.

Regarding *coupling*, Simon discussed the properties of *nearly decomposable subsystems*. "Near decomposability" means that "intracomponent linkages are generally stronger than intercomponent linkages" (1962: 106). Sometimes this tendency is treated almost as a way of defining a hierarchy, as in discussing how clusters of interaction in human societies "will identify a rather well-defined hierarchic structure" (1962: 88). In other sections, it is an empirical matter, as in the discussion of communication in organizations (1962: 103). Two questions seem to me to be worth asking in this context. First, it is not obvious that the natural decomposition of a system is invariant over time, or even unambiguous at a certain time. If a hierarchy is defined according to frequencies of interaction, there may be no stable hierarchy when interaction patterns are varied and varying. Second, measuring the strength of linkages is problematical. Frequency may be relevant for some purposes, whereas the importance of linkages may be more appropriate for others. For example, there may be more frequent interaction between a boss and his subordinates than between bosses. Nevertheless, the strategic weight of the latter may lead one to cluster the systems into bosses and subordinates, instead of the groups containing mixes of the two that Simon's discussion (1962: 106) of different frequencies of interaction at different levels of a social hierarchy seems to imply.

Finally, the example implies a *universal* and *one-way ordering*, so that the parts of the clocks are obviously subordinated to the whole, and do not serve as parts also in other systems. A small Chinese box cannot contain the larger one. This is a characteristic of nested, "material" hierarchies. The gene is a part of—contained in—the cell, the cell in the tissue, the tissue in the organ, and so on. Interestingly, this hierarchy, where the gene is at the "lowest" level, is turned upside down if we consider it as an information, rather than a material, system. It is a central dogma of genetic biology that information goes only from gene to cell, not the other way around. Thus, the subordinate part in terms of substance is the governor in terms of communication. (The universality of the ranking breaks down even further when we consider that this central dogma is now challenged. It appears that genes are indeed influenced by their surroundings.)

My imputation of clear ordering as a crucial component of Simon's use of hierarchy contrasts with his explicit inclusion of systems without subordination in his definition. Most of his examples, however, deal with formal—that is, with subordination—hierarchies. One could go one step further. In the definition of hierarchy, the critical words may be "composed of" or—for "complex system"—"made up of." If A is composed of many Bs, we would normally argue that B cannot be composed of As. Thus, there is a sense of subordination given by the type of relation implied in the verbs used.[8]

It seems that most of the points raised above in trying to save Tempus' reputation can be related to three assumptions underlying Simon's example. The *first* is an assumption of *pre-specification* and *stability*. Input, production process, and output are given and do not change over time. There is perfect harmony within the hierarchy, which is polluted only from the environment.

The *second* is an assumption of *instrumental* parts and their *additive influence* on the whole. The components do not have their own goals, and their contribution to the totality contains no surprises.[9] They are totally subordinated to the function of the total hierarchy, and finally to the will of its master. The *third* is the *universality* and *unidirectional* character of the hierarchy. There are not many superordinate systems to which a given part belongs, and there is no confusion as to what the top level, defining the totality, is.

THE HISTORICAL HERITAGE OF HIERARCHY: IS DIONYSIUS THE AREAOPAGITE STILL VALID?

It is interesting to note how closely the three sets of attributes summarized above conform to the essence of the first known use of the word "hierarchy." Dionysius the Areopagite (or pseudo-Dionysius, as he is sometimes called) invented the word in the fifth century AD and "defined" it in two treatises, on the celestial and the ecclesiastical hierarchy, respectively.[10] His pioneering contribution has, to my knowledge, never been noted in the field of organization studies. Dionysius presented the organization structure of heaven. A number of principles of hierarchy can be extracted from the texts, and they resemble those of Simon, as well as those implied in the structure of large organizations, to a striking degree.

Dionysius's hierarchy is *eternal* and *never-changing*. It is *perfect* and *harmonious*. It has *enemies outside* and needs to be protected by *secrecy and obscurity* from the uninitiated. The organization structure is *deep* (nine levels) and *unambiguous*. Order is clearly a vertical affair and a matter of *universal subordination*. A given angel is subordinated to his (her?) boss for all issues and purposes (no temporary project organization in heaven!). It is amusing to find that the principle of *not bypassing* the chain of command applies also to angels (but not to God). The purpose of it all is for the lower levels to *become as much like the highest* as possible. In ascending, it is important to "cry out with never silent lips ... the hymn of divine praise" (Dionysius 1981: 56). *Knowledge and perfection increase* as you move up the hierarchy, thereby justifying the *one-way flow* of communication, from the top and down. *The boss knows everything*, literally.

Dionysius's hierarchy differs in some respects from the watchmaker's. There is dynamism through scope for advancement, so that a part becomes a part on a higher level. The stark instrumentality of the clock mechanism is also moderated in a system where the entire order is sacred, and every component reflects some of this.[11] Undoubtedly the main principle, however, is "*vertical sealing off of units.*" The fall of an angel must not compromise the integrity of the superiors.

The parallelisms indicated may appear trivial. Is it not just normal that the meaning of a word such as "hierarchy" is relatively consistent over time? Is it not even commendable that it has retained most of its original significance? My quarrel is not with the fidelity to historical usage. The problem is rather that what was explicit and central to Dionysius is, with later authors, hidden as a set of implicit assumptions. Hierarchy is "technified" and "neutralized," which in itself is strange for a word so loaded with history and sacrament (see the Appendix to this chapter). In this way, we have inherited a propensity to take the meaning of word combinations such as "hierarchical classification system," "organizational hierarchy" (literally: sacred order of tools), and "hierarchy of goals" as self-evident. Thereby, we tend to blend and hide important assumptions and make them difficult to discern.

One additional assumption, a kind of "meta-assumption," is stated rather clearly by Dionysius: "Our hierarchy is a sacred *science, activity, and perfection* ..." (1981: 17, emphases added). Thus there is a hierarchy of *knowledge* as well as of *action* and of *being*, and the three coincide. Big action flows from the top and generates little actions by lesser beings, endowed with only partial knowledge. Here, in my view, we get closer to why hierarchy has been such a magnet for organizational theorists. The corporation has been seen as an instrument for processing information and dividing up work. Information and work are broken down into parts and handled by special units. The breakdown of information coincides with the breakdown of action. The result is a triple chain of organizational positions, information, and action. To generalize wildly: there are CEOs with brains, global and summarized information, and formulation of strategies at the top, and workers with legs or more limited brains, specific information, and implementation of tactics at the bottom.

For many firms today, it is obvious that this model applies less and less. Knowledge may be greater at the periphery and far "down" the command chain. Instead new strategies are developed, or emerging, in subunits. The locus of knowledge may not coincide with the locus of strategic initiative. In fact, managerial work consists largely in constantly rearranging structures and work processes so that knowledge and potential for action may meet. (Compare to the discussion in Zeleny 1987. The distinction between different types of "division of labor" goes in the same direction as my distinction between different hierarchical orders.) Scott (1987a: 40–45), in summarizing Weber's theory of bureaucracy and the criticisms against it, makes the point that in Weber's time technical competence and position were highly correlated, whereas today this is no longer the case. The staff–line distinction recognizes this, but perhaps "not so much a solution to the difficulty ... as a structural recognition of the distinctiveness of the two sources of authority sloughed over in Weber's analysis" (Scott 1987a: 44). My suggestion is to posit several "lines," and expect the degree of overlap to vary between organizations, and the relative criticality of the lines to vary as well, also over time.

It is not only a matter of separate dimensions (knowledge, action, work) overlapping, but also of the structuring of each dimension. Today we doubt that knowledge is fundamentally reducible to single bits. We also start to question whether new patterns emerge from big causes, cascading out in a hierarchy of smaller effects. Chaos theory is beginning to emphasize large effects of small causes ("the butterfly effect"), and the practical impossibility of deducing the former from the latter. Common experience of how new strategies emerge seems often to fit such a dynamic, rather than the hierarchical derivation of means from overarching ends (compare with Mintzberg 1973, and Mintzberg et al. 1976).

Analyses of the disadvantages of hierarchy and emphasis on the existence of more complex systems than the clock are of course common in the literature. "Control losses" in hierarchies and optimal structures for varying complexities of problems have been studied empirically (Williamson 1964; Bavelas 1951; Blau and Scott 1962; Perrow 1979; and many others). The intention has been to pinpoint crucial aspects of hierarchy, which are so obvious that they may escape undetected, and the questioning of which gives rise to new conceptions of organization. Therefore, how can the signs that hierarchy is being modified in MNCs be related to the conceptual discussion?

THE MNC AND ASSUMPTIONS OF HIERARCHY: THE EMERGENCE OF A HIERARCHICAL MODEL

An implicit point of view in the preceding discussion has been to reason in terms of organizational effectiveness. Hierarchy's consequences, rather than its causes, have been the main preoccupation. Now this perspective will be applied explicitly. I will argue that the MNC is confronting a world which largely invalidates the fundamental assumptions of hierarchy and of its benevolent effects. In turn, let us discuss the four assumptions of *pre-specified and stable tasks; instrumentality and additive influence by parts; unidirectionality*

209

and universality, and finally, the meta-assumption of *coinciding hierarchies of knowledge, action, and people.*

Pre-specification and stability

In the ethnocentric and polycentric MNC (Perlmutter 1965), tasks are indeed rather clear and stable. It is natural to build a pyramid with easily definable distinctions between headquarters and subsidiaries. Ethnocentricism implies sequential interdependence (Thompson 1967). Knowledge and initiative reside in the center, and more operational tasks in the periphery. Polycentrism suggests another, but equally clear, division of tasks. Headquarters is at the center of pooled interdependencies, and acts as a monitor and portfolio manager. However, in the geocentric case, the task of any one unit is much more complex, unstable, and intricately related to the tasks of other units. Interdependencies between "center" and subsidiaries, as well as among subsidiaries, become reciprocal. A design strategy that simply recommends incorporating such interlinkages in the same unit does not help very much. Too much becomes incorporated, since reciprocal interdependencies encompass many organizational units. The same problems confront the analyst or designer trying to map the organizational structure through frequencies of interaction.

If organization is perceived as a hierarchy of jobs (as in Weber's bureaucracy), the modern MNC constantly upsets the hierarchy, since a long-term specification of the role of any one organizational unit is unfeasible. One might take the argument one step further. The very *raison d'être* of the MNC is constantly to rearrange jobs and transactions, utilizing its infrastructural advantages of globality. In this sense, the MNC becomes a *meta-institution*.[12] It should not be understood as a particular solution in terms of the governance mode of Williamson's transaction cost theory (1975 and particularly 1981). Instead, it is better understood as a mechanism for constantly *selecting* governance modes for an array of innumerable and changing transactions. The MNC becomes a *selection mechanism* rather than a *selected mechanism*. This type of meta-institution is what is required when tasks, information, technological interfaces, and so on cannot be prespecified and must change at non-trivial speed.

The implication of all this is that no hierarchical ordering will be well suited to probable future tasks. Given the pernicious influence and indirect effects of any particular "freezing" of basic structure, it seems reasonable to argue that hierarchy must not be seen as one of the first strategies to manage complex information processing demands, as it is in Galbraith's (1973) analysis. (See for example Davidson and Haspeslagh (1982) on the difficulties of implementing an organization according to global product lines.)

Most recent suggestions for more flexible MNC management (Bartlett and Ghoshal 1986; Doz and Prahalad 1986; Hedlund 1986; White and Poynter 1990; Nonaka 1990) bring up the necessary multidimensionality of the organization structure. My argument here is that we need to go one step further and question the whole idea of stable dimensionality in the hierarchy. To exaggerate a bit, we need to consider the formal structure of the organization last, not first, as far as its efficiency in carrying out its tasks is concerned. This is not "simply" a matter of matrix organization. (See Hedlund (1986) for a discussion of this point.) There may, of course, be reasons other than efficiency for sticking to a permanent hierarchy: for example, the preservation of power for the top managers or the need to identify a center of accountability demanded by parties external to the firm.

Instrumentality and additivity

It is obvious that the subsidiaries of large MNCs cannot be seen only as instruments of the center, the headquarters, the corporate group, or whatever. Influential frameworks of analyzing the MNC take the anchoring in a host country environment as the critical factor against which any ambitions for global integration have to be balanced (Doz 1979).

Systematic or synergetic, rather than additive, coupling of subsidiaries to the rest of the corporation is implicit in the conception of a geocentric MNC. In polycentrism, one market can be given up and you simply have a slightly smaller company. In many industries today, it is impossible to consider strategies this way. Take away the US market, and you also influence scanning for R&D, competitive posture on third country markets, the supply of components, exchange rate vulnerability, and so on. The same argument may also apply across product lines. My discussion, however, applies primarily within only moderately diversified firms. In very heterogeneous organizations, the benefits of rich interaction are too minor to justify the efforts.

Human aspects reinforce the trend away from instrumental and additive views of the parts of the MNC. MNCs have some disadvantage compared with local companies in recruiting, a disadvantage that becomes further pronounced if and when the subsidiary becomes only a pawn in a superordinate game.

Unidirectionality and universality

It is not uncommon in MNCs to speak of a distributed network of "centers of competence." Subsidiaries are or become or are made specialized, and take on roles as global coordinators in some areas, whereas they may continue to be "soldiers" in others. Multiple hierarchies shift between products and issues, and over time intersect. In the extreme, there is no visible overall apex. Any unit is both a coordinating and directing center and a subordinated part, and the composition of roles changes often enough and overlaps to such an extent that a segregation into different hierarchical chains becomes impractical.

211

I shall not claim that any existing MNC resembles this extreme model. However, tendencies to assign global product mandates, tendencies to charge subsidiaries with new roles as strategic contributors, functional specialization over subsidiaries and countries, the use of international project teams, and interlocking-directorate types of management structures all move the MNC in this direction. (See, for example, Hedlund 1980; Bartlett and Ghoshal 1986.) Obviously, such trends will be more visible in MNCs from small home countries.

Coinciding knowledge, action, and people hierarchies

Many of the previous points can be related to the breakdown of the Dionysian construction of mirroring structures of knowledge, action, and "social" (if such a term is allowed among angels) position. Because of differing market environments and organizational histories, technological expertise often does not coincide with superior position in the organizational hierarchy. Innovation is increasingly likely to be generated from localized and diffused but globally motivated action rather than from tightly coordinated strategies formulated at the core. It is not possible to reduce the sum total of organizational knowledge to a filing cabinet, or a department, or a computer program at the top.

The question then becomes what the function of top management really is. Blau argues that "conditions in organizations that make the reliable performance of duties relatively independent of direct intervention by top management further the development of multilevel hierarchies," since then the problem that hierarchy can make the top executive lose touch will not matter so much (1968: 464). His argument assumes that some useful coordination task remains to be achieved, or that competition is inefficient enough to allow hierarchies to be established on "non-rational" grounds.

Now, the development of information technology has opened up new vistas for working with distributed knowledge and reliable multi-focal action,[13] without relying on layers of management for coordination. Managerial levels become unnecessary when information is available immediately (in time) and broadly (in physical and organizational space). It is now routine in advanced MNCs to have systems where individual sales orders are immediately fed into global logistical, manufacturing, and financial systems, and where many decision routines are automated and decision variables jointly optimized. The consequence is a drastic simplification in the number of formal managerial levels. Thus, this type of advanced technology makes hierarchy unnecessary, rather than relieving it of its drawbacks, as in Blau's (1968) discussion.

Such practically complex but conceptually simple cases of information technology may cloud the wider picture, however. In the long run, the consequences of wide access and possibilities for experimentation in combining

212

pieces of information are probably more important.[14] Multiple trial is the only way to explore the consequences of combinations of one technology with another, one set of competences with a market far away, and so on. Information technology makes this possible on a global scale. The approach is considered common sense in research laboratories, small high-tech firms (see Bahrami and Evans, 1987), and some professional organizations. Now, in much larger settings, it may be possible partly to substitute for the strict demands on physical proximity and intensive personal interaction by linking people and units through technical means.[15]

The organization in this perspective becomes an arena for creation and experimentation, rather than for the exploitation of given knowledge and other resources.[16] In a way, we are sketching the outlines of and structural prerequisites of global, large-scale entrepreneurialism. Schumpeter's (1947) long-run hypothesis was that the institutionalization of entrepreneurship would slowly grind the capitalist machine to a standstill, or at least result in a more mediocre capacity for change. However, technical advances may allow the design of institutions not envisioned by Schumpeter. It is significant that as late as 1973, when Galbraith writes about information systems and strategies for organization design, he explicitly calls for *vertical* information systems (my emphasis). Although he refers to probable incapacities for imagining new social systems, Galbraith buys into the Dionysian formula of knowledge as one hierarchy. (It is true, however, that he emphasizes lateral processes and structures in general.)

Arrow uses the important distinction between "terminal acts" and "experiments" developed by Raiffa and Schlaifer to contrast two very different kinds of decisions: "decisions to act in some concrete sense, and decisions to collect information" (1974: 49). Arrow emphasizes the trade-off between efficient terminal acts and rich experimentation, and does not at all see hierarchy, or any other structure, as the obvious solution: "The optimal choice of internal communication structures is a vastly difficult question" (1974: 54). In spite of this, in the chapter that follows this discussion he does not really take issue with the argument that "since transmission of information is costly ... it is cheaper and more efficient to transmit all the pieces of information once to a central place than to disseminate each of them to everyone" (1974: 68). This is seen as the classical argument for "authority."

The "polar alternative" for authority is claimed to be "consensus" (1974: 69). Consensus is viable when interests and information are identical in a group. I would argue that there are indeed many ways to move towards these conditions, by using modern technology and by intelligent redesign of incentive systems, including ownership structures. If, in addition to this, the modern organization has to shift the balance towards more experiments and fewer terminal acts, it is not at all obvious that information processing demands lead one to design authority structures. Of course, this is a familiar argument. The evidence is well summarized by Scott (1987a: 151–154). It seems as if the idea of experimentation and information seeking is not really carried through in the debate on authority, the advantages of which are more posited than argued.

Arrow emphasizes, as I have tried to do, religious beliefs in the acceptance of authority (1974: 64–65 in particular). Perhaps biases of the kind introduced by Dionysius can explain why his list (1974: 77) of "responsibility mechanisms" in modern organizations does not contain the conceivable alternative of responsibility to those governed, with an active role by the subordinates, for example as constituting the board of directors. Such circularity goes against the grain of hierarchy, but is not often mentioned, in spite of the fact that it does not contradict any of the basic lines of the analysis of information-processing demands.

As an aside, it is tempting to contrast the implications of an emphasis on experimentation with those of transaction cost theory. The boundaries of the firm (not the "hierarchy"!) will be determined by consideration of *optimum range and intensity of experimentation*, rather than by minimum cost of transacting and producing. The function of boundaries is partly the same; to ensure internalization of rents discovered and created, to handle incentive problems, and so on. Added emphasis is placed, however, on the tacit dimension of organizational competence (cf. Pavitt 1971). The many references to Polanyi's (1958) discussion of tacitness in economics and organization theory do not, in my view, stress adequately that Polanyi was talking about personal knowledge. The analysis and the challenges become more complex if tacitness is seen at a social level. A global firm may be seen as an investor in technical and human communications infrastructure and codes, where the interpretative capability is largely firm-specific and tacit. By definition, tacit knowledge cannot be easily codified, and is thus less amenable for assignation in hierarchical knowledge structures. And consequently, if social tacit knowledge is important, it follows that hierarchy is at least problematical as a reflection of the distribution of competence in the organization (see Arrow 1974: 55–56.)

ASPECTS OF HIERARCHY

I have argued that hierarchy can be challenged conceptually and theoretically, and some assumptions laid bare that make it seem less attractive as a design principle for certain kinds of systems and organizations. The modern MNC falls in the category of systems not benefited by hierarchical conception. It has also been claimed that tendencies in MNCs illustrate adaptations based on assumptions alternative to those constituting hierarchies.[17] From all of this is emerging a notion of an alternative organizing principle, which I call *heterarchy*.[18] A heterarchy is by definition a more ambiguous creature than the hierarchy. Still, it is possible to define some aspect of heterarchy in a more formal way.

1. Components in a heterarchy are related along three primary dimensions: knowledge, action, and position of authority.[19] The dimensions of most actual organization structures (geography, product, function, technology, and so on) are only proxies for the primary dimensions. It is necessary, whenever one specifies an order, also to specify along which dimension the order applies.
2. Units in a heterarchy may or may not be ordered in the same way along the three dimensions. The rule, rather than the exception, will be that the orders do not coincide. Thus, "management by exception" becomes a strange principle in a heterarchy.
3. The order will vary over time and circumstance. A given unit will be both Chief and Indian. Diagrammatically, hierarchy in its simplest form can be contrasted with heterarchy thus:

Hierarchy	Heterarchy		
A	A	B	C
B	B	A	B
C	C	C	A

4. The order will not necessarily be transitive. The organization will often be circular (Ackoff 1974). This is McCulloch's (1965) original idea developed in the 1940s, which is applied in Ogilvy (1977) and Schwartz and Ogilvy (1979). McCulloch hypothesizes that the human brain is so constructed that:

> Circularities in preference instead of indicating inconsistencies, actually demonstrate consistency of a higher order than had been dreamed of in our philosophy. An organism possessed of this nervous system—six neurons—is sufficiently endowed to be unpredictable from any theory founded on a scale of values. It has a heterarchy of values, and is thus internectively too rich to submit to a summum bonum.
>
> (McCulloch 1965: 43)

Later findings on the holographic properties of the brain point in the same direction as McCulloch's speculations. The most intelligent systems we know seem to be heterarchically organized. Again, schematically, we can represent the difference:

Hierarchy	Heterarchy
A	A
B	B
C	C
	A

Practical examples of heterarchical social systems are democratic political systems, employee share ownership, and many kinds of project councils and R&D boards in companies. In addition, computer programs have been described as heterarchical. (See Hofstadter 1980.)

5. The relations between units in a heterarchy may be of several kinds: A may issue commands to B, evaluate B, hold knowledge of importance to B, include B as a constitutive part, and so on. This is a consequence of multidimensionality. In addition, however, within the confines of the dimension of, say, action, we can conceive of different types of ordering. Act A may be an instruction leading to act B (such as McCulloch's neurons firing messages to each other). Act A may also be superordinate more in the sense of confirming or catalyzing a whole set of acts B, C, D, and so on. In my view, much of the problem with Simon's discussion has to do with the fact that the type of relation between subsystems is not specified.

The hierarchical model, as observed in organizational practice, obscures the differences between kinds of relation and puts the command structure as the primary one. A result of recognizing these distinctions is that the notion of rank order and verticality in themselves become less relevant, and at least "secularized."[20] The sum total is to create a situation where "management" is as much a horizontal as a vertical affair, and becomes part of every unit's and individual's task. If managerial competence is a scarce resource, this may lead to specialization of this function, as of every other job (cf. Williamson 1975: 47, 52). However, it is not clear why managers should be "above" those whose coordination needs they serve.

Hierarchy   Heterarchy
A   A   B   C
B
C

6. A heterarchy is given cohesion and is protected from mere anarchy primarily by normative integration (Etzioni 1975). Shared objectives and knowledge, and a common organizational culture and symbolism, are important mechanisms. Investments in communication systems, rotation of personnel, a bias for internal "promotion," and other human resource management strategies become increasingly important. Simon (1989), in discussing the balance between markets and organizations, emphasizes employees' identification with the organization, and criticizes transaction cost analysis for neglecting such aspects. However, Simon in this same paper emphasizes "specialization and the consequent hierarchization of authority" (1989: 22). I have tried to argue that specialization does *not* necessarily lead to hierarchy.

Simon introduces the concept of "docility" to characterize the attitude of individuals in organizations. To be docile is to be tractable, manageable, teachable. He confesses that he is not entirely happy with the term (1989: 13). No doubt it paints a brighter picture of human nature than the references to shirking, cheating, moral hazard, and opportunism in the property rights, agency cost, and transaction cost literature. Still, there are the contours of a curiously passive creature in the word and its referents. Heterarchy will have to rely also on more active and assertive organizational identification. Scott (1987a: 34) notes that "formalization makes allowances for the finitude of humans." The same point is made concerning government in general and scientific work. It is worth noting that industry leaders have now started wondering about how to tap into the positive sources of human motivation much more directly, perhaps to make allowances for the *infinitude* of human beings. For example, Jan Carlzon of SAS (1985) makes the distinction between two ways of managing: by *instruction*, by specifying *restrictions*, which makes it impossible for the managed to take responsibility; and by *information*, by specifying *opportunities*, which makes the employee take responsibility.

Instillation of common interests can and should also take the form of material incentives. A heterarchical MNC would do well to seriously consider global employee ownership of the "parent company."[21] Bonus systems can be designed to encourage system-wide responses and responsibilities commensurate with responsibilities.

In summary, and at the risk of launching unwieldy catch phrases, hierarchy as an alternative to hierarchy may be characterized as:

- multidimensional (knowledge, action, and position)
- asymmetrically ordered along the dimensions
- temporary subordination and simultaneous sub- and superordination
- non-transitivity, circularity
- horizontality
- normative, goal-directed integration.

The beginning of new metaphors for the large, complex firm

It seems as if the modern corporation has reached the limits of useful borrowing of concepts from other fields. Hierarchy came from the church;[22] strategies, line–staff distinctions, divisions, and many other things from the military; bureaucracy from the state. Is it not time that the private corporation invested in something on its own?

Blocking such progress are the half-digested techniques and metaphors of history and other fields of human effort. Scrutinizing "hierarchy" was meant

217

to indicate that the inheritance is not all to the good. The idea of heterarchy is partly to suggest formally definable aspects of alternative structures. It is also meant to imply a more encompassing notion of order, of which hierarchy is a special case defined by some rather strict assumptions. Heterarchy also aims to describe empirical reality—what actually goes on in the modern MNC—better than conceptions of hierarchy.

Other reconceptualizations of managerial activity are consistent with the drift of my argument. Nonaka's (1990) "information creation" (as distinct from information processing) is a step in a more dynamic view of what companies do and what it takes to do it. Morgan's (1986) critique of various views of "organization," suggesting "imaginizations" as one possible alternative concept, is also related to my discussion of the limits of instrumentality and mechanism.[23] Static conceptions of environment–organization interaction have long been challenged, notably by Weick (1979). Such ideas are akin to stressing the action dimension of heterarchy, and debating possibilities of pre-specification of tasks.

These broad discussions lead also to questioning the nature of "management." A first indication that this word is as loaded with partly outdated meaning as "hierarchy" is the etymology of the word. A quick search in the *Oxford English Dictionary* reveals that it originally had to do with breaking and training horses. (The word *manège* means the arena where horses go round and round, just like employees, with the trainer with the whip in the center, just like the manager.)[24]

If the world of heterarchy seems too messy to be a practical alternative, it may be a comfort to contemplate the possibility that non-hierarchy seems to work better in practice than in theory. The brain functions, perhaps heterarchically, in spite of our inability to grasp its mode of coordination. The naturalness of hierarchy thus may be much more a product of mental and perceptual biases than we like to admit. The conception that order requires ordering may also be contrasted with the view of a Canadian tribe of Indians, described by Miller (1955) and discussed in Bouvier (1984). Hell for them is a horrible place "where some human beings are in control of others." (The Western hell, as we know from successful interrogation by the Holy Inquisition, is very neatly organized, also in nine levels.[25]) The tribe does not even have a word for hierarchy.[26] A final reflection is that in Western languages, it seems difficult to find translations of the Greek word. We rely on the latitude of imprecision given by a silent consensus not to engage in conceptual archeology. The cost is, as I have argued, the unconscious adoption of a number of interesting but questionable assumptions and/or the complete stripping of the concept of any precise meaning.

APPENDIX

It is well beyond the scope of this paper and its author to speculate on the reasons for the shift in the meaning of hierarchy from sacred to secular. My own hunch is that the Enlightenment and science destroyed the deeper basis of a hierarchy of beings. However, for political and personal safety reasons, at least the top of the hierarchy was preserved. (Giordano Bruno was burnt partly for associating the new idea of infinity with the possibility that there might not be any particular distinctions in creation: "pantheistic immanentism.") The illogic of this (keeping the top) did not escape the great minds of the time. Leibniz wrote that:

> Sir Isaac Newton, and his followers, have also a very odd opinion concerning the work of God. According to their doctrine, God Almighty wants to wind up his watch from time to time; otherwise it would cease to move. He had not, it seems, sufficient foresight to make it a perpetual motion. Nay the machine of God's making is so imperfect, according to these gentlemen, that he is obliged to clean it now and then by an extraordinary concourse, and even to mend it, as a clockmaker mends his work.[27]

POSTCRIPT
By D. Eleanor Westney

Gunnar Hedlund himself pursued the ideas set forth in this chapter in the tragically few years left to him, both in terms of theoretical exposition of the central role of knowledge in the MNC (Hedlund 1994) and in analysis of cross-border product development projects (Hedlund and Ridderstrahle 1995).

The work since then that most creatively extends and expands on Gunnar's ideas is the research by Doz, Santos, and Williamson (2001) on the cross-border networks constructed by firms that are "born in the wrong place": that is, established outside the countries that contain lead markets and world-class centers of technology.

Notes

1   An earlier version of this paper was presented at the workshop on Organizational Theory and the Multinational Corporation at INSEAD on September 1–2 1989. The author wishes to thank W. Richard Scott, David Hawk, Bruce Kogut, and colleagues at IIB, particularly Maria Bolte, Peter Hagstrom, Lars Hakanson, Dag Rolander, and Karl Ahlander, for constructive criticism of earlier drafts.
2   However, Williamson (1975: 41–56) does discuss the relative merits of peer groups and "simple hierarchies," although the latter concept is not strictly defined. Chandler's (1962, 1977) analysis resembles that of the transaction cost analysts. "Managerial hierarchies" are seen as replacing markets, and the evolution of the large firm is described largely as replacing small hierarchies with bigger, more complex ones. The alternative is seen as a "federation of autonomous offices," so that coordination is assumed to require hierarchy, and the concept becomes almost synonymous to internal organization in general (see Chandler 1977: 1–12).
3   El Sawy (1985) is the first discussion of the firm as a hologram, as far as I know.

4 Note that in the following discussion the page references of Simon (1962) refer to the 1982 reprint of that volume.

5 Ackoff and Emery (1972) provide classifications in line with these ideas. See also the discussion of "nested hierarchies" on the one hand and those of "independently individuated entities" on the other in Depew and Weber (1985).

6 The watchmaker analogy is a very interesting one in that it pictures a world with a maker of perfect knowledge, a sort of omniscient God. His creation is frictionless and everything has its perfect place in it. Simon argues (1962: 93) that his theory assumes no teleological mechanism, "in spite of the overtones of the watchmaker parable." It seems that the parable of a watchmaker is irresistible for social as well as natural scientists. Cf. the remarks by Leibniz quoted in the Appendix, and Dawkins' (1986) "blind watchmaker."

7 See the history of navigation. The concept of navigation, which assumes reliable timekeeping, led to frenetic efforts to design robust clocks. Evolution could not work with a stable, ready part.

8 It is tempting but not possible here to get involved in the question of whether language itself is necessarily hierarchically structured, and whether the difficulties of defining non-hierarchy might have to do with this.

9 It may be argued that Simon's argument is exactly about the importance of independently existing parts, with which evolution can then play. However, the example assumes that the clockmaker *manufactures* the parts. He is *not* in the position of evolution, at least a non-teleological kind of evolution, having to contend with a historical mess of components not particularly useful a priori for any design at all. A better example would be to consider a complete ignoramus stumbling around in a junkyard, trying to get something interesting put together.

10 The contribution of Dionysius is sketched in Hedlund (1988), which relies on the translation and commentary by Thomas L. Campbell (Dionysius 1981).

11 Of course, hierarchy literally is translated as "rule through the sacred."

12 "Institution" is here used in a restrictive sense, "markets" and "hierarchies" in transaction cost theory being regarded as institutions. See also Hedlund (1986).

13 Cf. Prahalad and Doz (1987), and their "multi-focal MNC."

14 Hagstrom (1990) contains a discussion of un- and rebuilding and relocation of activities in MNCs as a consequence of modern information technology.

15 All experience tells us that this will not be *sufficient*. It needs to be complemented by close attention to global *human* communication systems. Nevertheless, "organized anarchies," "adhocracies," "free-form organization," and so on become possibilities also for large organizations. These may come to resemble "professional organizations." Analyses of coordination mechanisms in such organizations are akin to much of my discussion above. See Scott 1965 and 1987a: 236–239. Edgar Schein's work on the nature of managerial hierarchy in such contexts is also very relevant: see for example Schein 1989 and 2001.

16 See Hedlund and Rolander (1990), for further discussion of exploitation and experimentation strategies.

17 It is not the purpose of this paper to give an empirical review of the evidence, so the propositions must here stand only as hypotheses and examples.

18 I first discovered the concept in Ogilvy (1977), who refers to McCulloch (1965) as his source of inspiration. See also my own discussion (1986).

19 I have here selected anthropocentric concepts. It is possible that the aspects of heterarchy in social systems are also characteristic of a wider class of systems.

20 Of course, there are deep cultural forces protecting the sacred aspects of hierarchy. The relativistic view of relations between parts here propounded is not readily subscribed to in societies where the essence of the society is exactly the sanctity of authority relations. My argument is basically in terms of efficiency, not legitimacy.

21 Note that family metaphors are very common in MNC parlance: *daughter* companies, ask *mother* for money, come *home* for review, and so on. It should be apparent that such a metaphor does not necessarily imply unambiguous subordination ("*sub*sidiaries").

22 Of course, the military may also be cited as the source of hierarchy in substance if not in name. However, the insistence upon authority is complemented by emphasizing local, independent action in line with very overarching goals. The military is more hierarchic in peace than in war-time action (see for example Arrow 1974: 69).

23 "Organization" comes from "*organon*" which means, among other things, "tool."

24 Chuang-tzu has a chapter on horses' hooves, which argues that even in the training of horses, you should not "manage" too much. Half of the horses will die, for example. In Western orthodoxy, such germs of more indirect leadership principles are conspicuously absent. Lao Tzu, of course, also gives many examples of the virtues of non-action by the ruler, spontaneous order and vitality, and so on. Taoism may be the source of inspiration for new perspectives on management.

25 See Paine 1972, ch. 7.

26 The general question of cultural bias in the concept and practice of hierarchy is, of course, a very complicated one which cannot be discussed at length here. Works by Hofstede (1980a), Laurent (1983), and Maruyama (1978) seem particularly relevant among modern authors. Weber's work on religion and its relation to capitalism and bureaucracy also provides ample material.

27 From *The Leibniz-Clarke Correspondence*, ed. H. G. Alexander, quoted in Patrides 1973: 444.

11 Procedural Justice Theory and the Multinational Corporation

W. Chan Kim and Renée A. Mauborgne

The frontiers of debate concerning multinational corporations (MNCs) are increasingly shifting from resource-based advantages to advantages derived from strategic capability—the ability of multinational corporations to conceive and execute complex strategies (Prahalad and Doz 1987; Kim and Mauborgne 1993c, 1995). An MNC's strategic capability determines its ability to leverage the worldwide assets, distinctive competencies, and knowledge of its globally dispersed network of operations. While strategic capability is increasingly central to the success of MNCs, it presents an increasingly difficult challenge.

Traditionally, the MNC was viewed as a hierarchy. In this hierarchy, relations between the head office and its network of global operations were chiefly viewed as a governing mode, wherein tasks were achieved through legitimate rules, formal sanctions, authority, and the manipulation of rewards and punishments. However, as global operations have increasingly accumulated rich resources and competencies, grown in size, complexity, and inter-unit linkages, with non-trivial cultural and spatial distances separating them from the head office, the distinctive powers of hierarchy have declined (Hedlund 1986, Chapter 10 this volume; Kim and Mauborgne 1991, 1993b). While the degree of this decline varies by firm (for example, through the extent of organizational socialization in a firm), by industry (for example, in the extent to which technology is routine and tangible), and by culture (for example, in the extent to which cultural values support unconditional deference to authority), monitoring difficulties and control loss are on the rise across all MNCs, heightening the discretionary power of multinational managers.

Concurrent with multinationals' lessening of control over the actions of subsidiary units and the multinational managers that comprise them, the strategic requirements for global success demand increasingly high levels of intellectual and emotional cooperation across the multinationals' network of operations. If we reflect on the strategic prescriptions of effective global operations this becomes clear. These include dexterously shifting capital and resources across national units, cross-subsidizing global units to counter global rivals indirectly (Hamel and Prahalad 1985), institutionalizing fully standardized product offerings, marketing approaches, and commonly used distribution systems worldwide to allow for maximum global efficiencies

(Levitt 1983; Yip 1989), and consciously consolidating worldwide knowledge, technology, marketing, and production skills that can serve as engines for continuous new business development, innovation, and enhanced customer value (Prahalad and Hamel 1990). While these strategic requirements may be diverse (Ghoshal 1987), they are united in that their effective achievement rests on individual managers' consummate emotional and intellectual cooperation. Building on Williamson (1975), consummate cooperation, be it intellectual or emotional, reflects the willingness of managers to go beyond formally defined guidelines or minimally acceptable requirements to give their best for the benefit of the organization.

Consummate emotional cooperation is central to swift and coordinated actions and multinational managers' willing sacrifice of subsystem for system, and short-term for long-term, goals and priorities. When consummate emotional cooperation exists, MNCs can expect managers to execute strategic decisions to the best of their abilities even if those decisions are not parallel with multinational managers' individual self-interests. On the other hand, consummate *intellectual* cooperation motivates multinational managers' efficient and full exchange of knowledge, ideas, and innovations. When such cooperation prevails, we can expect a high level of learning across managers and strategic decisions of enhanced quality.

In MNCs' flexible, integrated network of global operations (Bartlett and Ghoshal 1989), where recourse to hierarchy is not only less feasible but also insufficient to motivate more than perfunctory cooperation, the critical question is how to build multinationals' strategic capability to achieve these two objectives. It is our contention that the theoretical discipline of procedural justice research (e.g. Thibaut and Walker 1975; Tyler and Caine 1981; Alexander and Ruderman 1987; Lind and Tyler 1988; Folger and Konovosky 1989; Tyler 1990), which is grounded in the fields of social psychology and law, may provide important insights into this issue. Procedural justice theory is concerned with how the dynamics of the decision process, in particular the perceived fairness of this process, affect individuals' attitudes and behavior.

There are two reasons for our conviction that procedural justice may well be a theoretical discipline of significance to the study of the modern multinational. The first concerns the unit of analysis of procedural justice research: the decision-making process and the individual. As the strategic capability of multinationals is increasingly embedded in dispersed and changing decision-making units which cut across geographic regions, functions, and businesses, process and people, not structure and systems, emerge as central determinants of multinationals' strategic capability (Bartlett and Ghoshal 1995). The second reason concerns the attitudinal and behavioral affects of procedural justice. Based on the recent theoretical advances of Kim and Mauborgne (1991, 1993a, 1993b, 1993c, 1995, 1996, 1997, 1998), the exercise of procedural justice can be predicted to positively enhance organizational members' consummate emotional and intellectual cooperation, and the effective conception and execution of strategic decisions in the multinational. Hence, we argue here that the exercise of procedural justice may well provide a way to induce the effective design and execution of strategic decisions, offering a potentially powerful, but so far unexplored, route to high performance in the multinational.

This chapter traces the theoretical heritage of procedural justice, discussing the two trends in the literature that start to move procedural justice into the domain of multinational corporations. Next we explore the recent advances in procedural justice research, developing the theoretical link between the exercise of procedural justice and consummate emotional and intellectual cooperation, high-quality strategic decision content and execution, and performance in the multinational. Finally, we discuss the multinational contexts in which the application and study of procedural justice could yield potentially profound insights into managing the modern multinational and building its strategic capability.

THE THEORETICAL HERITAGE OF PROCEDURAL JUSTICE

The historical antecedents of procedural justice theory are grounded in the seminal work of Thibaut and Walker (Thibaut et al. 1974; Thibaut and Walker 1975, 1978; Walker et al. 1974). The starting point of Thibaut and Walker's work was a concern with how the process by which decisions are reached exerts a powerful influence on human cognitions and behavior. This led them to embark on a systematic study of the psychology of social decision-making processes.

This seminal work of Thibaut and Walker represented a domain of social psychology that viewed the individual through a different, and in some respects new, lens. It regarded individuals as equally as concerned, if not more concerned, with matters of process as with outcomes. Accordingly, the central focus of Thibaut and Walker's analysis was how individuals' evaluations of ongoing social interactions are shaped by the dynamics of social process. Although there exist multiple aspects of social processes that may well influence, to a non-trivial extent, individuals' reactions to their social interaction, Thibaut and Walker concentrated on only one dimension: judgments that procedures and social processes are just.

Accordingly, Thibaut and Walker created the field of procedural justice by merging an interest in the psychology of justice with the study of process. More concretely, procedural justice theory concerns itself expressly with the "social psychological consequences of procedural variation, with particular emphasis on procedural effects of fairness judgments" (Lind and Tyler 1988: 7). It maintains that people care a great deal about the procedures by which outcomes are arrived at, and argues for the primacy of fair procedures per se.

Thibaut and Walker first explored the concern for procedural justice in legal and judicial settings: few domains have granted as much attention to questions of procedures and processes as has the law. This research provided the first unambiguous demonstration that variations in procedural justice per se indeed affect the attitudes and behaviors of those subject to a procedure. Specifically, Thibaut and Walker found that increases in procedural justice judgments result in salutary attitudinal and behavioral consequences, including better acceptance of, and compliance with, the resulting decision outcomes. This led them to conclude specifically that the exercise of procedural justice may well allow the legal process to "bind up the social fabric and encourage the continuation of productive exchange relations between individuals," and generally that the property of being fair and just may well be an important requisite for any model of decision making. Subsequent studies of procedural justice in legal settings have widely confirmed these findings (e.g. Lind et al. 1980; Tyler and Folger 1980; Casper, Tyler, and Fisher 1988; Tyler 1988, 1990).

Since the seminal research of Thibaut and Walker, two important trends in procedural justice research are particularly relevant here. One concerns the contexts in which procedural justice has been studied. As the theoretical work of Leventhal (Leventhal 1990; Leventhal, Karuza, and Fry 1980) brought to light, the scope of procedural justice judgments as a psychological phenomenon is not limited to legal issues. The concept can be extended to procedures in non-legal settings as well. This position, which was since echoed even more strongly in the work of Lind and Tyler (1988), provided an invaluable bridge between procedural justice concerns and a wide range of social settings. In essence, it untied procedural justice theory from its bondage to the legal domain, thereby clearing the way for more diverse applications of the theory. Researchers accordingly embarked on an increasing number of studies in non-legal settings: the political (e.g. Tyler and Caine 1981; Tyler, Rasinski, and McGraw 1985), educational (e.g. Tyler and Caine 1981), and interpersonal (e.g. Barrett-Howard and Tyler 1986). Consistently these works have found that concerns of procedural justice are central to individuals and have strong social psychological consequences.

Questions of how employees react to organizational procedures in business settings eventually attracted the attention of procedural justice researchers (Greenberg 1987a). For example, both Greenberg (1987b) and Folger and Konovsky (1989) applied the concept of procedural justice to the procedures used in performance evaluations for promotions and pay raise decisions. In another study, Tyler (1989) traced the impact of procedural justice judgments on the reactions of workers to corporate resource allocation and conflict resolution decision processes. Sheppard and Lewecki (1987) assessed executives' perceptions of procedural fairness in seven distinct "role domains" of managerial activity. In addition, issues of procedural justice have been extended in business settings to labor dispute resolution procedures (Sheppard 1984), grievance processes (Fryxell and Gordon 1989), personnel procedures (e.g., Folger and Greenberg 1985; Alexander and Ruderman 1987), and lay-off processes (Brockner et al. 1987). Without exception, these studies have provided support for Leventhal's assertion concerning the generality of procedural justice concerns; people, be they executives, middle-level managers, or lower-level employees, were consistently found to care a great deal about the justice of the procedures by which organizational decisions were reached.

The second trend that stands out in the literature is the migration of attitudinal effects examined and established in procedural justice research. While the initial studies on procedural justice confined their interest to the impact of procedural justice on outcome satisfaction, as the body of procedural justice research multiplied, concern has shifted from how procedural justice impacts lower-order attitudes like satisfaction to how it affects higher-order long-term attitudes. Procedural justice judgments have been shown to have positive and unambiguous effects on the higher-order attitudes of commitment (e.g. Alexander and Ruderman 1987; Brockner et al. 1987; Tyler 1989), trust (e.g. Greenberg 1987b; Folger and Konovsky 1989; Tyler 1989), and social harmony (e.g. Alexander and Ruderman 1987; Tyler and Griffin 1989) in organizational members subject to decision processes. Hence, not only the contexts but also the effects of procedural justice have widely suggested that procedural justice is an even more permeating concern than Leventhal himself had thought.

PROCEDURAL JUSTICE AND THE MULTINATIONAL CORPORATION

The above two trends, we would argue, start to make procedural justice an interesting and relevant theoretical lens for managing the modern multinational. Procedural justice, whose unit of analysis is the individual and decision-making processes, has not only been shown to exert a significant effect on managers in corporate settings, but it is increasingly recognized to be a powerful determinant of individuals' higher-order attitudes of commitment, trust, and social harmony so essential to the effective functioning of multinationals' networks of globally dispersed units. Collectively, they can be theorized to build a sense of community among global managers wherein kinship obligations replace quid pro quo attitudes toward exchange and interaction (Kim and Mauborgne 1991).

Lind and Tyler (1988) provide insight into why increases in procedural justice result in favorable changes in important attitudes and behaviors of organizational members. They assert that in forming important attitudes towards organizations, individuals implicitly adopt a long-term perspective of informed self-interest. A long-term perspective is taken because individuals recognize that social association (here the act of working together in an organization) requires that other people's outcomes and objectives sometimes be given priority, and that their own desires sometimes be post-poned or abandoned if all individuals are to continue to engage in the social interaction. But what then leads individuals to believe that, over the long term, their interests will be reasonably served by a given organization? Lind and Tyler assert that the perceived procedural justice of an organiza-tion's decision-making practices plays a powerful role in influencing this belief. If the procedures by which decisions are reached are perceived as fair, organizational members tend to develop a feeling of reassurance that their interests will be protected and advanced through the decision-making process. This leads individuals to believe that over the long term they will receive reasonable outcomes, even in the absence of short-term gains over an intermediate time frame. Consequently the conviction that an organi-zation's decision-making practices are procedurally just tends to foster loyalty to an organization, more harmonious relations, and generally posi-tive attitudes toward the organization as a whole and the authorities involved.

Kim and Mauborgne (1997, 1998, 2003) furthered the studies on this front by exploring why procedural justice matters in the context of strate-gic decision-making in multinationals and in business settings in general. In discussions of the importance of procedural justice, they found that executives' comments had traces of self-interest concerns. However, these concerns were complemented by statements of another nature: intellectual and emotional recognition. Interviewees' comments suggested that proce-dural justice was valued not so much because it was perceived to enhance the favorability of decision outcomes, but because it echoed managers' fundamental belief in recognizing individuals for their intellectual and emotional worth. On the one hand, individuals seek recognition of their value not as "labor," "personnel," or "human resources," but as human beings who are treated with full respect and dignity and appreciated for their individual worth regardless of hierarchical level. On the other hand, individuals seek recognition that their ideas are sought after and given thoughtful reflection, and that others think enough of their intelligence to explain their thinking to them. When individuals feel recognized for their intellectual and emotional worth, they are inspired to engage in voluntary cooperation and active knowledge sharing, which are essential to the orga-nization's success. This insight led Kim and Mauborgne to propose intel-lectual and emotional recognition theory as a theoretical bridge explaining the causal link between the exercise of procedural justice and higher-order attitudes and behaviors.

THE MEANING OF PROCEDURAL JUSTICE

Procedural justice can be conceptualized as the extent to which the dynamics of a decision process are judged to be fair. This conceptualization of procedural justice stands in accord with the general definition of procedural justice in the literature (see Lind and Tyler 1988). While the potential importance of due process is not without mention in multinational management literature (e.g. Prahalad and Doz 1987), Kim and Mauborgne (1991) were the first to systematically explore its meaning in the multinational context. In a field study of 63 multinational managers, they found procedural justice to be associated with five distinct characteristics. These are:

- that two-way communication exists in multinationals' strategic decision-making processes
- that strategic views can be legitimately challenged in the process
- that decision participants are knowledgeable of the local situation of each other
- that managers are provided with an account of the multinational's final strategic decisions
- that decisions are made consistently.

Taken together, these five characteristics lead multinational managers to judge the multinational's strategic decision-making process to be procedurally just.

Bilateral communication is central to procedural justice because it makes managers feel that their point of view was expressed and considered in reaching strategic decisions. With respect to the ability to challenge and refute strategic views, multinational managers view this as pivotal in bringing to light possible misperceptions or wrong assumptions made in the strategic decision process. Local familiarity is important because it is seen to provide a basic proof that global strategies were set with maximum knowledge of the ramifications of such actions at the local level. The provision of an account for final strategic decisions provides managers with an intellectual understanding of the rationale behind ultimate strategic decisions; especially valued is a sound explanation for why managers' views might have been overridden. Finally, consistent decision-making procedures are prized because they are thought to minimize behavior that participants define as shaped by politics and favoritism in the strategic decision process (Kim and Mauborgne 1993b).

These procedural justice components find support in the existing literature. They are conceptually similar to procedural justice indicators found to influence procedural justice judgments in a wide variety of settings and studies: bilateral communication (e.g. Thibaut and Walker 1975; Leventhal 1990; Greenberg 1986; Folger and Konovsky 1989), consistent application of procedures (e.g. Leventhal 1990; Sheppard and Lewicki 1987; Tyler 1988), ability to refute decisions (e.g. Leventhal 1990; Alexander and Ruderman 1987; Sheppard and Lewicki 1987), local familiarity (e.g. Greenberg 1986; Folger and Konovsky 1989), and the provision of an account (e.g. Bies and Shapiro 1987).

PROCEDURAL JUSTICE, CONSUMMATE EMOTIONAL COOPERATION, AND STRATEGY (DECISION) EXECUTION

Practical and theoretical ground has been developed to expect procedural justice to have a positive effect on consummate emotional cooperation and decision execution in multinationals. As Kim and Mauborgne (1991, 1993b) were conducting field research to understand what motivated subsidiary top management to execute global strategic decisions, they discerned a pattern in executives' responses. Subsidiary top managers who perceived the process by which global strategic decisions were reached to be procedurally just expressed a high level of commitment, trust, and social harmony toward one another (Kim and Mauborgne, 1991). They were committed to execute global strategic decisions not just to the letter, but in the spirit they embodied, engaging in consummate emotional cooperation. In this sense, procedural justice could be read to be associated with high normative value, creating what Weber (1946) referred to as a sense of legitimacy. In Weber's world, normative value or legitimacy influences a strong impact on individuals' internal motive system and can guide behavior even in the absence of externally driven incentives. These collective insights led Kim and Mauborgne to draw on the rich body of procedural justice research, and theorize the effect that process fairness exerts on multinational managers' consummate emotional cooperation and execution of decisions.

Several procedural justice studies are particularly relevant here. Tyler (1990) conducted a pioneering study that traced the effect of procedural justice on individuals' support for court decisions. It was arguably the first major study that went beyond attitudes to examine the behavioral effects of procedural justice judgments. Tyler focused on the effect of procedural justice on two distinct types of legitimacy, one that is conceptually similar to the higher-order attitude of trust, and the other to institutional commitment. His central proposition was that procedural justice judgments would augment both types of legitimacy, and through these, citizens' support for court decisions even in situations in which those decisions contradict personal perceptions of what is right, or are at odds with individuals' self-interests. We would argue here that Tyler's study thus begins to suggest that via higher-order attitudinal effects, procedural justice judgments inspire consummate emotional cooperation in the execution of decisions. This supports Katz's (1964) proposition that employees with positive psychological feelings toward organizations that go beyond instrumental concerns, will be motivated to go beyond perfunctory cooperation to perform their tasks to the best of their abilities.

More recent procedural justice studies offered some evidence that procedural justice judgments positively enhance five types of organizational citizenship behaviors ranging from sportsmanship to altruism (e.g. Moorman 1991;

Moorman et al. 1991). These behaviors can be interpreted as surrogate assessments of procedural justice's effect on consummate emotional cooperation. In an executive development program, Korsgaard, Schweiger, and Sapienza (1995) found, using a role-playing case simulation, that the exercise of procedural justice had a positive effect on executive participants' reported levels of commitment and trust, which were posited to engender high levels of cooperation, especially concerning the implementation of the resulting strategic decision.

In drawing on the results of their own field work and other procedural justice research, Kim and Mauborgne theorized that if procedural justice indeed positively impacts multinational managers' higher-order attitudes like commitment, trust, and social harmony, it should positively affect their execution of strategic decisions. Organizational commitment is essential for managers to identify with the global objectives of the enterprise and to pursue them to the best of their ability. Trust in head-office management heightens the propensity of managers to sacrifice subsystem for system, and short-term for long-term, priorities and considerations. Social harmony serves to strengthen the social fabric and inspire ongoing exchange relations of the effective and efficient kind between organizational members. Through its impact on higher-order attitudes, procedural justice could be expected to influence positively managers' consummate emotional cooperation and with this, the effective execution of strategic decisions.

Consider, for example, the underlying meaning of organizational commitment. When individuals are committed to an organization, they identify with its goals and objectives and pursue them to the best of their ability, in essence demonstrating a form of consummate emotional cooperation (e.g. Mowday, Steers, and Porter 1979). If attaining those goals and objectives requires that they execute strategic decisions to the best of their abilities, they are likely to do so. As the work of O'Reilly and Chatman (1986) brought to light, organizational commitment induces extra-role behavior or "prosocial" efforts on behalf of the organization. Employees with high organizational commitment demonstrate active commitment and cooperate fully to implement corporate decisions. Likewise the trust multinational managers have in head-office management may also positively affect decision execution. When multinational managers trust head-office managers, they are confident that the intentions and actions of the head office are guided by local concerns as well as by a concern with maximizing corporate revenues. Trust fosters a faith that, even if the head office's decisions are not in line with a multinational manager's interests at times, the head office's future support will compensate for any sacrifice required. Hence, trust could be predicted to promote consummate emotional cooperation and effective strategic decision execution.

Figure 11.1 provides a depiction of the overall theorized effects advanced in Kim and Mauborgne's research (1993a, 1993b, 1993c, 1996). For purposes of simplicity, control and moderating variables have been left out here.

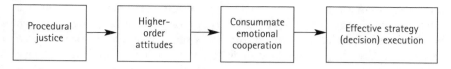

Figure 11.1 A procedural justice model of strategy (decision) execution

Based on a sample of over 100 multinational managers, Kim and Mauborgne not only established that the exercise of procedural justice in global strategic decision making positively affects multinational managers' compliance with strategic decisions via its effect on higher-order attitudes (Kim and Mauborgne 1993a, 1993b). Their subsequent study confirmed their prediction that these higher-order attitudes would induce consummate emotional cooperation or extra-role behavior in the execution of global strategic decisions (Kim and Mauborgne 1996). Multinational managers who perceived the global strategic decision-making process to be procedurally just were committed to cooperate fully in the execution of decisions that went beyond their individual self-interests or instrumental concerns on behalf of the organization. Their study also found empirical evidence that traditional incentives of resource allocations, structure, decision favorability, and rewards did not exert a significant effect on multinational managers' consummate emotional cooperation or extra-role behavior.

Hence, designing global strategic decision-making processes around the principles of procedural justice provides a powerful though overlooked way to induce the effective execution of strategic decisions. It allows MNCs to address the implementation issue up front, in the decision process. As Guth and MacMillan (1986) have suggested, corporate general management's failure to secure organizational members' motivation to implement corporate strategic decisions at the start can result in significant "counter effort" and "upward intervention," thereby reducing the quality of strategy implementation. Given the decline in the hierarchical properties of MNCs and global managers' concurrent rise in discretionary power, we would argue that the potential importance of procedural justice to strategy execution in MNCs is significant.

PROCEDURAL JUSTICE, CONSUMMATE INTELLECTUAL COOPERATION, AND STRATEGY (DECISION) CONTENT

If a procedural justice model of strategic decision making is to provide a powerful way to organize the decision process, then the design principles of procedural justice must be shown not only to induce the effective execution of the resulting strategies, but ideally also to have a salutary effect on the quality of the resulting global strategic decisions. An ideal strategy content in the absence of implementation means little; so too does effective implementation of a less than satisfactory strategy. The intellectual heritage of procedural justice research, however, has provided little insight on this issue. Procedural justice research, coming predominantly from the domain of law, politics, and social settings, had confined its assessment in this regard to whether the exercise of procedural justice has an impact on producing decision outcomes that were perceived to be fair. However, as procedural justice is studied in more and more business settings, the need to assess the decision-content implications of procedural justice becomes clear.

Kim and Mauborgne (1995) made a pioneering attempt to examine the decision content implications of procedural justice. As shown in Figure 11.2, procedural justice can be predicted to enhance consummate intellectual cooperation and the content of strategic decisions via its effect on higher-order attitudes on the one hand, and information processing on the other.

Consummate intellectual cooperation—the willingness of multinational managers to actively share their knowledge, innovative ideas, and expertise—has fast become an essential strategic asset. For consummate intellectual cooperation to be actualized, it can be argued that nothing less than an affirmative attitude toward cooperation will suffice. One reason is that knowledge and expertise are often viewed as power, and as such are not easily shared. Another reason is that the major benefits of internal diffusion of know-how accrue to recipients, not transmitters. Of course, were it possible for multinational managers to "sell" their knowledge and expertise to others, these problems might be overcome. However, this is often and perhaps usually infeasible. As know-how is largely an intangible asset, its value to a "purchaser" cannot be known until the purchaser has it, but once the knowledge is disclosed, the purchaser has acquired it without cost.

In the absence of economic incentives and with the presence of perceived power disincentives to diffuse knowledge and expertise, it follows that consummate intellectual cooperation will not transpire as long as quid pro quo

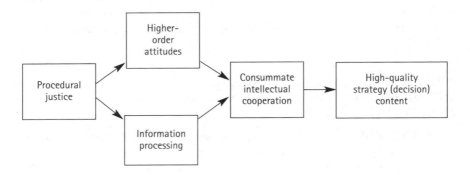

Figure 11.2 A procedural justice model of strategy (decision) content

attitudes to interactions among multinational managers prevail. Rather, the hoarding and withholding of knowledge and expertise are far more likely. Hence, to the extent that procedural justice positively influences higher-order long-term attitudes of commitment, trust, and social harmony among managers, heightened intellectual cooperation can be expected (Kim and Mauborgne 1993b). Building in part on the work of Mohr (1969), Ghoshal and Bartlett (1988) argued that social harmony or a cooperative atmosphere will foster active exchange of knowledge and ideas by making the sharing of knowledge and information a "desirable" activity to organizational members. Kim and Mauborgne found support for this proposition in all three phases of their three-stage study on multinational corporations. Their work suggests that, via its positive effect on higher-order attitudes, procedural justice may well exercise a positive effect on consummate intellectual cooperation and thereby on high-quality strategic decisions.

The second theoretical reason put forth to expect procedural justice to impact the content of strategic decisions positively can be traced to the inherent information-processing capabilities of procedural justice. Kim and Mauborgne (1993b, 1995) introduced information processing as a theoretical bridge to explore the impact of procedural justice on the quality of resulting strategic decisions. Information processing in organizations is generally defined as the gathering, interpreting, and synthesis of information in the context of organizational decision making (Galbraith 1973; Tushman and Nadler 1978). The view that decision-making units can be usefully viewed as information-processing systems originated in the work of Thompson (1967) but was more thoroughly developed by Galbraith (1973, 1977) and Tushman and Nadler (1978). Building on the open systems view of requisite variety, information-processing theory in essence states that, to be effective, a match must exist between the information-processing capacity of an organization and the information-processing requirements imposed by its environmental and strategic conditions (Duncan 1973; Daft and Lengel 1986; Galbraith 1973; Pennings 1975; Tushman and Nadler 1978).

Here the five dimensions of procedural justice were conceptualized as the critical variables determining the information-processing capability of a multinational's global strategic decision-making process (Kim and Mauborgne 1995). The dimensions of procedural justice identified previously have important implications for gathering, interpreting, and synthesizing strategic information. The over-riding strategic objectives of global strategy, on the other hand, can be seen as posing requisite requirements for information processing to design global strategies for multinationals that can meet these strategic objectives. In the spirit of information-processing theory, the central contention here was that if procedural justice enhances the kinds of strategic information necessary to achieve the global strategic objectives of the multinational, the exercise of procedural justice may well bear a positive influence on the design of effective global strategic decisions (Kim and Mauborgne 1993c, 1995).

Although numerous studies have used some form of information processing to link an organization's design to its environmental and strategic conditions (e.g. Burns and Stalker 1961; Lawrence and Lorsch 1967; Galbraith 1970; Van de Ven, Delbecq, and Koenig 1976; Tushman 1978; Smith et al. 1991), the studies of Duncan (1973) and Egelhoff (1982, 1988b) are particularly relevant here. Duncan (1973) conceptualized the dimensions of a decision unit's structure as the critical variables determining the information-processing capability of a decision unit. He theorized that if the information-processing capability of a decision unit matches the information-processing requirements imposed by the types of decisions a unit must make (routine versus non-routine) and the environmental conditions it faces, the decision unit will be effective and achieve its goals and objectives.

The second relevant work is that of Egelhoff (1982, 1988b). In his first study, Egelhoff (1982) set out to extend the current understanding of the relationship between the structure and strategy of multinational organizations using an information-processing perspective. Even more relevant is Egelhoff's (1988b) exploratory examination of the information-processing implications of planning processes. In this second study, Egelhoff sought to understand how business planning systems in multinationals are influenced by the strategy and environment of the organization. In short, not only did Egelhoff argue that planning systems are information-processing mechanisms but he also provided some preliminary evidence that in successful multinationals, planning systems tend to fit critical strategic conditions. Taken together, the studies of both Duncan and Egelhoff provide some evidence that an information-processing perspective is a meaningful conceptual basis to explore the effect of procedural justice in global strategic decision making on the quality of the resulting strategy content.

Kim and Mauborgne went on to explore whether the five dimensions of procedural justice foster the types of strategic information necessary to achieve multinationals' strategic objectives of balancing global and local perspectives, strategic renewal, and global learning. For example, the extent to which bilateral communication exists between managers involved in the multinational's strategy-making process could be expected to induce parties not only to transfer their distinctive points of view, knowledge, and expertise but also to hear out the opposite party. This diffusion and sharing of perceptions, knowledge, and ideas should promote a higher rate of global learning (Ghoshal and Bartlett 1988). At the same time, extensive two-way communication should likewise foster a better balancing of global efficiency and local responsiveness. Taking this logic one step further, the different backgrounds and orientations brought to bear by multinational managers should result in a more creative and thorough testing of the appropriateness of past successful strategic moves. In other words, two-way communication should heighten multinationals' ability to achieve global strategic renewal (Prahalad and Doz 1987).

Another example is the ability legitimately to challenge and refute strategic views. Granting global managers the right to challenge the head office's and each other's strategic views limits the ability of each party to dominate the decision process and crowd out the strategic views of others. As a result, a better balance between the global and local perspectives of decision partici-pants may well be struck. Beyond this, the ability to refute should create a restless, self-questioning atmosphere in the multinational. This would serve to break the inclination to maintain the status quo and simply assume the continuing merit of past strategic responses (Prahalad and Doz 1987). Consequently, a higher rate of global strategic renewal should also result.

A last illustration is the extent to which the head office provides a full account for its final strategic decisions. A comprehensive explanation of why strategic decisions are made as they are grants managers two things: a more comprehensive understanding of the cognitive maps of head-office man-agers, and a sound rationale for why their own perspective may have been accepted or rejected in the making of ultimate strategic decisions. In this way, the account serves as a feedback loop that perpetually informs and educates global managers, and gradually alters their conceptual lens for subsequent interpretations of the environment. Hence, the provision of an account should work to promote a greater rate of ongoing global learning (Daft and Weick 1984). At the same time, requiring the head office to provide an account of final strategic decisions assures organizational members that not only the head office but also all other perspectives were given due consider-ation in the making of strategic decisions. This should, in turn, prompt a higher level of balancing between these two perspectives in the making of ultimate strategic decisions.

Based on a detailed analysis of the information-processing capabilities of each of the five dimensions of procedural justice, Kim and Mauborgne (1993b, 1995) predicted that designing the decision-making process around the prin-ciples of procedural justice would have important implications for gathering, interpreting, and synthesizing the types of strategic information that are neces-sary to achieve the multinational's strategic objectives. Based on an empirical study of 63 global strategic decision-making units, Kim and Mauborgne found general support for the hypothesized relations. While their study was embed-ded in the context of multinationals' global strategic decision-making units, it shed light on how the content implications of procedural justice could be examined in diverse settings.

As stated previously, the items that multinational managers identified with procedural justice in global strategic decision making are consonant with the items used to represent the domain of procedural justice in a range of settings. This would suggest that the exercise of procedural justice in general provides an effective way to enhance the information-processing capability of decision processes, and thus could be expected to enhance the quality of resulting strategic decisions, irrespective of the specific context. At the same time, because procedural justice is generally associated with higher-order attitudes that can be read as precursors to consummate intellectual cooperation, further theoretical ground exists to expect a positive impact of procedural justice on decision content. This would suggest that the model presented in Figure 11.2 provides a potentially useful way to build procedural justice research across business settings.

In this light, Kim and Mauborgne's subsequent research explored the relevance of procedural justice in diverse business settings, ranging from corporate transformation and product innovation to company–supplier relations (Kim and Mauborgne 1997, 1998). Their research tested the generalizability of the two models introduced above. They found that the exercise of procedural justice exerts positive effects on both higher-order attitudes and information processing, which in turn creates consummate intellectual and emotional cooperation and positively impacts strategy (decision) content and execution. These effects are significant across the range of strategic decision-making contexts, including, but not limited to, joint ventures, cross-functional integration, process re-engineering, corporate transformation, innovation, corporate management, strategic alliances, and company–supplier relations. Kim and Mauborgne (1998) further explored the cognitive and motivational processes underlying procedural justice, and proposed the intellectual and emotional recognition theory, which provides the cognitive link underlying the positive correlations between the exercise of procedural justice and the quality of strategy (decision) content and execution found in empirical settings.

PROCEDURAL JUSTICE, STRATEGY (DECISION) CONTENT AND EXECUTION, AND PERFORMANCE

Collectively, the discussions above lead us to theorize that the exercise of procedural justice in multinationals' strategic decision processes provides a way to *simultaneously* design effective global strategic decisions on the one hand, and inspire global managers' effective execution of those decisions on the other. Through the impact of procedural justice on higher-order attitudes and information-processing capability, global strategic decisions of high quality can be expected. The exercise of procedural justice leads to strategic decisions that effectively embrace multinational missions of global learning, balancing global efficiency and local responsiveness, and global strategic renewal. The effective attainment of these multinational missions is a gateway to superior performance (e.g. Prahalad and Doz 1987; Bartlett and Ghoshal 1989). Likewise, the exercise of procedural justice produces strong intrinsic motivation to execute decisions to the best of one's abilities. Effective execution of strategic decisions is a key differentiator between high and low-performing organizations. Taken together, if procedural justice is able to influence both the quality of strategic decisions and their execution, designing global strategic decision processes around the principles of procedural justice should have a positive impact on performance.

Kim and Mauborgne (1993b) advanced a procedural justice model of performance based on the model presented in Figure 11.3. Again, for purposes of simplicity, relevant control and moderating variables considered in Kim and Mauborgne's original work have been omitted. In examining the performance implications of procedural justice in global strategic decision making, performance may well need to be viewed not only from the perspective of the "stand alone" performance of the decision unit, but also from the perspective of its contribution to overall corporate level missions and performance. Assessing performance in this way would take into account global strategic decision units' diverse roles and tasks within a multinational network. Kim and Mauborgne found empirical support for the hypothesis that the exercise of procedural justice in global strategic decision making leads to enhanced performance in global industries. Two-stage longitudinal data gathered from both head-office and subsidiary top management provided evidence that in global industries, where the demands for consummate emotional and intellectual cooperation among managers are especially prominent, the exercise of procedural justice plays an important role in enhancing performance.

Building and testing a procedural justice model of performance is especially important as procedural justice research increasingly migrates to the business context. Explicitly addressing performance heightens significantly the motivation for top managers to explore the significance of procedural justice in their management practices. To date, economic theories have dominated top managers' attention and action agenda, largely because they speak the consequential bottom line language of managers, while social psychological theories

Figure 11.3 A procedural justice model of performance: linking strategy (decision) content and execution

like procedural justice do not yet do so. Performance is critical because it is the central indicator on which managers are evaluated. Attitudes and behavior may be important, and managers do care about them, but given limited resources and time and the need to prioritize, managers' attention will first gravitate to factors shown to affect performance.

A procedural justice model of performance makes an important contribution to closing this gap, as does assessing the decision content implications of procedural justice. Doing so also enriches the intellectual tradition of procedural justice research by expanding its analysis beyond normative attitudes and behavior to embrace economic concerns of efficiency and effectiveness and high-quality decisions. Kim and Mauborgne's comparative case studies of plant transformations (1997) gathered further support for the proposed procedural justice model of performance.

Korine (1997) took another step in this direction. Using both deductive and inductive approaches, he examined the role of procedural justice in managing innovation teams, showing that the exercise of procedural justice in innovation team dynamics enhances their performance, including time to market, development, costs, customer satisfaction, and product quality. While we need to see more of this type of research in the future, there are strong grounds for believing that with refinements and further applications, the performance implications of procedural justice might be robust and at work across diverse business settings.

POTENTIALLY FRUITFUL AREAS FOR MARRYING PROCEDURAL JUSTICE RESEARCH AND THE STUDY OF THE MNC

As multinational corporations are characterized by increasing numbers of intra- and inter-organizational decision-making units whose success demands knowledge sharing and voluntary cooperation to produce decisions of high quality with effective execution, a multitude of settings open up where procedural justice could be fruitfully explored. Chief on this list would be the impact of procedural justice in international joint venture teams, cross-functional teams, and innovation or product-creation teams that cut across geographic regions. In these settings, the control, monitoring, and appraisal capability of multinationals is limited, and the importance of team/decision-making dynamics and individuals' internal willingness to cooperate is pre-eminent.

A review of the literature on any one of these types of decision-making unit repeatedly drives home the importance of trust, commitment, social harmony, and active knowledge sharing for their effective functioning and performance. What is far less well understood or addressed is the more practical question of just how multinational managers can go about creating these important higher-order attitudes and active idea diffusion. The theoretical tradition of procedural justice, in particular the recent advances that have been made in the multinational context, suggest that the exercise of procedural justice may represent a potentially powerful way to address this fundamental question of how.

From a company perspective, we can conclude that procedural justice is likely to be of most importance in those multinationals facing globalized competition and actively exercising global strategies. These face strong demands for extensive inter-unit exchanges and cooperation, swift actions in a globally coordinated manner, and the sacrifice of subsystem for system priorities and considerations. Specific examples of this might include:

- multinationals actively pursuing a strategy of core competence building (Prahalad and Hamel 1990) wherein the knowledge, technology, and production skills cultivated in each node of the global network must be actively shared and continuously consolidated worldwide
- multinationals aggressively exercising cross-subsidization across units to out-maneuver global competitors (e.g. Hamel and Prahalad 1985).

From a situational perspective the application of procedural justice is likely to be of greatest value in multinationals' most powerful and resource-rich decision-making units, as well as in those units that play a central but "unfavorable" role in multinationals' global strategies (such as a subsidiary unit asked to drop prices and sacrifice its own revenue to parry a global competitor's move in another subsidiary's market). To rephrase this, procedural justice is likely to yield the greatest gains in those decision-making units where commitment, trust, and social harmony are virtually indispensable to social order and the effective execution of global strategies.

CONCLUDING THOUGHTS

In this chapter we have argued that procedural justice, whose unit of analysis is the decision process and the individual, may provide important insights into managing the multinational corporation and building strategic capability. Designing global strategic decision-making processes around the principles of procedural justice provides a potentially powerful avenue to *simultaneously* achieve high-quality strategic decisions and their effective execution. This is traceable to the higher-order attitudes and information-processing capability associated with procedural justice, which foster consummate emotional and intellectual cooperation. Consummate emotional and intellectual cooperation is indispensable to high performance, not just in the multinational but in many forms of organization. Procedural justice builds a sense of community and imbues legitimacy in the decision-making process. It strikes at individuals' internal motivating code of what is right, creating a willingness in managers to go beyond formally prescribed roles and responsibilities to contribute to the best of their abilities. In this way group interest is maximized over individual self-interest in the making and executing of strategic decisions.

To the extent that high performance rests on (1) the increasing sacrifice of subsystem for system priorities and considerations; (2) swift actions in a globally coordinated manner; and (3) effective and efficient knowledge and idea exchange among the nodes of the multinational's global network, a procedural justice model of strategic decision making may offer important insights into achieving high performance in the multinational. Kim and Mauborgne's research on the performance implications of procedural justice provides an important first step in this direction. As more scholars follow this lead and explore the link between procedural justice and performance, new and important prescriptions will be advanced. We hope that this chapter will inspire much-needed research in this area.

Procedural justice can be seen as a form of loose coupling, because it allows global managers from across the multinational's network of operations to remain separate and yet simultaneously coupled. Hence, the results of procedural justice research can reinforce Weick's (1976) claim that loose linkages can be very effective in achieving the objectives of organizations. Procedural justice may well be one viable way to achieve this objective in the multinational in particular and business organizations in general.

To date, the field of international business, and multinational management in particular, has benefited little from the rich theoretical insights of social psychology. While the field of economics has been drawn on consistently, little research has looked to what the field of social psychology can offer to our understanding of how to manage multinational corporations effectively. However, as the hierarchical powers of MNCs continue to wane, global managers' tasks become increasingly less discrete and monitorable, and resource advantages take a back seat to strategic capability in explaining corporate performance, it is our contention that the field of social psychology can offer bountiful insights into new ways to manage the multinational.

Looking into the future, we are strongly convinced that procedural justice theory can offer rich insights into managing the multinational corporation and building strategic capability. It is our contention that the effects of procedural justice may well be profound in a wealth of multinational strategic decision settings, such as the increasingly prevalent and important horizontal inter-unit exchange relations, international joint ventures, and joint decision making that occurs across globally dispersed functional and divisional activities, as in the case of creating innovation. The title of this chapter reflects our growing conviction that rich managerial implications can be derived from the further development and application of procedural justice theory to the multinational. It is our hope that this chapter will serve as a humble beginning for what we envision to be a very long and fruitful road of studies on procedural justice in particular, and social psychology in general, in managing the multinational.

12 The Reproduction of Inertia in Multinational Corporations

Martin Kilduff

How do the members of a multinational organization organize themselves each day to replicate the interconnections, the hierarchies, the problems, the routines with which they are familiar? It would be a mistake to assume that the taken-for-granted structures of everyday life such as interpersonal relationships, chains of command, and exchange networks are re-formed effortlessly each day. In any large complex organization, such communicative structures only survive through constant use. Part of the use may be maintenance, as when friends telephone each other merely to "touch base" rather than to exchange information. The task of social reproduction is all the more difficult in the case of the multinational corporation (MNC) because it must be accomplished across national frontiers and cultural differences. In an MNC operating across many national borders with a variety of loosely coupled subsidiaries, considerable resources may have to be devoted simply to keeping routines and other structured behaviors reliable from day to day. Organizational inertia, from this perspective, is achieved only at great effort and cost (see for example Hannan and Freeman 1984: 152).

This chapter will focus on the MNC as an especially interesting arena for research into (1) the formation of norms and routines, (2) the reproduction of such norms and routines across national and cultural groups, and (3) the consequences—especially those that are unintended—of this reproduction. As many writers have pointed out, the MNC is characterized by greater diversity and complexity than those organizations operating within single national markets. Routines imprinted at the time of founding tend to persevere in all organizations (Stinchcombe 1965), but perseverance may be difficult to sustain in subsidiaries that are located in very different cultural milieus. Newcomers from different cultural backgrounds may repeatedly challenge behaviors that are taken for granted by the founder of the organization. Coordination in any organization tends to be facilitated by common procedures and assumptions. Such commonality may be more difficult to achieve and sustain in the MNC than in organizations operating within rather than across cultures.

In other words, inertia in the MNC does not occur by default, as a result of managerial complacency or as a natural consequence of growing organizational age and size. On the contrary, inertia is problematic: it is likely to be under continual challenge as subsidiaries open in new cultures and as the

241

employee population becomes increasingly diverse. Paradoxically such challenges to taken-for-granted procedures may actually strengthen those procedures by leading to an explicit commitment by organizational members to adhere to what have hitherto been implicit norms (cf. Bettenhausen and Murnighan 1985). Relative to mononational organizations, the MNC may use more resources to ensure the reliable reproduction of routines. The MNC, then, faced with continual disruptions to its inertia, may be less tolerant of heterogeneous attitudes and behavior than organizations operating in more homogeneous environments. Anecdotal evidence suggests that some of the most successful MNCs, such as IBM, are the most rigorous in enforcing procedures and norms across cultural settings.

The MNC is therefore an especially interesting arena in which to study the production and reproduction of routines and the possible consequences of this reproduction for both individual and corporate actors. Structuration theory (Giddens 1984) has proposed that institutions reproduce themselves through the purposeful actions of knowledgeable agents. In a separate but compatible line of work, the enactment approach describes how individual routines produce complex organizational phenomena (Weick 1979; Abolafia and Kilduff 1988). The present chapter approaches the question of the reproduction of inertia in MNCs using both the structuration and enactment perspectives.

STRUCTURATION THEORY

Background

As formulated in the writings of Giddens (1976, 1984), structuration theory focuses on how knowledgeable actors draw upon rules and resources in their social interactions to reproduce complex social systems unintentionally. The theory draws upon the classic sociology of Marx, Weber, and Durkheim, as well as upon the contemporary literature on interaction routines (Goffman 1959) in trying to understand how people recreate the institutions of society.

For Marx, human beings "make history, but not in circumstances of their own choosing" (quoted in Giddens 1984: xxi). Individual actors, pursuing their own ends, help sustain the very institutions of society within which they are constrained. It is this tension between voluntary, purposeful action, on the one hand, and institutional constraint, on the other, that structuration theory explores. From Durkheim, Giddens carries over the observation that an institution both pre-exists and outlasts the individuals who embody it at any particular moment. Institutionalized realities are social facts, according to Durkheim, which constrain individual action. Giddens adds an emphasis on the enabling properties of institutions. Social structures, such as language and bureaucracy, can imprison us in iron cages of outdated custom, as Weber has observed. But they can also enable us to communicate and to work efficiently.

To understand how human action is both constrained and enabled requires a focus on the routine, everyday behaviors of individuals. From Weber, Giddens adopts a strong emphasis on the meanings that actors place on the routines they enact, as well as a concern for the specific historical and geographical context within which action unfolds.

Analyses of meaningful situated action are best exemplified, according to Giddens, in the work of Erving Goffman. Goffman's writings carefully dismantle the apparently spontaneous flow of everyday activity into its routinized components. The organization, from Goffman's perspective, is composed of performance teams consisting of individuals who cooperate in staging routines (Goffman 1959: 79). Goffman focuses attention on the dramaturgical aspects of routine interactions, the way teams stage displays to enhance their positions in competition with other teams. Successful performances require skilful use of sign equipment, such as clothes, furniture, cars, offices, and so on. Expert management of such sign equipment can help support the definition of the situation that team members are attempting to enact.

Team performances, no matter how well rehearsed, are fragile attempts to create social reality and are constantly subject to disruptions from unforeseen contingencies. Everyday routine performances are held to high standards of "aptness, fitness, propriety, and decorum," by audience members (Goffman 1959: 55). Clearly, such standards vary dramatically across national boundaries, suggesting a rich field for the investigation of performance failures in MNCs between teams from different national subsidiaries. Indeed, much of the interest in dramaturgical analysis is on the myriad ways that impressions, those "delicate, fragile" things (Goffman 1959: 56), can be both created and discredited, and how team members cope with unexpected loss of face.

Structuration theory and routines as programmed responses

The emphasis in the work of Giddens and Goffman on routines and norms as personal resources used by conscious individuals in pursuit of their own ends is startlingly different from the usual treatment evident in the organizational behavior literature. The importance of routines in organizations was first extensively developed by March and Simon (1958), building on and reacting to the emphasis on the routines of manual labor evident in the scientific management tradition. March and Simon depicted the organization as a nested set of performance programs. At any particular level in the organization, decision makers faced with problems could invoke a repertoire of programmed responses from which they could choose the response that seemed most appropriate. From this perspective, organizational participants appear to be controlled by routines, as March and Simon (1958: 142) observe that "most behavior, and particularly most behavior in organizations, is governed by performance programs."

Cyert and March elaborated this view of organizational behavior and explicitly modeled it as a computer program (1963: 126). Not until the development of the garbage can model (Cohen, March, and Olsen 1972) did the Carnegie School researchers appear to recognize that individuals and coalitions could use routines to further their own interests whether or not the major problems facing the organization were being solved.

Nelson and Winter (1982) further develop the programmed model of organizational decision making. Echoing March and Simon (1958), Nelson and Winter (1982: 128) assert that "the behavior of firms can be explained by the routines that they employ." But several points of similarity between Giddens' conception and that of Nelson and Winter emerge. First, unlike the Carnegie School researchers, Nelson and Winter emphasize that organizational routines are opaque, rather than transparent. People may be purposively enacting routines without being able to articulate precisely what the routines consist of, much as people may be able to speak complex sentences without being able to explain the rules governing their production. Second, because knowledge of routines is largely tacit, the replication of routines across organizational boundaries is problematic (Nelson and Winter 1982: 118). Third, routines in organizations are not the mere instruments of management control emphasized by March and Simon (1958). Instead, as Giddens would agree, the set of routines in an organization represents a negotiated settlement of competing interests, a truce between potentially conflicting definitions of the situation.

Organizational inertia, then, is a function not merely of a market demand for reliability and accountability (cf. Hannan and Freeman 1984), or a consequence of imprinting at the time of founding (cf. Stinchcombe 1965), but may also be a consequence of the balance of internal tensions within the organization: "Adaptations that appear 'obvious' and 'easy' to an external observer may be foreclosed because they involve a perceived threat to internal political equilibrium" (Nelson and Winter 1982: 111).

Despite some similarities between Giddens' theory and the Nelson and Winter model, the structuration approach remains unusual in suggesting how the structured world of rules, regulations, norms, and customs is created and recreated through the routine, day-to-day interactions of purposeful individuals. The theory builds on the classic works of Marx, Weber, and Durkheim, but offers an interpretation that differs sharply from the functional synthesis proposed by Parsons (1937). Structuration theory, unlike much of the modern organizational culture literature, does not accept the Parsonian notion that actors internalize the shared values upon which social cohesion is said to depend. Structuration theory offers a more paradoxical explanation of the replication of social institutions, as the following discussion shows.

STRUCTURATION THEORY AND THE MULTINATIONAL CORPORATION

Language is a favorite analogy used by Giddens to illustrate how interacting individuals reproduce institutions: competent speakers of French unwittingly help to reproduce the language itself as they engage in conversation. Further, the language that is reproduced is an institution that has preceded and will survive the speakers. The rules of language production are opaque, even though competent speakers tend to obey these rules unerringly. Competent speakers can always tell you what they are trying to say, and why they are saying it, even though they cannot explain the rules that make speech possible.

A multinational corporation is also an institution that is reproduced in the interactions of knowledgeable actors. The MNC, like a language, can precede and survive the particular individuals whose interactions serve at any given time to reproduce it. The actors can always provide rationales for why they are doing what they are doing. They have theories about the institution and their relationship with it. From a structuration perspective, the actions of top managers, as much as those of the lowest subordinates, express underlying rules that may be opaque in their operation. Further, the individually motivated actions of participants in an institution such as a multinational serve to reproduce patterns of social relations of which the participants themselves may be unaware.

The emphasis of the theory, then, is on the recursiveness of institutional-ized reality, in contrast with the linear nature of each individual's life. Individual lives are linear in the sense that people age and die, whereas the institutions to which they belong may continue to be enacted by new generations of participants. The work of the MNC is continuously recreated as employees engage in routinized exchanges that enact the familiar characteristics of the institution. The enacted routines are the intended result of individual actions. Indeed, as part of the intentional reproduction of routine, actors reflexively monitor both their own activities and the activities of others. Each person is engaged in a skilled performance at work, in concert with others. Actors are alert to deviations from the expected performances, and intervene to repair slippage from expected enactments (Goffman 1959).

From a structuration perspective, language is situated action, in the sense that language use is embedded in local contexts of meaning. The reproduction of language is only possible through the activity of specific speech communities, within each of which speakers have mastered "the circumstances in which particular types of sentences are appropriate" (Giddens 1987: 200). The reproduction of language is likely to vary across speech communities in accordance with local variations in contexts of meaning. Indeed, this phenomenon is observable empirically in, for example, the differences in dialect and usage between communities located in neighboring counties in England.

The parallel between a language and an institution such as an MNC is not merely a fanciful metaphor. In a very real sense, an institution is expressed in its language use. March and Simon may have been the first to observe the reality-defining power of organizational vocabularies:

> The world tends to be perceived by the organization members in terms of the particular concepts that are reflected in the organization's vocabulary.... The particular categories and schemes of classification it employs are reified and become, for members of the organization, attributes of the world rather than mere conventions.
>
> (March and Simon 1958: 166)

One of the most obvious facts about multinational corporations is that subunits in different countries tend to employ different languages. The implication of the present discussion is that the attempt to maintain adherence to the same concepts across language boundaries is likely to prove extremely difficult to the extent that such concepts are embedded in the language patterns of particular speech communities. Within the same multinational enterprise, managers from different cultural backgrounds maintain culturally based frames of reference and resist the homogenizing effects of organizational membership (Hofstede 1980a, 1980b; Laurent 1983). When cultural differences are reinforced by language differences, fidelity to concepts and standards promulgated by corporate headquarters may be imperfect. Further, even if organizational members all accept the importance of a concept such as customer service, the interpretation of this concept is likely to vary widely. Discrepant interpretations of organizational norms can find support in the social networks through which norms are diffused (Krackhardt and Kilduff 1990).

Network members, drawing on shared normative frameworks, continually monitor interpersonal behavior. This monitoring can also be thought of as an individual difference variable (Snyder 1974, 1979). Some people are high self-monitors, in that they can skilfully adapt their behavior to the role demands of whatever setting they enter. Others are low self-monitors, preferring to enact roles that are relatively invariant across social settings. Low self-monitors are relatively insensitive to the social cuing of expected performance. In an MNC that is concerned with replicating similar institutional procedures across different cultures, such as a fast-food chain, the low self-monitor who lacks sensitivity to local demands might be an appropriate candidate for transfer across cultures. For the MNC that seeks to shape its subsidiaries to the perceived demands of each culture, a high self-monitor would be the appropriate candidate for transfer.

From a structuration perspective, a role in an organization is best understood as a range of prerogatives and obligations that the incumbent can activate (Giddens 1984: 84). The actor has discretion with respect to the aspects of the role he or she wishes to express. There is always the possibility of a skilled performer reinterpreting the role demands in a creative way to the benefit or the detriment of other actors in the system. In an MNC, for example, a creative CEO can interpret the role demands to balance stake-holders' interests in terms of fundamentally realigning away from a core business, such as oil, and toward a potential high-growth business, such as electronics. This creativity in role interpretation disrupts the reproduction of inertia and can threaten the survival of the organization even as it opens new opportunities (Tushman and Romanelli 1986).

The knowledgeability of actors in a system such as an MNC is a funda-mental tenet of structuration theory. Actors have a theoretical understanding of why they are doing what they are doing, and can provide rationales or accounts if asked. The knowledge of actors includes knowledge of the social conditions within which they act, such as the hierarchy of power relation-ships, for example. But actors also have a tacit, practical knowledge that is evident in their actions even though they are not able to articulate it. The distinction between the two types of knowledge is related to the familiar one between espoused theories and theories-in-use (Argyris and Schon 1978).

The espoused theories of organizational actors are expressed in accounts of action. From the structuration perspective, such accounts are themselves actions, designed to maintain social worlds (Garfinkel 1984; Heritage 1987). Accounts are social constructions that retrospectively interpret events in the light of normative expectations. The presentation of accounts is, from this perspective, part of the reflexive monitoring that sustains ongoing social reality. An account can be a weapon in the effort to maintain an interpretive and normative base for future action.

Theories-in-use are expressed in actions that can have both intended and unintended consequences. A major focus of structuration theory is on the unintended consequences of action, and how these consequences feed back into the system to constrain subsequent actions. For example, the CEO of a diversified multinational may respond to calls for clarification concerning how the decentralized decision-making system works by issuing detailed guidelines to subsidiaries and monitoring their implementation. His actions, however, tighten HQ control over decision making rather than loosen it. Thus, by clarifying the decentralized control policy, the CEO unintentionally undermines the policy.

It is important to emphasize that, from a structuration viewpoint, the unin-tended consequences of action do not have the latent function of system main-tenance and integration suggested by functional theories. Whereas functional theories (e.g. Merton 1936) show how seemingly irrational acts are not so irra-tional after all if they are considered in terms of the whole system, structura-tion theory focuses on what economists have called "perverse outcomes." For example, suppose an MNC wants to reduce labor costs and decides to shift production from the USA to a developing country. Other MNCs are doing the same thing, however, with the result that the wages in the developing country begin a rapid escalation, whereas labor costs in the USA begin to decline in real terms because of oversupply. By relocating to the developing country, therefore, the MNC helps to cause the very phenomenon—wage inflation—that it was trying to avoid.

Another hypothetical example: suppose a French MNC tries to penetrate the Japanese market by hiring local managers for the Tokyo office who can speak the language and who know the culture. The company is unable to attract the best-connected and most qualified applicants, however, because they prefer to work for the top Japanese companies. The MNC selects from an applicant pool significantly weaker than that of its rivals. The managers it hires are not as good as those of its major competitors. The result therefore is worsening of competitive position caused by the policy that was meant to prevent such deterioration.

These perverse outcomes are triggered by the actions of knowledgeable actors but are unintended. Often such perverse outcomes are remote in time and space from the triggering actions. Further, the unintended consequences are often part of a vicious circle that constrains subsequent actions. For example, as the competitive position of the Japanese division suffers because of inferior management, the applicant pool itself becomes less impressive, since good applicants are not attracted to poorly performing companies.

Knowledgeable actors in the process of reproducing the structures of the corporation use resources, both material and authoritative. Material resources, such as money and machinery, are familiar enough to students of organizations. Authoritative resources are potentially much more illuminating as a focus of study in MNCs. Authoritative resources consist of the capability to harness the activities of human beings and result from the "dominion of some actors over others" (Giddens 1984: 373). The MNC, its authority breaching the boundaries of nation states, invents for itself a governance structure that seeks to balance local demands and global vision, to paraphrase one book on the subject (Prahalad and Doz 1987). The ways in which this balancing act is maintained are fundamental to understanding the functioning of MNCs. Do subsidiaries of MNCs replicate the normative environment of their parent company, or do they adapt to the local environment in which they are geographically situated? Is there evidence of normative control from subsidiaries to headquarters?

The emphasis on the efforts of subordinates to control superiors is not accidental. In the structuration perspective, power is expressed in patterns of domination, and resources are the media through which power is exercised. Power in this formulation is not the sole prerogative of top management in the MNC. Subordinates also act to control superiors by managing resources in certain ways. For example, subsidiaries can control corporate headquarters by manipulating resource flows.

In any social system, understanding resource flows and power relationships requires an analysis of two aspects of social structure: the patterns of social relations, on the one hand, and the underlying codes of meaning, on the other. The patterns of social relations can be conveniently thought of in terms of two kinds of social networks: (1) the informal exchange relationships between interacting individuals and (2) the relationships across space and time between, for example, structurally equivalent individuals or entities. In an exchange relationship, individuals influence each other through personal contact, whereas in a structurally equivalent relationship, competing individuals may influence each other through envy-driven emulation in the absence of any direct contact (Burt 1987). To take one example of how these concepts might apply to MNCs, suppose an MNC has acquired a diverse group of previously autonomous companies and grouped them into business streams for administrative convenience. Units within each stream are compelled to see each other as more or less equivalent in relation to the headquarters. A social relationship of competition may commence, despite headquarters' efforts to foster cooperation.

A second aspect of structure consists of the norms that frame social encounters. These generalizable procedures enable the enactment of everyday life and constitute what one might call the culture of the system. The structuration perspective focuses on the "many seemingly trivial procedures followed in daily life" (Giddens 1984: 22) rather than on unusual rites and rituals. These procedures can have profound effects on social conduct.

The top management of some MNCs explicitly tries to manipulate the reproduction of the organization's culture. Indeed, a common recommendation of books aimed at top managers of MNCs is that they should intervene to change, mold, or otherwise shape the culture of the organization. From a structuration perspective, however, the organization's culture is expressed in the interactions and interpretations of knowledgeable actors, not in company handbooks, seminars, or CEO speeches.

The culture of the organization at any point in time can be understood as a set of social constructs negotiated among knowledgeable actors to anticipate and control the motivational and cognitive diversity in the organization (Krackhardt and Kilduff 1990; see also Wallace 1970: 36). Institutionalized traditions, set in place by the organization's founders, shape and are shaped by emergent beliefs and actions. The paradox is that freely interacting individuals tend to reproduce their version of the organization's culture, thus constraining the diversity of behaviors and cognition they allow themselves, often without any awareness of the constraints they enact. Management's attempts to disrupt radically taken-for-granted procedures in the name of "culture change programs" are likely to meet with resistance and resentment from those whose routines are threatened (see for example Siehl 1985). Organizational culture can only be an imperfect management control device because routinized procedures are transmuted and transmitted by social networks that operate outside of the formal organizational socialization and reward system (Krackhardt and Kilduff 1990).

In the MNC, the potential for subcultures to flourish with the support of local networks is tremendous. Members of these subcultures may believe that they, and not management, are enacting the traditions set in place by the founders. Management intolerance or ignorance of the diversity of interpretations and behaviors can lead to unanticipated organizational conflict (see for example Stoffle 1975; Whyte 1951). Given diverse cultural premises, the production of organization-wide routines may be difficult to achieve. The national origin of European managers, for example, significantly affects their view of proper management (Laurent 1983). Latin managers, compared with managers from Northern cultures, perceive authority, status, and power as attached not to institutional elements such as offices or functions but to individuals (Laurent 1986). In fact Latin managers, compared with their Northern European counterparts, are significantly less likely to take norms and rules for granted in organizations (Kilduff and Angelmar 1989). The MNC is an arena in which implicit theories of organizing are bound to conflict. Such conflicts may undermine the taken-for-granted legitimacy of organizational routines.

The mention of the effects of books about MNCs on the actions of members of MNCs raises the final aspect of structuration theory that is important to the discussion: the double hermeneutic. This is the process by which the results of social science affect the knowledgeable agents who are its subject matter. In the case of MNCs the process is clearly evident. Books about MNCs containing distillations of research on MNCs are targeted precisely at the practitioners who served as subjects. It becomes unclear whether innovations in MNC development result from research-based suggestions or managerial practice. In any case, a rigid distinction between theory on the one hand and subject matter by which theory can be tested on the other seems hopeless. From this perspective, even such apparently irrelevant aspects of social science research as the literary prowess of the author can have significant effects on future attempts to replicate findings, by increasing or decreasing the communication of implications to the subjects of study.

ENACTMENT AND STRUCTURATION

The structuration perspective suggests that routines are the key to understanding the functioning of any organization. These routines can be understood as programs or standard operating procedures (see e.g. March and Simon 1958). But these programs may be only imperfectly reproduced. The possibility of random variation in the reproduction of routines is not explicitly addressed in Giddens' (1984) model, but it is part of the ecological model of action proposed by Weick (1979). Random variations can alter routines so that diffusion across large, loosely coupled organizations may be imperfect. Just as in the children's game in which a message is systematically garbled as it is whispered from ear to ear, so in the MNC a routine transferred from one department to another may be transformed by the time it reaches a division in another country.

From both the enactment and the structuration perspectives, iterated individual acts produce and reproduce structure. One aspect of the structure of the organization is the rules that underlie the repeated actions and interactions of individuals. The structuration perspective tends to take these repeated interactions for granted as a starting point from which to investigate the consequences of such interaction. The enactment approach is much more interested in the evolution of such norms in arbitrary traditions (Weick and Gilfillan 1971), rational myths (Meyer and Rowan 1977), and national cultures (Kilduff and Angelmar 1989). From the enactment perspective, the same iterated behavior may occur for a variety of different reasons, and attention must be focused on the meanings attributed to behavior (Abolafia and Kilduff 1988). Apparent behavioral homogeneity can mask heterogeneous goals, assumptions, and values (Weick 1979; Donnellon, Gray, and Bougon 1985). The MNC, with its diverse mix of ethnic and national groups, offers an excellent arena in which to investigate the enactment, attribution, and regulation of norm-based behavior.

The enactment perspective and the structuration perspective are similar in their emphasis on the micro foundations of organizational structure in the purposeful behavior of individuals. Interacting individuals can create complex structures beyond the power of any one person to comprehend (Weick 1979). In Giddens' terms, a perverse outcome of individual action may be that it constrains one's future actions in ways that are neither anticipated nor welcomed. For example, Carlos is a graduate in biochemistry from the best university in Ecuador. To further his career, he obtains a job with a multinational pharmaceutical company that offers professional and career advancement far in excess of what domestic employers can offer. After two years of training overseas, however, he is sent back to Ecuador to negotiate with the Health Minister retail prices for a group of drugs urgently needed by the rural and urban poor in Ecuador. His corporate mission is to persuade the minister to agree to a high retail price for the drugs, and in this he is successful: his command of the language and culture, his personal contacts inside the country combined with the professional training he has received, make him an ideal representative of the MNC to the host government. But what has he achieved? He has succeeded in furthering the interests of the MNC at the expense of the people in his own country. His victory is also his loss. After six troubled months, he resigns abruptly to pursue an academic career.

In enactment theory, actors are said to create the environment that then impinges on their subsequent actions (Weick 1979). By combining this insight with structuration theory's emphasis on the individual's involvement in the reproduction of routines, one understands how an actor such as Carlos can create the conditions by which the structure of the institution constrains his choices. Carlos pursues his own ends at the same time as he recreates the structures of the organization that both enable and constrain. He pursues his own career even as he negotiates a high price for the drugs. If he finds himself trapped, then he has, in a sense, trapped himself.

In Weick's model, retrospective sense-making can change the meaning of action and lead an employee like Carlos either to quit the company or to become transformed into an organization man who sees the acquisition of high corporate profits from selling drugs to developing countries as completely ethical. There is also the possibility that individual or coalition action can force changes in rule-based behavior (Abolafia and Kilduff 1988). Carlos could succeed in changing the strategy of the MNC. Drugs could be donated to developing countries as a way of gaining international goodwill. The enactment perspective, relative to the structuration perspective, is more optimistic about the possibility of changing vicious circles through modifications in cognitive attributions and behavioral routines.

The transmission of routines in multinational organizations is problematic, because such routines are embedded in the interactions of specific individuals in specific places. Structuration theory suggests that the institutional authority of the MNC itself is an outcome of the everyday routine behavior of organizational participants who may or may not have internalized the values and norms promulgated by the top management team. Indeed, a central paradox exposed by both the enactment and structuration approaches is that organizational participants can actively participate in the reproduction of institutional arrangements with which they may fundamentally disagree. Within the international management literature, one dimension of this problem has been pursued, namely the headquarters–subsidiary balance of power: the pulls of the subsidiary to enlarge its autonomy and the countervailing efforts of the headquarters to maintain or increase control. The structuration approach suggests that the rational actor arguments used to explain headquarters–subsidiary relations can be subsumed within a larger, ongoing set of dynamics that make maintenance of MNC patterns problematic.

SUGGESTIONS FOR A RESEARCH AGENDA

There are two focal points where research on norms and routines in MNCs can make a powerful contribution to the further development of the structuration and enactment paradigms, and where the paradigms can guide research of critical importance in understanding the MNC as a complex organization. First, given the enormous power of MNCs to transform the earth and the lives of its people, a set of questions of broad popular, as well as scholarly, interest concerns the formation of norms and routines in MNCs. What are the norms and routines that govern behavior in these huge entities? From where do these norms and routines come? Is it possible to infer the rules that govern the routines? How are the norms and routines reproduced across national boundaries, and what kinds of distortions ensue? Different cultural groups within MNCs are likely to espouse quite different theories about management and organizing (Hofstede 1980a; Laurent 1983, 1986). Do these different espoused theories reflect different routinized practices? If such behavioral differences exist, what are the consequences of these differences? What are the conditions leading to high fidelity of reproduction of routines? To what extent are routines that appear startlingly different merely simple transformations of an underlying structural pattern? The research focus must not be on what top management declares the organizational philosophy or culture to be, but on the norms that are expressed by workers throughout the organization in both their behavioral routines and their accounts of action.

There are many ways to study the diffusion of norms from the headquarters to new subsidiaries. Certainly an ethnographic treatment of the diffusion process would reveal much about the possible mutations that norms might undergo in new settings. A social network analysis of the diffusion process would help embed norm transmission in ongoing patterns of relationships, and might reveal the extent to which the normative and social orders overlap.

The second research focus is on the apparently spontaneous social interactions between organizational teams in MNCs. These can be deconstructed into their routine dramaturgical elements—the realm charted by Goffman, Giddens, and Weick under the rubric of impression management, structuration, and enactment. This is also the realm of management decision making, organizational stratification, internal labor markets, leadership, and culture.

Within the MNC, each subsidiary can be considered a performance team. The preliminary step in a research effort would be to examine the identities and relationships of these teams. What kinds of routine performances are teams enacting for each other? How are impressions being managed? Are there interesting variations in the use of sign equipment?

As a way of understanding the pervasiveness of scripted behavior, a study of breaches of expected actions is instructive. Such breaches can reveal organization-wide coalitions whose interests may be strikingly opposed, even though their espoused theories are similar (Kilduff and Abolafia 1989). What kinds of performance disruptions can be observed, and what do these reveal about the staged nature of social reality? What kinds of slippages can be observed between back and front regions? What kinds of rewards are teams performing for?

Taking a more macro perspective on the routinized performances being enacted by teams in MNCs might lead to the question, "Of what results are teams unaware, in terms of consequences that are set in motion by their own enactments?" Research on unintended consequences looks at how unforeseen events are triggered. These unintended events can, in their turn, circumscribe future actions, because the actors remain unaware of the process they are enacting.

For example, one could analyze how an ecological disaster attributed to an MNC, such as the explosion of a chemical plant in a developing country, was the unwanted result of a series of apparently trivial routine decisions (see for example Perrow 1984). Disasters blamed on MNCs might be unintended consequences, remote in time and space, of routine decisions taken in cultural contexts very different from those in which the decisions are implemented. Similarly, one could examine how an institutionalized practice, such as the cultural domination of an MNC by one ethnic group, was sustained not only by the actions of the dominant group but also by the actions of the subordinate.

Alternatively, one could trace over time how a cumulated series of events (such as the serial acquisition of a diverse group of previously autonomous companies) is derived from a rather trivial and accidental occurrence. In such a case, the accounts that people give retrospectively, such as the attribution to a diversification strategy, can be profitably compared with the circumstances of the first acquisition.

Finally, and perhaps most ambitiously, the researcher can ask, "How is team activity embedded in and constitutive of the larger systems of meaning that collectively identify the MNC?" These larger systems include the political, structural, and cultural systems, as well as the technical systems of production. March and Simon's (1958) image of the organization as a nested set of routine performances can be used to define the ultimate aim of a study of MNC routines: to show how sets of purposeful behaviors interlock and interact to produce the complexity and diversity that distinguish this particular organizational form.

CONCLUSION

This brief review of structuration and enactment paradigms has two surprising implications for research on MNCs. First, the outpouring of books and articles offering advice to managers of MNCs can itself be a focus of a research effort aimed at understanding the knowledgeability of agents in MNCs. As a realm of discourse, the managerial literature constantly recreates the double hermeneutic between discourse and practice. The analysis of how this discourse affects the reproduction of institutionalized practices in MNCs would itself be a valuable exercise.

The second implication of this review is that MNCs can be interesting arenas for theoretically driven research. There can be no sociological or psychological theory of the MNC itself, however. MNCs are interesting because of the diversity and complexity of their routinized reproductions, but social reproduction itself, and the structures of everyday life that enable and constrain it, are features of every social system.

13 Mickey on the Move: Observations on the Flow of Culture in the Multinational Corporation[1]

John Van Maanen

As this collection of essays suggests, organizational theorists are just getting around to the serious study of the multinational corporation. As of yet they have not had much time for culture. But when culture does enter into the emerging representation of the MNC, it does so often as an all-purpose variable used to account for many of the problems faced by MNCs. Such firms by definition do business in different countries under vastly different conditions throughout the world; they must therefore enter into relations with people—as customers, employees, suppliers—from distinct national (and other) cultures who may have quite different ideas as to what the organization and their roles in relation to it are all about. This multinational character creates varying degrees of cultural complexity, confusion, and conflict when individuals and groups who do not share the same underlying codes of meaning and conduct come into contact with one another. These troubles may persist over time and even become amplified, thus leading to a good deal of distrust, disorder, hostility, and unraveling of corporate or local agendas. Viewed from this frame, organization theory applied to the MNC becomes then a search for those organizational forms that might obviate, obliterate, mediate, blunt, or otherwise soothe local interests in favor of corporate ones.

At the same time, organizational theorists are quick to point out the various incentives and advantages of operating on a transnational scale—markets to exploit, labor pools to tap, information sources to develop, and so on. Thus, in the very process of doing business internationally, a firm may also discover new ways of doing things and new things to do that make use of the varied cultural backgrounds of its members, suppliers, and customers. Cultural diversity is a resource for the firm. With this frame at play, organization theory applied to the MNC then becomes a search for organizational forms that preserve and capitalize on local knowledge, skill, and interest.

More than form is at issue, however. As many organizational theorists are only too happy to point out, an MNC also has a cultural character of its own (e.g. Ouchi and Wilkins 1985; Fine 1985; Bartlett 1986; Schein 2001). Here, the now hackneyed phrase "corporate culture" enters the analysis of multinationals as a way of indicating a sort of culture of cultures. The phrase carries a kind of hope and glory that is apparently appealing to some theorists, for it suggests that culture operates as a bonding device holding an organization together—the superglue that connects structural elements of a firm to its economic, political, and social strategies, and ultimately to the results it obtains from the marketplace (e.g. Ott 1988; Czarniawska-Joerges 1992; Martin 2002).

The view of culture put forth here is not quite so bold or unidirectional. I do not, for example, equate culture with homogeneity of thought and action across a diverse collection of people. Such a condition, were it to exist, might well indicate a lack of culture rather than a presence. Culture is a differentiating device as much as it is an integrating one. It is a means of marking differences and establishing boundaries, not erasing them. Culture concerns meaning systems, ideas, patterns of thought. It represents more a model for the behavior of members of a given group than a model of their behavior (Goffman 1974: 41).

All of this is to suggest that to consider seriously what culture is and what it is not takes us well beyond the usual leisure of the theory class in organization studies, where concepts are turned into variables and measurement proceeds apace. Culture is most distinctly not a variable in any conventional sense. If anything, it is more a sensitizing concept for organizational theorists, akin to the biologist's use of the term "life" or the physicist's notion of the term "force." It is central to the study of organization(s) but remains elusive. Once captured by a definition, it seems always to escape. This is not, however, for lack of effort.

CULTURE AS PROCESS AND PRODUCT

The study of culture—organizational or otherwise—has a reasonably long history. It is also a contentious history with a vast proliferation of approaches, empirical studies, concepts, theories, and legendary figures (heroes and villains). Although most scholars today would probably agree that culture comprises symbols through which alternative patterns of conduct are more or less encoded and, with some slack, produced, there is no orthodoxy to be found.[2] Virtually all the old definitions and theories surrounding culture are still commingling with the new. But, to follow the Wittgensteinian principle and look not for lexical meanings but for the ways the term culture is used in scholarly practice, two usages are apparent (Peterson 1990). One treats culture as a process, the other, as a product.

Culture as a process is an approach that derives from anthropology and sociology. It regards culture for the most part as codes of conduct embedded in or constitutive of the social life of a given group whose boundaries may be fixed and distinct or (increasingly) ambiguous and dispersed. Researchers within this intellectual tradition speak of the culture of a nation, a tribe, a corporation, a gang, a profession, an ethnic enclave, or a common pursuit followed by such nominal groups as surfers, tourists, evangelists, or drug dealers. Such codes are found by ethnographic observation, attitude surveys, content analysis of key documents, or studying patterns of cultural choice.[3]

Culture as a product is an approach that comes from the humanities, literary criticism in particular. These days it has a home in a wide variety of university-based cultural studies programs. It treats culture as something created; the result of individual or group activities that carry distinct symbolic properties with certain meanings attached for certain groups. Students of "high" culture look to the products of artists, scientists, intellectuals, architects, and so forth. Students of "low" culture look to the products of the media, advertising, fashion, fads, movies, television, and so on. Various interpretive approaches—historical studies, deconstruction, semiotics, hermeneutics, and the like—are used to uncover how the studied signs operate, what they teach, and how they use or are used by those exposed to them (Van Maanen 1995).[4]

These two approaches to culture rarely overlap. Those who study symbols do not ordinarily concern themselves with the social organization standing behind cultural productions, and those who examine production activities are relatively unconcerned with what such productions mean to those who consume or witness them.[5] This is a pity since even a modest convergence of interest between the two would add considerable depth to the empirical work going on in either domain. In the organizational research community, for example, it would be of more than passing interest to have a study that examined the products put forth by some of the celebrated, supposedly exemplary, organizational cultures. More relevant to the purposes here, however, would be the study of the influence the products or services offered by an MNC have on the host culture(s) in which it operates. From my perspective, culture needs to be treated as both process and product. This is not easy.

Part of the difficulty in bridging these approaches is in the mystery that surrounds the elusive mantra that is culture itself. Process or product, it is a loose concept that refers to the marking and classifying of the experienced world. It is as much a socially organized process as it is a collectively validated result. When located within a group, it provides members with images of their basic concerns, principles, ethics, and bodies of manners, rituals, ideologies, strategies, and tactics of self-survival, including certain notions of good deeds and bad, various forms of folklore and legends, and a set of ideas that allows something of a "consciousness of kind" to emerge such that rough boundaries of demarcation can be drawn between (and among) members and non-members. Culture is socially organized meaning that emerges from intimate and sustained human interaction. When interaction is tied to space, so too is culture.

The carriers of culture are individuals, and it is axiomatic among cultural theorists that culture is learned. The way we give logic to the world begins at birth with the gestures, words, tone of voice, noises, colors, smells, and body contact we experience; with the ways we are raised, washed, rewarded, punished, held in check, toilet trained, and fed; by the stories we are told, the games we play, the songs we sing, or rhymes we recite; the schooling we receive, the jobs we hold, and the careers we follow; right down to the very way we sleep and dream. Our culture is what is familiar, recognizable, habitual. It is "what goes without saying."

The tacit character of culture suggests that we are perhaps most aware of it when standing on or near its boundaries. When we speak of "our" culture, we often do so in terms of contrast—what it is not. At a societal level, when a Frenchman remarks, "American children are spoiled and impolite," he is referring not to American children per se but to the French conception of child raising and how the proper child ought to behave within French society. Likewise, if an American claims, "the French are rude and never let one finish their sentences," she is putting forth American rules for conversation. It is at the boundaries that cultural premises are brought into awareness. In this sense, only at the meeting places between cultures—where there is a breakdown, hitch, or hiccup—does one become alert to both the similarity (what one shares with others of one's own culture) and difference (what distinguishes one from those of other cultures) expressed by the always relational notion of culture.

Culture here, there, everywhere

Modern society complicates the study of culture. Indeed, the twenty-first century marks the end of a world that could, with some truth, be seen as a mosaic of separate cultures or societies with sharp, well-defined edges. The deep structure of modernity (or post-modernity for that matter) carries with it the idea that people are cut loose from their past and place (Castells 1997; Zachary 2000). Widespread urbanization, expanded literacy, bureaucratized work relations, new forms of mass communication, geographic and economic mobility, and the shifting character of the nation state are the surface features of such modernity. Advanced industrial societies contain a head-swirling mix of cultural groupings, from those grounded in ethnic and kinship identity to those resting on the mutual love of a particular labor or leisure. And most critically, these cultural groups not only bump up against each other but interpenetrate one another as well.

Such interpenetration can be seen as a cultural flow—the movement of cultural products and/or processes from a group familiar with them to one that is not. Much of this flow results in an increased awareness on the part of some people, and occurs in a relatively free, unsponsored, reciprocal, and rather spontaneous fashion in everyday life as differing cultural groups interact at work, in school, on the street, in shops, or in any place where people congregate. Contemporary society is such that people generally develop a fairly broad conception of other cultural processes and products by the same kind of listening, looking, and learning as they do within their own cultural group(s). The flow here is rather diffuse, uncentered, often reciprocal and multi-channeled (Becker 1982).

Culture also flows in a centered or command fashion. Some who have it wish to provide it to others. The flow here is relatively thin, unidirectional and often confined to particular narrow channels, yet nonetheless steady and frequently institutionalized. The state, for example, is an organizational form that tries—with varying degrees of success—to reach out toward its subjects and project the idea of a nation as a culture (Anderson 1983). Citizens are schooled in officially approved cultural matters normally associated with conceptions of history and tradition (conceptions that may in fact be spurious and quite controversial). Work organizations engage in an analogous process whenever their leaders set out deliberately to create a corporate culture which members are to demonstrate fealty to and embrace. The success of such culture building and transmission obviously depends on the history and traditions conveyed to particular clusters of recipients and the degree to which the state or the organization is a valued part of the life of its subjects.

Another centered flow of culture occurs in commercial spheres. Markets represent channels for cultural flows, as products and processes of one cultural group are offered to members of another cultural group. While culture may move by command, its reception is by no means assured or welcomed (Hannertz 1989, 1992). Of concern to us here is a basic sociological proposition that commodities or services sent forth by organizations to consumers or users have value beyond whatever function they perform or whatever labor value is associated with their production (Granovetter 1985; Etzioni 1988; DiMaggio 1990). A part of this value lies in the cultural meanings associated with particular goods and services. Culture can therefore flow for fun, profit, edification, or any other motive in our collective vocabularies.

An example of the reach cultural marketing can achieve is provided by MacCannell's (1976) fine ethnographic study of the contemporary tourist. He argues quite convincingly that objects in the modern world are increasingly invested with symbolic capital—so much so that even "pure experience" can be marketed. Culturally infused products that leave no physical trace such as the "fidelity" of a stereo, the "style" of a restaurant, the "feel" of a computer, the "ambiance" of a resort, or the "strong backbone, heady, full, complete, almost thick" properties of a vintage red wine are all goods that are sold on the "experience" they are said to deliver.

Cultural experience

This brings us (at last) to a degree of focus. I am concerned here not only with the flow of culture but also with the structure of cultural experience itself. The latter is, it seems, a hot item in the marketplace today and a topic of considerable interest to cultural theorists and to students of MNCs. Cultural experience is, of course, the stuff from which ethnographies presumably emerge, the stuff that tourists relentlessly pursue, and the stuff that is used—implicitly if not explicitly—to direct MNCs. It may also be what MNCs provide—knowingly or not—to customers in distant lands as well as to their employees who happen to be located in or sent to such lands.

Cultural experience contains a certain hip or gamy (even sexual) connotation beyond its scholarly ethnographic or instrumental market meanings. In brief, it implies the transformation of an original emptiness or skepticism on the part of a person or group into a belief or feeling that results from direct, first-hand involvement in a previously unknown, or at least partially unknown, social domain. Importantly, cultural experience in no way signals the gaining of competence in, or a conversion to, the social world in which the experience is initially marked. Rejection, distaste, amusement, ignorance, and befuddlement are all possible outcomes of such encounters. But such encounters do promote a kind of cultural awareness that was previously lacking.

Examples of cultural experience are not hard to locate. Conventional levels of analysis serve as guides. Driving down an interstate freeway in the USA might serve as a delightful individual experience to the visitor from Denmark—the more barren the landscape the better, since it would be "more American." Managers or technicians from the Netherlands working in Mexico City as representatives of an oil company subsidiary in that country partake in a cultural experience organized partly by their firm. Or to reverse the flow, Japanese students sitting about a local sake bar watching American sitcoms on TV may be having a cultural experience of a remarkable, or more likely unremarkable, sort. Certainly, in most of the world, few groups are immune to cultural experiences of this sort. What are we to make of them?

Two rough answers can be sketched out to these questions. Both must account for the organizer, the taker, and the channel associated with cultural experience. If we first examine the market as the channel of interest, a kind of global homogenization or integration theory surfaces as one answer. Cultural influences continuously pound away on the sensibilities of people, such that eventually bits and pieces of whatever indigenous cultures are associated with their life fade out, as they assimilate more and more of the cultural forms and meanings brought to bear on them from outside. Over time, the local character of culture is increasingly reduced, marginalized, or driven out in favor of transnational symbolic forms originating elsewhere. Everyday life as an organizer of cultural experience must compete with more distant sources of cultural experience whose organizers (and senders) seek to spread as widely as possible. Given the resources and willingness to invest in such a project, the culture-conscious MNC systematically replicates itself wherever it goes, by pounding away on those who work in its subsidiary units.

This is cultural imperialism pure and simple. The high-tech culture of the industrialized world, with powerful organizational backing, faces a more or less defenseless, small-scale variety of national and folk culture whose members are slowly but surely lured or coerced into dependency.

Homogenization comes from a center-to-periphery flow of cultural experience, bringing about something of a world culture that is, by and large, a version of contemporary industrial society. This is a zero-sum game where the loss of culture shows itself most distinctly in the least organized and powerless communities. All the while, the more organized and powerful grow increasingly similar, coming to shape, share, and signal the world culture.

The global homogenization thesis has a good deal going for it—not the least its simplicity. But another answer to this question is possible. This answer concentrates on the flow of culture in everyday life where a good deal of stability and local values persist. Cultural experiences that do not easily fold into the patterns of thought and action on this level are (1) unmarked entirely and thus have no influence, (2) rejected out of hand as culturally inappropriate and unattractive, or (3) eventually brought into line through transformations and adjustments of one sort or another. Culture may still flow from the center outward, along a market channel, but there is a corruption down the line so that the core of the penetrated culture is left untouched. The local core may even be recharged, reinvigorated, and made more aware and assertive of its own character and perspective as a result of such contact, displaying its own inherent strengths and adaptive abilities in the face of alien ways. Everyday life thus colonizes the center (or market) rather than vice versa, reshaping the imported culture to its own specifications.

Organization, culture, and the MNC

Both homogenization and resistance theories are popular. Each has several variants and thoughtful adherents in a number of scholarly camps. Both view the current expansion of MNCs in uneasy terms. Homogenization suggests the gradual decline of global diversity through the growth of a highly rationalized and commodified world culture. The resilience of local culture perspective implies a Balkanized world order where mutual respect, understanding, or common ground across cultures are not to be expected. Evidence for both views is readily available.

Some students of MNCs, for example, point to the relative success some firms have had in creating a centralized global operation, where control of the firm is securely in the hands of those enthroned at headquarters, and the look and feel of subsidiary activities throughout the world are quite similar.[6] Managers and employees alike share corporate aims, and the local policies and practices of the firm are more similar than not. These homogenized MNCs take advantage of what is regarded as a convergence of consumer preferences worldwide, sophisticated information technologies, the benefits of scale economies, and the corporate dedication and competence displayed by a similarly trained and motivated workforce to keep in check far-flung subsidiaries, to distribute and sell common products throughout the world, and to keep decision making in line with firm criteria originating in corporate headquarters. The power to ignore, bypass, or shape and mold culture is taken for granted.

Other MNC watchers have become enchanted with a more heterogeneous model of global operations, one more in touch with the cultural resistance scenario outlined above.[7] They point to the growing strength of the forces of localization, including the dependence of MNCs on host governments, the eagerness of some MNCs to "capture" local innovation and creativity, and the apparent stubborn objections of consumers in some markets to standardized products and practices. The disadvantages—economic and social—of large-scale production are highlighted, along with the needs of MNCs for cultural expertise in order to operate effectively in unfamiliar societies. The heterogeneous MNC becomes the model operation. Independent and relatively self-sufficient national (or subnational) subsidiaries are emphasized, and a highly pluralistic version of the MNC is the result. Authority is dispersed across the organization, and the culture flow from the center outward is more or less constrained.

Qualifications and contingencies can be tied to both models. Most students would agree that all MNCs bear something of a cultural stamp that originates in the society where the organization was first designed (Laurent 1983, 1986). The greater the economic power of this society, the larger and older the organization, the more obvious the stamp (Chandler 1986). At the periphery, the older and larger the subsidiary, the more likely it is that the unit will be marked by local or country-specific modifications (Stopford and Wells 1972). MNCs involved in the manufacture and sale of global products are apparently more likely to suffer from strong, centralized, corporate controls than MNCs involved in numerous regionalized consumer product businesses (Robinson 1967). MNCs headquartered in small countries are apt to be less ethnocentric than those from large countries, and hence the flow of culture may be more symmetric or reciprocal (Hedlund 1986). Certainly complexity of the organizational form itself enters the picture, since the total number of ties between the center and periphery may act as a constraint on the center's ability to tighten any or all links (Nohria and Ghoshal 1989).

What comes out of such studies is the notion that MNCs are virtually always faced with hard choices. They can, if senior managers wish, work toward a highly centralized operation on a global scale and attempt with more or less success to rein in subsidiary operations through the construction of a "strong" corporate culture designed and communicated from the center outward. Or they can choose to cut loose operations on the periphery, allowing subsidiaries relatively great flexibility in terms of policy and procedure. Most popular now are various mixed models: firms can therefore learn to "think locally and act globally" or "think globally and act locally," depending on the kind of strategic models that are used by the managers who direct the activities of the firm (Prahalad and Doz 1987). The homogeneous parts of the MNC develop in response to intensive corporate socialization, rapid transfer and rotation of managers across selected units of the firm, strict reporting and evaluation procedures tied to common reward systems, elaborate corporate-wide rituals organized to promote feelings of commonality and shared purposes and the like. The heterogeneous parts of the MNC lift, downplay, or ignore such practices and encourage local autonomy. Strategically, it is all a matter of choosing a goal and then following the proper formula. Or is it?

The problem for cultural theorists as well as organizational strategists with all this commonsense organization theory is that it either trivializes culture by reducing its relevance to something that is thought to be fully under the control of a few, and exported, if necessary or desired, to the many, or it enshrines culture as impenetrable, unique, unfathomable, always local, and essentially timeless and omnipresent. Both views are entirely too simple, and a considerably more nuanced view of the workings of MNCs is needed.

A revisionist perspective directs attention to specific cultural interaction sites in the firm where different marking, classifying, and meaning-making devices are put to work in particular places at particular times. High variability is quite likely to be the result of such a focus, with the exceptional and peculiar showing up in contrast to either the local autonomy stories or those of homogenization. Such particularity, however, leaves us only a collection of highly diverse stories to tell. So given my aims here, some attention needs to be paid to an overall conceptualization of the flow of culture that incorporates a sense of the general.

To this end, I will tell a tale of culture on the move. The story reaches for the general in its depiction of just how one culture attends to the imports of another. The level of analysis is relatively broad, working across national or societal boundaries. But the considerations that enter at this level are relevant all the way down the chain of cultural groupings. The story concerns a common practice of MNCs, namely the packing-up of an operation and product developed at home and shifting it lock, stock, and barrel elsewhere. The hope always is that it will perform as well (or better) in its new surroundings as in the old. Examples are everywhere: Volvo goes to Russia, Mitsubishi comes to Palo Alto, Club Med goes to Paradise. My story concerns the exporting of Disneyland, a product (and cultural experience) of some fame, into several new and culturally distinct contexts.

MICKEY'S GLOBAL VISION[8]

At first glance, Tokyo Disneyland is a physical and social copy of Disneyland in Southern California—a clone created 6000 miles distant, and perhaps something of a cultural bomb dropped on perfect strangers. The castle, the flags, the rides, the entertainment, the orderly waterways and impeccably clean grounds, the ever-smiling ride operators and Disney characters that prance about charming the old and young alike; even the crowds, the traffic, the smog, the lengthy waits for attractions, the summer heat, the suburban sprawl surrounding the park, all seem in harmony with the spirit and letter of the almost 50-year-old original. Even the gate receipts for this detailed replica met and exceeded expectations from the day the Tokyo park opened. Walt's world travels well, it seems—so well, in fact, that another version opened outside Paris in 1992 and yet another copy is set to open in Hong Kong in 2005.

Global homogenization appears to be working here. Culture—at least a theme park form of American pop culture—is flowing from the West to the East quite smoothly and easily. On the surface, at least, the culture codes at work and on display at Disneyland move gracefully into a vastly different societal context and perform the same wonders they perform at home. For observers of the MNC, this may seem a fortunate turn of events since it provides a rather visible, happy, and public stage on which to examine the cultural exchange process. Moreover, it appears to be close to a pure case of emulation and adoption, given that Disney was lavishly courted, warmly welcomed, and provided numerous favors when choosing to locate in Japan, France, and Hong Kong. This is not a case therefore of the center forcing itself on the periphery.

Disneyland is perhaps a glimpse of the coming world culture; a commodified and highly standardized cultural product built on the Coca-Colonizing forces of Western, particularly American, consumer values (Baudrillard 1983). The increased traffic in culture and the apparently asymmetric transfer of meaning systems and symbolic forms give way to an empire of signs ruled by those who produce and export the world's most desirable goods and services. This is a sort of context-free reading of the global fascination with American popular culture and the universal desire for the cultural experience a visit to Disneyland provokes. Indeed, Disney products and images have long been part of a world culture, and are virtually impossible to escape anywhere. Mickey Mouse cartoons are seen in Balinese villages amid rice paddies and oxen (Myerhoff 1983). Children's candies are sold in Italy wrapped in packages adorned with the familiar cast of Disney characters (Iyer 1988). Disneyfication operates with an apparent vengeance in Latin America where millions on millions of *Donald Duck* comic books are distributed (Dorfman and Matterlart 1975). In many respects, the Disney corporate logo of the globe with mouse ears is hardly an idle boast.

Context-dependent explanations for the workings of culture flow seem antiquated, downright quaint, when employed to explain how Disneyland has been able to move into foreign territory. Japan is, for example, a prime player in the world economy, highly sophisticated and self-conscious culturally, careful, almost xenophobic, about the importation of things foreign, and the possessor of one of history's oldest, most subtle cultures founded on a sense of exclusivity, hierarchy, and obligation (Benedict 1946; Nakane 1970; Fukutake 1981). Japan is certainly not a cultural dumping ground for the West, or likely to respond well to expressions of American individualism and its associated colonial, paternal, and patriotic images. Yet when Disney officials expressed an interest in providing some home-country attractions, such as a "Samurai Land" to replace one of its American attractions, or a ride and narrative based on the classic Japanese children's story "The little peach boy," the Japanese partners in Tokyo Disneyland resisted strenuously and insisted on a duplicate American version, thus retaining (presumably) the cultural purity of the original (Raz 1999; Brannen 1992). The streams of local visitors to the park would then seem to validate the idea that Disney's cultural products and experience work in the same way across two radically dissimilar contexts, effectively and effortlessly transcending cultural boundaries.

This is certainly the spin put on the story by corporate officials. Consider the comment by a public relations spokesperson at Tokyo Disneyland: "We really tried to avoid creating a Japanese version of Disneyland....To us, Disneyland represents the best America has to offer" (quoted in Brannen 1992). Such remarks explicitly suggest that the Japanese managers of Disneyland believe they have created a replica, and implicitly they suggest that the imported Disney version retains its original influence and meaning. Similar stories are told by company representatives at Disneyland Paris and Hong Kong, who take care to publicly stress the "universal appeal" of Disneyland.

The market conquers all in this sterling tale of an excellent company and product. However, if we look somewhat closer and in more detail—beyond the sales figures and surface similarities of the parks—certain interesting contradictions to this presumed unproblematic one-way flow of culture begin to appear. My contention is that these contradictions are instructive and shed considerable light on just how "cultural experience" is sorted out, sold, and received. To understand this flow of culture requires first an appreciation for the "Disney experience" in its indigenous locale.

Mickey at home

Disneyland first opened its gates in July 1955. It has been a remarkable economic success and become something of a national institution. One student of American culture notes that the definition of "good parents" in the USA turns, in part, on whether or not Mom and Dad have visited Disneyland with their children (Real 1977). And its appeal to foreign visitors as an "authentic" American site representing the best the country has to offer is apparent in this quote from an editorial in the normally dyspeptic and reserved London-based publication the *Economist*:

> Builders, architects, city planners, managing directors from around the
> world should all be forced in chains if necessary to find out from Mickey
> Mouse how one can create an environment in which laughter flourishes and

well-being is created. If Mickey Mouse were elected mayor, the efficiency of local government would increase by several hundred percent.

(quoted in Harrington 1979)

Disneyland is, in this view, a product—part movie theater, part tourist site, part shopping mall, part museum, part stage production, part playground, part shrine, part ceremony, part spectacle, part festival, and so on. It has been subject to countless assessments of culture critics who, although not always impressed by its wonders, do manage to agree on a number of unifying themes standing behind the product—themes that seemingly integrate and make meaningful a visit to the park on the part of the millions that crowd the grounds each year.[9]

Most begin by noting the order, safety, and cleanliness at Disneyland, and the marked contrast these features bear to contemporary urban life in America (Watts 1997; Fjellman 1992; Marin 1977; Myerhoff 1983; Schickel 1968). The rectangular grid of the city is replaced in the park by graceful, curved walkways. Motorists become pedestrians. The drab industrial and metropolitan landscape is replaced by bright colored buildings done up in ebullient and whimsical forms and covered by sumptuous ornaments and thousands of twinkling lights that turn night into day. The crowded, disorderly, fear-inspiring city scenes of ordinary life are transformed within the park to obedient, friendly queues and the peaceful strolling of people kept secure by unarmed, unobtrusive, yet ever-present and smiling park police. Work clothes give way to leisure garb. Adults take the role of children on rides designed to rekindle youthful memories, while children take on adult roles by driving snarling miniature automobiles on toy freeways, exploring deep space, and making family decisions about what to do next. The frontier town of yesteryear is no longer dusty, dirty, and rather formless, but becomes prim, tidy, and "what it should have been" by virtue of its scrubbed, freshly-painted, simple, and sweet look.

In the American context, Disneyland is a topsy-turvy world that highlights in its physical and social design a long string of semiotic contrasts that set the park off as a sought-after cultural experience for patrons: work/play, adult/child, dirty/clean, poverty/wealth, dangerous/safe, rude/civil, cold/warm, routine/festive, and so on (Van Maanen 1991; Gottdiener 1982; King 1981). These contrasts of America/Disneyland create the differences on which the park's claim to be "the happiest place on earth" rests. To make good on this claim requires the banishment of all signs of decay, crime, confusion, discontent, pain, or struggle in the park's design, and the reduction wherever possible of social and stylistic diversity on the part of customers and employees alike.

The layout of the park conveys a high degree of thematic integration well known to visitors. Dominating the landscape from the center is Sleeping Beauty's Castle with streets radiating outward, Versailles-like, into the four lands, each representing something of a distinct stage of life: Fantasyland for

266

early childhood where the attractions are small-scale and built on mythical, imaginary fables quite familiar to American children; Frontierland for adolescence where cowboy tales of the Wild West are re-enacted through the hourly shooting of the glum desperado by the smug sheriff, and summertime romps recreated on Tom Sawyer's Island; Adventureland for young adulthood where a test of courage against the strange and savage is presented as an Indiana Jones trek up-river into the dark, unexplored territories of the world; and Tomorrowland for adulthood where the dream of science and technology conquers all and personable robots cavort alongside humans.

The castle and hub of the park is reached by a walk through Main Street, an imaginative (but pickled) recreation of a midwestern railroad town at the turn of the twentieth century, full of quasi-Victorian shops selling modern merchandise. Between Adventureland and Frontierland lies New Orleans Square, which Walt Disney claimed "is just like the 1850s original Vieux Carré but a lot cleaner" (Lowenthal 1985: 321). And in the backwoods of Disneyland sits Bear Country and its reminder of the rural, "hayseed" relatives of the Mom and Pop entrepreneurs who made it to Main Street.

To the American visitor, each of the lands and constituent elements fits rather well-worn and comfortable mythical and historical narratives. Fantasyland, for example, embodies the classic children's literature of the West that has been culturally strip-mined by Disney via movies, books, and television programs. The verbal and visual images of Perrault, Collodi, Milne, and Barrie are now thoroughly familiar as Disney's Cinderella, Pinocchio, Winnie-the-Pooh, and Peter Pan. In Frontierland, a Frederick Turner version of America is conveyed by its relentless Westward-Ho imagery of rugged individualism and hardships overcome. Adventureland reminds visitors of the exploration saga of a Stanley and Livingstone sort as they journey through a lush, tropical jungle where elephants wave their trunks on cue and headhunting is still in style. The stories are conventional, stereotypical American versions of their world and its inhabitants.

This mythology underlying Disneyland images and narratives is a form of what Myerhoff (1983) usefully labels "hyperculture," a collective form of expression that overstates and overclarifies some cultural interpretation. There is certainly nothing subtle to Americans about Disneyland. The stories told in and by the park are exaggerated, inflated versions of events, aggrandized to the point of parody. The imagination provided at Disneyland is complete. Little room is left for the spontaneous or disarrayed. Lavish panegyric productions are staged to evoke both patriotism and nostalgia. Iconography is worked out in minute, common-denominator detail such that the partaker of gloom in the Haunted Mansion is, for instance, greeted by willows (for sadness), twisted oaks (for transitory life), dark, pod-like vehicles (for departure), and black-clad attendants (for morticians). Seemingly nothing is left to chance: each rock, tree, and plant in the park is numbered and assigned a proper role.

The communicative work that takes place inside the park serves to distinguish Disneyland from other (and earlier) theme parks. In contemporary America, Disneyland emerges as an island of calm sanity and safety in troubled times. The forces of decay are arrested, sexual innuendos are all but banished, liquor is taboo, evil is overcome, the innocent prevail, disorder is tamed, the future is clarified, the past cleaned up, and, in general, the perverse world of doubt, fear, and unfair competition outside the gates is held at bay. Turn-of-the-(twentieth)-century amusement parks in America performed much the same kind of symbolic work, but the reversals were different, almost an inversion of the symbolic work at Disneyland. Old parks developed from the background of a relatively stern Victorian heritage that stressed self-control, rationalism, industriousness, and delayed gratification, and thus worked to create feelings of spontaneity, intensified emotion, release, and a scornful, mocking attitude toward the culture outside the park (Adams 1991; Harris 1990; Kasson 1978).

Two emblematic attractions at Disneyland—also found at Tokyo Disneyland—serve nicely as concrete instances of the hypercultural statements found in the park, and will help illustrate and unpack something of the cultural experience the park offers to its American customers. First, consider the tame imagery presented by "It's a small world," an attraction first built by Disney for the New York World's Fair in 1964 and then rebuilt a year later at Disneyland. The cuteness and adorableness that permeates every amusement in the park is particularly clear in this attraction. The patrons enter a castle-like structure through a large and elegant topiary garden of plant life shaped into animal forms. They ride in small boats through a cartoon-like array of moving dolls dressed in native costumes that represent a selected variety of world cultures. The dolls spin and sing repetitively what is surely one of the most nauseating tunes of all time—"It's a small world after all." The dolls portray the "children of the world" in miniature. They are uniform in size, appearance, and mannerisms except for marginal differentiations of race, nationality, and dress. The marking is simple and redundant, cultural signs that Americans have long been accustomed to through children's literature, movies, television, and comic books. Holland is coded by tulips and bells, Japan by fans and kimonos, India by temples and saris. The faces are, however, basically Anglo-Saxon, even when intended to signal Chinese, Latino, or Arabic. The facial markers are mere hints that point to the possible existence of differences, but since the differences are so slight, they could not possibly be taken to be of serious consequence. A sort of insidious ethnocentrism is obvious in the infantilization of the world's cultures, where all human differences are superficial and benign. Americans are notably absent in this display except as passive observers of the scene, blissfully drifting past the world of young, diminutive, ebullient, bright-eyed, innocent, and lovable "Others."

If "Small world" is a hypercultural message of simplicity and harmony, of sweet differences and unity in the world, the Adventureland "Jungle cruise" is less reverential and more explicit toward some of the world's cultures. The racial themes and imperialist mentality of the late nineteenth and early twentieth centuries are built into this attraction, from the scenic constructions on the banks of the river to the words and phrases of the animated spiel that accompanies each cruise. The voyage departs next to a pile of plastic human skulls, beneath shields, spears, totems, and other symbols of some nameless but faintly menacing region beyond white settlement. The adventure consists mostly of short takes of mechanized people of color and wildlife as encountered in the river and along its banks. One scene places four members of a safari atop a pole with a horned rhinoceros threatening to impale them from below. The members of the party are three Africans who stare minstrel-like at the animal beneath them, faces glazed with fear and eyes protruding. At the very top of the pole, furthest from the rhino and danger, perches the white safari leader.

Disneyland is, of course, made up of thousands on thousands of hypercultural statements. Any one sign may give way to diverse readings, but when bundled all together, the teachings are abundantly clear. The overt messages and themes come back to the same concerns: friendliness, optimism, the civilization of the frontier, the ultimate victory of good over evil, the beauty and power of America, the importance of efficiency, cleanliness, order, and courtesy, the importance of staying in line (figuratively and literally), the triumph of modern technologies (particularly transportation technologies), and so forth. What is celebrated at Disneyland and what is being taught come together under labels such as patriotism, cultural superiority, and the trivialization of differences across the globe. America shines and spreads its light on the world, and the exotic is reduced to familiar terms. All this is packaged in a fashion that is thematically consistent, rather banal, closely scrutinized and controlled, and licensed by broad middle-class values of harmony and order.

The same production is replicated as the Magic Kingdom in Orlando, Florida. The second park opened in 1969, and now, with its peripheral attractions, Epcott Center, Paradise Island, MGM-Disney Studios, and numerous Disney-owned and operated hotels and fun zones adjacent to the park, the total complex in Orlando outdraws Disneyland by a large—almost two to one—margin. Walt Disney World is, in fact, second only to Washington DC in the number of tourists it attracts within the United States each year (Birnbaum 1989). Its construction, however, sets Disneyland apart as the "original," giving it the measure of authenticity that only a copy can provide.

The copy is not perfect. The scale is larger and some attractions, such as the Matterhorn bobsleds, are still found only at Disneyland. The Magic Kingdom lacks the intimacy of Disneyland but when combined with the other tourist sites on the grounds at Walt Disney World, it becomes part of an activity menu that lengthens the average visitor's stay to a matter of days rather than hours. One observer likens the complex to "Mickey Mouse on Steroids" (Fjellman 1992: 21).

Some (modest) differences within the park are visible as well. Sleeping Beauty's Castle is replaced by the bigger, more photogenic, and splendid version, Cinderella's Castle. Some of the rides, such as Big Thunder Mountain, are longer and slightly more harrowing. Others are thin replicas, such as the Pirates of the Caribbean, which is much more elaborate, lengthy, and entertaining at Disneyland. Still, despite small changes in design and its bloated size, the cultural experience for American visitors to the two parks is much the same. The context does not shift radically, nor do visitors seemingly notice much difference—beyond scale—in the two parks (Foglesong 2001; Watts 1997). What the park in Walt Disney World provides, however, is a measure of choice for those about to construct yet another copy of Disneyland.

Mickey goes to Tokyo

Disneyland went international in 1983 with the opening of its Tokyo operation. As noted earlier, it claims to be a near-perfect copy of the Disneyland production minus a few of the original's attractions. There are some recognized modifications, but these are imports selected from the Magic Kingdom instead of Disneyland (such as Cinderella's Castle and the Mickey Mouse Theater). In terms of organizational control, it is as decentralized as they come—the Oriental Land Company, a Japanese development and property management firm, took full control shortly after the park was built and now provides Walt Disney Enterprises with a rough 10 percent cut of Tokyo Disneyland's profits from admissions, food, and merchandise sales. A small American management team ("Disnoids") is deployed in Japan as advisors and consultants to keep the park in tune with Disney doctrine, and the firm hires a handful of non-Japanese employees, mainly Americans, as "cast members" (entertainers, craftspeople, and characters) strategically scattered throughout the park. The question now to be raised concerns the flow of culture from the West to the East. To what extent does Tokyo Disneyland mean the same thing to its new patrons as it means to its old?

In a nutshell, Tokyo Disneyland does not work—indeed cannot work—in the same way as its American counterpart. Although certain principles of cultural flow hold steady, the meanings attached by visitors to the forms that flow shift significantly, and whereas an American strolling through Frontierland may be gently reminded of a romanticized and nostalgic view of his or her past, the Japanese patron ambling through Westernland can have no such cultural experience. This is not to say that the symbols and Disney narratives are meaningless in the Japanese context. Such a view could not begin to explain the popularity of the park, which today outdraws Disneyland in California by several million customers each year. But what does appear to be happening is the recontextualization of the American signs so that the Japanese are able to make them their own. This process may be highly general, and something of the norm for cultural transformations.

270

Most observers of modern Japan note the country's penchant for the importation of things foreign, from public bureaucracies (Westney 1987) to fashion (Stuart 1987) to popular sports (Whiting 1977). In fact, Japan's wide-scale adoption of things American is now something of a universal cliché. The choice of imports is, however massive, highly selective. Thus the consumption of foreign goods in Japan seems less an act of homage than a way of establishing a national identity by making such imports their own through combining them in a composite of all that the Japanese see as the best in the world. Some of this conspicuous consumption correlates with significant increases in per capita disposable income and what appears to be a new and more relaxed attitude among the Japanese toward leisure and play (Fallows 1989; Emmott 1989). But whatever the source of this omnivorous appetite, the Japanese seem unworried that their cultural identity is compromised by such importation.

Not to be overlooked, however, are the subtle, sometimes hidden ways in which alien forms are not merely imported across cultural boundaries but in the very process turned into something else again, and the indigenous and foreign are combined into an idiom more consistent with the host culture than the home culture. Two features of the way Disneyland has been emulated and incorporated in the Japanese context are apparent. Each suggests that Tokyo Disneyland takes on a rather different meaning for workers and customers alike in its new setting.

First, Disneyland is made comfortable for the Japanese in ways that contrast with its California and Florida counterparts. In some ways, the fine-tuning of the park's character follows a domestication principle familiar to anthropologists, whereby the exotic, alien aspects of foreign objects are set back and de-emphasized, replaced by an intensified concern with the more familiar and culturally sensible aspects (Shweder 1991; Wallace 1985; Douglas 1966). Thus the safe, clean, courteous, efficient aspects of Disneyland fit snugly within the Japanese cultural system and can be highlighted. Disneyland as "the best of America" suits the Japanese customer, with its underscored technological wizardry and corporate philosophy emphasizing high-quality service. Providing happiness, harmony, and hospitality for guests by a staff that is as well groomed as the tended gardens in the park is certainly consistent with Japanese practices in other consumer locales (Vogel 1979; Taylor 1983; Dore 1987). The legendary *sotto voce* of the Japanese service provider is merely a modest step away from the "people specialist" of planned exuberance and deferential manners turned out by the University of Disneyland in the United States—at least in theory if not always in practice (Van Maanen 1991). And "Imagineering," a Disney oxymoron used to designate the department responsible for the conceptual development and design of park attractions—"the engineers of imagination"—is used in Japan, as in the USA, without a touch of irony or awareness of contradiction.

If anything, the Japanese have intensified the orderly nature of Disneyland. If Disneyland is clean, Tokyo Disneyland is impeccably clean; if Disneyland is efficient, Tokyo Disneyland puts the original to shame by being absurdly efficient. Whereas Disneyland is a vision of order, sanitized, homogenized, and precise, Tokyo Disneyland is even more so, thus creating, in the words of one observer, "a perfect toy replica of the ideal tinkling, sugarcoated society around it, a perfect box within a box" (Iyer 1988: 333). One of the charms of Disneyland to American visitors is the slight but noticeable friction between the seamless perfection of the place and the intractable, individualistic, irredeemable, and sometimes intolerable character of the crowd. In the midst of its glittering contraptions and mannerly operatives are customers strolling about wearing "shit happens" or "dirty old man" T-shirts. Tourists in florid tent dresses and country-club attire share space in the monkey car of Casey Jones's Circus Train with tattooed bikers and spiked Goths. Elderly retirees with seasonal passes sit serenely on Main Street watching gum-snapping teenagers make out as they all await the arrival of the evening parade. Park police—dressed as US marshals or tin-horn cops—chase down the little criminals of Disneyland on Tom Sawyer's Island or Main Street as irate parents screech at their offspring to wipe the chocolate off their faces and keep their hands off the merchandise. Some parents manage to curb their youngsters' enthusiasm and wanderlust by attaching them to a leash, others simply track them down after several ear-shattering screams fail to bring them in. For the Disneyland patron, such contrasts give life to the park and provide a degree of narrative tension.

In Tokyo, the shadow between the ideal and reality is not so apparent. Adults and children bend more easily toward the desired harmonious state, and out-of-order contrasts are few and far between inside (and, perhaps, outside) the park. This is a society where the word for wrong means "different" and "the nail that sticks out is the nail that must be hammered down" (Bayley 1976; Kamata 1980; White 1987). To the extent that there is order in Disneyland, it is welcomed as a contrast to the outside world; order in Tokyo Disneyland is expected and largely taken for granted, so that the park glides effortlessly rather than lurching self-consciously toward its fabled efficiency. Iyer summarizes his visit to Tokyo Disneyland in the following way:

> There was no disjunction between the perfect rides and their human riders. Each was as synchronized, as punctual, as clean as the other. Little girls in pretty bonnets, their eyes wide with wonder, stood in lines, as impassive as dolls, while their flawless mothers posed like mannequins under their umbrellas. [They] waited uncomplainingly for a sweet-voiced machine to break the silence and permit them to enter the pavilion—in regimented squads. All the while, another mechanized voice offered tips to ensure that the human element would be just as well planned as the man-made: Do not leave your shopping to the end, and

try to leave the park before rush hour, and eat at a sensible hour, and do not, under any circumstance, fail to have a good time.

(Iyer 1988: 317–318)

Failures to have a good time are rare, partly because of the way Tokyo Disneyland has rearranged the model to suit its customers. Despite its claims as a duplicate, a number of quite specific changes have taken place. The amusement park itself is considerably larger than Disneyland (124 acres to 74). As a result, it loses some of the intimacy that is so uncharacteristic in the Southern Californian setting, and instead gives off a feeling of conspicuous spaciousness rather unusual in greater Tokyo, where it seems every square inch is fully utilized. Disneyland's fleet of Nautilus-like submarines is missing, perhaps because of Japan's deep sensitivity to all things nuclear. There are few outdoor food vendors in the park but over 40 sit-down restaurants, about twice as many as in Disneyland. It is considered rude to eat while walking about in Japan, the munching of popcorn in the park being apparently the only exception.

Several quite distinctive and popular attractions have been added in Tokyo, each quite explicit about which culture is, in the final analysis, to be celebrated in the park. One, incongruously called "Meet the world," offers not only a history of Japan but also an elaborate defense of the Japanese way. In this regard, it is not unlike Disneyland's "Meet Mr Lincoln," where visitors are asked at one point to sing along with the mechanical icon a passionate version of "America the beautiful." In Meet the world, a sagacious crane guides a young boy and his sister through the past, pausing briefly along the way to make certain points such as the lessons learned by the Japanese cave dwellers ("the importance of banding together") or the significance of the samurai warrior ("we never became a colony") or the importance of early foreign trade ("to carry the seeds offered from across the sea and cultivate them in our own Japanese garden"). Another site-specific attraction in Tokyo Disneyland is the "Magic Journeys" trip across five continents, which culminates, dramatically, in the adventurer's return to "our beloved Japan where our hearts always remain."

Another altogether fascinating yet unique attraction to Tokyo Disneyland is situated inside Cinderella's Castle, and is organized as a tightly packed mystery tour through a maze of dark tunnels, fearsome electronic tableaus, and narrow escapes. Groups of about 15 to 20 visitors are escorted through this breathless 13-minute adventure in the castle by lively tour guides who, in the climactic moment of the tour, select a single member of the group to do battle with evil. The chosen hero or heroine is provided with a nifty laser sword and, backed by inventive special effects and timely coaching from the tour guide, manages to slay an evil sorcerer just in the nick of time. The group is thus spared, free again for further adventures in the park. The attraction ends with a mock-solemn presentation of a medal to the now bashful group savior, who leads everyone out the exit after passing down an aisle formed by applauding fellow members of the mystery tour.

It is hard to image a similar attraction working in either Disneyland or Disney World. Not only would group discipline necessary to ensure that all members of the tour would start and end together be lacking, but selecting a sword bearer to do battle with the Evil One would quite likely prove to be a considerable test for a tour guide when meeting with a characteristic American chorus of "me, me, me" coming from children and adults alike. The intimacy, proximity, and physical, almost hands-on, interaction between customers and amusement sources found in Tokyo Disneyland are striking to a visitor accustomed to the invisible security and attention given to damage control so prevalent in the US parks. Tokyo Disneyland puts its guests within touching distance of many of its attractions so that a customer who wished to could easily deface a cheerful robot, steal a Small World doll, or behead the Mad Hatter. This blissful respect for the built environment at Tokyo Disneyland allows ride operators to take more of an exhibitory stance to their attraction than a custodial one, which is often the perspective of Disneyland operatives (Van Maanen and Kunda 1989).

Other distinctly Japanese touches include the white gloves for drivers of the transportation vehicles in the park, a practice drawn from the taxi and bus drivers in Japan; name tags for employees featuring last names rather than first names; a small picnic area just outside the park for families bringing traditional box lunches to the park, a reminder of family customs in Japan and a compromise to the Disney tradition of allowing no food to be brought into the park; and subtitles in Japanese for most of the English-language street and attraction signs. All ride soundtracks and spiels are, of course, in Japanese, and several American visitor students of the park report considerably more ad-libbing by Japanese ride operators than by their American counterparts (Raz 1999; Brannen 1992).

Such concessions to the Japanese guest contrast with the proclamation of a pure copy. One might argue that such changes are minor adjustments in keeping with the fundamental marketing techniques of both capitalistic societies, namely, tailoring the product to its audience. But it is also important to keep in mind that even the notion of consumer capitalism in the two contexts varies systematically.

Main Street USA, for example, has become, in Tokyo, the World Bazaar. Little remains of the turn-of-the-century midwestern town of Walt's slippery memory. The World Bazaar is quite simply an enormous, modern, up-scale shopping mall where many of the products (and possibilities) of the five continents are brought together in a postmodern Disney collage that is distinctly Japanese. Few modest trinkets are on sale at the World Bazaar; instead, costly, high-status items are offered, all bearing an official Disney label and wrapped in Tokyo Disneyland paper suitable for the gift-giving practices of the Japanese (as outlined by Brannen 1992). Frontierland's presentation of the continental expansion of the USA has given way to Westernland, which is apparently understood only through the Japanese familiarity with the Wild West imagery of American movies, television, and pulp fiction. Thus to the same extent that nostalgia, patriotism, and historical narratives provide the context of meaning for visitors to Disneyland, visitors to Tokyo Disneyland are made comfortable through devices of their own making. Although the structure may appear quite similar, the meaning is not.

The second feature of the emulation process in Tokyo Disneyland runs counter to some of our more optimistic (or at least calming) beliefs about the workings of cultural flows. Tokyo Disneyland serves as something of a shrine in Japan to Japan, an emblem of self-validating beliefs in the cultural values and superiority of the Japanese. Disneyland at home serves as such an American shrine, but it is, of course, America that is celebrated. How is it that a painstaking near-copy of what is undeniably an American institution— like baseball—can function to heighten the self-awareness of the Japanese?

The answer lies in the workings of culture itself, for it is a differentiating device, a way of marking boundaries. Tokyo Disneyland marks cultural boundaries in a variety of ways. One already mentioned is the outdoing of Disneyland in the order-keeping domain. The message here is simply, "Anything you can do, we can do as well (or better)." One of the character-istic features of modern Japan is its drive toward perfection, and it has built a Disneyland that surpasses its model in terms of courtesy, size, efficiency, cleanliness, and performance. Were the park built more specifically to Japanese tastes and cultural aesthetics, it would undercut any contrast to the original in this regard. Although Disneyland is reproduced in considerable detail, it is never deferred to entirely, thus making the consumption of this cultural experience a way of marking the boundaries between Japan and the USA. Japan has taken in Disneyland only, it seems, to take it over.

Consider also another cultural flow analogous to the way Disneyland itself treats the foreign and exotic. Tokyo Disneyland maintains, indeed amplifies, self-and-other contrasts consistent with Japanese cultural rules. Only Japanese employees wear name tags in the park; the foreign (Western) employees do not. Americans hired to play Disney characters such as Snow White, Cinderella, Prince Charming, Alice in Wonderland, Peter Pan, and the Fairy Godmother are nameless, thus merging whatever personalized identities they may project with those of their named characters. Other Western employees such as crafts-people (glass blowers, leather workers, and so on), dancers, magicians, musi-cians, and role-playing shopkeepers also remain tagless. Musicians play only American songs—ranging from the Broadway production numbers such as "Yankee doodle dandy" put on the large stage settings of the park to the twangy country and western tunes such as "Stand by your man" played in a fake saloon of Westernland. During the Christmas season, songs such as "Rudolph the red-nosed reindeer," "Silent night," and the "Hallelujah chorus" of Handel's *Messiah* are piped throughout the appropriately festooned park, as a portly American Santa Claus poses for snapshots with couples and families who wait patiently in long queues for such a photo opportunity. That the *gaijin* (literally, "outside person") employees ordinarily speak only English while playing their roles furthers their distinctiveness in the setting. Mary Yoko Brannen (1992) writes of these practices:

> Rather than functioning as facilitators of the Disneyland experience like their Japanese counterparts, gaijin employees are put on display. Gaijin cast members are displayed daily in a group at the place of honor at the front of the Disneyland parade, and gaijin craftspersons are displayed throughout the day at their boxed-in work stations not unlike animals in cages at the zoo.

The same general practice is followed at Disneyland, but of course the roles are reversed, and the "others" are constructed out of different cultural building blocks. Just as blacks are notable at Disneyland and Disney World primarily for their absence from the productions and the work force, Koreans are conspicuously absent in Tokyo Disneyland—victims, it seems, of the racial politics of Asia. Villains of the Disney narratives produced in the USA seem always to speak and act with vaguely foreign personae and accents, typically, but not always, Russian or German; evil in Tokyo Disneyland is represented by *gaijin* witches, goblins, and ghosts whose accents are distinctly non-Japanese. Such a practice of sharply separating *gaijin* from society mirrors other Japanese cultural productions such as the popular television shows devoted to portraying *gaijin* stupidities (Stuart 1987) or the practice of limiting the number of baseball players on professional teams to a few *gaijin* players per team (Whiting 1989). The outsiders may be accorded respect but they are not to come too close, because the culture provides no easy space for them. One does not become Japanese any more than one can eat steak with chopsticks.

These contrasts in meaning across the two parks could be extended considerably. The point, however, is not to enumerate all the amplifications, reversals, or twists in meaning but to note their rather pervasive presence. The perspective presented here is that the Japanese cultural experience in Tokyo Disneyland is akin to a "foreign vacation" with a number of comforting homey touches built in. The perfect copy of Disneyland turns out to be anything but perfect at the level of signification. If Disneyland sucks the difference out of differences by presenting an altogether tamed and colonized version of the people of other lands (who are, when all is said and done, just like the good folks at home in Los Angeles or Des Moines), Tokyo Disneyland celebrates differences by treating the foreign as exotic. These "others" are to be understood only in terms of the fact that they are not Japanese and not, most assuredly, like the good people of Osaka or Kyoto. In this regard, both parks are isolated by a belief in their own cultural superiority. Perhaps it would be asking too much of a commercial enterprise to question such a belief, since the corporate aim in both settings is, in crude terms, to build and manage an amusement park to which people will come (and come again), to be run assembly-line fashion through its attractions and stripped of their money.

In the cracks, however, Tokyo Disneyland offers some intriguing lessons in culture flow beyond the mere fact of its existence. First, the representation of "the best in America" in Japan breaks some new ground, and contributes modestly to what might be called postmodernism, by combining cultural elements in new ways and then allowing customers and workers alike to develop the logic of their relationship. Thus Mickey Mouse, a symbol of the infantile and plastic in America, can come to stand for what is delightful and adorable in Japan, and can be used to sell adult apparel and money-market accounts. This is not simply a matter of the Japanese appropriating Mickey, but rather signals a process by which a selected alien import is reconstituted and given new meaning.

Second, such cultural flows are ongoing matters. Mickey Mouse has been hanging around Japan for a long time. His current cultural status has a long history. Working out the cultural meaning of Tokyo Disneyland is also a long-term affair. Many of the distinctly Japanese characteristics of the park were absent when the gates were first thrown back.

Third, not only are cultural meanings worked out rather differently in a new setting than they were in the old (and such adaptation takes time), but as culture flows continue, people on both sides of the border become more aware of their own culture (and its contradictions) as they increase their awareness of the other culture (and its contradictions). The traffic flow is messy, but as culture moves back and forth, people on both sides may discover new ways to do things that might not be apparent from either culture. People are not passive in relation to culture as if they merely receive it, transmit it, express it. They also create it, and new meanings may eventually emerge as cultures interpenetrate one another. The notions of family entertainment, safe thrills, and urban leisure will surely never be the same in Japan since Tokyo Disneyland has appeared on the scene. The changes, however, might occur swiftly. For example, a poll in Japan taken only five years after the park opened reported that over 50 percent of the Japanese adults, when asked "where they experienced their happiest moment in the last year," responded by saying, "Tokyo Disneyland" (Iyer 1988).

On the other hand, the view that cultural influence moves strictly along the tracks of massification—mass media, mass production, mass marketing, and mass consumerism—ushering in a global culture that spells the eclipse of national and local cultures is certainly discredited by Tokyo Disneyland. As anthropologists have long known, this view is naive to the point of banality. As Westney (1988: 6) wisely notes: "Our understanding of the emulation process is painfully inadequate."

A useful term that may have the correct connotations is suggested by Hannerz (1989, 1992) and Rosaldo (1989), who use the notion of "creolization" to describe the ongoing historically cumulative inter-relatedness between interacting cultures—in particular among cultures where one or several may at the moment have the upper hand in terms of social and economic power. Thus, although the dominant Disney parent had the clout to bring the subordinate Tokyo Disneyland to life, the daughter organization in this tale of cultural blending infused the park with its unique and highly situated character. Creolization may be a rough metaphor, but it nicely captures the fact that cultures, like languages, can be of mixed, rather than pure and highly distinct, character (Holm 1988: 13–68). Creole cultures emerge and develop as people actively take part in bringing about a synthesis of codes to increase cultural affinities between interacting people as each is better understood by the other, thus facilitating a passage of more cultural imports and exports—"l'appetit vient en mangeant."

With creolization, a kind of open-endedness might hold, so that participants in mixed cultural contexts need not sacrifice their social heritage or local knowledge, but may become competent in a multicultural enterprise that is marked by reciprocal cultural flows. The American and Japanese observe each other at Tokyo Disneyland (and Disneyland), and whereas the Americans may mythologize and learn from the splendid service provided at the park, the Japanese may honor and learn from the ingenuity and charm of the park design and attractions. In the process, both may open themselves up so that culture flows back and forth more freely and new ways of doing things come forth.

Mickey goes to Paris

Euro Disney—now Disneyland Paris—opened to great fanfare in April 1992. Located in Marne-la-Vallée, 32 kilometers east of Paris, it is, on the surface much less a duplicate of Disneyland in its design than Tokyo. Part of this is due to the insistence of the French government that the park have some "decided French touches" and due, in another part, to Disney's own market research and best guesses as to what would play well for the 310 million Europeans within two hours' flight of the park. In short, a different kind of cultural sensibility is operating in Disneyland Paris than in Tokyo Disneyland, such that the cultural contrasts, blends, and conflicts are more noticeable in France than in Japan.

The cultural sensibility on the part of both the French and the Americans is however anything but gentle or generous. Nor is it modest. The European story is in fact still playing out, but a good part of the story is now well known, and it unfolded as a result of what can only be considered a rough beginning. The unprecedented success of Tokyo Disneyland led Disney's senior managers and its board of directors to believe they had a sure-fire global winner (a golden goose) on their hands, and Europe seemed the most appropriate and potentially most lucrative place to locate the next Disneyland. And this time Disney executives were determined not to let others reap most of the profits, as was the case in Tokyo.

The lessons Disney took away from Japan, however, had little to do with cultural recontextualization and more to do with cultural massification. Convinced that Disneyland was in fact a "global product," the company marched into France as a corporate colonizer, sure of its might and right. The choice of the Paris site was announced in 1985. After extensive negotiations with the French government, the final contract for a US$2 billion park—whose costs eventually ballooned to US$5 billion—was signed in 1987.[10] What seemed to drive much of the company's actions during its early years in France were two simple but troubling assumptions: "If we build it they will come" and "the bigger we build it, the better."

The business press began to carry stories about possible problems for Euro Disney as early as 1989, when the launch of Euro Disney shares in Paris was met by a group of egg-throwing protesters who managed to pelt Michael Eisner in full view of the press. Potato farmers and local residents in Marne-la-Vallée staged a number of well-attended protests and generated a good deal of public sympathy for what they claimed was a governmental give-away of their lands and way of life. When Disney began hiring staff for the park, the press carried stories about the demanding conduct and dress code on which Disney insisted, to the dismay of its employees. The company ran into some highly publicized disputes with 16 of its French contractors, which threatened to delay the scheduled opening and were sent to arbitration. Construction costs escalated, largely a result of Disney's desire to build an "architectural masterpiece" in Europe with no frills spared.

The eagerness of the French government to attract Disney was not matched however by French intellectuals. As cultural historian Richard Pells put it:

> When the park opened in April 1992, writers competed with one another to see whose denunciations were the most hyperbolic. A "cultural Chernobyl" exclaimed the theater director Ariane Mnouchkine. "A terrifying giant's step toward world homogenization," the philosopher Alain Finkielkraut declared. To another commentator, Euro Disney was "a horror made of cardboard, plastic, and appalling colors, a construction of hardened chewing gum and idiotic folklore taken straight out of comic books written for obese Americans." According to the French intellectuals, Disney commercialized the fairy tales of children everywhere, thereby stifling their dreams and preparing them to become mere spectators and consumers.... Worst of all, Disneyland was no longer over there, across the ocean, in America, the home of mass culture. Now it was right here, in the heart of French civilization, practically within the boundaries of Paris itself.
>
> (Pells 1997: 311–312)

Such criticisms were not abated by Disney's efforts to make the park more varied and "European" than its counterparts elsewhere. Several innovations in Disneyland traditions appear in the park. Tomorrowland is gone. It has been replaced by Discoveryland (and later imported back to the original—without the name change—as part of the 1998 renovations in Anaheim). The shift was a result, in part, of Disney market surveys showing that Europeans hold an ambivalent and skeptical attitude toward the wonders of modern science and technology (Sassen 1989). Discoveryland draws on the imagery of Jules Verne, Leonardo da Vinci, and H. G. Wells to find the future in the past, and abandons the gleaming, crisp, militaristic Tomorrowland look of other parks. The Jungle Cruise is not longer around in the European park to remind visitors of their colonial past. Perhaps Disney surveys showed that Third World "natives" are less amusing to the French, English, or Dutch than to the Americans or Japanese. Identifications for the origins of the various narratives and fairy tales presented in the park, absent elsewhere, are prominent in Paris, where the corporation agreed (reluctantly) to acknowledge the rightful authors—but not the imagery—of its expropriated children's tales (Grover 1997: 191–192). In Paris, Snow White now speaks German, Sleeping Beauty rests in her French chateau (*Le Château de la Belle au Bois Dormant*), Pinocchio reclaims his Italian heritage, and Peter Pan flies not from Los Angeles but from London again.

The critics have not been charmed or silenced by Disney's face work and expensive and sometimes rather elaborate revisions in the park design. Some still regard the project as a form of "creeping Americanism," and are disturbed less by the attractions and look of the park than by, for example, the tasteless fast food available on the grounds and having to eat it from tables and chairs bolted to the floor. In what has turned out to be altogether clairvoyant, local politicians and community leaders in the region voiced their concerns early on about "externalities" and the possible Orlando-ization of the region—the traffic and crowds the development would attract, as well as the potential build-up of unwanted urban problems in the region.

The troubles inside the park seemed only to get worse after the opening. While the expected number of paying guests came to the park (about 11 million the first year), they complained about the lack of restaurant space, the disorderly and lengthy queues, and the lack of the friendly service that the park's advertising and their experience of the Disney Parks in the USA had led many of them to expect. Vigilant and veteran Disney observers were not impressed either with the park's performance. Brannen and Wilson (1996: 104) were apparently shocked when they visited Disneyland Paris in 1995, almost three years after the opening.

> On three out of five visits we noticed bathroom stall doors to be broken and the bathrooms themselves untidy, smiles from service people at restaurants on the park were not only uncommon but in one instance a

food server got into a squabble with a customer over whether she had paid or not, and the grounds themselves were littered, with few sidewalk sweepers in sight (a notable fixture at other Disney parks).

(Brannen and Wilson 1996: 104)

The relative ease with which the Disney service culture of "the happiest place on earth" was transferred to Tokyo did not prepare the company for the challenges of implementing it in France. One early press story (Toy, Marmot, and Grover 1990) carried the following anecdote:

> Disney University, a feature of all company parks, has launched the standard day-and-a-half course in Disney culture, plus job training that can last weeks. "We have to do more explaining in class," admits David Kanally, director of the university's Paris branch. Sessions often erupt into debates. One group of French students spent 20 minutes discussing how to define "efficiency." Says Kanally: "That wouldn't happen in Orlando."

The angry employee reaction to the dress and conduct code, and the public protests voiced in the press, forced Disney eventually to relax some of its restrictions. But even so, in 1995, the park was charged with violating French labor law in its efforts to impose its dress code on its French employees. French labor law has thus far proved to be an unanticipated impediment for Disney in other ways, for it contains far more limitations on the use of part-time and contingent workers than Disneyland is accustomed to in the USA or Japan. Of Disney's some 12,000 employees in the European park today, only about 3000 are part-timers (close to a reversal of the full-time/part-time ratios of other parks). The French courts also consider illegal some of the major control tools much favored by American managers: the allocation of valued overtime work to the most effervescent and reliable workers, and the speedy dismissal of those who fail to meet the Disney standards.

All has not been entirely antagonistic however. While trade unions in France have often been difficult for Disney management, they do occasionally surprise. After the "storm of the century" blew through the Ile de France during the Christmas holidays in 1999, causing extensive damage, a bitter work stoppage involving 10,000 Disney employees was suspended by union leaders so that Cast Members could get back to work restoring the park. "Given the disastrous state of the park it would be unreasonable to continue the protest" said a union leader at the time (*International Herald Tribune*, December 31 1999).

Customers are not unmindful of the front-stage (and back-stage) debates occurring at the park. But it is doubtful that such matters are of overriding concern to them. Certainly, as noted, attendance targets have been met for most of the park's history. Indeed, Disneyland Paris is now—

and has been for almost ten years—the most popular European tourist destination by a large measure. But the company has continued—and continues—to lose money. Part of the problem is the accumulated debt that the company faces. In 2003, for example, reacting to a tourist slow-down from the Iraq war, the SARS scare, and the economic slump in Europe, Disney agreed to forgo licensing fees and royalties for the year, and the company cautioned investors for the third time in the past decade that it might not have enough cash to pay debts owed to its banks (*New York Times*, August 1 2003). While there is little likelihood that Disney will ever face insolvency in France, given the continuous and strong political backing it gets at the national level in France and its role as an important employer in the Paris region, the company has yet to fully come to terms and manage its way out of the troubling conditions it faces.

Many of these difficulties reflect cultural mistakes and misunderstandings. Visitors do not spend as much time or money in the park as their counterparts in the USA or Japan. During the early years of the enterprise, they did not stay in the six (now seven) expensive themed hotels that Disney owned, since there were few reasons for people to linger at a park that could easily be seen in a day or less. The crowds spent far less on souvenirs and food, since so many of them were "day trippers" who preferred to spend their time and money in Paris or elsewhere. Americans and Japanese, it turns out, are willing to spend much more on their relatively short vacations than are Europeans, who enjoy much longer—and for that reason, cheaper by the day—vacations. Moreover, the French (and Europeans generally) are much less willing to pull their children out of school for a special vacation trip (as in the USA) or to see school trips to Disneyland as an appropriate educational experience (as in Japan).

Disney exacerbated these problems by its pricing policies. Staying at one of the Disney hotels was for years more expensive than staying at a comparable hotel in Paris. Souvenirs were of the low-quality, high-price variety. And admissions charges were for some time considerably higher than in the US parks. It seems that Disney pricing policies were based initially on the costs of building and running a larger than necessary complex, rather than based on what customers were willing to bear. The ambitions of Disney—"to make Paris a side trip"—were, in retrospect, rather unattainable if not foolish.

Almost from the beginning, it was clear Euro Disney was in quite serious trouble. Massive losses accumulated over the first few years of operations, and few believed that the early 1990s recession was the sole cause. A new chief executive, Philippe Bourguignon, was appointed in 1994 to stem the financial bleeding. The first rescue package proposed by Disney was indignantly rejected by the most important French stakeholders in Euro Disney, the banks. The rescue package that was finally approved called for a moratorium on the royalties going to Disney, at home as well as on the interest payments to the banks (*Economist*, April 13 1996: 66–67). A step in Bourguignon's turn-around effort was taken when the ill-fated name Euro

Disney was abandoned in favor of "Disneyland Paris." But, as most analysts pointed out, the rescue package and the new name would work only if the park was able to draw more customers, get them to spend more, and at the same time cut its operating costs.

The reorganization story in Paris is a continuing one. Disney is by no means out of hot water yet. Opening the 2nd Gate in 2002—Walt Disney Studios Park—has certainly helped boost attendance some and pushed hotel revenues up, for there are now more reasons for visitors to spend more time (and money) on the grounds. Disney has also been increasing the number of attractions in the park, and trimming the workforce where possible. It has also been adding a number of experienced French and European managers to help run the park.

Other changes have occurred as Disneyland Paris continues to localize and hence learn across borders. Advertising, originally following the Euro Disney intention to "reach out to all of Europe," has increasingly focused on national markets. Features of the park that appeal, say, to Germans are not the same ones that draw Dutch or British visitors. This has turned out to be vital since only about 40 percent of the park's visitors to date are from France, with 17 percent from Belgium, Luxembourg, and the Netherlands, 15 percent from Britain, and 10 percent from Germany. Wine was added to the menu, a much remarked-on omission that had annoyed the French, for it displayed the company's apparent disregard for the country's taste and culture, and its none-too-subtle assumption that whatever works in the USA would work in France.

Perhaps most important, ticket prices have been reduced and discounts, special promotions and events (such as Bastille Day, Christmas, and Oktoberfest celebrations) have come to play an important role in attracting nearby customers. Seasonal fluctuations are more extreme at Disneyland Paris than at the other parks, so boosting attendance during slack winter months (or paring back operations) is crucial. The local population remains Disney's trump card, and nurturing this customer base will make or break the park in the long run. Integrating a visit to Disneyland Paris into the leisure routines of French families within driving distance of the park will provide the repeat visitor foundation —"France first"—on which sizeable and predictable revenues depend. Experience, experiments, and a willingness to innovate are crucial here, as is guidance from regional and community leaders in both public and private sectors.

At the moment, it seems that Disney has shrunk the size of its American flag and tried with some success to put aside a few of its more home-bound cultural assumptions. This is of course a tricky matter of degree, for certainly a part of Disneyland Paris's appeal remains its American look and feel, however loath some Europeans may be to openly express such desire. In sum, cross-border learning at Disneyland Paris has been slow and irregular, marked by peaks and valleys, and associated more with the shifting mix of managerial personnel and their whims than with a gradual accumulation of useful organizational memory and culturally sensitive practices. The bottom line is that there is still some distance to travel before Disneyland Paris and the people who visit and work there feel entirely comfortable, and on their way to achieving the kind of success both the French and Americans who first entertained the project had imagined.

Mickey goes to Hong Kong

In the USA, Mickey Mouse is rather soft and round, cuter and better behaved than in Tokyo, where he is rather muscular, smart, and bratty. In Paris, he is cooler, thinner, and seemingly more urbane. Even in America, Mickey has changed over the years from a cruel and cocky mouse to a sweet, innocent, and more childlike mouse. How he will appear in China is a question of some relevance to the sort of cultural experience that is in store for the paying guests to the Fifth Disneyland, under construction at Penny's Bay on Lantau Island in Hong Kong.

Slated to open in 2005, Hong Kong Disneyland provides an opportunity to see what the Disney organization has learned in two tries about the design, export, and management of what it takes to be its premier global product: the theme park. If the past provides lessons for the future, Disney has now over 20 years of experience in the international theme park trade to draw on—of both success and failure. What has it learned that will play well for the over six million residents of Hong Kong? What has it learned that will help or hinder the organization as it moves into the cosmopolitan gateway to (and from) mainland China?

While the project is not yet complete as of writing this in late 2004, a good deal of background information is available that may shed light on further developments. The "deal" was first announced in 1999. The building of Hong Kong Disneyland is estimated to cost somewhere close to US$4 billion. The project is backed by the Hong Kong government which will be the majority stockholder (57 percent). Roughly two billion dollars goes for land reclamation, road building, ferry connections, water treatment plants, artificial reefs, and other infrastructure necessary for the construction and operation of the new park. Disney, however, will control the design, manage the park and share—with 43 percent ownership—in the revenue stream generated by the enterprise. As in France, the Disney organization has near-total control of the show and property (about 300 acres).

The park under construction will be smaller than those in either Tokyo or Paris. The workforce required when Hong Kong Disneyland is up and running is estimated to be around 5000, and the company says it needs to attract only five or six million customers a year to break even—anticipated to grow to about ten million by 2020. This represents about half the workforce and draw expected in the early stages of other Disneylands. One-third of the guests are likely to come from Hong Kong, one-third from China, and one-third from other Asian countries. In terms of park design, the deal makers in Hong Kong ordered up the "original Disneyland" and were uninterested, it seems, in any unique Chinese touches beyond some of the cuisine served in the park and respect for local traditions. Ostensibly, this will be no test for the Imagineers of Disneyland, since the creative demands on the company in Hong Kong are slight.

Part of these prenuptial agreements on design and content may be because Disney products—including Disneyland—are rather well known in the region. Disney TV shows and cartoon characters have long been popular in Hong Kong, and Disney has been beaming several much watched prime-time children's show throughout China since the late 1980s. Of course pirated versions of Disney movies and videos are everywhere in Asia, thus providing another sort of "synergy" for marketing Disneyland (a boost in familiarity that may or may not be welcomed by Disney executives).

Wasko, Phillips, and Meehan (2001) conducted a global survey of college students from 53 separate countries on the brand awareness of Disney products. Their results show the Chinese, no less than the Europeans or Japanese, to be quite familiar with Disney characters, narratives, movies, and merchandise. Moreover, the broad meanings read into these cultural artifacts also appear quite similar across countries. Indeed the strongest findings in Wasko's survey were the near-universal recognition of Disney products and the commonly shared understandings of what Disney means across the globe. For example, 93 percent of the respondents said Disney promoted "Fantasy and Fun;" 88 percent agreed that Disney represented "Happiness," "Magic," and "Good over Evil"; and 80 percent thought Disney stood for "Family," "Imagination," and "Love/Romance." In short, Disney carries a set of core meanings and values that Wasko claims are understood in the same way almost everywhere, and these are the same ubiquitous values that the organization itself emphasizes in its sales and marketing work.

This seems to be something of a cuddly form of globalization. Contact with Disney occurs for most in early childhood, but is persistent, intense, and now inter-generational. From this perspective, Disney is accepted in part because its products and values appear friendly, innocent, and compatible with local culture, such that watching a Disney video or carrying a Mickey Mouse pencil box does not feel like something that is being imposed from the outside, but rather as something that people choose individually to fit comfortably into their patterns of everyday life. Seeing Disney products (including theme parks) as "natural" and somehow imbued with common and benign values does not, however, eliminate either ambiguity or criticism. Being seen as supportive of, say, "family values" does not specify what values in particular are to be furthered in a local context, nor does the somewhat sacred status of Disney products and perceived content make criticism of the company's market saturation and business practices impossible.

It is in the domain of particulars that Disney's planned move to Hong Kong becomes most interesting. In this regard, the shift in family values that has more or less transformed East Asia over the past 20–30 years is relevant. In Hong Kong, a long economic boom began in the 1970s as the then British territory moved from a low-wage, light-industrial colonial outpost to a regional center for financial services and high-technology industries. A professionalized, white-collar middle class began to rapidly replace the post-war working class of Hong Kong. By the mid-1970s, the majority of residents were living in small, hard-working, nuclear families, preoccupied with their own lives and children, rather than a wider network of kin.

This has produced what Watson (1997) calls a generation of "Little Emperors and Empresses": children who grow up in small (striving) middle-class families, rather isolated from their extended ties, and hence garner a good deal of the attention, affection, and support of two parents (and sometimes four grandparents as well). Children in Hong Kong are not only much loved and fussed about as a rule, but are regarded as independent decision makers and control substantial economic resources. A local study Watson cites from the *South China Morning Post* (December 2 1995) notes that Hong Kong parents gave junior-high-school-aged children an average of over US$100 a month to spend on snacks and entertainment. Surely such indulgence bodes well for Hong Kong Disneyland. Hong Kong is a relatively wealthy society, its families are small, and children clearly have spending power.

Next door to Hong Kong are 1.3 billion people in mainland China. Most of course cannot hope to visit Hong Kong Disneyland, but residents just across the border in the Shenzhen Special Economic Zone are surely on the Disney map of potential paying guests. Shenzhen was one of the first regions in the People's Republic to benefit from Deng Xiaoping's economic reforms—beginning in the early 1980s—and the area has become something of a boom town, where all the material products of the good life, including luxury apartments, the latest fashions from New York and Paris, fine hotels, and flashy discothèques are available to a few. China's single-child policy no doubt amplifies the "Little Emperors and Empresses" phenomenon in the area, and recent policy changes at the national level now allow residents of the four largest cities in China—Beijing, Shanghai, Guangzhou, and Shenzhen—to travel to Hong Kong on their own as tourists instead of having to come only on officially approved business trips or with centrally approved and organized tours (*New York Times*, August 15 2003).

All is not rosy however. The Disney organization itself has occasionally run into trouble in China. Its 1999 film *Mulan*, expected to be an artistic success, box-office smash, and something of a cultural breakthrough in China, fell flat. When screened in China, the animated film, a Westernized version of a much beloved Chinese folktale in which the key characters looked American and lived happily ever after, annoyed political leaders, the public, and critics alike. The movie did poorly among Chinese audiences in the USA as well. Trying to explain Disney's miscalculation of just how accepting the people and the country would be for the film, one local observer noted:

> Every child in China grows up with the legend of Fa Mulan but they couldn't identify with the movie and they couldn't recognize the characters because they were drawn for an international audience. Mulan looked more like Pocahontas than the average Chinese face.
>
> (*International Herald Tribune*, June 16 1999)

Perhaps more serious and troubling are the difficulties Disney ran into in 1997 when releasing the Martin Scorsese film *Kundun* about the Dalai Lama. Political leaders in Beijing objected to the film's content and distribution not in China (where, of course, it was not shown) but in the USA. Disney, to its credit, did not knuckle under and pull the film. Although the movie flopped at the box office and was rather quickly withdrawn from the market, Disney worried enough about offending the political sensitivities of the Chinese government (and being "blacklisted") that it hired the former US Secretary of State Henry Kissinger to re-establish cordial relations for the firm in Beijing after the film ran its course. Shuttle diplomacy, it seems, is useful for more than peacekeeping missions among nations. Such diplomacy may well become a necessary part of Disney's operation in Hong Kong.

In terms of the local response to the building of Hong Kong Disneyland, most of the population appears pleased at present. Language will be less of a problem for Disney than in Paris, given Hong Kong's long colonial past under British rule. Bilingual speakers are common, and most of the Hong Kong population is comfortable with English. Young people may well take to Disneyland as they took to McDonald's in the late 1970s, and flock to the park precisely because it offers a cultural experience that is (at least initially) foreign and distinctively not Chinese (Watson 1997). And to adults, Disneyland carries considerable symbolic value as a high-quality, safe, clean, modern, family-oriented, and desirable place to visit.

As is true elsewhere, many in Hong Kong see the park as a high-profile and high-powered magnet that will draw visitors to the region. It adds also to the list of leisure options and potential pleasures available to residents of Hong Kong, one of the most tightly packed and stressful cities in the world in which to live. And for some, the park is seen as a way to help preserve the novel and unique status of the former territory, which is now in danger of losing its long-standing international flavor. Disneyland, many feel, will lift the appeal of Hong Kong as a tourist destination, particularly among families, teenagers, and honeymooners.

Not all in Hong Kong are quite so enamored with the cultural experience the park will offer. Some local politicians have taken Disney (and the government) to task for not fully sharing information about the negotiated agreement and explaining the costs of the project to the public. Some cultural elites as well as some business leaders have expressed concern over the foreign influence Disney represents—a blatant example of cultural imperialism in their view—and argue that embracing yet another Disneyland sends the wrong message to both the local population and the world. Hong Kong has its own vibrancy and heritage, they say, and bringing Disneyland to town is but a "pointless parody of American kitsch" (*International Herald Tribune*, June 16 1999). And, intellectuals, as always, have joined the fray, suggesting that Hong Kong might be better served by offering tourists a taste of Tang Dynasty poetry, Sichuan cooking, and silk fashions than thrill rides, cartoon characters, and mouse ears. None of these Disneyland critics are likely to be disarmed either when reading that Michael Eisner's ebullient confidence in the project is based—at least partly—on his conviction that "the Chinese people love Mickey no less than Big Mac" (*Los Angeles Times*, June 6 2002).

But popular culture of a local sort thrives in Hong Kong too, and Disneyland may well fit nicely into this milieu. Like Tokyo, Hong Kong is itself a major center for the production of transnational culture. The Hong Kong fashion industry influences clothing in Los Angeles, Bangkok, and Paris. The "Cantopop" music that originates in Hong Kong is heard and enjoyed throughout Asia. Hong Kong is also the third largest producer in the world of movies, and the birthplace of the Kung Fu film genre. Most significantly perhaps, Hong Kong is now emerging as a center for television production in Asia. This is surely a world that those in the Disney organization will know.

Regarding Disneyland's workaday operations in Hong Kong, there are a few matters of concern. Labor, however, is probably not one of them. Not only is a talented and attractive young workforce available within the region, there are few reasons to suspect that part-time labor will be frowned on. Moreover, a huge, well-educated, and hungry workforce is close at hand, and the regime in Hong Kong that has bet on Disneyland's economic success might, if necessary, do away with some of the messy obstructions that organizations in more democratic societies must deal with as a matter of course—striking trade unions, active consumer movements, irksome property rights advocates, and so on. As for the management of the park, the number of veteran Hong Kong and Asian executives that make up the management structure of the park is proportionately higher than was that of French and European managers at Disneyland Paris in its early days. The American presence in Hong Kong is slight and low key. This should help ease cooperation with contractors, suppliers, potential customers, workers, and other groups, and perhaps foster a speedy localization of the enterprise.

While operational problems seem of slight concern to Disney officials at the moment, environmental and social problems do not. Disney faces more than a few of them in Hong Kong. For instance, construction of Disneyland Hong Kong calls for a good deal of landfill, earth moving, underwater dynamiting, and dredging. Waters around the construction site are now polluted. White dolphins are dying and fish stocks are dwindling (some say disappearing). It appears that like the farmers in France who suffered when Disneyland Paris arrived, the livelihood of local fishermen is threatened. In 2001, a Disney spokeswoman said of the situation:

> To date, there is no evidence that links the current issues the fishermen are raising to the reclamation at Penny's Bay. The government continues to monitor this. They've put measures in place on site to address this issue. They've assured us they are taking it seriously.
>
> (Reuters News Service, November 21 2001)

The response is familiar, and strikingly reminiscent of Disney's corporate stance on social problems elsewhere—notably Orlando and Paris. The company's public position—ridiculed in environmental circles and in some Hong Kong newspapers as obdurate and obstructionist—is that such matters are external to the company and hence of little managerial concern ("let the government take care of it"). Such a policy is no doubt cost-effective but might well have negative consequences in the long run, especially in the Hong Kong context where antagonism between the public and private sectors is less pronounced (or expected) than in the USA (or, for that matter, in Japan or France). Big Asian companies are expected by most to promote the general welfare of the communities in which they operate. Hong Kong now represents an odd mixture of socialism and capitalism, and Disney may have much to learn.

There may be some more modest lessons in store for Disney in terms of its service-providing routines as well. As in France, the "grin and wave" approach to people processing within the park may strike some potential employees and customers as a bit over the top. Watson (1997) points out that consumers in Hong Kong are often suspicious of clerks and other service personnel who laugh and smile on the job. Hong Kong residents, it seems, place a high value on expressions of "seriousness," and workers are expected to assume a demeanor that conveys determination and unflappability to show they are paying full attention to what they are doing. The result is apparently more frowning than smiling among service providers. Hence the congeniality and familiarity that cast members are more or less famous for in other Disney parks (with the significant exception of Paris) may not be as well received in Hong Kong as will the projection of other qualities admired in the local culture—directness and competence.

All in all, however, the economic prospects for Hong Kong Disneyland appear fairly bright. Visiting the park from Hong Kong or mainland China will hardly be viewed as an act of cultural treason. A large and apt workforce is available, and potential customers seem thrilled at the prospects of having their own Disneyland. Modest mis-steps and cultural misunderstandings will occur, of course, and one hopes that learning on the part of the company, the government, the financial backers, and the consumers will be swift (and open-ended). More problematic perhaps are the long-term consequences for both Disney and Hong Kong. If the formula of moving from the exotic to the ordinary works out, what will Disney have brought to the region and the region to Disney? Will "chewing-gum jobs" proliferate and create a drain on available social services, as in Orlando? Will traffic congestion and pollution further strain an already pressed metropolis, as in Tokyo? Will cultural standards fall as Mickey Mouse ascends, as many in Paris would argue? Will Hong Kong's valued contribution to an independent Asian entertainment industry be reduced, as Disney, with its seemingly unlimited financial resources, enters into the scene? Will Hong Kong Disneyland prove to be a good corporate citizen or merely a greedy, rapacious American? These (and many more) questions are all in play.

A world with mouse ears?

At the limit, a global community is an impossible condition. It would prevail only if people the world over were to share a mutually intelligible and homogeneous culture. While the world is certainly shrinking as communication and transportation technologies proliferate and trade barriers are reduced, we are nowhere close to either mutual intelligibility or homogeneity. What we have seen of Disney and its travels around the world to date suggests as much.

What has occurred in the various parks, and no doubt will occur in Hong Kong, is more a process of localization than globalization. Some elements of the Disney way are accepted, some rejected, some changed, and some ignored. Moreover, it has been a slow and gradual, and despite Disney's hopeful intentions and efforts, a thoroughly two-way process. And while the initial stages of cultural learning have for all parties been highly significant, they have not been fully determinative of the long-term success or failure of Disney's cross-border ventures. As we have seen, culture—as a set of ideas, reactions, assumptions, and expectations—is itself constantly changing as people and groups change.

Predictability in this domain is problematic at best. How Disneyland is used and what it means in Hong Kong will be different from how it is used and understood elsewhere. And these differences are likely to grow rather than shrink with the passage of time, as each park takes on its own special character as result of the constant interactions among managers, designers, employees, customers, environmentalists, politicians, policy makers, social critics, and the like. While the ties of culture to place have been loosened in the late twentieth and early twenty-first centuries, they have not gone away, and local identities are still much valued. Businesses that forget about such matters are likely to pay a stiff price.

Culture is, of course, not a fixed condition, and thus cultural learning is at best a most uncertain process, a continual flow of shifting ideas and things. Cultural products—like Disneyland—and the meanings we attach to them are at any moment the result of unremitting change, coming from the interplay of the past and present, the familiar and strange, the local and distant. If this interplay is intensifying, as the materials on Disney suggest, the consequences of moving cultural products and services developed in one land to another are probably less predictable than ever (and they have never been particularly predictable anyway).

THE STRUCTURE OF CULTURE

What does all this culture-mongering about the amusement trade have to do with the altogether serious and instrumental MNC? An answer must begins with the very definition of a multinational firm. To take an all-purpose definition:

> The MNC is the quintessential case of the dispersed firm with individual components located in a number of autonomous political units. These organizational sub-units or subsidiaries are often embedded in highly heterogeneous environmental conditions and have developed under very different historical circumstances.
>
> (Ghoshal and Nohria 1990: 322)

Such a definition features complexity, differentiation, and implicitly at least, suggests a good deal of variation in terms of the relations that hold between and among organizational units of the center and the periphery. Cultural diversity is a given. Within this context, a good deal of debate takes place as to what structural form best suits the MNC. In pursuing this question, the debate takes into account a rather long (and growing) list of contingent conditions—market, industry, strategy, governmental policies, consumer trends, and so forth.

On this list of "contingent conditions" too is "corporate culture." In terms of reach or range, corporate culture can be seen to stretch from strong to weak culture. Strong cultures are those that allegedly limit subsidiary discretion; direct firm actions from the center; export similar management practices, products, and administrative routines from corporate headquarters to subsidiaries; and in general exercise considerable control and discipline over the operations of all units comprising the firm. Weak cultures are presumably everything the strong cultures are not. Their principal characteristics would seem to be local autonomy and relative freedom for subsidiary units.

The appeal to managers and organizational theorists of the so-called strong culture standing behind the MNC is obvious. An organization with a culture of its own that inspires loyalty to a common pursuit would presumably reduce local peculiarities, promote uniform practices, and, most optimistically, transcend all those annoying, culturally induced behavioral differences that result from maintaining operational outposts throughout the world. In theory, strong cultures can be encouraged by a variety of mechanisms such as the regular and relatively swift rotation of personnel to and from the center and around the subsidiaries, encouragement of long-term employment within the firm, extensive use of headquarters-programmed training and development activities to help build a strong sense of identity and commitment to the firm on the part of employees, common management systems for performance appraisal, and reward practices, extensive international seminars that bring members of the periphery together regularly and enhance the spread of common objectives, the use of common language throughout the firm, and so forth. This is a sort of Holy Roman Empire version of the MNC, such that if it operated according to plan, a marketing manager of, say, a corporation headquartered in Paris would feel just as comfortable working in Hong Kong, Nairobi, or San Francisco. Ouchi's (1981b) dream of the "clan" form of organization nicely conveys this strong-culture perspective.

At the other end of the continuum sit those MNCs supposedly sporting weak cultures at the center, and thus promoting independence on the part of some, if not all, subsidiaries. Many of the organization types suggested in DiMaggio's (2001) useful collection of readings about the twenty-first century firm fall here, and feature such characteristics as highly differentiated management practices across subsidiaries, low levels of personnel rotation, small corporate staffs, and little sustained contact between headquarters and peripheral units. Loyalty adheres to the local unit to which one is assigned, and whatever attachments individuals have toward the MNC itself are primarily formal, distant, and calculative.

As is implied by the mechanisms supposedly associated with each organizing mode, culture, strong or weak, is a matter of social engineering. Ethnocentricism—whether from the center or from the periphery—can be rooted out or built in. It is all really a matter of managerial choice. Even mixed modes or designer organizations especially tailored to meet global business demands are possible, such that strong cultures with multiple centers, the "postmodern, holographic, heterarchy" of Hedlund (1986) or the "post-bureaucratic firm" of Heckscher and Donnellon (1994) emerge as normative possibilities.

There is perhaps some truth to these ideas of managerial discretion. At the extreme one could perhaps blow away annoying local peculiarities by staffing the outposts of all operations with loyal functionaries from headquarters, and then locking them up so that no contact and corruption of plans and practices could ooze in from the local sites. Or conversely, one could lock out headquarters officials and dictates. Endless variations on these strategic designs can be (and are) put forth. All represent a rather tired working-out of the dubious postulates of structural-functionalism—a view arguing that similar structures produce similar behavior.

This functionalist perspective on the MNC over-emphasizes form or appearances, and pays inadequate attention to the meaning or substance of behavior. My "Mickey on the move" tale was put forth here to try to undercut such a view. Culture is not social structure. To consider the proper structural configuration of the MNC in terms of the corporate culture seen to be encouraged by such a configuration, or to situate the study of MNCs within a context that subordinates (or elevates) localism, ethnicity, or national culture to macrosocial forces such as authority systems, rationalization, universalization, or market forces, would be to rehash stale debates. Culture must be treated as it is symbolically constructed, represented, understood, and used by a group. This sidesteps the definitional problems posed by a search for a structural model of the MNC as a specific form of social organization. Organizational structures do not in themselves provide meaning for people; this is why so many organizations designed to create culture or community as a cure for fragmentation, conflict, underachievement, or alienation are doomed to failure.

Culture is an ordinary word that, when imported into organizational studies, causes enormous difficulty. A good part of this difficulty is that culture implies simultaneously both difference and similarity—a group of people who (1) have something in common with each other that (2) distinguishes them from other people. The use of the term is in fact always occasioned by the desire or need to express such a relational idea. Pushed into service in the world of organizations, boundary problems surface immediately. The problems are, for example, not simply, "Are those working for company X different from those working for company Y?" but, "How different is a company X engineer from another company X engineer?" In other words, is the boundary dividing one company from another more meaningful to an employee than the boundary that distinguishes him or her from another within the same firm? An engineer from a sales representative? A field service engineer from one in product development? A headquarters-based engineer from a Paris-based engineer? A Paris-based engineer from a Tokyo-based engineer? And so on. As one moves "down" the scale toward the domain of day-in and day-out associations, the referents of the boundary become less apparent to the outsider, until they may become entirely invisible (Van Maanen and Barley 1984).

But as one moves down the ladder of collective grouping, the referents may also become more salient and important to company members, because they relate more directly to the intimate parts of their life, and perhaps refer increasingly to the more obvious, substantial, and experiential aspects of their cultural identities, which are, in all probability, multiple. Conversely, as one moves up the scale, culture is approached more as a rhetorical front. When CEOs refer to their firm as "a family," or government leaders refer to the "European Community," or British officials lay claim to the cohesion among Pakistanis, Canadians, Tanzanians, and the British Islanders in the name of "the Commonwealth," they may often be regarded as indulging the rhetoric and stating an aspiration that is all too obviously missing in what is commonly called reality. But when workers in a machine shop talk of "their group," ride operators at Disneyland speak of "their crew," stockbrokers mention "their club," or R&D managers denote "their project," they may refer to an entity, a felt reality, invested with all the sentiments attached to friendship, kinship, citizenship, colleagueship, neighborhood, familiarity, jealousy, envy, and rivalry as they inform the social processes of everyday life. At this level, culture is more than an oratorical abstraction; it hinges crucially on feeling and consciousness.

CORPORATE CULTURE REVISITED

Much of the talk surrounding corporate culture—especially the talk that is peddled to stockholders and the business press—is thin gruel indeed. Official versions of corporate culture usually emerge from self-conscious managerial efforts to discover and reconstruct a heritage and identity for the firm—part, perhaps, of a search for authenticity and a felt need to contrast one's own organization with others of too similar ilk. Such a history serves as a collective counterpart to individual memory, and both are highly selective renditions of the past. By claiming a culture, the past can be fumigated, cleaned up, and an ever-so-nice history developed. As Susan Sontag (1979: 22) writes, "Just wait until now becomes then and you'll see how happy we were." Corporate culture in this sense is little more than a version of how corporate officials would like their organization to appear. Using the culture construct to frame such efforts is often an attempt to legitimize a rather problematic claim.

Serious portraits of corporate cultures reveal a far more interesting, complicated, and divisive world than that put forth by managerially loaded accounts.[11] Such studies increasingly focus on the "organization of diversity," and present few portraits of womb-like cultures surrounding an obedient society of saints. Culture in the raw is lively, contentious, unpredictable. Strong culture is achieved only by great efforts, and even then it is problematic, since strong culture flowing from the top (or center) may embargo progress, retard change, deny differences, and by filtering out undesirable elements, create a kind of collective blindness. Weak culture is more a matter of allowing cultures at levels below corporate headquarters to go their own way, sometimes in splendid isolation. Activities are coordinated only when precious resources are threatened. Culture is everywhere and always relevant in organizational life, but there is no obvious or natural level of analysis from which to observe it.

Organizations, like societies, are sometimes mistakenly deemed to have a totality or consensus because of their small size, low level of structural differentiation, acceptance on the part of most of the group of a relatively few models of action, highly stable environments in which habits and routines continue to work well, and/or isolation from other groups. When culture emerges from face-to-face interaction among a group of people who, for example, don't move around much and have little contact with outsiders, it is simple to think of culture in consensual terms—too simple. Such a view is misleading because consensus is, in many ways, a form of death at the group level, since it can not provide a group with alternatives, dynamics, or the imagination required for meeting shifting conditions. Culture is a differentiating device in organizations, a way of marking differences within and between groups all the way up and all the way down the analytic scale. Any social organization highly differentiated at the structural level—such as MNCs—but homogeneous on the level of culture would be emptied of all cultural meaning.

SOME FINAL WORDS

With this revisiting of corporate culture in mind, what are we to make then of the role culture plays in the MNC? Five points are worth making. First, the effect of culture on performance, particularly economic performance, is probably drastically over-estimated. At the international level, for example, whatever country is on top at the moment seems always to make too much of it by moralizing about the cultural reasons for its own success. Until the early 1980s, for example, Westerners observing East Asia usually concluded that its culture(s) could never adapt to modern industrial capitalism. Confucianism, the willingness to sublimate the individual's interest to the group, the role allowed elders, the respect for the past—all traits now cited to explain the various economic booms in East Asia—were used earlier to explain why these countries could never catch up. Similar discourse goes on in organizations, as the worth of a corporate culture rises and falls with its economic success. The champ-to-chump transformation of many of those sterling corporate cultures celebrated by Peters and Waterman in 1982—and mourned by Peters in 1987—is a case in point.

Second, even if a correlation between economic performance and strong corporate culture were to exist, it is not clear what it might mean. Corporate culture in the MNC can be strong in at least two ways. One version contains all the elements of an old, colonial, ethnocentric model whereby the center merely replicates itself in its subsidiaries. This model, like its close relatives in governmental, religious, and military domains, seems always to contain the seeds of its own destruction because of the resentment and resistance it engenders when on the move. Another more sophisticated version suggests that a sort of globalized corporate culture is possible, which builds on the cultural differences and knowledge represented in subsidiary operations but essentially transcends them by drawing all parts of the MNC together in pursuit of common goals. Such goals are not necessarily imposed from the center and shipped to the periphery. They may develop from interaction among those in diverse sectors of the MNC. There are of course enormous practical and analytic difficulties with such a model, not the least being the very high level of abstraction at which it is cast. But such a model may very well represent the best advice available to the managers of MNCs, given the fact that research on the cultural side of MNCs still remains largely on the science fiction side of the house.[12]

Third, to the extent that the above global model emphasizes the slow, mutual acquisition of culture through processes of give and take rather than simply trying to ram culture down through the corporation by means of coercive persuasion, it holds certain possibilities and potential. Coercive persuasion as cultural transmission puts great faith in agents—missionaries, mothers, brothers, corporate trainers, business schools, top managers, schoolteachers—and the design of socialization settings and processes through which an agent's work is supposedly accomplished (Schein 1961; Van Maanen and Schein 1979). Corporate culture as something to be propagated from on high and effectively transmitted throughout the organization assumes the existence of a rather timeless, well-specified body of knowledge that everyone in the organization could, at least in theory, know.[13] Yet, as studies looking closely at the acquisition of culture suggest, no one ever gets or even needs it all (e.g. Becker et al. 1961; Spradley 1970; Hannerz 1992; Shore 1996). Acquisition occurs throughout the organization on far less than a one-to-a-customer basis. The flow of culture is ongoing, part of the political, social, and economic life within (and certainly beyond) the firm, and therefore always moving in several directions at once. The distinctiveness of the organization is then a matter of degree, as cultural affinities across domains may be discovered along, for example, product, professional, geographic, divisional, or personal dimensions. A concern for the acquisition of culture also seems in keeping with the multinational character of MNCs, where employees do not renounce their various cultural citizenships when coming to work for the firm, but add to their cultural experiences (and presumably competencies) and those of the organization as a result of their participation.

Fourth, as to the impact of MNCs on the societies in which they operate, even the most transcendent, global, participative, sensitive, and cheerful MNC raises problems that can not be casually dismissed. MNCs are powerful and resourceful actors on the world's stage, and they do disrupt, alter, and influence the patterns of culture wherever they operate. So powerful are they that continuing to think of them in national terms may be a mistake. After all, capital now moves on computers across borders as if such entities as Japan, France, Brazil, and the USA did not exist. In this global moment, perhaps it is foolish to worry about societal labels when Toyota meets the payroll in Kentucky and McDonald's opens fast-food concessions in Beijing. The world is perhaps turning into one big marketplace, with the Great Wall becoming the Great Mall, much to the delight of the homogenization theorist.

Such a result is doubtful. The resilience of culture constructed from a people's history, customs, and the materials of their everyday life throughout the world is not to be denied. Recontextualization may well be less predictable or effective than outright rejection. The resurgence of ethnic, religious, and national identities in the wake of colonialism and repression was one of the most obvious global trends in the late twentieth century. Perhaps such resurgence and the resulting differentiation and self-consciousness among cultures can be managed so that all cultures learn from each other, and slowly but surely, through contact, exchange, and an emergent form of creolization, grow more comfortable with one another. This might allow a kind of postmodern "Utopia of differences" to be established on a global basis. Is this Utopia possible? This is really a question for Professors Derrida, Lyotard, and Baudrillard. But since an answer (and a conclusion) is only a few keystrokes away, I will provide one here. It is my fifth and (mercifully) final point.

Whatever a Utopia of differences might mean and produce, it would ultimately depend on the ability of people of differing cultures to enter into a very deep dialogue with one another and to do so on an entirely equal footing. If, for example, the problems of an MNC are seen as obstacles that separate people of distinct cultural backgrounds, and these obstacles are then treated first and foremost as objects of analysis to be understood rather than ignored, squashed, pushed aside, or otherwise bulldozed over, then the possibility emerges that a deconstruction of cultures—"ours" as well as "theirs"—can occur, and a reconstruction based on the authentic and appreciated differences between and among people can develop. In this way, MNCs might contribute to the emergence of a world culture that reflects such a Utopia of differences.

This is, alas, highly unlikely to take place anywhere, let alone within an MNC. The MNC is not in the deconstruction business. It operates in differing regions of the world for gain, not for study or for improving intercultural understandings. It operates by choice on those who often have no choice. As long as the idea of a common goal originating in some center and moving outward pervades the MNC, differences are likely to continue to be ignored, denied, covered up, and otherwise regarded in mostly unfavorable terms. Such differences will continue to exist, of course, and will play out in a variety of ways. But they will not be seen as a source of fundamental value and a mark of our common condition. There may be ways to manage these differences more respectfully and with perhaps greater appreciation as to what they may contribute to the organization as a whole. Yet without confronting and altering the sense of self and other that runs deep and virtually everywhere in the MNC, such differences will not be understood.

Notes

1 This chapter is a substantial revision of "The flow of culture: Some notes on globalization and the multinational corporation" which appeared as Chapter 12 in the
   first edition of this volume. The revision is modest analytically but extensive empirically. The "Disneyland experience" plays a much greater role in this chapter than
   before, largely because there is so much more of it available to discuss than when
   the previous edition went to press. The company has been quite busy in the international culture trade over the past decade. Disney has now been operating its park
   in France since 1992, and plans to soon open the fifth Disneyland in Hong Kong.
   Moreover, Tokyo Disneyland has grown considerably. All this thickens the plot. As
   before, I have received a good deal of aid, comfort, and criticism from the unlucky
   readers of my Disney tales generally, and on an earlier draft of this chapter in particular. I have tried to be reasonably responsive to this friendly fire. Comments from
   Eleanor Westney, Ed Schein, Mary Yoko Brannen, Andre Laurent (my co-author
   from the previous edition), Gideon Kunda, John Weeks, Tony DiBella, and Jane
   Salk have been especially helpful here (and elsewhere).

2 My view follows the "interpretive turn" taken by many students of culture over
   the past 30 or so years. This perspective is set forth nicely by Geertz (1973, 1995)
   and is broadened by Rabinow and Sullivan (1987) and Rosaldo (1989). Such a
   view highlights the difficulties posed for native and analyst alike in "reading" culture, and thus treats culture as considerably more problematic, contentious, and
   varied than earlier approaches. One result of this shift is that the functionalist view
   of a given social structure is seldom seen in current sociological or anthropological work beyond the four-color introductory textbooks. This functionalist view
   emphasizing the "replication of uniformity" approach to culture has given way to
   a more particularistic "organization of diversity" approach, wherein attention is
   paid to the contrasting habits, motives, customs, and so forth that coexist within,
   or mark, group boundaries (Wallace 1970).

   One implication to be drawn from recent cultural studies is that the homogeneity
   and monolithic nature of culture as portrayed in the classic ethnographic monographs was overdone (Marcus and Fischer 1986; Clifford 1988). Especially pertinent
   to the materials presented here is the observation that the common-denominator
   people so prevalent in the classic ethnographic texts on the remote and isolated societies of the world have become far less prevalent in contemporary texts, since ethnographers have moved closer to home to do their work, where they perhaps know
   more of what is going on around them. Like the natives they study, current ethnographers have great difficulty stuffing the knowledge they gain of others into simple
   categories. A brief summary of some of the twists and turns in ethnographic thought
   and practice is found in Van Maanen (1988: 13–44).

3 A list of ethnographic studies in this domain would be long indeed. Recent exemplary monographs within the relatively narrow range of organization studies
   include Weeks's (2004) close study of a British bank; Kunda's (1992) reading of
   a once celebrated culture associated with a high-tech engineering firm; Kondo's
   (1990) portrait of work, gender, and identity in Japan; Jackell's (1988) treatment
   of the moral precepts held by US corporate managers; Biggart's (1989) lively look
   at direct sales organization; Traweek's (1988) comparative analysis of how high-
   energy physics is conducted in the United States and Japan; and Halle's (1984)
   close study of a New Jersey chemical plant. Classic examples of such work are
   found in Gouldner (1954), Dalton (1959), and Becker et al. (1961).

4 Recent exemplars in this realm are not hard to locate. Some favorites of mine
   in the organizational studies domain include Gusfield's (1981) decoding of
   drunk driving enforcement practices in the USA, Latour's (1987) reading of

the products of laboratory science, and Yates's (1989) historical treatment of the social consequences of various office technologies. Broader examples of interpretive cultural work include Sahlins (1981), Leach (1976), and Wallace (1978). A good general introduction to this side of the cultural studies house in sociology is found in Becker and McCall (1990).

5 Notable exceptions include Manning's (1989) concern for the causes and consequences of the codes and practices of police dispatchers, Becker's (1982) treatment of the multiple worlds supporting the craft and social production of art, and MacCannell's (1976) ethnographic reading of modern tourists, tourist sites, and the rapidly growing tourist industry. It is also worth noting in this regard that journalists are often interested in matching cultural practices to cultural products. Consider, for example, the social world created by trying to beat Las Vegas roulette, as revealed by Bass (1985), the late 1960s life of the high-church priests of hippiedom and acid as chronicled by Wolfe (1968), and what "getting out in front of the price performance curve" in the computer industry means to those who engineer the products, as told by Kidder (1981). All three of these journalistic examinations involve a good deal of fieldwork and acute sensitivity to both sides of the cultural studies division identified in the text.

6 Global homogenization as played out in the MNC is something of an imperialistic call to order issued by headquarters. Of historical interest, an unintentionally insightful example of just such a process is provided by Kuin's (1972) look at "Unileverization," where the key to Unilever's economic success worldwide at the time was said to be the adoption of a common language throughout the firm (English), intensive training, standard reporting formats, regular rotation of managers around the world, common goals and operating practices across subsidiaries, and the provision of long-term employment contracts for managerial and professional staff. More recent and scholarly attempts to build the generic and successful "global organization" are found in Galbraith and Lawler (1993); Goold and Campbell (2002); and Nadler and Tushman (1997). These attempts are put forth in much the same spirit and frame as the "Unilever Way." It is worth noting as well that the rather famous Hofstede (1980a) study claiming to have discovered deep cultural differences across the globe was conducted at IBM, an organization noted at the time for its obsession with corporate control and standardization.

7 Global heterogeneity as cultural resistance no doubt takes many forms. In the case of the MNC it is perhaps best thought of as a noticeable drift by subsidiary units away from directions sought by headquarters. Such drift may be intentional or unintentional, but the result is a degree of operational autonomy for subsidiary organizations. The management literature typically treats such drift as nearly pathological. It is ordinarily seen as a troubling problem about which something ought to be done (immediately). That so much attention is devoted to trying to regulate such drift suggests that the global heterogeneity scenario sketched out in the text is more than the wishful dream of those academic culture watchers who, it seems, are forever rooting for diversity. See, for example, Edstrom and Galbraith (1979), Jaeger (1983), and Montagna (1990) for illustrative studies of policies and practices designed to increase the control of headquarters over drift-prone subsidiaries in the MNC.

8 The analysis that follows in the text is based on a number of methods, none of which are to be found in any respectable method textbook. Some are altogether opportunistic and retrospective, such as my two and a half year work stint as a ride operator at Disneyland in the late 1960s, periodic visits to the US park(s), and a short visit to Tokyo Disneyland (accompanied by a translator). I have also spent considerable time at Disneyland Paris while on sabbatical from MIT in France.

The work on Hong Kong Disneyland reported here is based on library time and a few interviews with individuals familiar with the project. My methods in the USA and Japan are covered in more depth in Van Maanen 1991, 1992, and 1995.

9 Among the more engaging and challenging interpretations of the myth, magic, and mystery of Disneyland not mentioned in the section text are Wasko 2001; Watts 1997; Britton 1989; Eco 1986 (20–56); Moore 1980; Real 1977 (44–90); Shearling and Stenning 1985; Spinelli 1987; and Wolf 1979. This is but a drop in a very large bucket.

10 Although Disney was eager to reap the potential profits from the enterprise, executives of the firm were no more enthusiastic than they had ever been about assuming much of the risk. Therefore the financial structure for the new park was a complicated one. A finance company was set up as the owner of the park in which Disney took a 17 percent stake. A separate company, Euro Disney, was formed to operate the park, of which 49 percent was owned by the Walt Disney Company. To help raise capital, the rest of the shares of Euro Disney were listed on the Paris stock exchange and available to the public at an opening share price of US$11.50 (quickly rising to its all-time high of US$18). Disney had paid about US$1.50 for each of its shares, a fact that, when it became known in the wake of a falling share price in the 1990s, caused considerable public criticism. Foreshadowing the discussion in the text, Euro Disney shares were selling on the Bourse in the summer of 2004 at about US$0.60 a share (and have been around this level for years). See Solomon (1994) for a more extensive discussion. The deal-cutting in Paris is also covered well by Grover (1997) and Watts (1997). For the company view of things, see Michael Eisner (1998).

11 Good examples in this regard are relatively easy to find. Some of my recent favorites not yet mentioned include Adler and Adler (2004); Tucker (1999); Fine (1996); Morrill (1995); Allison (1994); Leidner (2003); Young (1991); and Smith (1990).

12 There are of course enormous difficulties involved in conducting intensive, in-depth cultural studies of transnational organizations. Their intimidating size and geographic spread make traditional ethnographic techniques appear helplessly inadequate. At the moment, however, the development of business case studies seems to be far and away the most common approach bearing evidence of the cultural character of the MNC. This situation should perhaps wake slumbering ethnographers, for however inadequate they may feel exploring the turf of the MNC, their methods are far superior to the reliance of most case writers on a plant tour, an overnight visit, a handful of soft interviews, and the sanguine collection of company-produced documents. Some engaging ideas on just how such studies might be pursued are provided in Marcus (1998).

13 This model assumes that culture can be transmitted in a reasonably uniform way such that individuals are either socialized or not. If socialized, the idea is that they will all behave in the same way under the same circumstances (Van Maanen and Schein 1979). Culture is therefore provided on a one-to-a-customer basis, and customers have little choice as to what to accept or reject. Culture comes as a package deal. It is the case, however, that no one learns a culture in quite the same way even within a single cultural tradition (Schwartz 1981; Wolcott 1982). Recognition of the inevitable slippage in any socialization program has pushed theorists toward an "acquisition" rather than "transmission" model of cultural learning (Ochs 1988; Wolcott 1990; Shweder, 1991; Van Maanen, 2004).

References

Abolafia, M. L. and Kilduff, M. (1988) "Enacting market crisis: the social construction of a speculative bubble," *Administrative Science Quarterly* 33:2, pp. 177–193.

Ackoff, R. L. (1974) *Redesigning the Future*, New York: Wiley.

Ackoff, R. L. and Emery, F. E. (1972) *On Purposeful Systems*, Chicago: Aldine.

Adams, J. A. (1991) *The American Amusement Park Industry: A History of Technology and Thrills*, Boston, Mass.: Twayne.

Adams, J. S. (1965) "Inequity in social exchange," in L. Berkowitz (ed.), *Advances in Experimental Social Psychology 2*, New York: Academic Press.

Adler, P. and Adler, P. (2004) *Paradise Laborers: Hotel Work in the Global Economy*, Ithaca, NY: Cornell University Press.

Aharoni, Y. (1966) *The Foreign Direct Investment Decision*, Boston, Mass.: Harvard Business School.

Alchian, A. and Demsetz, H. (1972) "Production, information costs, and economic organization," *American Economic Review* 62, pp. 777–795.

Aldrich, H. E. (1972) "An organization–environment perspective on cooperation and conflict in the manpower training system," in R. C. Sarri and Y. Hasenfeld (eds), *The Management of Human Services*, New York: Columbia University Press.

Aldrich, H. E. (1976) "Resource dependence and interorganizational relations: Relations between local employment service offices and social service sector organizations," *Administration and Society* 7, pp. 419–454.

Aldrich, H. E. (1979) *Organizations and Environments*, Englewood Cliffs, N.J.: Prentice-Hall.

Aldrich, H. E. (1981) "Organization-sets, action-sets, and networks: Making the most of simplicity," in P. C. Nystrom and W. H. Starbuch (eds), *Handbook of Organizational Design*, London: Oxford University Press, pp. 385–408.

Aldrich, H. E. and Marsden, P. V. (1988) "Environments and organizations," in N. J. Smelser (ed.), *Handbook of Sociology*, Newbury Park, Calif.: Sage.

Aldrich, H. E. and Pfeffer, J. (1976) "Environments of organizations," *Annual Review of Sociology* 2, pp. 79–105.

Aldrich, H. E. and Whetten, D. (1981) "Organisation-sets, action-sets, and networks: making the most of simplicity," in P. C. Nystrom and W. H. Starbuck (eds), *Handbook of Organizational Design*, London: Oxford University Press, pp. 385–408.

Alexander, S. and Ruderman, M. (1987) "The role of procedural and distributive justice in organizational behavior," *Social Justice Research* 1, pp. 177–198.

Allen, T. J. (1978) *Managing the Flow of Technology: Technology Transfer and the Dissemination of Technological Information within the Research and Development Organization*, Cambridge, Mass.: MIT Press.

Allison, A. (1994) *Nightwork: Sexuality, Pleasure, and Corporate Masculinity in a Tokyo Hostess Club*. Chicago: University of Chicago Press.

Allison, P. D. (1984) *Event History Analysis: Regression for Longitudinal Event Data*, Beverley Hills, Calif.: Sage.

References

Anand, J. and Kogut, B. (1997) "Technological capabilities of countries, firm rivalry, and foreign direct investment," *Journal of International Business Studies* 28, pp. 445–465.

Anderson, B. (1983) *Imagined Communities*, London: Verso.

Anderson, E. and Gatignon, H. (1986) "Modes of foreign entry: A transaction cost analysis and propositions," *Journal of International Business Studies* 17:3, pp. 1–26.

Anderson, E. and Oliver, R. (1987) "Perspectives on behavior-based versus outcome-based salesforce control systems," *Journal of Marketing* 51, pp. 76–88.

Ansoff, H. I. (1965) *Corporate Strategy: An Analytic Approach to Business Policy for Growth and Expansion*, New York: McGraw-Hill.

Anthony, R. and Dearden, J. (1980) *Management Control Systems*, Homewood, Ill: Irwin.

Aoki, M. (1988) *Information, Incentives, and Bargaining in the Japanese Economy*, Cambridge: Cambridge University Press.

Argyris, C. and Schon, D. A. (1978) *Organizational Learning*, Reading, Mass: Addison-Wesley.

Arpan, J. S. and Ricks, D. A. (1986) "Foreign direct investment in the U.S., 1974–1984," *Journal of International Business Studies* 17:3, pp. 149–154.

Arrow, K. J. (1974) *The Limits of Organization*, New York: W. E. Norton.

Arrow, K. J. (1985) "The economics of agency," in J. W. Pratt and R. J. Zeckhauser (eds), *Principal and Agents: The Structure of Business*, Boston, Mass: Harvard Business School Press, pp. 37–54.

Astley, W. G. and Van de Ven, A. H. (1983) "Central perspectives and debates in organization theory," *Administrative Science Quarterly* 28, pp. 265–273.

Bacharach, S. B. and Aiken, M. (1976) "Structural and process constraints on influence in organizations: A level specific analysis," *Administrative Science Quarterly* 21, pp. 623–642.

Bahrami, H. and Evans, S. (1987) "Stratocracy in high technology firms. Special issue on organizational approaches to strategy," *California Management Review* 30:1, pp. 51–66.

Baliga, B. and Jaeger, A. (1984) "Multinational corporations: control systems and delegation issues," *Journal of International Business Studies* 15:3, pp. 25–40.

Barkema, H. G., Bell, J. H., and Pennings, J. M. (1996) "Foreign entry, cultural barriers, and learning," *Strategic Management Journal* 17, pp. 151–166.

Barley, S. R. (1983) "Semiotics and the study of occupational and organizational cultures," *Administrative and Science Quarterly* 28, pp. 393–413.

Barley, S. R., Meyer, G. W., and Gash, D. C. (1988) "Cultures of culture: Academics, practitioners, and the pragmatics of normative control," *Administrative Science Quarterly* 33: 24–60.

Barney, J. and Ouchi, W. (1986) *Organizational Economics*, San Francisco: Jossey-Bass.

Barrett-Howard, E. and Tyler, T. R. (1986) "Procedural justice as a criterion in allocation decisions," *Journal of Personality and Social Psychology* 50, pp. 296–304.

Bartlett, C. A. (1979) "Multinational structural evolution: The changing decision environment in international divisions," unpublished doctoral dissertation, Harvard Business School.

Bartlett, C. A. (1981) "Multinational structural change: evolution versus reorganization," in L. Otterbeck (ed.), *The Management of Headquarters–Subsidiary Relationships in Multinational Corporations*, Aldershot, England: Gower, pp. 121–146.

Bartlett, C. A. (1983) "MNCs: Get off the reorganization merry-go-round," *Harvard Business Review* 61:2, pp. 138–146.

Bartlett, C. A. (1986) "Building and managing the transnational: The new organizational challenge," in M. E. Porter (ed.), *Competition in Global Industries*, Boston, Mass.: Harvard Business School Press, pp. 367–404.

302

References

Bartlett, C. A., Doz, Y., and Hedlund, G. (eds) (1990) *Managing the Global Firm*, London: Routledge.

Bartlett, C. A. and Ghoshal, S. (1986) "Tap your subsidiaries for global reach," *Harvard Business Review* 64:6, pp. 87–94.

Bartlett, C. A. and Ghoshal, S. (1989, revised ed. 1998) *Managing Across Borders: The Transnational Solution*, Boston, Mass.: Harvard Business School Press.

Bartlett, C. A. and Ghoshal, S. (1990) "Matrix management: Not a structure, a frame of mind," *Harvard Business Review* 68:4, pp. 138–145.

Bartlett, C. A. and Ghoshal, S. (1995) "Changing the role of top management: Beyond systems to people," *Harvard Business Review* May–June, pp. 132–142.

Bass, T. A. (1985) *The Eudaemonic Pie*, Boston, Mass.: Houghton Mifflin.

Baudrillard, J. (1983) *Simulations*, New York: Semiotext(e).

Baum, J. A. C. and Amburgey, T. (2002) "Organizational Ecology," in J. A. C. Baum (ed.) *The Blackwell Companion to Organizations*, Oxford: Blackwell Publishers, pp. 304–326.

Bavelas, A. (1951) "Communication patterns in task-oriented groups," in D. Lerner and H. D. Lasswell (eds), *The Policy Sciences*, Stanford, Calif.: Stanford University Press, pp. 193–202.

Bayley, D. (1976) *Forces of Order*, Berkeley, Calif.: University of California Press.

Becker, H. S. (1982) "Culture," *Yale Review* 71, pp. 513–528.

Becker, H. S., Greer, B., Hughes, E. C., and Strauss, A. (1961) *Boys in White*, Chicago, Ill.: University of Chicago Press.

Becker, H. S. and McCall, M. M. (1990) *Symbolic Interaction and Cultural Studies*, Chicago, Ill.: University of Chicago Press.

Beer, M. and Davis, S. (1976) "Creating a global organization, failures along the way," *Columbia Journal of World Business* 11:2, pp. 72–84.

Bendix, R. (1956) (1974) *Work and Authority in Industry*, Berkeley: University of California Press.

Benedict, R. (1946) *The Chrysanthemum and the Sword*, Chicago, Ill.: University of Chicago Press.

Bennett, D. C. and Sharpe, K. E. (1979) "Agenda setting and bargaining power: The Mexican state vs. transnational automobile companies," *World Politics* 32, pp. 57–89.

Benson, J. K. (1975) "The interorganizational network as a political economy," *Administrative Science Quarterly* 20, pp. 229–249.

Bettenhausen, K. L. and Murnighan, J. K. (1985) "The emergence of norms in competitive decision making groups," *Administrative Science Quarterly* 30, pp. 350–372.

Bies, R. J. and Shapiro, D. L. (1987) "Interactional fairness judgements: The influence of causal accounts," *Social Justice Research* 1, pp. 199–218.

Biggart, N. W. (1989) *Charismatic Capitalism*, Chicago, Ill.: University of Chicago Press.

Biggart, N. W. and Guillén, M. F. (1999) "Developing difference: Social organization and the rise of the auto industries of South Korea, Taiwan, Spain, and Argentina," *American Sociological Review* 64:5, pp. 722–747.

Birnbaum, S. (1989) *Steve Birnbaum's Guide of Disneyland*, Boston, Mass.: Houghton Mifflin.

Birkenshaw, J. M. (1997) "Entrepreneurship in multinational corporations: The characteristics of subsidiary initiatives," *Strategic Management Journal* 18:3, pp. 207–229.

Birkenshaw, J. M. (1998) *Multinational Corporate Evolution and Subsidiary Development*, London: Macmillan.

Blainey, G. (1984) "The history of multinational factories in Australia," in A. Okochi and T. Inoue (eds), *Overseas Business Activities, Proceedings of the Fuji Conference*, Tokyo: University of Tokyo Press.

References

Blau, P. M. (1968) "The hierarchy of authority in organizations," *American Sociological Review* 33, pp. 453–467.

Blau, P. M. (1970) "A formal theory of differentiation in organizations," *American Sociological Review* 35, pp. 201–218.

Blau, P. M. and Scott, W. R. (1962) *Formal Organizations*, San Francisco: Chandler.

Boddewyn, J. J. (1988) "Political aspects of MNE theory," *Journal of International Business Studies* 19:3, pp. 341–363.

Bohn, R. (1988) "Learning in noisy manufacturing environments: An alternative to the learning curve," Working Paper No. 88–070, Boston, Mass.: Harvard Business School.

Bourgeois, J. (1979) "Toward a method of middle-range theorizing," *Academy of Management Review* 4:3, pp. 443–447.

Bouvier, P. L. (1984) "Subjectivity and the concept of hierarchy: The dominant paradigm and the prevailing work system," in *Proceedings from the International Conference of Society for General Systems Research*, June, New York.

Bower, J. L. (1970) *Managing the Resource Allocation Process*, Boston, Mass.: Harvard Business School Division of Research.

Bower, J. L. (1987) *When Markets Quake*, Boston, Mass.: Harvard Business School Press.

Boyd, B. K. and McSween, C. B. (1988) "Once more into the breach: A meta-analytic review of the relationship between strategic planning and performance," paper presented at the Annual Meeting of the Western Academy of Management, Big Sky, Mass., March 24–26.

Boyd, R. and Richerson, P. (1985) *Culture and the Evolutionary Process*, Chicago: University of Chicago Press.

Brannen, M. Y. (1992) "Bwana Mickey: Constructing cultural consumption at Tokyo Disneyland," in J. Tobin (ed.), *Remade in Japan: Consumer Tastes in a Changing Japan*, New Haven: Yale University Press.

Brannen, M. Y. and Wilson, J. M. (1996) "Recontextualization and internationalization: Lessons in transcultural materialism from the Walt Disney Company," *CEMS (Community of European Management Schools) Business Review* 1, 1.

Bresser Pereira, L. C. (1993) "Economic reforms and economic growth: Efficiency and politics in Latin America," in L. C. Bresser Pereira et al. (eds), *Economic Reforms in New Democracies*, Cambridge: Cambridge University Press, pp. 15–76.

Britton, D. (1989) "The dark side of Disneyland," *Art Issues* 4, pp. 13–22; 5, pp. 3–17.

Brockner, J., Grover, S., Reed, T., DeWitt R., and O'Malley, M. (1987) "Survivors' reactions to layoffs: We get by with a little help for our friends," *Administrative Science Quarterly* 32:4, pp. 526–541.

Brooke, M. Z. and Remmers, H. L. (1970) *The Strategy of Multinational Enterprise*, New York: Elsevier.

Brown, M. and Philips, P. (1986) "The decline of the piece-rate system in California canning," *Business History Review* 60, pp. 564–601.

Brown, N. O. (1947) *Hermes the Thief: Evolution of a Myth*, Madison: University of Wisconsin.

Buckley, P. J. (1988) "The limits of explanation: Testing the internationalization theory of the multinational enterprise," *Journal of International Business Studies* 19, pp. 181–193.

Buckley, P. J. and Casson, M. (1976) *The Future of the Multinational Enterprise*, London: Macmillan.

Buckley, P. J. and Casson, M. (1986) *The Economic Theory of the Multinational Enterprise*, London: Macmillan.

Burenstam Linder, S. (1961) *An Essay on Trade and Transformation*, New York: Wiley.

Burns, T. and Stalker, G. M. (1961) *The Management of Innovation*, London: Tavistock.

References

Buroway, M. (1979) *Manufacturing Consent*, Chicago, Ill.: University of Chicago Press.

Burt, R. S. (1978) "Stratification and prestige among elite experts in mathematical sociology circa 1975," *Social Networks* 1, pp. 105–158.

Burt, R. S. (1987) "Social contagion and innovation: Cohesion versus structural equivalence," *American Journal of Sociology* 92, pp. 1287–1335.

Burt, R. S., Minor, M. J., and Associates (eds) (1983) *Applied Network Analysis: A Methodological Introduction*, Beverly Hills, Calif.: Sage.

Calvet, A. L. (1981) "A synthesis of foreign direct investment theories and theories of the multinational firm," *Journal of International Business Studies*, Spring–Summer, pp. 43–59.

Camacho, A. and Persky, J. J. (1988) "The internal organization of complex teams," *Journal of Economic Behavior and Organization* 9, pp. 367–380.

Cantwell, J. (1989) *Technological Innovations and Multinational Corporations*, Cambridge, Mass.: Blackwell.

Capon, N., Christodoulou, C., Farley, J. U., and Hulbert, J. M. (1987) "A comparative analysis of the strategy and structure of United States and Australian corporations," *Journal of International Business Studies* 18, pp. 51–74.

Cardoso, F. H. and Faletto, E. [1973] 1979. *Dependency and Development in Latin America*. Berkeley, Calif.: University of California Press.

Carley, K. (1986) "An approach for relating social structure to cognitive structure," *Journal of Mathematical Sociology* 12:2, pp. 137–189.

Carlzon, J. (1985) *Riv Pyramiderna*, Stockholm: AB Bonniers.

Carroll, G. R. (1983) "Dynamic analysis of discrete dependent variables: A didactic essay," *Quality and Quantity* 17, pp. 425–460.

Carroll, G. R. (1984) "The specialist strategy," *California Management Review* 3, pp. 126–137.

Carroll, G. R. (1987) *Publish and Perish: The Organizational Ecology of Newspaper Industries*. Greenwich, CT: JAI Press.

Carroll, G. R. (ed.) (1988) *Ecological Models of Organizations*, Cambridge, Mass.: Ballinger.

Carroll, G. R. and Hannan, M. T. (2000) *The Demography of Corporations and Industries*. Princeton: Princeton University Press.

Carroll, J. and Delacroix, J. (1982) "Organizational mortality in the newspaper industries of Argentina and Ireland: An ecological approach," *Administrative Science Quarterly* 27, pp. 169–198.

Carroll, J., Delacroix, J., and Goodstein, J. (1988) "The political environments of organizations: An ecological view," in B. M. Staw and L. L. Cummings (eds), *Research in Organizational Behavior* 10, pp. 359–392.

Casper, J. D., Tyler, T. R., and Fisher, B. (1988) "Procedural justice in felony cases," *Law and Society Review* 22, pp. 483–507.

Casson, M. (1987) *The Firm and the Market*, Cambridge, Mass.: MIT Press.

Castells, M. (1997) *The Power of Identity*, London: Blackwell.

Caves, R. E. (1971) "International corporations: The industrial economics of foreign direct investment," *Economica* 38, pp. 1–27.

Caves, R. E. (1982) *Multinational Enterprise and Economic Analysis*, Cambridge: Cambridge University Press.

Caves, R. E., Crookell, H., and Killing, J. (1982) "The imperfect market for technology licenses," *Oxford Bulletin of Economics and Statistics* 45:3, pp. 249–267.

Chakravarthy, B. S. and Lorange, P. (1991) *Managing the Strategy Process: A Framework for a Multibusiness Firm*, Englewood Cliffs, N.J.: Prentice-Hall.

Chandler, A. (1962) *Strategy and Structure: Chapters in the History of the American Industrial Enterprise*, Cambridge, Mass.: MIT Press.

References

Chandler, A. (1977) *The Visible Hand: The Managerial Revolution in American Business*, Cambridge, Mass.: Harvard University Press.

Chandler, A. (1986) "The evolution of modern global competition," in M. E. Porter (ed.), *Competition in Global Industries*, Boston, Mass.: Harvard Business School Press, pp. 405–448.

Chandler, A. (1990) *Scale and Scope: The Dynamics of Industrial Capitalism*, Cambridge, Mass.: Harvard University Press.

Chandler, A. D. and Daems, H. (eds) (1980) *Managerial Hierarchies: Comparative Perspectives on the Rise of the Modern Industrial Enterprise*, Cambridge, Mass.: Harvard University Press.

Channon, D. F. (1973) *The Strategy and Structure of British Enterprises*, Boston, Mass.: Division of Research, Graduate School of Business, Harvard University.

Child, J. (1973) "Strategies of control and organizational behavior," *Administrative Science Quarterly* 18, pp. 1–17.

Clark, G. (1984) "Authority and efficiency: The labor market and the managerial revolution of the late nineteenth century," *Journal of Economic History* 44:4, pp. 1069–1083.

Clifford, J. (1988) *The Predicament of Culture*, Cambridge, Mass.: Harvard University Press.

Cohen, M. D., March, J. G., and Olsen, J. P. (1972) "A garbage can model of organizational choice," *Administrative Science Quarterly* 17, pp. 1–25.

Cole, R. E. (1978) "The late-developer hypothesis: An evaluation of its relevance for Japanese employment patterns," *Journal of Japanese Studies* 4:2, pp. 247–265.

Coleman, J. S. (1966) "Foundations for a theory of collective decisions," *American Journal of Sociology* 71, pp. 615–627.

Contractor, F. J. and Lorange, P. (1988) *Cooperative Strategies in International Business*, Lexington, Mass.: Lexington Books.

Cook, K. S. (1977) "Exchange and power in networks of interorganizational relations," *Sociological Quarterly* 18, pp. 62–82.

Cook, K. S., Emerson, R. M., Gilmore, M. R., and Yamashigi, T. (1983) "The distribution of power in exchange networks: Theory and experimental results," *American Journal of Sociology* 89, pp. 275–305.

Crozier, M. (1964) *The Bureaucratic Phenomenon*, Chicago, Ill.: University of Chicago Press.

Crozier, M. and Friedberg, E. (1980) *Actors and Systems: The Politics of Collective Action*, Chicago, Ill.: University of Chicago Press.

Cvar, M. R. (1986) "Case study in global competition: Patterns of success and failure," in M. E. Porter (ed.), *Competition in Global Industries*, Boston, Mass.: Harvard Business School Press, pp. 483–515.

Cyert, R. M. and March, J. G. (1963) *A Behavioral Theory of the Firm*, Englewood Cliffs, N.J.: Prentice-Hall.

Czarniawska-Jorges, B. (1992) *Exploring Complex Organizations: A Cultural Perspective*, Newbury Park, Calif.: Sage.

Daft, R. L. and Lengel, R. H. (1986) "Organizational information requirements, media richness and structural design," *Management Science* 32:5, pp. 554–571.

Daft, R. L. and Macintosh, N. B. (1981) "A tentative exploration into the amount and equivocality of information processing in organizational work units," *Administrative Science Quarterly* 26:2, pp. 207–224.

Daft, R. L. and Weick, K. E. (1984) "Toward a model of organizations as interpretation systems," *Academy of Management Review* 9:2, pp. 284–295.

Dahl, R. (1957) "The concept of power," *Behavioral Science* 2, pp. 201–215.

Dalton, M. (1959) *Men Who Manage*, New York: Wiley.

References

Daniels, J. D., Pitts, R. A., and Tretter, M. J. (1984) "Strategy and structure of U.S. multinationals: An exploratory study," *Academy of Management Journal* 27:2, pp. 292–307.

Daniels, J. D., Pitts, R. A., and Tretter, M. J. (1985) "Organizing for dual strategies of product diversity and international expansion," *Strategic Management Journal* 6, pp. 223–237.

Davidson, D. (1989) *Corporate Culture and Organizational Effectiveness*, San Francisco: Jossey-Bass.

Davidson, W. (1976) "Patterns of factor-saving innovation in the industrialized world," *European Economic Review* 8, pp. 207–217.

Davidson, W. H. and Haspeslagh, P. (1982) "Shaping a global product organization," *Harvard Business Review*, pp. 125–132.

Davis, S. (1974) "Two models of organization: Unity of command vs. balance of power," *Sloan Management Review* 16:1, pp. 29–40.

Davis, S. M. and Lawrence, P. R. (1977) *Matrix*, Reading, Mass.: Addison-Wesley.

Dawkins, R. (1986) *The Blind Watchmaker*, Burnt Mill, Harlow: Longman.

Deal, T. E. and Kennedy, A. A. (1982) *Corporate Cultures*, Reading, Mass.: Addison-Wesley.

Delacroix, J. and Carroll, G. (1983) "Organizational foundings: An ecological study of the newspaper industries of Argentina and Ireland," *Administrative Science Quarterly* 28, pp. 274–291.

Delios, A. and Henisz, W. J. (2000) "Japanese firms' investment strategies in emerging economies," *Academy of Management Journal* 43, pp. 305–323.

Delios, A. and Henisz, W. J. (2003) "Political hazards, experience and sequential entry strategies: The international expansion of Japanese firms, 1980–1998," *Strategic Management Journal* 24:12, pp. 1153–1164.

Demsetz, H. (1988) "The theory of the firm revisited," *Journal of Law, Economics, and Organization* 4:1, pp. 141–161.

Depew, D. J. and Weber, B. H. (eds) (1985) *Evolution at a Crossroads: The New Biology and the New Philosophy of Science*, Cambridge, Mass.: MIT Press.

Depke, D. (1989) "Suddenly, software houses have a Big Blue buddy," *Business Week* 3118, August 7, pp. 68–69.

Deutsch, K. (1966) *The Nerves of Government: Models of Political Communication and Control*, New York: Free Press.

DiMaggio, P. J. (1986) "Structural analysis of organizational fields: A blockmodel approach," *Research in Organizational Behavior* 8, pp. 335–370.

DiMaggio, P. J. (1988) "Interest and agency in institutional theory," in R. Friedland and A. F. Robertson (eds), *Beyond the Marketplace*, Chicago, Ill.: Aldine.

DiMaggio, P. (1990) "Cultural aspects of economic action," in R. Friedland and A. F. Robertson (eds), *Beyond the Marketplace*, Chicago, Ill.: Aldine.

DiMaggio, P. (ed.) (2001) *The Twenty-first-century Firm: Changing Economic Organization in International Perspective*, Princeton: Princeton University Press.

DiMaggio, P. J. and Powell, W. W. (1983) "The iron cage revisited: Institutional isomorphism and collective rationality in organizational fields," *American Sociological Review* 48, pp. 147–160.

DiMaggio, P. J. and Powell, W. W. (1991) *The New Institutionalism in Organizational Analysis*, Chicago, Ill.: University of Chicago Press.

Dionysius, the Pseudo-Areopagite. (1981) *The Ecclesiastical Hierarchy*, trans. and annot. T. L. Campbell, Lanham, Md.: University Press of America.

Dobbin, F. R., Edelman, L., Meyer, J. W., Scott, W. R., and Swidler, A. (1988) "The expansion of due process in organizations," in L. G. Zucker (ed.), *Institutional Patterns and Organizations: Culture and Environment*, Cambridge, Mass.: Ballinger.

307

Doner, R. F. (1991) *Driving a Bargain: Automobile Industrialization and Japanese Firms in Southeast Asia*, Berkeley: University of California Press.

Doner, R. F. (1992) "Limits of state strength: Toward an institutionalist view of economic development," *World Politics* 454, pp. 398–431.

Donnellon, A., Gray, B., and Bougon, M. G. (1985) "Communication, meaning, and organized action," *Administrative Science Quarterly* 31, pp. 43–55.

Dore, R. P. (1973) (1974) *British Factory Japanese Factory: The Origins of National Diversity in Industrial Relations,* Berkeley: University of California Press.

Dore, R. P. (1983) "Goodwill and the spirit of market capitalism," *British Journal of Sociology* 34:4, pp. 459–482.

Dore, R. (1987) *Taking Japan Seriously,* Stanford: Stanford University Press.

Doremus, P. N., Keller, W. W., Pauly, L. W., and Reich, S. (1998) *The Myth of the Global Corporation*, Princeton, N.J.: Princeton University Press.

Dorfman, A. and Matterlart, A. (1975) *How to Read Donald Duck*, New York: International General.

Douglas, M. (1966) *Purity and Danger,* London: Routledge and Kegan Paul.

Doz, Y. (1976) "National policies and multinational management," doctoral dissertation, Harvard Business School.

Doz, Y. (1978) "Managing manufacturing rationalization within multinational companies," *Columbia Journal of World Business* 8:3, pp. 82–94.

Doz, Y. (1979) *Government Control and Multinational Strategic Management: Power Systems and Telecommunications Equipment,* New York: Praeger.

Doz, Y. (1980) "Strategic management in multinational companies," *Sloan Management Review* 21:2, pp. 27–46.

Doz, Y. (1986) *Strategic Management in Multinational Companies,* Oxford: Pergamon.

Doz, Y., Bartlett, C. A., and Prahalad, C. K. (1981) "Global competitive pressures vs. host country demands: Managing tensions in multinational corporations," *California Management Review* 23:3, pp. 63–74.

Doz, Y. and Prahalad, C. K. (1981) "Headquarters influence and strategic control in MNCs," *Sloan Management Review* 23:1, pp. 15–29.

Doz, Y. and Prahalad, C. K. (1984) "Patterns of strategic control in multinational corporations," *Journal of International Business Studies* 15:2, pp. 55–72.

Doz, Y. and Prahalad, C. K. (1986) "Controlled variety: A challenge for human resource management in the MNC," *Human Resource Management* 25:1, pp. 55–72.

Doz, Y. and Prahalad, C. K. (1987) "A process model of strategic redirection in large complex firms: The case of multinational corporations," in A. Pettigrew (ed.), *The Management of Strategic Change*, Oxford: Blackwell.

Doz, Y. and Prahalad, C. K. (1988) "Quality of management: An emerging source of global competitive advantage?" in N. Hood and J. E. Vahlne (eds), *Strategies in Global Competition*, London: Croom Helm.

Doz, Y., Prahalad, C. K., and Hamel, G. (1990) "Control, change and flexibility: The dilemma of transnational collaboration," in C. A. Bartlett, Y. Doz, and G. T. Hedlund (eds), *Managing the Global Firm*, London: Routledge.

Doz, Y., Santos, J., and Williamson, P. (2001) *From Global to Metanational: How Companies Win in the Knowledge Economy*, Boston, Mass.: Harvard Business School Press.

Duncan, R. B. (1973) "Multiple decision-making structures in adapting to environmental uncertainty: The impact of organizational effectiveness," *Human Relations* 26, pp. 273–291.

Dunkin, A. (1989) "Now salespeople really must sell for their supper," *Business Week* 3117, July 31, pp. 1–50.

References

Dunning, J. H. (1973) "The determinants of international production," *Oxford Economic Papers* 25:3, pp. 289–336.

Dunning, J. H. (ed.) (1974) *Economic Analysis and the Multinational Enterprise*, London: Allen and Unwin.

Dunning, J. H. (1977) "Trade, location of economic activity and the multinational enterprise: A search for an eclectic approach," in B. Ohlin, P. O. Hesselbom, and P. J. Wiskman (eds), *The International Allocation of Economic Activity*, London: Macmillan.

Dunning, J. H. (1980a) "Toward an eclectic theory of international production: Some empirical tests," *Journal of International Business* 11:1, pp. 9–31.

Dunning, J. H. (1980b) "Explaining changing patterns of international production: In defense of the eclectic theory," *Oxford Bulletin of Economics and Statistics* 42, pp. 269–295.

Dunning, J. H. (1981a) *The Eclectic Theory of the MNC*, London: Allen and Unwin.

Dunning, J. H. (1981b) *International Production and the Multinational Enterprise*, London: Allen and Unwin.

Dunning, J. H. (1986) *Japanese Participation in British Industry: Trojan Horse or Catalyst for Growth*, Dover, NH: Croom Helm.

Dunning, J. H. (1993) *Multinational Enterprises and the Global Economy*, New York: Addison-Wesley.

Dunning, J. H. and Pearce, J. A. (1985) *Profitability and Performance of the World's Largest Industrial Companies*, London: Financial Times.

Durkheim, E. (1933) *The Division of Labor in Society*, New York: Free Press.

Dutton, J. E. and Jackson, S. (1987) "Categorizing strategic issues: links to organizational action," *Academy of Management Review* 12, pp. 76–90.

Dyas, G. P. and Thanheiser, H. T. (1976) *The Emerging European Enterprise: Strategy and Structure in French and German Industry*, London: Macmillan.

Eccles, R. G. (1981) "The quasifirm in the construction industry," *Journal of Economic Behavior and Organization* 2, pp. 335–357.

Eccles, R. G. and Crane, D. B. (1987) "Managing through networks in investment banking," *California Management Review* 30:1, pp. 176–195.

Eccles, R. G. and White, H. (1988) "Price and authority in inter-profit center transactions," *American Journal of Sociology* 94 (Supplement), pp. 17–51.

Eco, U. (1986) *Travels in Hyperreality*, New York: Harcourt Brace Jovanovich.

Edstrom, A. and Galbraith, J. (1979) "Transfer of managers as a coordination and control device in multinational organizations," *Administrative Science Quarterly* 22, pp. 248–263.

Edwards, R. C. (1979) *Contested Terrain: The Transformation of the Workplace in the Twentieth Century*, New York: Basic Books.

Egelhoff, W. G. (1982) "Strategy and structure in multinational corporations: An information processing approach," *Administrative Science Quarterly* 27:3, pp. 435–458.

Egelhoff, W. G. (1988a) "Strategy and structure in multinational corporations: A revision of the Stopford and Wells Model," *Strategic Management Journal* 9:1, pp. 1–14.

Egelhoff, W. G. (1988b) *Organizing the Multinational Enterprise: An Information Processing Perspective*, Cambridge, Mass., Ballanger.

Eisenhardt, K. (1985) "Control: Organizational and economic approaches," *Management Science* 31, pp. 134–149.

Eisenhardt, K. (1988) "Agency- and institutional-theory explanation: The case of retail sales compensation," *American Management Journal* 31:3, pp. 488–511.

Eisenhardt, K. (1989) "Agency theory: An assessment and review," *Academy of Management Review* 14:1, pp. 57–74.

References

Eisenstadt, S. N. (1966) *Modernization: Protest and Change*, Englewood Cliffs, N.J.: Prentice-Hall.

Eisner, M. (with T. Schertz) (1998) *Work in Progress*, New York: Random House.

El Sawy, O. A. (1985) "From separation to holographic enfolding," paper presented to TIMS meeting, May, Boston.

Emerson, R. M. (1962) "Power–dependence relations," *American Sociological Review* 27, pp. 31–41.

Emmott, B. (1989) *The Sun Also Sets*, New York: Simon and Schuster.

Etzioni, A. (1961) (1975) *A Comparative Analysis of Complex Organizations*, New York: Free Press of Glencoe.

Etzioni, A. (1988) *The Moral Dimension*, New York: Free Press.

Evan, W. M. (1967) "The organization-set: Toward a theory of interorganizational relations," in J. D. Thompson (ed.), *Approaches to Organizational Design*, Pittsburgh, Pa.: University of Pittsburgh Press, pp. 173–191.

Evan, W. M. (ed.) (1976) *Interorganizational Relations*, Harmondsworth, England: Penguin

Evans, P. (1979) *Dependent Development*, Princeton, N.J.: Princeton University Press.

Evans, P. E. and Doz, Y. (1989) "The dualistic organization," in P. Evans, Y. Doz, and A. Laurent (eds), *Human Resource Management in International Firms*, London: Macmillan.

Fallows, J. (1989) *More Like Us*, Boston, Mass.: Houghton Mifflin.

Fama, E. F. and Jensen, M. C. (1983) "Separation of ownership and control," *Journal of Law and Economics* 26:2, pp. 301–326.

Fayerweather, J. (1960) *Management of International Operations: Text and Cases*, New York: McGraw-Hill.

Fayerweather, J. (1978) *International Business Strategy and Administration*, Cambridge, Mass.: Ballinger.

Fine, G. A. (1985) "Negotiated orders and organizational cultures," *Annual Review of Sociology* 10, pp. 239–262.

Fine, G. A. (1996) *Kitchens: The Culture of Restaurant Work*, Chicago: University of Chicago Press.

Fiol, C. M. and Lyles, M. A. (1985) "Organizational learning," *Academy of Management Review* 10, pp. 803–813.

Fischer, D. H. (1970) *Historians' Fallacies*, New York: Harper Colophon.

Fjellman, S. M. (1992) *Vinyl Leaves: Walt Disney World and America*, Boulder, Co: Westview.

Flaherty, T. (1986) "Coordinating international manufacturing and technology," in M. E. Porter (ed.), *Competition in Global Industries*, Boston, Mass.: Harvard Business School Press, pp. 83–109.

Fligstein, N. (1990) *The Transformation of Corporate Control*, Cambridge, Mass.: Harvard University Press.

Foglesong, R. (2001) *Married to the Mouse: Walt Disney World and Orlando*, New Haven, Conn.: Yale University Press.

Folger, R. (1977) "Distributive and procedural justice: Combined impact of 'voice' and improvement on experienced inequity," *Journal of Personality and Social Psychology* 35, pp. 108–119.

Folger, R. and Greenberg, J. (1985) "Procedural justice: An interpretative analysis of personnel systems," in K. Rowland and G. Ferris (eds), *Research in Personnel and Human Resources Management III*, Greenwich, Conn.: JAI Press.

Folger, R. and Konovsky, M. (1989) "Effects of procedural and distributive justice on reactions to pay raise decisions," *Academy of Management Journal* 32:1, pp. 115–130.

Folger, R., Rosenfield, D., Grove, J., and Corkran, L. (1989) "Effects of "voice" and peer opinions on responses to inequity," *Journal of Personality and Social Psychology* 37, pp. 2253–2261.

Fombrun, C. J. (1983) "Attributions of power across social network," *Human Relations* 36:3, pp. 493–508.

Fouraker, L. E. and Stopford, J. (1968) "Organization structure and multinational strategy," *Administrative Science Quarterly* 13, pp. 57–70.

Franko, L. G. (1976) *The European Multinationals: A Renewed Challenge to American and British Big Business*, Stamford, Conn.: Greylock.

Freeman, J. H. and Boeker, W. (1984) "The ecological analysis of business strategy," *California Management Review* 26:3, pp. 73–86.

Freeman, J. H., Carroll, G., and Hannan, M. T. (1983) "The liability of newness: Age dependence in organizational death rates," *American Sociological Review* 48, pp. 692–710.

Freeman, J. H. and Hannan, M. T. (1983) "Niche width and the dynamics of organizational populations," *American Journal of Sociology* 88, pp. 1115–1145.

Freeman, L. C. (1979) "Centrality in social networks: Conceptual clarification," *Social Networks* 2, pp. 215–239.

Fruin, M. (1992) *Competitive Strategies and Cooperative Structures: The Japanese Enterprise System*, New York: Oxford University Press.

Fryxell, G. E. and Gordon, M. E. (1989) "Workplace justice and job satisfaction as predictors of satisfaction with union and management," *Academy of Management Journal* 32:4, pp. 851–866.

Fucini, J. J. and Fucini, S. (1990) *Working for the Japanese: Inside Mazda's American Auto Plant*, New York: Free Press.

Fukutake, T. (1981) *Japanese Society Today*, Tokyo: University of Tokyo Press.

Gagliardi, P. (ed.) (1990) *Symbols and Artifacts*, New York: de Gruyter.

Galbraith, J. R. (1969) "Organization design: An information processing view," Working Paper 425–469, Sloan School of Management, MIT.

Galbraith, J. R. (1970) "Environmental and technological determinants of organization design," in J. W. Lorsch and P. R. Lawrence (eds), *Studies in Organization Design*, Homewood, Ill.: Irwin, pp. 113–139.

Galbraith, J. R. (1973) *Designing Complex Organizations*, Reading, Mass.: Addison-Wesley.

Galbraith, J. R. (1977) *Organization Design*, Reading, Mass.: Addison-Wesley.

Galbraith, J. R. and Lawler, E. E. (1993) *Organizing for the Future: The New Logic for Managing Complex Organizations*, San Francisco: Jossey-Bass.

Galbraith, J. R. and Nathanson, D. A. (1978) *Strategy Implementation: The Role of Structure and Process*, St. Paul, Minn.: West Publishing.

Garfinkel, H. (1984) *Studies in Ethnomethodology*, Cambridge, England: Polity Press.

Gastanaga, V. M., Nugent, J. B., and Pashamova, B. (1998) "Host country reforms and FDI inflows: How much difference do they make?" *World Development* 26:7, pp. 1299–1314.

Gates, S. and Egelhoff, W. (1986) "Centralization in headquarters–subsidiary relationships," *Journal of International Business Studies* 17:2, pp. 71–92.

Geertz, C. (1963) *Peddlers and Princes: Social Development and Economic Change in Two Indonesian Towns*, Chicago, Ill.: University of Chicago Press.

Geertz, C. (1973) *The Interpretation of Cultures: Selected Essays*, New York: Basic Books.

Geertz, C. (1995) *After the Fact*, Cambridge, Mass.: Harvard University Press.

Gelsanliter, D. (1990) *Jump Start: Japan Comes to the Heartland*, New York: Farrar, Straus and Giroux.

References

Gereffi, G. (1978) "Drug firms and dependency in Mexico: The case of the steroid hormone industry," *International Organization* 32, pp. 237–286.

Gereffi, G. (1989) "Rethinking development theory: Insights from East Asia and Latin America," *Sociological Forum* 4:4, pp. 505–533.

Gereffi, G. (1990) "Paths of industrialization: An overview," in G. Gereffi and D. L. Wyman (eds), *Manufacturing Miracles*, Princeton, N.J.: Princeton University Press.

Gerschenkron, A. (1962) *Economic Backwardness in Historical Perspective*, Cambridge, Mass.: Harvard University Press.

Ghemawat, P. and Spence, A. M. (1986) "Modeling global competition," in M. E. Porter (ed.), *Competition in Global Industries*, Boston, Mass.: Harvard Business School Press, pp. 61–79.

Ghoshal, S. (1986) "The innovative multinational: A differentiated network of organizational roles and management processes," unpublished doctoral dissertation, Harvard Business School.

Ghoshal, S. (1987) "Global strategy: An organizing framework," *Strategic Management Journal* 8, pp. 425–440.

Ghoshal, S. and Bartlett, C. A. (1988) "Creation, adoption, and diffusion of innovations by subsidiaries of multinational companies, *Journal of International Business Studies* 19:3, pp. 365–387.

Ghoshal, S. and Bartlett, C. A. (1990) "The multinational corporation as an interorganizational network," *Academy of Management Review* 15:4, pp. 603–625.

Ghoshal, S. and Nohria, N. (1990) "Internal differentiation within multinational corporations," *Strategic Management Journal* 10:4, pp. 323–338.

Giddens, A. (1976) *New Rules of Sociological Method*, New York: Basic Books.

Giddens, A. (1984) *The Constitution of Society*, Berkeley, Calif.: University of California Press.

Giddens, A. (1987) "Structuralism, post-structuralism and the production of culture," in A. Giddens and J. H. Turner (eds), *Social Theory Today*, Stanford, Calif.: Stanford University Press, pp. 195–223.

Gilpin, R. (1987) *The Political Economy of International Relations*, Princeton, N.J.: Princeton University Press.

Ginsberg, A. (1990) "Connecting diversification to performance: A sociocognitive approach," *Academy of Management Review* 15, pp. 514–535.

Glendon, M. A., Gordon, M. W., and Osakwe, C. (1994) *Comparative Legal Traditions*, St. Paul, Minn.: West.

Goffman, E. (1959) *The Presentation of Self in Everyday Life*, New York: Doubleday.

Goffman, E. (1974) *Frame Analysis*, New York: Harper and Row.

Golding, A. M. (1971) "Semiconductor industry in Britain and the United States: A case study in innovation, growth and diffusion of technology," unpublished PhD dissertation, University of Sussex, Brighton.

Goold, M. and Campbell, A. (2002) *Designing Effective Organizations: How to Create Structured Networks*, San Francisco: Jossey-Bass.

Gottdiener, M. (1982) "Disneyland: A Utopian urban space," *Urban Life* 11, pp. 139–162.

Gouldner, A. (1954) *Patterns of Industrial Bureaucracy*, New York: Free Press.

Graham, E. and Krugman, P. (1989) *Foreign Direct Investment in the United States*, Washington: Institute for International Economics.

Granovetter, M. (1973) "The strength of weak ties," *American Journal of Sociology* 81, pp. 1287–1303.

Granovetter, M. (1985) "Economic action and social structure: The problem of embeddedness," *American Journal of Sociology* 91:3, pp. 481–510.

Granovetter, M. (2001) "A theoretical agenda for economic sociology," in M. F. Guillén, R. Collins, P. England, and M. Meyer (eds), *Economic Sociology for a New Millennium*, New York: Russell Sage Foundation.

References

Greenberg, J. (1986) "Determinants of perceived fairness of performance evaluations," *Journal of Applied Psychology* 71, pp. 340–342.

Greenberg, J. (1987a) "A taxonomy of organizational justice theories," *Academy of Management Review* 12:1, pp. 9–22.

Greenberg, J. (1987b) "Using diaries to promote procedural justice in performance appraisals," *Social Justice Research* 1, pp. 219–234.

Greenberg, J. and Folger, R. (1983) "Procedural justice, participation, and the fair process effect in groups and organizations," in P. Paulus (ed.), *Basic Group Process*, New York: Springer-Verlag.

Grover, R. (1997) *The Disney Touch: Disney, ABC and the Quest for the World's Greatest Empire*, rev. edn, Chicago: Irwin.

Guillén, M. F. (1994) *Models of Management: Work, Authority, and Organization in a Comparative Perspective*, Chicago: University of Chicago Press.

Guillén, M. F. (2000a) "Business groups in emerging economies: A resource-based view," *Academy of Management Journal* 43:3, pp. 362–380.

Guillén, M. F. (2000b) "Corporate governance and globalization: Is there convergence across countries?" *Advances in International Comparative Management* 13, pp. 175–204.

Guillén, M. F. (2000c) "Organized labor's images of multinational enterprise: Divergent ideologies of foreign investment in Argentina, South Korea, and Spain," *Industrial and Labor Relations Review* 53:3, pp. 419–442.

Guillén, M. F. (2001a) "Is globalization civilizing, destructive or feeble? A critique of five key debates in the social-science literature," *Annual Review of Sociology* 27.

Guillén, M. F. (2001b) *The Limits of Convergence: Globalization and Organizational Change in Argentina, South Korea, and Spain*, Princeton, N.J.: Princeton University Press.

Gupta, A. K. and Govindarajan, V. (1991) "Knowledge flows and the structure of control within multinational corporations," *Academy of Management Review* 16:4, pp. 768–792.

Gupta, A. K. and Govindarajan, V. (2000) "Knowledge flows within the multinational corporations," *Strategic Management Journal* 21:4, pp. 473–496.

Gurr, T. R. and Jaggers, K. (2000) *Polity98 Project: Regime Characteristics, 1800–1998* [online] www.bsos.umd.edu/cidcm/polity.

Gusfield, J. (1981) *The Culture of Public Problems*, Chicago, Ill.: University of Chicago Press.

Guth, W. D. and MacMillan, I. C. (1986) Strategy implementation versus middle management self-interest. *Strategic Management Journal* 7, pp. 313–327.

Haggard, S. (1989) "The political economy of foreign direct investment in Latin America," *Latin American Research Review* 24, pp. 184–208.

Haggard, S. (1990) *Pathways from the Periphery: The Politics of Growth in the Newly Industrializing Countries*, Ithaca, NY: Cornell University Press.

Hagstrom, P. (1990) "New information systems and the changing structure of MNCs," in C. S. Bartlett, Y. Doz, and G. Hedlund (eds), *Managing the Global Firm*, London and New York: Routledge.

Hall, R. H., Clark, J. P., Giordano, P. C., Johnson, P. V., and Roekel, M. V. (1977) "Patterns of interorganizational relationships," *Administrative Science Quarterly* 22:3, pp. 457–471.

Halle, D. (1984) *America's Working Man,* Chicago, Ill.: University of Chicago Press.

Hamel, G. (1990) "A theory of competitive collaboration," doctoral dissertation, University of Michigan.

Hamel, G. and Prahalad, C. K. (1985) "Do you really have a global strategy?" *Harvard Business Review* July–August, pp. 139–148.

Hamel, G. and Prahalad, C. K. (1989) "Strategic intent," *Harvard Business Review*, 67:3, May/June, pp. 63–76.

313

References

Hamel, G. and Prahalad, C. K. (1990) "The core competence of the corporation," *Harvard Business Review* 68:3, pp. 79–91.

Hamilton, G. G. and Biggart, N. W. (1988) "Market, culture, and authority: A comparative analysis of management and organization in the Far East," *American Journal of Sociology* 94, S52–S94.

Hannan, M. T. and Freeman, J. (1977) "The population ecology of organizations," *American Journal of Sociology* 82, pp. 929–964.

Hannan, M. T. and Freeman, J. (1984) "Structural inertia and organizational change," *American Sociological Review* 49, pp. 149–164.

Hannan, M. T. and Freeman, J. (1989) *Organizational Ecology*, Cambridge, Mass.: Harvard University Press.

Hannerz, U. (1989) "Scenarios of peripheral cultures," paper presented at the Symposium on Culture, Globalization and the World-System, State University of New York at Binghamton, April 1.

Hannerz, U. (1992) *Cultural Complexity: Studies in the Social Organization of Meaning*, New York: Columbia University Press.

Harrigan, K. (1985) *Strategies for Joint Ventures*, Lexington, Mass.: Lexington Books.

Harrington, M. (1979) "To the Disney station," *Harper's*, January, pp. 35–39.

Harris, N. (1990) *Cultural Excursions*, Chicago, Ill.: University of Chicago Press.

Harvey-Jones, J. (1988) *Making it Happen: Reflections on Leadership*, Glasgow: Fontana/Collins.

Hayek, F. (1945) "The use of knowledge in society," *American Economic Review* 35, pp. 519–530.

Heckscher, C. A. and Donnellon, A. (eds) (1994) *The Post-Bureaucratic Organization*, Newbury Park, Calif.: Sage.

Hedlund, G. (1980) "The role of foreign subsidiaries in strategic decision-making in Swedish multinational corporations," *Strategic Management Journal* 9, pp. 23–26.

Hedlund, G. (1981) "Autonomy of subsidiaries and formalization of headquarters–subsidiary relationships in Swedish MNCs," in L. Otterbeck (ed.), *The Management of Headquarter Subsidiary Relationships in Multinational Corporations*, Aldershot: Gower, pp. 25–78.

Hedlund, G. (1986) "The hypermodern MNC: A heterarchy?" *Human Resource Management* 25, pp. 9–35.

Hedlund, G. (1988) "The first theory of hierarchy: Contemplation of its pervasiveness in modern business life," Research Paper 88/4, Institute of International Business.

Hedlund, G. (1994) "A model of knowledge management and the N-form corporation," *Strategic Management Journal, Special Issue on "Strategy—Search for New Paradigms,"* pp. 73–90.

Hedlund, G. and Ridderstrale, J. (1995) "International development projects: Key to competitiveness, impossible, or mismanaged?" *International Studies of Management and Organization* 25:1/2, pp. 158–184.

Hedlund, G. and Rolander, D. (1990) "Action in heterarchies: New approaches to managing the MNC," in C. A. Bartlett, Y. Doz, and G. Hedlund (eds), *Managing the Global Firm*, London and New York: Routledge.

Heenan, D. A. and Perlmutter, H. V. (1979) *Multinational Organization Development: A Social Architecture Perspective*, Reading, Mass.: Addison-Wesley.

Henisz, W. J. (2000a) "The institutional environment for economic growth," *Economics and Politics* 12, pp. 1–31.

Henisz, W. J. (2000b) "The institutional environment for multinational investment," *Journal of Law, Economics and Organization* 16, pp. 334–364.

Henisz, W. J. (2000c) *The Political Constraint Index Database* [online] http://www.management.wharton.upenn.edu/henisz/POLCON/ContactInfo.html.

References

Henisz, W. J. and Delios, A. (2001) "Organizational, imitative and network learning about the policy environment: Plant location decisions of Japanese multinational corporations, 1990–96," Working Paper, Wharton School.

Henisz, W. J. and Williamson, O. E. (1999) "Comparative economic organization— within and between countries," *Business and Politics* 1:3, pp. 261–277.

Hennart, J. F. (1982) *A Theory of Multinational Enterprise*, Ann Arbor: University of Michigan Press.

Hennart, J. F. (1988) "Upstream vertical integration in the aluminium and tin industries," *Journal of Economic Behavior and Organization* 9, pp. 281–299.

Hennart, J. F. (1989) "A model of the choice between firms and markets," Working Paper, Wharton School.

Herbert, T. T. (1984) "Strategy and multinational organization structure: an interorganizational relations perspective," *Academy of Management Review* 9, pp. 259–270.

Herbst, P. G. (1974) *Socio-Technical Design*, London: Tavistock.

Heritage, J. C. (1987) "Ethnomethodology," in A. Giddens and J. H. Turner (eds), *Social Theory Today*, Stanford, Calif.: Stanford University Press, pp. 224–272.

Herriot, S., Levinthal, D., and March, J. (1985) "Learning from experience in organizations," *American Economic Review Papers and Proceedings* 75, pp. 298–302.

Herzberg, F., Mausner, B., and Snyderman, B. B. (1959) *The Motivation to Work*, New York: Wiley.

Hill, C. W. L. and Kim, W. C. (1988) "Searching for a dynamic theory of the multinational enterprise; A transaction cost model," *Strategic Management Journal* 9, pp. 93–104.

Hirsch, P. M. (1972) "Processing fads and fashions: An organization-set analysis of cultural industry systems," *American Journal of Sociology* 77, pp. 639–659.

Hirsch, S. (1976) "An international trade and investment theory of the firm," *Oxford Economic Papers* 28, pp. 258–270.

Hofstadter, D. R. (1980) *Godel, Escher, Bach: An Eternal Golden Braid*, New York: Penguin.

Hofstede, G. (1980a) *Culture's Consequences: International Differences in Work-Related Values*, Newbury Park, Calif.: Sage.

Hofstede, G. (1980b) "Motivation, leadership and organization: Do American theories apply abroad?" *Organizational Dynamics*, Summer, pp. 42–63.

Hofstede, G. (1991) *Culture and Organizations*, New York: McGraw-Hill.

Holm, J. (1988) *Pidgins and Creoles, Vol. 1*, New York: Cambridge University Press.

Homans, G. (1974) *Social Behavior: Its Elementary Forms*, 2nd edn, New York: Harcourt, Brace.

Hoogvelt, A. and Puxty, A. G. (1987) *Multinational Enterprise: An Encyclopedic Dictionary of Concepts and Terms*, London: Macmillan.

Hout, T., Porter, M. E., and Rudden, E. (1982) "How global companies win out," *Harvard Business Review*, September–October, pp. 98–108.

Hrebiniak, L. G. and Joyce, W. J. (1985) "Organizational adaptation: Strategic choice and environmental determinism," *Administrative Science Quarterly* 30:3, pp. 36–49.

Huber, G. P. (1982) "Organizational information systems: Determinants of their performance and behavior," *Management Science* 28:2, pp. 138–155.

Huber, G. P. (1990) "A theory of the effects of advanced information technologies on organizational design, intelligence, and decision making," *Academy of Management Review* 15, pp. 47–71.

Hulbert, J. M. and Brandt, W. K. (1980) *Managing the Multinational Subsidiary*, New York: Holt, Rinehart and Winston.

Hymer, S. (1960) "The international operations of national firms," dissertation, MIT; published Cambridge, Mass.: MIT Press, 1976.

315

Hymer, S. (1970) "The efficiency (contradictions) of multinational corporations," *American Economic Review* 60, pp. 441–448.

Hymer, S. H. (1976) *The International Operations of National Firms: A Study of Direct Investment*, Cambridge, Mass.: MIT Press.

ICRG (1996) *International Country Risk Guide: Political and Financial Risk Tables*, East Syracuse, NY: Political Risk Services Group.

Inglehart, R. and Baker, W. E. (2000) "Modernization, cultural change, and the persistence of traditional values," *American Sociological Review* 65, pp. 19–51.

Iyer, G. R. (1997) "Comparative marketing: An interdisciplinary framework for institutional analysis," *Journal of International Business Studies* 28:3, pp. 531–561.

Iyer, P. (1988) *Video Nights in Kathmandu*, New York: Vintage.

Jackell, R. (1988) *Moral Mazes*, New York: Oxford University Press.

Jaeger, A. M. (1983) "The transfer of organizational culture overseas," *Journal of International Business Studies* 14:2, pp. 91–105.

Janis, T. I. (1972) *Victims of Groupthink*, Boston: Houghton Mifflin.

Jensen, M. C. and Meckling, W. H. (1976) "Theory of the firm: Managerial behavior, agency costs and capital structure," *Journal of Financial Economics* 3, pp. 305–360.

Jones, M. O., Moore, M. D., and Snyder, R. C. (eds) (1988) *Inside Organizations*, Newbury Park, Calif.: Sage.

Kadushin, C. (1978) "Introduction to macro-network analysis," manuscript, Columbia University Teacher's College.

Kamata, S. (1980) *Japan in the Passing Lane*, New York: Random House.

Kanter, R. (1972) *Commitment and Community*, Cambridge, Mass.: Harvard University Press.

Kasson, J. F. (1978) *Amusing the Millions*, New York: Hill and Wang.

Katz, D. (1964) "The Motivational Basis of Organizational Behavior," *Behavioral Science* 9, pp. 131–146.

Kidder, T. (1981) *Soul of the New Machine*, Boston, Mass.: Little Brown.

Kilduff, M. and Abolafia, M. Y. (1989) "The social destruction of reality: Organizational conflict as social drama," Working Paper 89/24, Fontainebleau, France: INSEAD.

Kilduff, M. and Angelmar, R. (1989) "Shared history or shared culture? The effects of time, culture, and performance on institutionalization in simulated organizations," Working Paper 89/05, Fontainebleau, France: INSEAD.

Kim, W. C. and Mauborgne, R. A. (1988) "Becoming an effective global competitor," *Journal of Business Strategy*, January–February, pp. 33–37.

Kim, W. C. and Mauborgne, R. A. (1989) "Assessing the administrative forms for managing the modern multinational," Michigan Business School: mimeo.

Kim, W. C. and Mauborgne, R. A. (1991) "Implementing global strategies: The role of procedural justice," *Strategic Management Journal*.

Kim, W. C. and Mauborgne, R. A. (1993a) "Procedural justice, attitudes, and subsidiary top management compliance with multinationals' corporate strategic decisions," *Academy of Management Journal* 36:3, pp. 502–526.

Kim, W. C. and Mauborgne, R. A. (1993b) "Making global strategies work," *Sloan Management Review* Spring, pp. 11–27.

Kim, W. C. and Mauborgne, R. A. (1993c) "Effectively conceiving and executing multinationals' worldwide strategies," *Journal of International Business Studies* 24:3, pp. 419–448.

Kim, W. C. and Mauborgne, R. A. (1995) "A procedural justice model of strategic decision making: Strategy content implications in the multinational," *Organization Science* 6:1, pp. 44–61.

Kim, W. C. and Mauborgne, R. A. (1996) "Procedural justice and managers' in-role and extra-role behavior: The case of the multinational," *Management Science* April, pp. 499–515.

Kim, W. C. and Mauborgne, R. A. (1997) "Fair process: Managing in the knowledge economy," *Harvard Business Review* 75:4, pp. 65–75.

Kim, W. C. and Mauborgne, R. A. (1998) "Procedural justice, strategic decision making, and the knowledge economy," *Strategic Management Journal.* 19, pp. 328–338.

Kim, W. C. and Mauborgne, R. A. (2003) "How to earn commitment," in J. Pickford (ed.), *Mastering People Management: Your Single Source Guide to Becoming a Master of People Management,* Financial Times/Prentice Hall, pp. 123–126.

Kimberly, J. (1975) "Environmental constraints and organizational structure: A comparative analysis of rehabilitation organizations," *Administrative Science Quarterly* 20, pp. 1–9.

Kimura, Y. (1989) "Firm specific strategic advantages and foreign direct investment behavior of firms," *Journal of International Business Studies* 10:2, pp. 296–314.

Kindleberger, C. P. (1969) *American Business Abroad,* New Haven and London: Yale University Press.

Kindleberger, C. P. (1973) *International Economics,* 5th edn, Homewood, Ill.: Irwin.

King, M. J. (1981) "Disneyland and Walt Disney World: Traditional values in futuristic form," *Journal of Popular Culture* 15, pp. 116–140.

Klein, B., Crawford, R., and Alchian, A. (1978) "Vertical integration, appropriable rents, and the competitive contracting process," *Journal of Law and Economics* 21, pp. 297–326.

Klein, S., Frazier, G. L., and Roth, V. J. (1990) "A transaction cost analysis model of channel integration in international markets," *Journal of Marketing Research* 27, pp. 196–208.

Kmetz, J. L. (1984) "An information-processing study of a complex workflow in aircraft electronics repair," *Administrative Science Quarterly* 29, pp. 255–280.

Kobrin, S. J. (1976) "The environmental determinants of foreign direct manufacturing investment; An ex-post empirical analysis," *Journal of International Business Studies* 7, pp. 29–42.

Kobrin, S. (1982) *Managing Political Risk Assessment: Strategic Response to Environmental Change,* Berkeley: University of California Press.

Kobrin, S. (1987) "Testing the bargaining hypothesis in the manufacturing sector in developing countries," *International Organization* 41, pp. 608–638.

Kobrin, S. (1988) "Expatriate reduction and strategic control in American multinational corporations," *Human Resource Management* 27:1, pp. 63–75.

Kobrin, S. J., Basek, J., Blank, S., and La Palombara, J. (1980) "The assessment and evaluation of noneconomic environments by American firms: A preliminary report," *Journal of International Business Studies* 11, pp. 32–46.

Kocka, J. and Siegrist, H. (1979) "Die hundert groessten deutschen Industrieunternehmen im spaeten 19. und fruehen 20. Jarhhundert. Expansion, Diversifikation und Integration im internationalen Vergleich," in N. Horn and J. Kocka (eds), *Law and the Formation of the Big Enterprises in the 19th and Early 20th Centuries,* Goettingen: Vandenhoeck & Ruprecht.

Koestler, A. (1978) *Janus—A Summing Up,* New York: Random House.

Kogut, B. (1983) "Foreign direct investment as a sequential process," in C. Kindleberger and D. Andretsch (eds), *The Multinational Corporation in the 1980s,* Cambridge, Mass.: MIT Press, pp. 38–56.

Kogut, B. (1985a) "Designing global strategies: Comparative and competitive value added chains," *Sloan Management Review,* Summer, pp. 15–28.

Kogut, B. (1985b) "Designing global strategies: Profiting from operational flexibility," *Sloan Management Review,* Fall, pp. 27–38.

Kogut, B. (1988) "Country patterns in international competition: Appropriability and oligopolistic agreement," in N. Hood and J. E. Vahlne (eds), *Strategies in Global Competition*, London: Croom-Helm.

Kogut, B. (1989) "A note on global strategies," *Strategic Management Journal* 10, pp. 383–389.

Kogut, B. (1990) "The permeability of borders and the speed of learning among countries," *Globalization of Firms and the Competitiveness of Nations*, Crafoord Lectures, University of Lund.

Kogut, B. (1991) "Country capabilities and the permeability of borders," *Strategic Management Journal* 12, pp. 33–47.

Kogut, B. (1992) "National organizing principles of work and the erstwhile dominance of the American multinational corporation," *Industrial and Corporate Change* 1, pp. 285–326.

Kogut, B. (ed.) (1993) *Country Competitiveness: Technology and the Organization of Work*, Oxford: Oxford University Press.

Kogut, B. and Chang, S. J. (1991) "Technological capabilities and Japanese foreign direct investment in the United States," *Review of Economics and Statistics* 73, pp. 401–413.

Kogut, B., Shan, W. J., and Walker, G. (1990) "The structuring of an industry: embeddedness among bio-technology firms," mimeo.

Kogut, B. and Singh, H. (1988) "The effect of national culture on the choice of entry mode," *Journal of International Business Studies* 19:3, pp. 411–432.

Kogut, B. and Zander, U. (1992) "The knowledge of the firm and the replication of technology," *Organization Science* 3, pp. 383–397.

Kogut, B. and Zander, U. (1993) "Knowledge of the firm and the evolutionary theory of the multinational enterprise," *Journal of International Business Studies* 24, pp. 625–645.

Kogut, B. and Zander, U. (1995) "Knowledge, market failure and the multinational enterprise: A reply," (with U. Zander), *Journal of International Business Studies* 26:2, pp. 417–426.

Kolde, E. J. (1985) *Environment of International Business*, 2nd edn, Boston, Mass.: Kent.

Kondo, D. (1990) *Crafting Selves: Power, Gender, and Discourses of Identity in a Japanese Workplace*, Chicago: University of Chicago Press.

Korine, H. D. (1997) "Managing innovation teams: A procedural justice perspective," unpublished doctoral dissertation, INSEAD.

Korsgaard, A., Schweiger, D., and Sapienza, H. (1995) "Building commitment, attachment, and trust in strategic decision-making teams: The role of procedural justice," *Academy of Management Review* 38:1, pp. 60–84.

Kostova, T. and Zaheer, S. (1999) "Organizational legitimacy under conditions of complexity: The case of the multinational enterprise," *Academy of Management Review* 24:1, pp. 64–81.

Krackhardt, D. (1989) "Graph theoretical dimensions of the informal organization," presentation at the European Institute of Business Administration, Fontainebleau, France: INSEAD.

Krackhardt, D. and Kilduff, M. (1990) "Friendship patterns and culture: The control of organization," *American Anthropologist* 92, pp. 142–154.

Kreps, D. (1984) "Corporate culture and economic theory," Working Paper, Stanford Graduate School of Business, Stanford University.

Kristensen, P. H. and Zeitlin, J. (2005) *Local Players in Global Games: The Strategic Constitution of a Multinational Corporation*. Oxford: Oxford University Press.

Kuin, P. (1972) "The magic of multinational management," *Harvard Business Review*, Nov–Dec., pp. 89–97.

References

Kunda, G. (1992) *Engineering Culture: Control and Commitment in a High-Tech Corporation*, Philadelphia: Temple University Press.

Kyriazi, G. (1981) *The Great American Amusement Parks*, Los Angeles: Castle Books.

La Porta, R., Lopez-de-Silanes, F., and Shleifer, A. (1999) "Corporate ownership around the world," *Journal of Finance* 54:2, pp. 471–517.

La Porta, R., Lopez-de-Silanes, F., Shleifer, A., and Vishny, R. (1998) "Law and finance," *Journal of Political Economy* 106:6, pp. 1113–1155.

La Porta, R., Lopez-de-Silanes, F., Shleifer, A., and Vishny, R. (1999) "The quality of government," *Journal of Law, Economics and Organization* 15, pp. 222–279.

La Tour, S. (1978) "Determinants of participant and observer satisfaction with adversary and inquisitorial modes of adjudication," *Journal of Personality and Social Psychology* 36, pp. 1531–1545.

Landsberger, Henry A. (1961) "The horizontal dimension in bureaucracy," *Administrative Science Quarterly* 6, pp. 299–332.

Latour, B. (1987) *Science in Action*, Cambridge, Mass.: Harvard University Press.

Laumann, E. O., Glaskiewicz, J., and Marsden, P. V. (1978) "Community structure as interorganizational linkages," *Annual Review of Sociology* 4, pp. 455–484.

Laumann, E. O., Marsden, P. V., and Prensky, D. (1983) "The boundary specification problem in network analysis," in R. S. Burt, M. J. Minor, and associates (eds), *Applied Network Analysis: A Methodological Introduction*, Beverly Hills, Calif.: Sage.

Laumann, E. O. and Pappi, F. (1976) *Networks of Collective Action: A Perspective on Community Influence Systems*, New York: Academic Press.

Laurent, A. (1983) "The cultural diversity of Western conceptions of management," *International Studies of Management and Organization* 13, pp. 75–96.

Laurent, A. (1986) "The cross-cultural puzzle of international human resource management," *Human Resource Management* 25, pp. 91–102.

Lawrence, C. (1983) "Nissan's way," *Miami Herald*, June 26, p. 5F.

Lawrence, P. R. and Dyers, D. (1983) *Renewing American Industry: Organizing for Efficiency and Innovation*, New York: Free Press.

Lawrence, P. R. and Lorsch, J. W. (1967) *Organization and Environment*, Homewood, Ill.: Irwin.

Lazarsfeld, P. F. and Menzel, H. (1961) "On the relation between individual and collective properties," in A. Etzioni (ed.), *Complex Organizations: A Sociological Reader*, New York: Holt, Rinehart and Winston, pp. 499–516.

Leach, E. R. (1976) *Culture and Communication*, Cambridge: Cambridge University Press.

Lehman, E. W. (1975) *Coordinating Health Care: Explorations in Interorganizational Relations*, Beverly Hills, Calif.: Sage.

Leidner, R. (2003) *Fast Food, Fast Talk: Service Work and the Routinization of Everyday Life*. Berkeley: University of California Press.

Lessard, D. and Lightstone, J. B. (1986) "Volatile exchange rates can put operations at risk," *Harvard Business Review*, July–August, pp. 107–114.

Leventhal, G. S. (1990) "What should be done with equity theory? New approaches to the study of fairness in social relationships," in K. Gergen, M. Greenberg, and R. Willis (eds), *Social Exchange: Advances in Theory and Research*, New York: Plenum Press.

Leventhal, G. S., Karuza, J., and Fry, W. R. (1980) "Beyond fairness: A theory of allocation preferences," in G. Mikula (ed.), *Justice and Social Interaction*, New York: Springer-Verlag.

Levinthal, D. (1988) "A survey of agency models of organization," *Journal of Economic Behavior and Organization* 9, pp. 153–185.

Levitt, B. and March, J. G. (1987) "Organizational learning," *Annual Review of Sociology* 14, pp. 319–340.

References

Levitt, T. (1983) "The globalization of markets," *Harvard Business Review* 61:3, pp. 92–102.

Li, J. and Guisinger, S. (1990) "Comparative business failures of foreign controlled firms in the United States," paper presented at the Doctoral Consortium for International Management, American Adademy of Management Conference, San Francisco, August 11–15.

Liberman, L. and Torbiörn, I. (2000) "Variances in staff-related management practices at eight European country subsidiaries of a global firm," *International Journal of Human Resource Management* 11, pp. 37–59.

Lincoln, J., Hanada, M., and McBride, K. (1986) "Organizational structures in Japanese and U.S. manufacturing," *Administrative Science Quarterly* 31, pp. 338–364.

Lind, E. A., Kurtz, S., Musante, L., Walker, L., and Thibaut, J. W. (1980) "Procedure and outcome effects on reactions to adjudicated resolution of conflicts of interests," *Journal of Personality and Social Psychology* 39, pp. 643–653.

Lind, E. A. and Tyler, T. R. (1988) *The Social Psychology of Procedural Justice*, New York: Plenum Press.

Lorange, P., Scott Morton, M. S., and Ghoshal, S. (1986) *Strategic Control*, West Publishing, St Paul, Minn.

Lowenthal, D. (1985) *The Past is a Foreign Country*, Cambridge: University of Cambridge Press.

Lubatkin, M., Calori, R., Very, P., and Veiga, J. (1998) "Managing mergers across borders: A two-nation exploration of a nationally bound administrative heritage," *Organization Science* 9:6, pp. 670–684.

Luustorinen, R. and Welch, L. (1989) "Internationalization: Evolution of a concept," *Journal of General Management* 14, pp. 34–55.

MacCannell, D. (1976) *The Tourist*, New York: Schocken Books.

Madhok, A. (1996) "The organization of economic activity: Transactions costs, firm capabilities, and the nature of governance" *Organization Science* 7:5, pp. 577–590.

Magee, S. P. (1977) "Information and the multinational corporation: An appropriability theory of direct foreign investment," in J. N. Bhagwati (ed.), *The New International Economic Order: The North–South Debate*, Cambridge, Mass.: MIT Press, pp. 317–346.

Mahini, A. and Wells, L. T. (1986) "Government relations in the global firm," in M. E. Porter (ed.), *Competition in Global Industries*, Boston, Mass.: Harvard Business School Press, pp. 391–314.

Manning, P. K. (1989) *Signifying Calls*, Cambridge, Mass.: TMIT Press.

March, J. G. and Olsen, J. P. (1980) *Ambiguity and Choice in Organizations*, 2nd edn, Oxford: Oxford University Press.

March, J. G. and Simon, H. A. (1958) *Organizations*, New York: Wiley.

Marcus, G. E. (1998) *Ethnography through Thick and Thin*, Princeton, N.J.: Princeton University Press.

Marcus, G. E. and Fischer, M. (1986) *Anthropology as Cultural Critique*, Chicago, Ill.: University of Chicago Press.

Marin, L. (1977) "Disneyland: A degenerate Utopia," *Glyph I*, Johns Hopkins Textual Studies, Baltimore, Md.: Johns Hopkins University Press, pp. 50–66.

Martin, J. (2002) *Organizational Culture: Mapping the Terrain*, Thousand Oaks, Calif.: Sage.

Martinez, J. and Jarillo, J. C. (1989) "The evolution of research on coordination mechanisms in multinational corporations," *Journal of International Business Studies*, Fall, 20:3, pp. 489–514.

Maruyama, M. (1978) "The epistemological revolution," *Futures*, June, pp. 240–242.

Mathias, D. (1978) "The role of the logistics system in strategic change," unpublished doctoral dissertation, Harvard Business School.

McClelland, D. (1961) *The Achieving Society*, New York: Free Press.

McCulloch, W. (1965) *Embodiments of Mind*, Cambridge, Mass.: MIT Press.

McManus, J. C. (1972) "The theory of the international firm," in G. Paquet (ed.), *Multinational Firm and the Nation State*, Don Mills, Ontario: Collier Macmillan.

Merton, R. K. (1936) "The unanticipated consequences of purposive social action," *American Sociological Review* 1: 6, pp. 894–904.

Meyer, J. W. and Hannan, M. T. (1979) *National Development and the World System: Educational, Economic, and Political Change 1950–1970*, Chicago: University of Chicago Press.

Meyer, J. W. and Rowan, B. (1977) "Institutionalized organizations: Formal structures as myth and ceremony," *American Journal of Sociology* 83, pp. 340–363.

Meyer, J. W. and Scott, W. R. (1983) *Organizational Environments: Ritual and Rationality*, Beverly Hills, Calif.: Sage.

Meyer, J. W., Scott, W. R., and Deal, T. E. (1983) "Institutional and technical sources of organizational structure: Explaining the structure of educational organizations," in J. W. Meyer and W. R. Scott (eds), *Organizational Environments: Ritual and Rationality*, Beverly Hills: Sage, pp. 45–70.

Meyer, M. W. and Zucker, L. G. (1989) *Permanently Failing Organizations*, Newbury Park, Calif.: Sage.

Mezias, S. J. (1990) "An institutional model of organizational practice: Financial reporting in the Fortune 200," *Administrative Science Quarterly* 35:3, pp. 431–457.

Miller, W. (1955) "Two concepts of authority," *American Anthropologist* 57, pp. 271–289.

Mintzberg, H. (1973) *The Nature of Managerial Work*, New York: Harper and Row.

Mintzberg, H. (1979) *The Structuring of Organizations*, Englewood Cliffs, N.J.: Prentice-Hall.

Mintzberg, H., Raisinghani, D., and Theoret, A. (1976) "The structure of 'unstructured' decision processes," *Administrative Science Quarterly* 21, pp. 246–275.

Mirrlees, J. (1976) "The optimal structure of incentives and authority within an organization," *Bell Journal of Economics* 7, Spring, pp. 105–131.

Mitchell, J. C. (1973) "Networks, norms and institutions," in J. Boissevain and J. C. Mitchell (eds), *Network Analysis*, The Hague: Mouton, pp. 15–35.

Mohr, L. B. (1969) "Determinants of innovation in organizations," *American Political Science Review* 63, pp. 111–136.

Montagna, P. (1990) "Accounting rationality and financial legitimation," in S. Zukin and P. DiMaggio (eds), *Structures of Capital*, Cambridge: Cambridge University Press, pp. 227–260.

Monteverde, K. and Teece, D. J. (1982) "Supplier switching costs and vertical integration in the automobile industry," *Bell Journal of Economics* 13, pp. 206–213.

Moore, A. (1980) "Walt Disney's world: Bounded ritual and the playful pilgrimage center," *Anthropological Quarterly* 53, pp. 207–218.

Moorman, R. H. (1991) "The relationship between organizational justice and organizational citizenship behaviors: Do fairness perceptions influence employee citizenship?" *Journal of Applied Psychology* 76, pp. 845–855.

Moorman, R. H., Organ, D. W., and Niefhoff, B. P. (1991) "Do fairness principles influence employee citizenship? A report of two studies on the relationship between three dimensions of organizational justice and organizational citizenship behavior," paper presented at the annual meeting of the Academy of Management Journal, Miami Beach Florida.

Moran, T. H. (ed.) (1985) *Multinational Corporations: The Political Economy of Foreign Direct Investment*, Lexington, Mass.: Lexington Books.

References

Morgan, G. (1986) *Images of Organization*, Newbury Park and London: Sage.

Morgan, G., Kristensen, P. H., and Whitley, R. (eds) (2001) *The Multinational Firm: Organizing across Institutional and National Divides*, Oxford: Oxford University Press.

Morrill, C. (1995) *The Executive Way: Conflict Management in a Corporation*, Chicago: University of Chicago Press.

Mowday, R. T., Steers, R. M., and Porter, L. W. (1979) "The measurement of organizational commitment," *Journal of Vocational Behavior* 14, pp. 224–247.

Myerhoff, B. (1983) "The tamed and colonized imagination in Disneyland," unpublished paper, Department of Anthropology, University of Southern California.

Nadler, D. A. and Tushman, M. L. (1997) *Competing by Design: The Power of Organizational Architecture*, New York: Oxford University Press.

Nakane, C. (1970) *Japanese Society*, Berkeley: University of California Press.

Negandhi, A. R. and Baliga, R. (eds) (1980) *Functioning of the Multinational Corporation*, Oxford: Pergamon Press.

Negandhi, A. R. and Baliga, R. (1981) "Internal functioning of American, German and Japanese multinational corporations," in L. Otterbeck (ed.), *The Management of Headquarter Subsidiary Relationships in Multinational Corporations*, Aldershot: Gower, pp. 107–120.

Nelson, R. (ed.) (1993) *National Innovation Systems*, New York: Oxford University Press.

Nelson, R. and Winter, S. (1982) *An Evolutionary Theory of Economic Change*, Cambridge, Mass.: Harvard University Press.

Newman, W. H. (1975) *Constructive Control*, Englewood Cliffs, N.J.: Prentice-Hall.

Nishiguchi, T. (1989) "Strategic dualism: An alternative in industrial societies," unpublished dissertation, Nuffield College.

Nohria, N. and Ghoshal, S. (1989) "The MNC as a differentiated network," unpublished paper, Boston, Mass.: Harvard Business School.

Nohria, N. and Ghoshal, S. (1997) *The Differentiated Network: Organizing Multinational Corporations for Value Creation*, San Francisco: Jossey-Bass.

Nohria, N. and Venkatraman, N. (1987) "Interorganizational information systems via information technology: A network analytic perspective," Working paper 1909–87, MIT, Sloan School of Management.

Nonaka, I. (1990) "Managing globalization as a self-renewing process: Experiences of Japanese MNCs," in C. A. Bartlett, Y. Doz, and G. Hedlund (eds), *Managing the Global Firm*, London and New York: Routledge.

Norman, R. (1976) *Management and Statesmanship*, Stockholm: SIAR.

North, D. (1981) *Structure and Change in Economic History*, New York: Norton.

North, D. (1990) *Institutions, Institutional Change, and Economic Performance*, New York: W. W. Norton.

North, D. and Thomas, R. (1973) *The Rise of the Western World: A New Economic History*, Cambridge: Cambridge University Press.

Ochs, E. (1988) *Culture and Language Development*, New York: Cambridge University Press.

Ogilvy, J. (1977) *Multidimensional Man*, New York: Oxford University Press.

Ohmae, K. (1985) "The global logic of strategic alliances," *Harvard Business Review* 67:2, pp. 143–154.

Ohmae, K. (1990) *The Borderless World: Management Lessons in the New Logic of the Global Marketplace*, New York: Harper Collins.

O'Reilly, C. and Chatman, J. (1986) "Organizational commitment and psychological attachment: The effects of compliance, identification, and internalization on prosocial behavior," *Journal of Applied Psychology* 71, pp. 492–499.

References

Orru, M., Woolesey Biggart, N., and Hamilton, G. G. (1991) "Organizational isomorphism in East Asia: Broadening the new institutionalism," in P. DiMaggio and W. W. Powell (eds), *The New Institutionalism in Organizational Analysis*, Chicago: University of Chicago Press.

Orru, M., Biggart, N., and Hamilton, G. (1997) *The Economic Organization of East Asian Capitalism*, Thousand Oaks, Calif.: Sage.

Ott, S. (1988) *The Organization Culture Perspective*, Reading, Mass.: Addison-Wesley.

Ouchi, W. (1977) "The relationship between organizational structure and organizational control," *Administrative Science Quarterly* 22, pp. 95–113.

Ouchi, W. G. (1978) "The transmission of control through organizational hierarchy," *Academy of Management Journal* 21:2, pp. 173–192.

Ouchi, W. G. (1979) "A conceptual framework for the design of organizational control mechanisms," *Management Science* 25:9, pp. 833–848.

Ouchi, W. G. (1980) "Markets, bureaucracies and clans," *Administrative Science Quarterly* 25, pp. 129–141.

Ouchi, W. G. (1981a) "A framework for understanding organizational failure," in J. Kimberly and R. Miles (eds), *The Organizational Life Cycle*, San Francisco: Jossey-Bass, pp. 395–430.

Ouchi, W. G. (1981b) *Theory Z*, Reading, Mass.: Addison-Wesley.

Ouchi, W. G. and Wilkins, A. L. (1985) "Organizational culture," *Annual Review of Sociology* 11, pp. 367–411.

Ozawa, T. (1980) "Japanese world of work: An interpretive survey," *MSU Business Topics*, Spring, pp. 45–54.

Paine, L. (1972) *The Hierarchy of Hell*, New York: Hippocrene Books.

Pareto, V. (1976) *Sociological Writings*, Oxford: Blackwell.

Parsons, T. (1937) *The Structure of Social Action*, Glencoe, Ill.: Free Press.

Pattee, H. (1970) "The problem of biological hierarchy," in C. H. Waddington (ed.), *Toward a Theoretical Biology III*, Chicago: Aldine, pp. 117–136.

Paul, J. K. (ed.) (1984) *High Technology International Trade and Competition*, Park Ridge, N.J.: Noyes Publications.

Pavan, R. J. (1972) "The strategy and structure of Italian enterprise," doctoral dissertation, Harvard Graduate School of Business.

Pavitt, K. (1971) "The multinational enterprise and the transfer of technology," in J. H. Dunning (ed.), *The Multinational Enterprise*, London: Allen and Unwin, pp. 61–85.

Pells, R. H. (1997) *Not Like Us: How Europeans have Loved, Hated, and Transformed American Culture since World War II*, New York: Basic Books.

Pennings, J. M. (1975) "The relevance of the structural-contingency model for organizational effectiveness," *Administrative Science Quarterly* 20, pp. 393–410.

Perlmutter, H. V. (1965) "L'enterprise internationale: Trois conceptions," *Revue Economique et Sociale*, no. 23.

Perlmutter, H. V. (1969) "The tortuous evolution of the multinational corporation," *Columbia Journal of World Business*, 4, pp. 9–18.

Perlmutter, H. and Trist, E. (1986) "Paradigms for societal transition," *Human Relations*, 39:1, pp. 1–27.

Perrow, C. (1979) (1986) *Complex Organizations*, 2nd edn, New York: Random House.

Perrow, C. (1984) *Normal Accidents: Living with High-Risk Technologies*, New York: Basic Books.

Perrow, C. (1986) *Complex Organizations: A Critical Essay*, 3rd edn, New York: Random House.

Peters, T. J. (1987) *Thriving on Chaos*, New York: Knopf.

Peters, T. J. and Waterman, R. H. Jr. (1982) *In Search of Excellence*, New York: Harper and Row.

Peterson, R. (1990) "Symbols and social life," *Contemporary Sociology*, 19, pp. 498–500.

Pfeffer, J. R. (1981) *Power in Organizations*, Marshfield: Pittman.

Pfeffer, J. R. and Salancik, G. R. (1974) "The bases and use of power in organizational decision making: The case of a university," *Administrative Science Quarterly* 19, pp. 453–473.

Pfeffer, J. R. and Salancik, G. R. (1978) *The External Control of Organizations: A Resource Dependency Perspective*, New York: Harper and Row.

Polanyi, M. (1944 Reprinted 1957) *The Great Transformation*, Boston, Mass.: Beacon Press.

Polanyi, M. (1958) *Personal Knowledge*, Chicago, Ill.: University of Chicago Press.

Porter, M. E. (1986) *Competition in Global Industries*, Cambridge, Mass.: Harvard Business School Press.

Porter, M. E. (1990) *The Competitive Advantage of Nations*, New York: Free Press.

Powell, W. W. (1985) *Getting Into Print: The Decision-Making Process in Scholarly Publishing*, Chicago, Ill.: University of Chicago Press.

Powell, W. W. (1988) "Institutional effects on organizational structure and performance," in L. G. Zucker (ed.), *Institutional Patterns and Organizations: Culture and Environment*, Cambridge, Mass.: Ballinger, pp. 115–138.

Poynter, T. A. and Rugman, A. M. (1982) "World product mandates: How will multinationals respond?" *Business Quarterly* 47:3, pp. 54–61.

Prahalad, C. K. (1975) "The strategic process in a multinational corporation," unpublished doctoral dissertation, School of Business Administration, Harvard University.

Prahalad, C. K. (1976) "Strategic choices in diversified MNCs," *Harvard Business Review*, July–August, pp. 67–78.

Prahalad, C. K. and Doz, Y. (1980) "Strategic management of diversified multinational companies," in A. Negandhi (ed.), *Functioning of the Multinational Corporation*, New York: Pergamon Press, pp. 77–116.

Prahalad, C. K. and Doz, Y. (1981) "An approach to strategic control in MNCs," *Sloan Management Review*, Summer, pp. 5–13.

Prahalad, C. K., and Doz, Y. (1987) *The Multinational Mission: Balancing Local Demands and Global Vision*, New York: Free Press.

Prahalad, C. K. and Hamel, G. (1990) "The core competence of the corporation," *Harvard Business Review* 90:3, pp. 79–93.

Pratt, J. and Zeckhauser, R. (1985) "Principals and agents: An overview," in J. Pratt and R. Zeckhauser (eds), *Principals and Agents: The Structure of Business*, Cambridge, Mass.: Harvard Business School Press, pp. 1–35.

Provan, K. G. (1983) "The federation as an interorganizational linkage network," *Academy of Management Review* 8, pp. 79–89.

Provan, K. G., Beyer, J. M., and Kruytbosch, C. (1980) "Environmental linkages and power in resource dependence relations between organizations," *Administrative Science Quarterly* 25, pp. 200–225.

Rabinow, P. and Sullivan, A. (eds) (1987) *Interpretive Social Science*, 2nd edn, Berkeley: University of California Press.

Ragin, C. C. (1987) *The Comparative Method*, Berkeley, Calif.: University of California Press.

Raz, A. (1999) *Riding the Black Ship: Japan and Tokyo Disneyland*, Cambridge, Mass.: Harvard University Press.

Real, M. (1977) *Mass-Mediated Culture*, Englewood Cliffs, N.J.: Prentice Hall.

Reibstein, L. (1987) "Firms trim annual pay increases and focus on long term," *Wall Street Journal*, April 10, p. 25.

324

References

Reynolds, T. and Flores, A. (1989) *Foreign Law,* Littleton, Colo.: Rothman.

Ritti, R. R. and Silver, J. H. (1986) "Early processes of institutionalization: The dramaturgy of exchange in interorganizational relations," *Administrative Science Quarterly* 31, pp. 25–42.

Robinson, R. D. (1967) *International Management,* New York: Holt, Rinehart and Winston.

Robinson, R. D. (1978) *International Business Management: A Guide to Decision Making,* 2nd edn, Hinsdale, ill.: Dryden Press.

Robock, S. H., Simmons, K.., and Zwick, J. (1977) *International Business and Multinational Enterprise,* Homewood, Ill.: Irwin.

Rogers, E. (1971) *Diffusion of Innovations,* New York: Free Press.

Rohlen, T. P. (1974) *For Harmony and Strength,* Berkeley: University of California Press.

Rosaldo, R. (1989) *Culture and Truth,* Boston, Mass.: Beacon Press.

Rosenzweig, P. and Singh, J. (1991) "Organizational environments and the multinational enterprise," *Academy of Management Review* 16:2, pp. 340–361.

Roumasset, J. and Uy, M. (1980) "Piece rates, time rates, and teams," *Journal of Economic Behavior and Organization* 1, pp. 343–360.

Rueda-Sabater, E. (2000) "Corporate governance and the bargaining power of developing countries to attract foreign investment," *Corporate Governance* 8, pp. 117–124.

Rugman, A. M. (1980) "A new theory of the multinational enterprise: Internationalization versus internalization," *Columbia Journal of World Business,* Spring, pp. 23–29.

Rugman, A. M. (1981) *Inside the Multinationals: The Economics of Internal Markets,* New York: Columbia University Press.

Sabel, C., Herringel, G., Kazis, R., and Deeg, R. (1987) "How to keep mature industries innovative," *Technology Review* 90:3, pp. 26–35.

Sahlins, M. (1981) *Historical Metaphors and Mythical Realities,* Ann Arbor: University of Michigan Press.

Sassen, J. (1989) "Mickeymania," *International Management,* November, pp. 32–34.

Sayrs, L. W. (1989) *Pooled Time Series Analysis,* Newbury Park, Calif.: Sage.

Schein, E. H. (1961) *Coercive Persuasion,* New York: Norton.

Schein, E. H. (1989) "Reassessing the 'divine rights' of managers," *Sloan Management Review,* Winter, pp. 63–68.

Schein, E. H. (2001) *Organizational Culture and Leadership,* 3rd edn, San Francisco: Jossey-Bass.

Schickel, R. (1968, rev. 1985) *The Disney Version,* New York: Simon and Schuster.

Schumpeter, J. A. (1947) *Capitalism, Socialism and Democracy,* 2nd edn, New York: Harper.

Schwartz, P. and Ogilvy, J. (1979) "The emergent paradigm: Changing patterns of thought and belief," *Analytical Report: Values and Lifestyles Program* 7, April.

Schwartz, T. (1981) "The acquisition of culture," *Ethos* 9, pp. 4–17.

Scott, W. R. (1965) "Field methods in the study of organizations," in J. G. March (ed.), *Handbook of Organizations,* Chicago: Rand McNally, pp. 261–304.

Scott, W. R. (1983) "Health care organizations in the 1980s: The convergence of public and professional control systems," in J. W. Meyer and W. R. Scott (eds), *Organizational Environments: Ritual and Rationality,* Beverly Hills, Calif.: Sage, pp. 99–113.

Scott, W. R. (1987a) *Organizations: Rational, Natural, and Open Systems,* 2nd edn, Englewood Cliffs, N.J.: Prentice-Hall.

Scott, W. R. (1987b) "The adolescence of institutional theory," *Administrative Science Quarterly* 32, pp. 493–511.

References

Scott, W. R. (1995) *Institutions and Organizations*, Thousand Oaks, Calif.: Sage.

Scott, W. R. (1998) *Organizations: Rational, Natural, and Open Systems*, Upper Saddle River, N.J.: Prentice-Hall.

Scott, W. R. and Meyer, J. W. (1983) "The organization of societal sectors," in J. W. Meyer and W. R. Scott (eds), *Organizational Environments: Ritual and Rationality*, Beverley Hills, Calif.: Sage, pp. 129–153.

Scott, W. R. and Meyer, J. W. (1989) "The rise of training programs in firms and agencies: An institutional perspective," Stanford University Working Paper.

Sehlinger, B. (1985) *The Unofficial Guide to Disneyland*, New York: Prentice Hall.

Seiler, E. (1984) "Piece rate vs. time rate: The effect of incentive on earnings," *Review of Economics and Statistics* 66:3, pp. 363–375.

Shapiro, A. (1984) "The evaluation and control of foreign affiliates," *Midland Corporate Finance Journal*, Spring, pp. 13–25.

Shearling, C. D. and Stenning, P. C. (1985) "From the panopticon to Disney World," in R. Ericson (ed.), *Perspectives in Criminal Law*, Toronto: University of Toronto Press, pp. 335–349.

Sheppard, B. H. (1984) "Third-party conflict intervention: A procedural framework," in B. M. Staw and L. L. Cummings (eds), *Research in Organizational Behavior*, Vol. 6, Greenwich, Conn.: JAI Press.

Sheppard, B. H. and Lewicki, R. J. (1987) "Toward general principles of managerial fairness," *Social Justice Research* 1, pp. 161–176.

Shore, B. (1996) *Culture in Mind: Cognition, Culture, and the Problem of Meaning*, New York: Oxford University Press.

Shweder, R. A. (1991) *Thinking through Cultures: Expeditions in Cultural Psychology*, Cambridge, Mass.: Harvard University Press.

Siehl, C. (1985) "After the founder: An opportunity to manage culture," in P. Frost, L. F. Moore, M. R. Louis, C. C. Lundberg, and J. Martin (eds), *Organizational Culture*, Beverly Hills, Calif.: Sage, pp. 125–140.

Simon, H. (1962) "The architecture of complexity," *Proceedings of the American Philosophical Society* 106, pp. 467–482.

Simon, H. (1973) "The organization of complex systems," in H. Pattee (ed.), *Hierarchy Theory*, New York: Braziller.

Simon, H. A. (1977) *The New Science of Management Decision*, rev. edn, Englewood Cliffs, N.J.: Prentice-Hall.

Simon, H. (1981) *The Sciences of the Artificial*, Cambridge, Mass.: MIT Press.

Simon, H. (1989) "Organizations and markets," Working Paper, Carnegie-Mellon University.

Singh, J. V., House, R. J., and Tucker, D. J. (1986) "Organizational change and organizational mortality," *Administrative Science Quarterly* 31, pp. 587–611.

Singh, J. V. and Lumsden, C. J. (1990) "Theory and research in organizational ecology," *Annual Review of Sociology* 16, pp. 161–195.

Smith, K. G., Grimm, C. M., Gannon, M. J., and Chen, M. J. (1991) "Organizational information processing, competitive responses, and performance in the U.S. domestic airline industry," *Academy of Management Journal* 34, pp. 60–85.

Smith, V. (1990) *Managing in the Corporate Interest: Control and Resistance in an American Bank*, Berkeley: University of California Press.

Snyder, M. (1974) "The self-monitoring of expressive behavior," *Journal of Personality and Social Psychology* 30, pp. 526–537.

Snyder, M. (1979) "Self-monitoring processes," *Advances in Experimental Social Psychology* 12, pp. 85–128.

Solomon, J. (1994) "Mickey's trip to trouble," *Newsweek*, February 14, pp. 34–38.

Sontag, S. (1979) *On Photography*, London: Penguin.

References

Spicer, A., McDermott, G., and Kogut, B. (2000) "Entrepreneurship and privatization in Central Europe," *Academy of Management Review* 25, pp. 630–649.

Spinelli, M. L. (1987) "Disneyland and Old Sturbridge Village," paper presented to the Northeastern Anthropological Association, Amherst, Mass.

Spradley, J. P. (1970) *You Owe Yourself a Drunk: An Ethnography of Urban Nomads*, Boston: Little, Brown.

Stallings, B. (1990) "The role of foreign capital in economic development," in G. Gereffi and D. Wyman (eds), *Manufacturing Miracles*, Princeton, N.J.: Princeton University Press, pp. 55–89.

Starbuck, W. (1983) "Organizations as action generators," *American Sociological Review* 48, pp. 91–102.

Steinbruner, J. (1974) *The Cybernetic Theory of Decision: New Dimensions of Political Analysis*, Princeton, N.J.: Princeton University Press.

Stevens, G. V. G. (1974) "The determinants of investment," in J. H. Dunning (ed.), *Economic Analysis and the Multinational Enterprise*, New York: Praeger, pp. 47–88.

Stiglitz, J. E. (1987) "Learning to learn, localized learning and technological progress," in P. Dasgupta and P. Stoneman (eds), *Economic Policy and Technological Performance*, New York: Cambridge University Press.

Stimson, J. A. (1985) "Regression in space and time: A statistical essay," *American Journal of Political Science* 29:4, pp. 914–947.

Stinchcombe, A. L. (1965) "Social structure and organizations," in J. March (ed.), *Handbook of Organizations*, Chicago: Rand McNally, pp. 142–193.

Stockey, J. (1983) *Vertical Integration and Joint Ventures in the Aluminium Industry*, Cambridge, Mass.: Harvard University Press.

Stoffle, R. W. (1975) "Reservation-based industry: A case from Zuni, New Mexico," *Human Organization* 34, pp. 217–225.

Stopford, J. M. and Wells, L. T. Jr. (1972) *Managing the Multinational Enterprise: Organization of the Firm and Ownership of Subsidiaries*, New York: Basic Books.

Stopford, J. M., Dunning, J., and Haberich, K. O. (1980) *The World Directory of Multinational Enterprises*, New York: Facts on File.

Stuart, P. M. (1987) *Nihonsense*, Tokyo: Japan Times.

Suárez, S. (2000) *Does Business Learn? Tax Breaks, Uncertainty, and Political Behavior*, Ann Arbor, Mich.: University of Michigan Press.

Suárez, S. (2001) "Indebted industrialization," *Encyclopedia of International Political Economy*, London and New York: Routledge, pp. 742–743.

Sundaram, A. and Black, J. S. (1992) "The environment and international organization of multinational enterprises," *Academy of Management Review* 17:4, pp. 729–757.

Swidler, A. (1985) "Culture in action," *American Sociological Review* 51, pp. 273–286.

Taylor, C. T. and Silberston, Z. (1973) *The Economic Impact of the Patent System*, Cambridge: Cambridge University Press.

Taylor, J. (1983) *Shadows of the Rising Sun*, New York: William Morrow.

Teece, D. J. (1980) "Economies of scope and the scope of the enterprise," *Journal of Economic Behavior and Organization* 1, pp. 223–247.

Teece, D. (1983) "A transaction cost theory of the multinational enterprise," in M. Casson (ed.), *The Growth of International Business*, London: Allen and Unwin.

Teece, D. (1985) "Multinational enterprise, internal governance and economic organization," *American Economic Review* 75, pp. 233–238.

Teece, D. J. (1986) "Transaction cost economies and the multinational enterprise," *Journal of Economic Behavior and Organization* 7, pp. 21–45.

Terpstra, V. (1982) *International Dimensions of Marketing*, Boston, Mass.: Kent.

Thibaut, J. and Walker, L. (1975) *Procedural Justice: A Psychological Analysis*, Hillsdale, N.J.: Erlbaum.

Thibaut, J. and Walker, L. (1978) "A theory of procedure," *California Law Review* 66, pp. 541–566.

Thibaut, J., Walker, L., La Tour, S., and Houlden, P. (1974) "Procedural justice as fairness," *Stanford Law Review* 26, pp. 1271–1289.

Thomason, G. F. (1966) "Managerial work roles and relationships, Part I," *Journal of Management Studies* 3, pp. 270–284.

Thompson, J. D. (1967) *Organizations in Action*, New York: McGraw-Hill.

Tichy, N. M., Tushman, M. L., and Fombrun, C. (1979) "Social network analysis for organizations," *Academy of Management Review* 4, pp. 507–519.

Tilton, J. (1971) *The International Diffusion of Technology: The Case of Semiconductors*, Washington DC: Brookings Institute.

Tolbert, P. S. (1985) "Resource dependence and institutional environments: Sources of administrative structure in institutions of higher education," *Administrative Science Quarterly* 30, pp. 1–13.

Tönnies, F. (1887) (1963) *Community and Society*, New York: Harper and Row.

Toy, S., Marmot, M., and Grover, R. (1990) "An American in Paris: Can Disney work its magic in Europe?" *Business Week*, March 12, pp. 34–38.

Toyne, B. and Nigh, D. (eds) (1997) *International Business: An Emerging Vision*, Columbia, SC: University of South Carolina Press.

Traweek, S. (1988) *Beamtimes and Lifetimes*, Cambridge, Mass.: Harvard University Press.

Tucker, J. C. (1999) *The Therapeutic Organization*, New York: Oxford University Press.

Tuma, N. B. and Hannan, M. T. (1984) *Social Dynamics: Models and Methods*, New York, Academic Press.

Tushman, M. L. (1978) "Technical communication in research and development laboratories: Impact of project work characteristics," *Academy of Management Journal* 21, pp. 624–645.

Tushman, M. L. and Nadler, D. A. (1978) "Information processing as an integrating concept in organizational design," *Academy of Management Review* 3, pp. 613–624.

Tushman, M. and Romanelli, E. (1986) "Organizational evolution: A metamorphosis model of convergence and reorientation," in L. L. Cummings and B. M. Staw (eds), *Research in Organizational Behavior* 7, Greenwich, Conn.: JAI Press, pp. 177–222.

Tyler, T. R. (1988) "What is procedural justice?: Criteria used by citizens to assess the fairness of legal procedures," *Law and Society Review* 22:1, pp. 301–355.

Tyler, T. R. (1989) "Using procedures to justify outcomes: Managing conflict and allocating resources in work organizations," Northwestern University Working Paper.

Tyler, T. R. (1990) *Why People Obey the Law*, New Haven, Conn.: Yale University Press.

Tyler, T. R. and Caine, A. (1981) "The influence of outcomes and procedures on satisfaction with formal leaders," *Journal of Personality and Social Psychology* 41, pp. 642–655.

Tyler, T. R. and Folger, R. (1980) "Distributional and procedural aspects of satisfaction with citizen–police encounters," *Basic and Applied Social Psychology* 1, pp. 281–292.

Tyler, T. R. and Griffin, E. (1989) "Managing the allocation of scarce resources: Using procedures to justify outcomes," Northwestern University Working Paper.

Tyler, T. R., Rasinski, K., and McGraw, K. (1985) "The influence of perceived injustice on support for political authorities," *Journal of Applied Social Psychology* 15, pp. 700–725.

United Nations Conference on Trade and Development (UNCTAD) (1994) *World Investment Report 1994: Transnational Corporations, Employment, and the Workplace*, New York: United Nations.

References

UNCTAD (1999) *World Investment Report 1999*, New York: United Nations.

Van de Ven, A. H., Delbecq, A. L., and Koenig, R. (1976) "Determinants of coordination modes within organizations," *American Sociological Review* 41, pp. 322–338.

Van de Ven, A. H. and Walker, G. (1984) "The dynamics of interorganizational coordination," *Administrative Science Quarterly* 29, pp. 598–621.

Van Maanen, J. (1975) "Police socialization: A longitudinal examination of job attitudes in an urban police department," *Administrative Science Quarterly* 20, pp. 207–228.

Van Maanen, J. (1988) *Tales of the Field*, Chicago, Ill.: University of Chicago Press.

Van Maanen, J. (1989) "Whistle while you work," paper presented at the American Anthropological Association Annual Meeting, November, Washington DC.

Van Maanen, J. (1991) "The smile factory," in P. Frost, L. Moore, M. Louis, C. Lundberg, and J. Martin (eds), *Reframing Organization Culture*, Newbury Park, Calif.: Sage, pp. 58–76.

Van Maanen, J. (1992) "Displacing Disney" *Qualitative Sociology.* 15:1, pp. 5–36.

Van Maanen, J. (1995) "Trade secrets," in R. H. Brown (ed.), *Postmodern Representations: Truth, Power, and Mimesis in the Human Sciences and Public Culture*, Urbana, Ill.: University of Illinois Press, pp. 118–138

Van Maanen, J. (2004) *Identity Work: Notes on the Personal Identity of Police Officers.* Unpublished paper.

Van Maanen, J. and Barley, S. (1984) "Occupational communities," in B. Staw and L. L. Cummings (eds), *Research in Organization Behavior,* Vol. 6, Greenwich, Conn.: JAI Press, pp. 287–365.

Van Maanen, J. and Kunda, G. (1989) "Real feelings," in B. Staw and L. L. Cummings (eds), *Research in Organization Behavior,* Vol. 11, Greenwich, Conn.: JAI Press, pp. 43–104.

Van Maanen, J. and Schein, E. H. (1979) "Toward a theory of organizational socialization," in B. Staw and L. L. Cummings (eds), *Research in Organization Behavior,* Vol. 1, Greenwich, Conn.: JAI Press, pp. 209–269.

Vancil, R. (1973) "What kind of management control do you need?" *Harvard Business Review,* March–April, pp. 75–86.

Vernon, R. (1966) "International investment and international trade in the product cycle," *Quarterly Journal of Economics* 80:2, pp. 190–207.

Vernon, R. (1971) *Sovereignty at Bay: The Multinational Spread of U.S. Enterprise,* New York: Basic Books.

Vernon, R. (1979) "The product cycle hypothesis in a new international environment," *Oxford Bulletin of Economics and Statistics* 41, pp. 255–267.

Vogel, E. F. (1979) *Japan as Number One*, Cambridge, Mass.: Harvard University Press.

von Hippel, E. (1988) *The Sources of Innovation*, Oxford: Oxford University Press.

Walker, G. (1985) "Network position and cognition in a computer software firm," *Administrative Science Quarterly* 30, pp. 103–130.

Walker, L., La Tour, S., Lind, E. A., and Thibaut, J. (1974) "Reactions of participants and observers to modes of adjudication," *Journal of Applied Social Psychology* 4, pp. 295–310.

Walker, L., Lind, E. A., and Thibaut, J. (1979) "The relation between procedural and distributive justice," *Virginia Law Review* 65, pp. 1401–1420.

Wallace, F. A. C. (1970) *Culture and Personality*, New York: Random House.

Wallace, F. A. C. (1978) *Rockdale*, New York: Knopf.

Wallace, F. A. C. (1985) "Rethinking technology 'and' culture," paper prepared for the Mellon Seminar on Technology and Culture, University of Pennsylvania, Department of Anthropology.

Wallerstein, I. (1979) *The Capitalist World Economy*, Cambridge: Cambridge University Press.

Walster, E., Berscheid, E., and Walster, G. W. (1973) "New directions in equity research," *Journal of Personality and Social Psychology* 25, pp. 151–176.

Warren, R. L. (1967) "The interorganizational field as a focus for investigation," *Administrative Science Quarterly* 12, pp. 369–419.

Wasko, J. (2001) *Understanding Disney: The Manufacture of Fantasy*, London: Blackwell.

Wasko, J., Phillips, M., and Meehan, R. (eds) (2001) *Dazzled by Disney? The Global Disney Audience Project*, New York: Leicester University Press.

Watson, A. (1974) *Legal Transplants*, Charlottesville, Va.: University of Virginia Press.

Watson, J. L. (ed.) (1997) *Golden Arches East: McDonald's in East Asia*, Palo Alto, Calif.: Stanford University Press.

Watts, S. (1997) *The Magic Kingdom: Walt Disney and the American Way of Life*, Boston, Mass.: Houghton Mifflin.

Weber, M. (1922/1978) *Economy and Society*, Berkeley, Calif.: University of California Press.

Weber, M. (1946) *From Max Weber: Essays in Sociology*, ed. H. H. Gerth and C. Wright Mills, New York: Oxford University Press.

Weeks, J. (2004) *Unpopular Culture: The Ritual of Complaint in a British Bank*, Chicago: University of Chicago Press.

Weick, K. E. (1976) "Educational organizations as loosely coupled systems," *Administrative Science Quarterly* 21, pp. 1–19.

Weick, K. E. (1979) *The Social Psychology of Organizing*, 2nd edn, New York: Random House.

Weick, K. E. and Gilfillan, D. P. (1971) "Fate of arbitrary traditions in a laboratory microculture," *Journal of Personality and Social Psychology* 17, pp. 179–191.

Welge, M. (1987) "Subsidiary autonomy in multinational corporations," in D. Van Den Bulcke (ed.), *International Business Issues*, Proceedings of the 13th annual meeting of EIBA, Antwerp.

Werner, S. (2002) "Recent developments in international management research: A review of 20 top management journals," *Journal of Management* 28, pp. 277–305.

Westney, D. E. (1987) *Imitation and Innovation: The Transfer of Western Organizational Patterns to Meiji Japan*, Cambridge, Mass.: Harvard University Press.

Westney, D. E. (1988) "Isomorphism, institutionalization and the multinational enterprise," paper presented at the Academy of International Business Annual Meeting, October, San Diego, California.

Westney, D. E. and Sakakibara, D. (1985) "Competitive study of the training, careers, and organization of engineers on the computer industry in Japan and the United States," MIT–Japan Science and Technology Program, MIT: mimeograph.

Westney, D. E. and Zaheer, S. (2001) "The multinational enterprise as an organization," in A. M. Rugman and T. L. Brewer (eds), *The Oxford Handbook of International Business*, Oxford: Oxford University Press, pp. 349–379.

White, M. (1987) *The Japanese Educational Challenge*, New York: Free Press.

White, R. E. and Poynter, T. A. (1990) "Organizing for world-wide advantage," in C. A. Bartlett, Y. Doz, and G. Hedlund (eds), *Managing the Global Firm*, London and New York: Routledge, pp. 95–116.

Whiting, R. (1977) *The Chrysanthemum and the Bat*, New York: Vintage.

Whiting, R. (1989) *You Gotta Have Wa*, New York: Vintage.

Whitley, R. (1992) *Business Systems in East Asia: Firms, Markets, and Societies*, London: Sage.

Whitley, R. (1999) "Globalization and business systems," in *Divergent Capitalisms: The*

Social Structuring and Change of Business Systems, Oxford: Oxford University Press, pp. 117–136.

Whyte, W. F. (1951) *Pattern for Industrial Peace*, New York: Harper and Row.

Wilkins, M. (1970) *The Emergence of the Multinational Enterprise: American Business Abroad from Colonial Era to 1914*, Cambridge, Mass.: Harvard University Press.

Williams, C. R. (1967) "Regional management overseas," *Harvard Business Review* 45, pp. 87–91.

Williamson, O. E. (1964) *The Economics of Discretionary Behavior: Managerial Objectives in a Theory of the Firm*, Englewood Cliffs, N.J.: Prentice-Hall.

Williamson, O. E. (1970) *Corporate Control and Business Behavior*, Englewood Cliffs, N.J.: Prentice Hall.

Williamson, O. E. (1975) *Markets and Hierarchies: Analysis and Antitrust Implications*, New York: Free Press.

Williamson, O. E. (1981) "The economics of organization: The transaction cost approach," *American Journal of Sociology* 87, November, pp. 548–577.

Williamson, O. E. (1985) *The Economic Institutions of Capitalism*, New York: Free Press.

Williamson, O. E. and Ouchi, W. G. (1981) "The markets and hierarchies program of research: Origins, implications, prospects," in W. Joyce and A. Van de Ven (eds), *Organizational Design*, New York: Wiley, pp. 347–370.

Winter, S. (1981) "Attention allocation and input proportions," *Journal of Economic Behavior and Organization* 2, pp. 31–46.

Wolcott, H. F. (1982) "The anthropology of learning," *Anthropology and Education Quarterly* 13 (special issue).

Wolcott, H. F. (1990) "Propriospect and the acquisition of culture," unpublished paper, University of Oregon, School of Education.

Wolf, J. C. (1979) "Disney World: America's vision of Utopia," *Alternative Futures* 2, pp. 72–77.

Wolfe, T. (1968) *The Electric Kool-Aid Acid Test*, New York: Farrar, Straus and Giroux.

Womack, J. P., Jones, D. T., and Roos, D. (1990) *The Machine that Changed the World*, New York: Rawson Associates.

Wood, R. and Bandura, A. (1989) "Social cognitive theory of organizational management," *Academy of Management Review* 14, pp. 361–384.

Woodward, J. (1965) *Industrial Organization: Theory and Practice*, New York: Oxford University Press.

Yates, J. (1989) *Control Through Communication*, Baltimore: Johns Hopkins University Press.

Yeung, H. (1997) "Business networks and transnational corporations: A study of Hong-Kong firms in the ASEAN region," *Economic Geography* 73:1, pp. 1–25.

Yip, G. S. (1989) "Global strategy … in a world of nations?" *Sloan Management Review*, Fall, pp. 29–41.

Young, M. (1991) *An Inside Job: Policing and Police Culture in Britain*, Oxford: Clarendon.

Zachary, G. P. (2000) *The Global Me*, New York: Public Affairs Press.

Zaheer, S. (1995) "Overcoming the liability of foreignness," *Academy of Management Journal* 38:2, pp. 341–363.

Zaheer, S. and Mosakowski, E. (1997) "The dynamics of the liability of foreignness," *Strategic Management Journal* 18:6, pp. 439–464.

Zaheer, S. and Zaheer, A. (1997) "Country effects on information seeking in global electronic networks," *Journal of International Business Studies* 28:1, pp. 77–100.

Zajac, E. J. and Olsen, C. P. (1993) "From transaction cost to transactional value analysis: Implications for the study of interorganizational strategies" *Journal of Management Studies* 30, pp. 131–145.

Zald, M. N. (1970) "Political economy: A framework for comparative analysis," in M. N. Zald (ed.), *Power in Organizations*, Nashville, Tn.: Vanderbilt University Press, pp. 221–261.

Zeitz, G. (1980) "Interorganizational dialects," *Administrative Science Quarterly* 25, pp. 72–88.

Zeleny, Y. M. (1987) "Management support systems: Towards integrated knowledge management," *Human Systems Management* 7, pp. 59–70.

Zucker, L. G. (1977) "The role of institutionalization in cultural persistence," *American Sociological Review* 42, pp. 726–743.

Zucker, L. G. (1983) "Organization as institutions," in S. Bacharach (ed.), *Advances in Organizational Theory and Research*, Vol. 2, Greenwich: JAI Press, pp. 1–43.

Zucker, L. G. (1987) "Institutional theories of organization," *Annual Review of Sociology* 13, pp. 443–464.

Zucker, L. G. (ed.) (1988) *Institutional Patterns and Organizations: Culture and Environment*, Cambridge, Mass.: Ballinger.

Zucker, L. G. (1989) "Combining institutional theory and population ecology: No legitimacy, no history," *American Sociological Review* 54:4, pp. 542–545.

Index